MOSES AS POLITICAL LEADER

Moses as Political Leader

Aaron Wildavsky

With a foreword by
Yoram Hazony

Shalem press
Jerusalem and New York

Third Printing, 2015

First published in 1984 as *The Nursing Father:*
Moses as a Political Leader. Second edition 2005.
Book and cover design: Erica Halivni
Cover picture: Preparatory sketch of
Moses Before the Burning Bush by Raphael.
Copyright © Alinari Archives/Corbis

Printed in Israel

ISBN 978-965-7052-31-0

CONTENTS

Foreword by Yoram Hazony   ix

Introduction   3

1. **Slavery**   30
   Passive People, Passive Leader

2. **From Slavery to Anarchy**   70
   Learning from Pharaoh What Not to Do

3. **From Anarchy to Equity**   103
   Leadership in the Golden Calf, the Spies, and the Akedah

4. **From Equity to Hierarchy**   138
   The Institutionalization of Leadership

5. **The Leader Disappears into the Book**   171
   Why Moses Does Not Get to the Promised Land

Conclusion: Leadership as a Function of Regime   205

Epilogue: A Speculation on the Survival of the Jewish People   244

Acknowledgments   263

Notes   266

Index   300

For my grandparents and my grandchildren

FOREWORD

Aaron Wildavsky's *Moses as Political Leader* was the first book-length study of the political thought of the Bible by a contemporary scholar of politics. The reissuing of this pathbreaking work, coinciding with the twentieth anniversary of its original publication in 1984, offers us an opportunity to take stock of what has—and what has not—taken place in the fledgling discipline of Jewish political studies in the two decades since then.

To get such a picture, one must begin by coming to terms with the same phenomenon that greeted Wildavsky when he began writing about Moses: Strange as it may seem, political thought and the history of political ideas are taught in most universities almost without reference to the Hebrew Bible. One may consult virtually any textbook on the subject, but in this respect they are almost always the same. Political philosophy is presented as a tradition that begins in pre-Socratic Greece, and proceeds from there to Plato and Aristotle, to the Greek and Roman philosophic schools, and to the political thought of Christianity, as found in the New Testament and the writings of the Church fathers. The intellectual story line then continues through medieval political thought such as that of Thomas Aquinas, and finally the modern philosophies of writers such as Hobbes, Locke, and Rousseau. This is the case in traditional presentations of the canon such as that of George Sabine. But it is also true of more recent revisions of the canon such as those proposed by Leo Strauss and Sheldon Wolin.[1] Regardless of where one looks, one is presented with a picture that treats the contribution of the Hebrew Bible to the political ideas of the West in a few dismissive sentences, or else with none at all.

What is wrong with such a presentation of history? There are at least two problems with it. The first is strictly *historical* in nature. As a matter of empirical fact, the Western tradition of political thought seems to have developed in constant dialogue with, and under the constant influence of, the Hebrew scriptures. This is certainly true of the authors of the New Testament, the Church fathers, and later Christian political thinkers. But it is at least as true of early modern writers such as Bodin, Cunaeus, Grotius, Selden, Milton, Hobbes, Harrington, and Locke, whose work is the basis for the modern state, and all of whom make extensive reference to the Hebrew scriptures in their political writings.[2] Even Rousseau seems to have tried his hand at the political interpretation of Hebrew scripture.[3] In all these cases, we find the thinkers of the West struggling to gain an understanding of politics with the assistance of the Hebrew Bible. Yet there is almost no echo of this intellectual effort in the history of Western political ideas.

But underlying this strictly historical problem is another, deeper issue, which comes into sight as soon as one tries to understand *why* there is no reference to the Hebrew Bible in the traditional picture of the history of Western political thought. What is it, exactly, that prevents the Bible from being treated as "political philosophy"? After all, it seems to be preoccupied with precisely those matters that are of concern to political theorists: War and peace, justice and injustice, rulers and ruled, obedience and disobedience, power and right, individual and state, empire and anarchy. Moreover, these topics are not treated in an arbitrary fashion. It is difficult to read the biblical texts without being impressed that there are messages and insights the authors intended to teach concerning these subjects. On its face, then, it would seem that there must be a biblical political teaching, something that could be called the "political philosophy of the Hebrew Bible," and that could be compared to the political philosophy of other classic and modern sources. Yet if there is such a thing, hardly anyone seems to know what it might be.

The absence of the Hebrew Bible from the study of political thought is thus a historical problem, but it rests on a second, *philosophical* problem—the question of what can be considered a legitimate source of political and moral truth. Clearly, there is some hesitation concerning the texts of the Bible that places them beyond the pale. To be sure, almost everyone seems willing at least to pay lip service to the notion that what we call the West is a civilization based on the fusion of Hebraic and Greek ideas. Yet the Hebraic contribution is generally relegated to a narrow band of theological concepts. Some unnamed barrier prevents the political ideas of the Bible, as well as the historical influence of these ideas, from being deemed a subject worthy of systematic study.

This unwillingness to treat the political teachings of the Hebrew Bible seriously stems, it seems, from the general devaluation of the Bible as a source of truth—a trend associated with Spinoza and the more radical wing of the Enlightenment, but which has now become widely accepted even by those who have never given the matter much thought. At the heart of this view is an account of the Bible that follows medieval philosophy in making a sharp distinction between those works that are the product of *revelation*, and those that are the product of *reason*. But whereas medieval thinkers hoped to show that both revelation and reason could lead to the truth, Enlightenment thinkers discounted revelation and implied that reason alone should be the basis for man's search for truth. Such a way of thinking had an immediate and dramatic result: As a book that had been traditionally considered a work of "reason," Plato's *Republic*, for example, was held to be worthy of being studied for the truths it might contain; whereas the biblical Book of Judges, which had been held to be a work of "revelation," was deemed unworthy of being studied for the truths it might contain. This manner of evaluating the worth of various books has proven to be one of the most enduring prejudices of the Enlightenment. And it is this prejudice that has apparently determined what ideas are to be taught as "philosophy," and what influences are to be regarded as meaningful in the history of ideas, for over two hundred years.

Now, this point of view suffers from a troubling internal contradiction. For it insists on maintaining a distinction between revelation and reason, even as it denies that there ever was such a thing as revelation. It says, in other words: Let us assume that there never was any such thing as revelation, so that all books are equally works of the human mind. But then, having said that all books are equally works of the human mind, it reimposes the supposedly discredited category of revelation in order to refer to those works of the human mind that can be known, a priori, not to be the source of truths worth considering. Thus it transpires that what was once an honorific, used by God-fearing individuals to grant a special status to their most cherished books, is maintained even up to the present day as an empty stigma, whose purpose is to demarcate a class of works from which it is believed we can learn nothing.

In this, the heritage of the Enlightenment, as it has existed until recently in many academic disciplines, is very far from a consistent humanistic approach, which seeks wisdom and insight wherever it is to be found. Such an approach would wish to judge each and every work by the worth of its content, rather than by the label that was applied to it in a bygone age. Such an approach would set aside the medieval distinction between revelation and reason, and study the Bible without prejudice, and with an eye to what wisdom and insight may be found in the text.

Such an approach has been long in coming. But its time has finally come. The last generation has seen a gradual but pronounced movement away from the certitude that the Hebrew Bible deserves the stigma that has been attached to it for the past two centuries. In a number of academic disciplines, it has become increasingly acceptable for scholars to entertain the hypothesis that the books of the Bible were the product of intelligent and reasonable minds, and that they can in fact be studied for the wisdom they reflect and the truths they contain. In the area of political thought, this change in intellectual atmosphere began to make itself felt two decades ago as the result of the pioneering books of Aaron Wildavsky, followed by those of Michael Walzer, Daniel Elazar, and others.

As far as I am aware, the first contemporary effort to make a systematic study of the Jewish political tradition, including the political thought of the Bible, took place in academic seminars conducted by Daniel Elazar in the late 1970s. But the possibility of a systematic exposition of the political thought of the Bible was not demonstrated to a broad audience until the publication of Aaron Wildavsky's *Moses as Political Leader* (1984), and of Michael Walzer's *Exodus and Revolution* (1985). These book-length treatments of the political career of Moses offered a modern academic audience the first glimpse of the intellectual depth underlying the thesis that the Hebrew Bible is a significant political work. These works, buttressed by the outstanding reputation of the scholars who stood behind them, opened the way to what has since become a steadily growing movement towards the reclamation of the Hebrew Bible in the study of politics.

Aaron Wildavsky came to the study of Moses after he was already among the world's most respected political scientists. Born in Brooklyn in 1930 to a family of Ukrainian Jewish immigrants, he received his undergraduate education at Brooklyn College, went on to study at the University of Sydney on a Fulbright scholarship, and then to Yale University, where he received his doctorate in 1958. After teaching for a few years at Oberlin College, Wildavsky moved to the University of California at Berkeley, where he served as professor of political science and public policy for thirty years, until his death in 1993.

In his long academic career, Aaron Wildavsky was author, co-author, or editor of 39 books, including respected contributions to the study of the functioning of government, public policy, and cultural theory. Perhaps his best-known work was in the field of public administration, in which *The Politics of the Budgetary Process* (1964), *Implementation* (1973), and *The Private Government of Public Money* (1974) did much to create an entire academic discipline devoted to understanding and improving the making of government policy. With Nelson Polsby, he co-authored *Presidential Elections* (1964), a more popular work that made the findings of political science accessible to college students and the general public, and was revised every four years to keep its data and conclusions fresh. In *Risk and Culture* (1982, co-authored with anthropologist Mary Douglas), and in a series of subsequent works, Wildavsky developed a cultural theory of politics that sought to explain political practice across civilizations as a function of the interplay among a small number of core factors that shape political regimes and the transitions from one regime to another.

In these and other writings, Wildavsky showed himself to be a daring innovator, who sought to reshape the subject matter of academic research so as to turn its attention to the real world beyond itself. It was this same impulse that, in the late 1960s, brought him to read the Bible for its political teachings. The period was that of the Vietnam War and the civil rights movement, and the campuses were seething with a politics of moral indignation, whose high-mindedness constantly threatened, in Wildavsky's view, to career into intellectual despotism. The most pressing issue, as he saw it, was for students and faculty alike to confront the relationship between the call to revolution and subversion of the existing order, on the one hand; and the need to preserve one's humanity in the face of this call, on the other. In order to grapple with this dilemma, he sought political and literary works whose subject was the "moral leader whose high aspirations lead him to the edge of despair or despotism, but who maintains his humanity in the end." As he writes in his introduction to *Moses as Political Leader*, "a little looking convinced me that social science research had little to offer in response. Besides, it was too cold. Whatever I had been doing obviously had not penetrated the audience I had tried to reach" (p. 6 of this edition).

The search for texts dealing directly with these issues brought him to the Hebrew Bible, whose political teachings are in fact preoccupied with the twin threats of despotism and anarchy that follow hard upon the heels of Moses' righteous revolution. Wildavsky describes the passion for the biblical text as something that may have been lying dormant in him; his grandparents were Orthodox Jews and his father, a skeptic, loved to recount stories from the Bible. But it was the recognition that there are times and places where the biblical political teaching is simply more relevant than that familiar to us from other sources that seems to have hit him the hardest. "There it was, just what I had been looking for—or, perchance, what had been looking for me—fanaticism with a moral purpose... My first question was, what gave Moses the right to have all those people killed?" (p. 7).

As Wildavsky describes it, he now began reading the biblical text on the supposition that it was a serious treatment of politics. In the years that followed, he found that this intuition of biblical relevance was upheld by an exacting study of the books of the Hebrew Bible. The result was *Moses as Political Leader*, which brought before the academic community the unprecedented claim that the books of Moses can be read as advancing a relevant and coherent political teaching.

It is easy to underestimate how revolutionary this claim was—and still is. I have already mentioned the weight of the existing canon of political thought, which militates with such force against the acceptance of the Hebrew Bible as a political text of real significance. But there are other factors that Wildavsky's thesis had to contend with as well. Most significant was the profusion of scholarly work on the Bible itself since the time of Wellhausen, which has consistently viewed the biblical text as a patchwork of editorial scraps cut from previously existing sources. It is of the nature of critical studies of this kind to assume a sharp dichotomization between any given, hypothetical source and its neighbor—for if the sources in their original form did not disagree sharply, then how would one be able to tell them apart once they had been fused into the biblical text as we now have it? The natural tendency of such work is therefore to see the final text as internally incoherent (even as it assumes that each of the original sources was *highly* coherent): The many sources become a kind of cacophony of internal disputation within the text, and whatever meaning or teaching it might otherwise have been thought to contain tends to dissolve in the face of this noise. The plain sense of the final text is, in other words, sacrificed in order to get at the supposed meanings of the various hypothetical sources from which it is understood to have been composed.

Wildavsky quotes a famous passage from Sigmund Freud's *Moses and Monotheism* (1939), which can easily serve as an example of the effect such source criticism has had on the capacity of scholars, and of educated individuals generally, to credit the possibility that the biblical text offers a coherent message of any kind. Here is Freud on his own use of the biblical text:

> When I use Biblical tradition here in such an autocratic and arbitrary way, draw on it for confirmation whenever it is convenient, and dismiss its evidence without scruple when it contradicts my conclusions, I know full well that I am exposing myself to severe criticism concerning my method and that I weaken the force of my proofs. But this is the only way in which to treat material whose trustworthiness—as we know for certain—was seriously damaged by the influence of distorting tendencies. Some justification will be forthcoming later, it is hoped, when we have unearthed those secret motives. Certainty is not to be gained in any case, and, moreover, we may say that all other authors have acted likewise.[4]

As Wildavsky points out, this suspicion of the text—these ruminations on its lack of "trustworthiness," on the "damage" done to it by "distorting tendencies," on the "secret motives" that were in play during the editing process—quickly deteriorates into a kind of hermeneutic nihilism, which leaves one with little choice but to conclude that the text as a whole can't really mean anything at all. In this way, we arrive at a kind of tyranny of the hypothetical sources from which the Bible is thought to have been compiled, such that the study of these sources rises up and destroys any possibility of studying the text as a whole.

The past thirty years, however, have seen a pronounced movement of writers in a number of disciplines against this tyranny of the sources. An important milestone in this direction was the movement called "canonical criticism," associated with the work of Brevard Childs and his colleagues, which has turned attention towards the coherence of specific books of the Bible and of the overall biblical canon.[5] Another was the introduction of the Hebrew Bible into the academic study of literature by Robert Alter and others, which has done much to revive the recognition that the Bible consists of coherent texts, often composed with extraordinary care.[6] Of significance, too, is the work of scholars such as Donald Harman Akenson, who has proposed that at least the first half of the Bible was ultimately the work of a single hand, assembled with the aim of advancing a single, unified teaching.[7] Although these scholars write with different concerns in view and reach a wide range of conclusions, they nevertheless represent a marked trend towards an understanding according to which the Bible was composed intelligently, so that a coherent meaning might reasonably be discerned in it.

In a sense, then, Wildavky's *Moses as Political Leader* was the natural consequence of a larger trend. But it was also one of the most daring expressions of this trend. For *Moses as Political Leader* not only seeks to demonstrate that the biblical narrative is intelligently assembled and coherent. It advances the claim that the teaching that emerges from this narrative is itself worthy of study—not only stylistically or historically, but also philosophically. As he writes:

> My book intends... to use biblical teachings about leadership to improve current understanding of that elusive yet essential activity. For these purposes, therefore, questions of origins—Who wrote the Bible? How was it written or rewritten? What ideological axes did the various hypothetical authors-cum-editors have to grind?—are subordinate to questions of content—Does the leadership perspective help us understand the Bible? What does the Torah teach about leadership? How valuable is this teaching? ... [M]y concern is with explicating the content of the

Mosaic Bible as it bears on substantive issues.... The important limits
are not the absence of eyewitnesses (or other corroborating data, which
might tell us more about the actual events), but rather the limits of
imagination and insight that can make the Bible speak in a meaningful voice (p. 20).

As is clear from this passage, Wildavsky believed that the question
of principal interest with regard to the biblical text is not who edited it,
but whether it has something important to say. To answer *this* question,
what is needed is to read the text as a whole, and with an eye towards
understanding what it is trying to teach. When one pursues this avenue
of research with imagination and insight, Wildavsky believed, the ideas
being advanced in the text come through loud and clear, and issues of
editorial history naturally remove themselves to the sidelines.

Of course, the books of Moses are not written in the form of an
Aristotelian treatise. They are presented as a narrative, and to discern a
political teaching in them, one must first assume that general truths can
be taught in the narrative form. In this, Wildavsky follows other modern
commentators on the Bible such as Umberto Cassuto and Nehama Leibowitz, who have argued that the biblical narrative is extremely sensitive
to the development of circumstance, power relations, personality, and
moral understanding over time. Recognition of this fact permits one to
understand the biblical characters as learning and growing in the course
of their experiences. And what they learn can also be a lesson to us. This
is no less true of Moses, and Wildavsky argues that the gradual development of Moses' political understanding over the course of the narrative
from Exodus to Deuteronomy permits us to understand the biblical text
as a kind of "primer" in government (p. 10). Through the medium of the
biblical text, we experience unrestricted monarchy (in Egypt), anarchy (in
the wilderness, when the people choose to be led by a golden statue in
the shape of a calf), and a regime Wildavsky calls political *equity*—essentially an egalitarian republic—in which Moses is little more than the
first among equals (in the rebellion of Korah). At each step, there are
evident reasons that Moses, as political leader, cannot continue under the
burden of the preceding political constellation. In this way, we are led
inexorably to the conclusion that Moses has little choice but to adopt
the final, hierarchical arrangement in which his rule is ameliorated by the
appointment of the assembly of elders—roughly, what we would today
call a limited or constitutional monarchy (p. 165).

In making this argument, Wildavsky imputes to the biblical text an awareness of and concern for governmental forms often thought to have been born only later, in Greece. And he attributes to the books of Moses a clear preference as to the form of the desired regime, this preference being justified not by arbitrary divine decree, but by the workings of reason as it responds to experience.

Of particular interest is Wildavsky's recognition that the biblical texts understand Hebrew politics as being perpetually poised between replication of Egypt's tyranny, on the one hand; and a slide into complete anarchy, on the other. As Wildavsky points out, when the Bible refers to Egypt as "the house of bondage," it refers not only to the enslavement of the Hebrews, but to a vertical political order that amounted to enslavement of most of the Egyptians as well. For a people recently liberated from this order, "the likely alternative" seems to be complete anarchy, and therefore dissolution (p. 33). The narrative reaches its climax at the golden calf, when Moses, having descended from the mountain, calls upon those loyal to him to kill their idolatrous brothers. As a result of this bloodshed, order is restored, but at the cost of Moses turning the sword on the very people he had sought to liberate from Pharaoh. The governmental forms Wildavsky calls *equity* and *hierarchy* are understood as the biblical text's alternatives to the installation of a regime like that of Egypt, a regime of "permanent purge" (p. 160).

This same question regarding the appropriate governmental form applies no less to the man who is to lead and govern the people, Moses. Wildavsky points out that at the outset, Moses has before him only two models of the individual's involvement in politics: The model of absolute passivity, which he inherits from the experience of bondage, and which Wildavsky finds embodied in the figure of Aaron (p. 121), who yields before the anarchic yearnings of the people and fashions for them an idol of gold; and the model of absolute authority, which he inherits from his familiarity with the god-king, Pharaoh (p. 112). The crucial question is whether there is a kind of political authority that is somewhere between these two poles, but nonetheless stable enough to endure. As Wildavsky emphasizes, the desire for the establishment of a human political authority of this kind is the basis for what is portrayed as God's ongoing effort to persuade Moses to take responsibility for events (e.g., "Wherefore criest thou unto me? Speak unto the children of Israel, that they go forward," Exodus 14:15). But it is also the basis of God's insistence on checking

Moses' tendency to seek unlimited power for himself. (pp. 171ff.) Moses struggles against both sides of this bargain, finally reconciling himself to the fact that a mature politics requires the assumption of ultimate responsibility, and yet without the benefit of ultimate power (p. 105).

A common caricature of biblical politics suggests that God gets mixed up in politics in order to strengthen absolute government. But Wildavsky presents the political thought of the Bible as moving in precisely the opposite direction. Pharaoh had no need of the Hebrew God to strengthen his absolute government; on the Egyptian view of things, Pharaoh was God, and that gave him all the authority he needed for absolute rule. As Wildavsky correctly realizes, the Hebrew God enters into politics not to support absolute government but to impose limits on its authority. God's appearance entails the establishment of a higher standard against which the acts of Pharaoh can be judged. But it also entails the establishment of a standard against which the acts of Moses can be judged. The introduction of this higher standard into the political realm is that which permits the limitation of Moses' power, thereby preventing the establishment of Moses as the first in a line of absolute rulers in Israel.

Wildavsky wrote two books on the political philosophy of the Bible: *Moses as Political Leader* and his later *Assimilation Versus Separation* (1993),[8] which deals with the political teaching of the Joseph narrative in Genesis. He had also planned on writing a third book on the political teachings of the story of David, but this was a work he did not succeed in completing before his death. (Elements of this work appear in the Epilogue Wildavsky added to *Moses as Political Leader*, which appears at the end of this volume under the title "A Speculation on the Survival of the Jewish People.") In all this work, he maintained his posture of quiet but firm defiance of the conventional wisdom, according to which the Bible could not possibly have a coherent political teaching. And this posture served as an aid and an inspiration to others.

The impact of Wildavsky's book stems, in part, from the fact that its revolutionary approach was backed up by Michael Walzer's *Exodus and Revolution*, which appeared shortly afterwards. Walzer, who writes that he read an early draft of Wildavsky's book,[9] emphasized a different aspect of the Pentateuchal political teaching, focusing on the books of Moses as a manifesto for revolution and political change. But his method was strikingly similar to that of Wildavsky's studies of the Bible. As he wrote:

> In returning to the original text, I make no claims about the substantive intentions of its authors and editors, and I commit myself to no specific view of the actual history. What really happened? We don't know. We have only this story.... The effort of modern critics to disentangle authorial traditions, to identify earlier and later fragments within the narrative, has not in my view produced a better understanding.... 'At no point,' as Northrop Frye has written, 'does [this effort] throw any real light on how or why a poet might read the Bible'—and it is no more help to a political theorist.[10]

The fact that scholars of the stature of Wildavsky and Walzer were willing to go out on this limb had an immediate and telling effect. When I was in graduate school studying political theory in the late 1980s, these books on the political thought of the Bible were already well known. This is not to say they had had a discernible effect on what was being taught as political philosophy—in my department, or anywhere else. But the perspective these books represented was understood to be legitimate. And when I proposed to write a doctoral dissertation on the political philosophy of the biblical Book of Jeremiah, at least some of my teachers responded with enthusiasm. I had the honor of having Wildavsky as a member of my dissertation committee.

My experience was by no means unique, and within a few years, works seeking to advance our understanding of the political thought of the Bible began appearing on a regular basis, both at the hands of students of political philosophy, and of other writers who became inspired to join in the effort of reviving our understanding of the biblical political teaching. Among these works are Shmuel Trigano, *Philosophie de la Loi* (1991); William Safire's book on Job, *The First Dissident* (1992); Wildavsky's book on the Joseph narrative, *Assimilation Versus Separation* (1993); Daniel Elazar, *Covenant and Polity in Biblical Israel* (1995); Yoram Hazony, *The Dawn: Political Teachings of the Book of Esther* (1995); Ira Sharkansky, *Israel and Its Bible: A Political Analysis* (1996); Alan Mittleman, *The Scepter Shall Not Pass from Judah* (2000); Michael Walzer, Menachem Lorberbaum, and Noam Zohar, eds., *The Jewish Political Tradition* (2000, 2003); Norman Podhoretz, *The Prophets* (2002); and Leon Kass, *The Beginning of Wisdom: Reading Genesis* (2003).

These works follow divergent paths, and not surprisingly, some are more persuasive than others. Nevertheless, when one considers the pattern to which this list gives expression, it is evident that something significant has happened in the wake of Wildavsky's early work. It is now obvious that the treatment of the Hebrew Bible as a work of political thought was no passing whim, but a serious proposition concerning the history of political ideas and the subject matter of political philosophy. I do not mean to say that this proposition has been established to anyone's satisfaction. Most of these studies cannot be regarded as definitive. Moreover, even when taken together, they hardly scrape the surface of what may reasonably be called the political thought of the Hebrew Bible. On the contrary, these works reflect only the beginning of the road to a clear understanding of the "political philosophy of the Bible" in all its dimensions. In addition, with respect to the effort to place the Hebrew Bible within the overall history of political thought in the West, this enterprise has begun in earnest even more recently, and one can only look forward to its development as a natural extension of the current exploration of the political thought of the Bible.[11]

There is, in short, much work that remains to be done before the Hebrew Bible finds its way into university courses, textbooks, and academic discourse as a significant political work in the history of the West. But when this happens—and it now seems clear that this is only a matter of time—this achievement will redound to the enduring credit of Aaron Wildavsky's first foray into the field.

Yoram Hazony
Jerusalem
November 2004

MOSES AS POLITICAL LEADER

INTRODUCTION

I am attracted to the study of Moses for many reasons, three of which are related to leadership. The first is that the Mosaic experience is comprehensive, spanning the spectrum of regimes and the types of leadership associated with them. The second is that Moses, far from being beyond us, was full of human faults, from passivity to impatience to idolatry. There are good reasons why he did not get to the Promised Land. The third is that Moses was a leader who taught his people to do without him by learning how to lead themselves. And this, in my opinion—which may be biased, because I am a professor—is the highest stage of leadership.

In this book, I argue two theses: first, that understanding of the Mosaic Bible may be enhanced by treating it as a teaching on political leadership; second, that our understanding of leadership may be improved by considering it as an integral part of different political regimes. Moses' experience reveals the dilemmas of leadership under the major types of rule, from slavery in Egypt to anarchy before the Golden Calf episode to equity (association without authority) in the desert, until his final effort to institutionalize hierarchy.

Viewing leadership as a function of regime, as the Bible does, can pull the modern social science study of leadership out of the morass of particularism in which its emphasis on the characteristics of leaders and their situations has left it mired. Scripture and secular studies of

leadership share an interest in the situations under which different leaders
are tested, but the Bible includes the one indispensable element missing
from modern leadership studies—politics. To be sure, there is endless
fascination in how these modern studies treat the micropolitics of thrust
and maneuver. Only the Bible, however, is fundamentally concerned with
the macropolitics of regimes—the grand politics that guide and shape
the behavior of leaders and followers. My task is to show that these
patterns of rule are not only musings of my imagination (which, with
generous borrowings from others, they surely are) but also, by marshal-
ing episode upon episode, that they are directly derived from the biblical text.[1]

WHY ME?

After I had started work on this manuscript, knowing that I was in more
than usual need of help, I spoke about the study and sent chapters out
for review to a considerable number of people. More than anything else,
they wanted to know why a political scientist with no evident qualifications for the task (I sharpen politer queries) would be so intensely
interested in this subject.

Why have I written this book? The question implies others: Can we
learn from Moses about leadership? Is it possible to study Moses? How?
By trying to answer these questions, I can explain my intent, if not my
accomplishment.

Long before I became a political scientist, I belonged to a family
whose roots went deep into Hebrew tradition. My paternal grandfather,
Israel Wildavsky, graduated from a religious academy. He was a rabbi—
though so far as I know he never practiced—who began as a teacher of
religion for children and spent most of his life in Poltava in the Ukraine
as proprietor of a wholesale dry goods store. Orthodox to the core, he
was honored by the Jewish community with the informal title of Reb
Yisroel. He lived a long life, dying with my grandmother during the
early days of the Nazi invasion.

My maternal grandfather, Mordechai Brudnow, graduated from a
yeshiva and was also orthodox. He spent his life studying the oral tradition. He did not work in the sense of remunerative employment, being

supported by his wife, who apparently considered it a privilege to have a scholar in the house. They spent their last years in the Holy Land. Born in America, I never knew my grandparents.

Sender Wildavsky, my father, a skeptic to the bone, followed the traditions of a community with which he identified wholeheartedly, but he lacked belief. On Yom Kippur, the Day of Atonement, he blew the shofar (the ram's horn) when asked, but I doubt he expected anyone outside the synagogue to hear. My father sent me to Hebrew school, was glad of my bar mitzvah, and wanted me to marry a Jewish girl, but was otherwise uninterested in religious observance. He did like to tell Bible stories of a sentimental and edifying kind (he was particularly effective with Ruth and Naomi) but not those involving the fire and thunder of a Moses.[2]

My mother, Eva, also followed the forms, blessing the candles on Friday evenings and attending services on holidays. But her heart was in Russian culture. My mother's people mattered a great deal to her; religion per se did not. Make of this what you will. Perhaps passions skip a generation.

I did go to a Hebrew school, where we learned something about the holidays, a little about prayers, but nothing of the language. We sounded the words without knowing what they meant. I liked the services, or at least the songs and chants, but that was about it. Something may have been starting to take root at that time, but if so I was not directly aware of it.

Of more recent and more direct influences, I can be a bit more precise. A small seed was planted at Brooklyn College, where M.J. Benadette, an authority on Sephardic (Spanish and North African) Jewry, gave a superb course on world literature. On a paper I submitted about Don Quixote, Professor Benadette wrote that it showed an interest in biblical themes that should be developed. Of course, I did not do so, but in my senior year I did write a prize essay about the work of Reinhold Niebuhr called "Sin and Politics." I mention this only because there is no telling what a positive suggestion by a teacher can do.

Later I found myself teaching at the University of California in Berkeley. The free-speech movement there was a traumatic episode, disrupting ordinary patterns and engendering much soul-searching. As soon as I realized what the movement was about, I was opposed, seeing in it a forerunner of the fanaticism that seemed to be sweeping the world.

What were we professors professing if we gave up our classrooms to be used, in the terminology of the times, as launching pads for political action? Rightly or wrongly, I believed that my arguments had merit, but I am reasonably certain they convinced no one. The war in Vietnam had driven out discussion.

One of the few advantages scholars have over other people is the opportunity to work out public problems in private research. The key to the era of which I am speaking appeared to be fanaticism. A little looking convinced me that social science research had little to offer in response. Besides, it was too cold. Whatever I had been doing obviously had not penetrated the audience I had tried to reach. Perhaps, I thought, an approach through literature would generate a warmer response. First, I looked for something about plain old-fashioned political fanaticism—writing in which each side is convinced the other must be consigned (by the first side, of course) to oblivion. After much browsing, a suggestion from Lewis A. Dexter led me to Sir Walter Scott's *Old Mortality*. Better than Dostoevsky's *The Possessed*, James' *Princess Cassamassima*, or Conrad's *Under Western Eyes*, in my opinion (though I despair of getting anyone who has heard only of *Ivanhoe* to read it), *Old Mortality* reveals the travails of ordinary people caught between rival religious and political fanatics during the Scottish civil wars. Score one.

Then I sought a portrayal of the fanaticism of insistence, of reiteration, of pure will. This I found in the French film *Last Year at Marienbad*. In that movie, in a world of pure logic, sans emotion, where hotel corridors lead nowhere and trees cast no shadows, a person who perseverates in an evident untruth may prevail.

Still I was dissatisfied. Was there, I wondered, no depiction of the good fanatic, of fanaticism with a justification? Even better, was there not an epic about a moral leader whose high aspirations lead him to the edge of despair or despotism, but who maintains his humanity in the end? Alas, I had no luck.

Then, during a sabbath service at the small orthodox synagogue in Berkeley, I listened to that week's portion of the Pentateuch (the five books of Moses, called by Jews the Torah, meaning *teaching*), which concerned the Golden Calf. When Moses comes down the mountain and sees the Hebrew people cavorting before the Calf, he slams down the tablets containing the law, calls for supporters, asks every man to kill his guilty brother, has the calf ground up and mixed with water, and makes the people eat it.

There it was, just what I had been looking for—or, perchance, what had been looking for me—fanaticism with a moral purpose. This was 1970, the fall after the spring of the invasion of Cambodia, when a resolution of mine in the faculty senate opposing the use of classrooms for political purposes lost by something like 450 to 50.

For the next five years, I read and reread the Golden Calf episode, aided by the Gideons, who see to it that there is a King James Bible in virtually every hotel room in America. My first question (taken up in Chapter 3) was, what gave Moses the right to have all those people killed?

By the middle 1970s, I had gotten as far as the Book of Exodus; it was the first time I had tried to read a whole book of the Bible as if it were about something other than strange genealogies and peculiar practices. Other books of the Bible followed; each new reading forced me to reformulate earlier hypotheses and to branch out, trying to see things whole, unifying my experiences with those set down in the Bible. In time, the Bible became not only a teaching for those accustomed to it but a Torah for me as well.

WHY MOSES?

I am often asked whether contemporary people can learn about leadership from the Mosaic[3] experience. Everyone recognizes the effrontery of implying that Moses has specific advice about current difficulties. No one expects to hear what Moses would do about the West Bank or strategic arms limitation or energy prices. Advice on how to think about leadership in general, rather than what to do in particular, is presumably what we want. This is fortunate, because Moses neither got nor offered direct didactic advice on leadership. Learning how to interrogate experience, past and present, is the essence of the Mosaic method. Leaders must be continual participants in their own education.

It is not, however, the leader per se but the successful leader who is of primary interest to social scientists. In this view, success, not failure, defines leadership. Social scientists study deciding rather than learning because social scientists assume that leaders already know what to do. In a word, current understanding of leadership is not at all Mosaic.

The advantage of the biblical account is that it offers not just one but several different Moseses, responding to many different challenges under several political regimes. The Bible provides various models of leadership, which allow for the expansion and contraction that is demanded by the characteristics of different regimes, as well as by the situations confronting leaders and followers. In the biblical view, as I shall show, different cultures or ways of life contain strong implications for how leaders shall behave in regard to followers. If the answer to the problem of social order is to institutionalize inequality, then one already knows a good deal about leadership; it is part of a regime based on hierarchy. If the culture is anarchistic, based on bidding and bargaining, leadership may last only until the immediate purpose is satisfied, after which a new contract with other leaders may be struck. Should the culture involve rejection of authority, as in the regime I call equity, it will not be easy for anyone to lead. Think of regimes as political cultures, the shared values justifying the political practices that uphold different ways of life.[4]

The Mosaic conception treats leadership as a multi-story edifice on which future generations can build as they learn how to interrogate their new experiences in altered conditions. It is wholly appropriate, therefore, that Moses learns mostly from failure.

According to Martin Buber, the Bible "is the history of God's disappointments." He goes on to say that "the biblical point of view... proclaims that the way... from the Creation to the Kingdom is trod not on the surface of success, but in the deep of failure."[5] Goethe suggested that the Hebrews must have spent only two years wandering in the desert, for nothing else, in his words, could "save, justify and honor" Moses' leadership. Otherwise, as Alfred D. Low puts Goethe's views, Moses is "bound to appear incompetent."[6] Moses' mistakes are almost his most important legacy. Inasmuch as he is imperfect—teaching faith but falling into idolatry at Meribah—we are given opportunities to learn from his errors.

Error is inevitable; but the Mosaic tradition takes error as a challenge to learning rather than as a cause for despondency in defeat. We, too, can entertain hypotheses and broach old questions in new ways. Indeed, this healthy balance between the events and texts of tradition and the necessity for new interpretations is one aspect of leadership that we can learn from Moses. Though our hypotheses will never quite hit the mark, we can learn from our own mistakes, adding them to those our forefathers made.

Learning from failure is discounted by theories of leadership that show leaders learning only (or mainly) from success. Yet learning from success is more difficult and less appropriate than learning from failure. Successes may be ascribed to many elements outside of one's own actions; success breeds the temptation to repeat the same actions in a less appropriate context. Nothing could be further from the Mosaic view: difficulty and disappointment punctuate Moses' entire career. Never easy with the rod of leadership, Moses is equally reluctant to take it up and to lay it down. Plagued by his own people as he had once plagued Pharaoh, Moses suffers their rebellion from the time he leaves Egypt until, rebelling against God's leadership himself, he is denied entrance to the Promised Land. Mosaic leadership, then, does not offer a series of successful solutions but rather a set of perennial problems that may be mitigated from time to time but can never be resolved. Moses moves through several political regimes, seeking but never finding the ideal balance among them. In the same way, Jews are commanded to seek God, though they will never find Him; the journey is as important as the destination.

Thus, in contrast to many leadership studies, I will not focus on Moses' particular traits. As Martin Buber realized, "The Bible does not concern itself with character, nor with individuality, and one cannot draw from it any description of characters or individualities. The Bible depicts something else, namely, persons in situations."[7] This brings us closer to what is known as situation theory in leadership studies but, again, my approach differs. For, as my brief synopsis of his "career" already indicates, Moses is interesting precisely because he is often unwilling or unable to lead; resolving his personal problem of passivity helps his people solve their problem of identity.

Leadership is not acknowledged except as it is tested under stress. In the attempt to practice leadership, the character of leaders is shaped by the nature of the regimes under which they act. Evil regimes cannot produce good leaders. Whether the good man can be an effective leader in a regime for which he is unsuited is a dilemma that Moses has to resolve. It is in this nexus—the tension between leaders who may or may not fit regimes—that the Bible is concerned with political personality.

We benefit, therefore, in two ways by viewing the Bible in part as a primer on leadership. On the one hand, we understand more about the Bible by focusing on leadership as a central problem in the relations of God, Moses, and the Hebrew people—that is, on the ideal, the leader, and the followers. On the other, we find that the Bible compellingly stages the issues, such as the need for direction versus the abuse of power, that still figure in our contemporary concerns about leadership.

Whether there is a meaningful correspondence between aspects of Mosaic experience and our own depends not only on what Moses did, but on what we make of it. Are we interested in forming expectations about the extent and limits of leadership under different types of rule? If so, the Bible presents as wide a panorama as can be found—from despots to anarchists, from the most to the least moral. Ambivalence about leadership—yearning to be led while fearing to be oppressed—is a theme that spans the centuries. When, as Moses did and we do, repeated calls for leadership are heard, even as the emerging leaders are being attacked, one knows that the existing regime incorporates important elements of equality. Caught between competing concepts—regimes that stress equality versus those based on hierarchy—we may better appreciate the dilemma of Moses and his often errant followers, who were similarly in conflict.

Immediately, however, the question arises of whether we—author and reader—can learn from Moses. He talks to God, but we have not been in touch lately. If Moses has God to call out to, it is fair to ask to whom secular leaders can appeal. Is Moses incomparable, then, because there is no human being, let alone a leader, to whom he can be compared? Are the instructions intended for Moses or the teaching he intends for us impossible to follow because Moses had that line to God? Is this a fatal impediment in learning about leadership (or anything else) from Moses? Need the origin of his inspiration, in other words, fatally impede the relevance of his teaching for us?

Does the relevance of Einstein's theories, I would ask in return, depend on his ability to explain the sources of his creativity? It is no more relevant to biblical study to ask how we get our hypotheses (by inspiration or perspiration) than it would be to judge scientists by whether they can explain how they arrived at original ideas.[8]

Whether leaders rely on God or intuition or social science, their aims are similar. Whether one chooses to speak of God (as I do), or of higher principles, or of the unknown (as an agnostic might), the dilemmas of leadership remain the same. To see that this is so, one need only look at leadership from the different viewpoints of believers and agnostics.

Consider the ordeal of the moral leader.[9] People of conscience (for example, Moses at the burning bush) often wonder why they have to be so burdened; conscience restricts their freedom, denies them pleasure, and troubles them without respite. God is Moses' conscience (indeed, the product of his conscience, if you like), and Moses explicitly wishes the divine finger would point to someone else. But since God refuses to choose another, Moses finds himself obliged to lead his people. Conscience will not let him quit.

Moses' problems come from his people's rejection of his moral injunctions; how can a moral leader guide a people who do not share his precepts? How can Moses make his conscience the conscience of the entire population? Since God has not delegated His power to Moses, poor Moses has only his wits and his personality to help him. From time to time, God intervenes directly to lend a hand, but for the most part Moses is on his own. What is more, Moses is obliged to act morally; his adversaries are not. To say the least, he has a hard job.

By learning how to learn from failure, Moses succeeds, though forbidden to taste the first fruits of his success by entering the Promised Land. That would be to contaminate the purity of his motives; he was supposed to act because of conscience (that is, God), not for reward. That is the essence of Judaism: God is to be obeyed because obedience is proper, not because we will be rewarded.

CAN WE STUDY MOSES?

I am frequently asked how one can learn about Moses. This is a friendly query, but its mixed tone of wonder and incredulity (half the askers desiring to understand, half doubting that it is possible) suggests that a contemporary book about the Bible has a long way to go before it can penetrate a modern consciousness. The basic difficulty is no less powerful for being pedestrian: most people no longer read the Bible.[10] The unity and coherence of the Pentateuch has been challenged by modern biblical scholarship for over two hundred years. The historical existence of Moses has been denied. The very claim that there is a Mosaic body of thought has been rejected in favor of the notion that different accounts from widely varying historical epochs have been loosely joined by later editors to form a puzzling pastiche of contradictory thoughts.

The most distinguished biblical critic of our time, Gerhard von Rad, states the consensus in no uncertain terms:

> The literary analysis of the Pentateuch... results in the distribution of this picture of Israel's early history over several major source-documents, which often diverge considerably in details, and the oldest of which, the Jahwist,... at best recounts 300 years at least after the events what took place prior to the settlement in Canaan. Nevertheless, following Wellhausen, even scholars whose approach was highly critical still clung substantially to the unilinear sequence of events represented by the bondage in Egypt, Sinai, the wandering in the wilderness, and the entry into Canaan; they also regarded Moses as Israel's authoritative leader throughout these stages. But a complete change has come over this picture as the result of the investigation of the history of traditions; and this has only been brought into full play in our time. In spite of its often very thoroughgoing criticism, previous historical research nevertheless still believed it possible to grasp the actual historical course of events, in its basic features at any rate, by a more or less immediate penetration behind the literary presentation. But this has turned out to be mistaken.[11]

There may have been no Moses, the implication is, and, therefore, we would not be able to learn about him by reading the Bible.

The critical questions are two: Is it possible to reconstruct what actually happened (the historicity question)? Who actually wrote what, when, and with what bias (the authorship question)?

For over a century, biblical criticism has been concerned with the origins and authorship of these ancient texts. This scholarship has shown that there was not one text but several, which were edited, combined, and recombined and reflect later as well as earlier influences. The "higher critics" have argued that the Bible was a product of numerous editors writing long after the events had taken place. Thus a massive effort was launched to rediscover whatever was left of the original accounts. Increasingly, the Bible has been analyzed in terms of its own development.

The difficulties created by modeling inquiry upon evolution without a principle of selection are legion. The available evidence cannot prove who wrote or edited what.[12] There is as much disagreement over sources as over substance. The exercise proves little for the believer; however altered the final form, the Bible now represents Holy Writ. For the skeptic, on the other hand, both the official Bible and scholarly criticism of it are on shaky ground. Attributing authorship to Moses legitimized the Torah, but there is no authoritative way to decide between the opposed views of critics.

The historicity of the Bible may be maintained by minimizing the role of the redactors, as its editors are called. But there is no need to deny creative collective composition.

When the orthodox say Moses wrote the Pentateuch (except, perhaps, for the last paragraphs describing his burial, which are attributed to Joshua), they mean it literally—Moses, the man of God, wrote "the words of this law in a book, until they were finished" (Deut. 31:24). Yet it is obvious that portions of the Pentateuch show awareness of future events. Parts of Leviticus, for example, deal with rituals appropriate for a central cult such as the temple and not for a tribe in the desert. And it would have been difficult for Moses to have written his own obituary. All this, and much more, has been known by commentators through the ages. Why, then, do they persist in saying Moses wrote the entire Torah? It is a matter of faith, surely, but it is more than that.

Ascribing authorship to Moses is the guarantee of the authenticity of Scripture. To say that Moses did not write it is to say that these experiences are not genuine. No books of Moses, no people of the book, no people.

Imagine what scientific activity would be like if no new hypotheses were permitted or, equally bad, if all hypotheses were considered equal. Without tradition, every new hypothesis supersedes everything that has gone before. Change is equivalent to a new mode of science or a new religion. Either change would have to be suppressed or there would be nothing to pass on except flux. By affirming the axiom of Mosaic authorship, changes in interpretation may be accommodated without rejecting the heritage.

In one sense, there is less difficulty with source criticism than meets the eye. It would be contrary to Mosaic teaching to deny the future a part to play in the past. No doubt other traditions embodied in books—the Bible mentions many other documents, such as the Book of the Wars of the Lord, which have been lost—were put together by later generations, in the process adding their own special insights and interests.

Today, though we no longer alter the text directly, we do so indirectly by translation and interpretation, as I am doing now. As John Henry Cardinal Newman said, "It is in point to notice also the structure and style of Scripture, a structure so unsystematic and various, and a style so figurative and indirect, that no one would presume at first sight to say what is in it and what is not.... And as it is owned the whole scheme of Scripture is not yet understood, so, if it ever comes to be understood, before the 'restitution of all things,' and without miraculous interpositions, it must be in the same way as natural knowledge is come at."[13] Let us be clear about what Newman is saying. By "natural knowledge," he means use of reason, hypothesis, evidence—whatever proves helpful in making sense out of the world in general and a rich biblical text in particular. In traditional Jewish thought as well, every generation, according to its own understanding, holds that its interpretation is part of what the Torah teaches.

The ability of future generations to make the text answer their questions, without distorting it beyond recognition, is part of the Bible's power. As with any fundamental text, what the Bible is depends partly on what it contains and partly on what each generation makes of it. Just as theories are part of our conception of the physical world, so the varied interpretations of the Bible are part of the meaning, which has to be in us as well as in the text, if we are to hold a dialogue with it. There is no lack of "data" in the Bible—only, in view of human limitations, an absence of creativity among interpreters.

Divergent views are traditional in biblical interpretation. No interpretation is unqualifiedly correct. The Babylonian Talmud tells of a rabbi arguing a legal point against majority opinion. Convinced he is right, the rabbi demands that God bear witness that his view is correct, and a concurring voice comes from heaven. The other rabbis answer, however, that the Torah is not in heaven and that on earth the majority should decide the disputed point.[14] Decisions are not correct but rather are agreed or disagreed upon; there is no ultimate right answer on earth, only the temporary assent of informed opinion. The same could be said of politics or, for that matter, of science.

The authority of the Bible as a religious text and the authority of Moses as a political leader raise comparable questions. Each is dependent on readers and followers to flesh out, and to act on, meanings. Whether leaders are followed or scriptures believed depends not only on an initial act of faith in trying something new and unproved but on subsequent experience in adapting ideas and following indicated directions. Society is not static, and neither is interpretation. Without continuous interpretation in the light of changing circumstance, it would be impossible to maintain the integrity of any original conception. Stability requires change.

What principles of interpretation are appropriate for the Torah as a book of instruction? The modern sage (as learned expositors of the Torah are called) Nehama Leibowitz sums up a lifetime of experience and centuries of tradition by saying, "There is one golden rule of interpretation: the particular can only be explicated in terms of its general context."[15] What more could a social scientist ask?

This book on leadership, which is designed to convey the Mosaic teaching in a general form, is intendedly scientific and therefore subject to the charge that it is more Greek than Hebrew. Am I, indeed, "trying to stuff biblical time into Greek space"?[16] The point is reminiscent of the longstanding debate in anthropology over whether peoples without modern technology are thereby convicted of being primitive in thought as well. Not so. Reason is hardly a monopoly of modern life. What is necessary is a method appropriate to making sensible the products of other cultures in ways comprehensible in ours.

STRUCTURAL ANTHROPOLOGY
AND RABBINIC RULES ARE ALIKE

By far the most powerful fieldwork methods in the social sciences are those of the structural anthropologists. Undeterred by gaps or apparent contradictions in chronology, able to accommodate dreams and fables, considering variants of the same story as clues to meaning, structural anthropologists take seriously the task of discovering the inner coherence of a way of life. Episodes are compared wherever they occur or however they appear, on the assumption that what matters most to people is how they ought to behave toward one another and how these values are to be embodied in their social practices.

The traditional rabbinic interpreters of the Bible, with centuries of practice, also sought to uncover layers of meaning by comparing biblical episodes. Perhaps it is not surprising, then, that the methods of structural anthropology turn out to be almost a carbon copy of the rules of rabbinic interpretation as these have been handed down in the last two thousand years. These rules, called *middoth*, were codified by various rabbis and have been made available to us in Hermann Strack's great work on the Talmud.[17] Because they care about the moral meaning of the Bible as a guide to social relations, the rabbis, like the man who spoke prose, have all along been practicing the best social science there is!

Edmund Leach's celebrated monographic article on the legitimacy of Solomon is useful to us because it uses an anthropological method—structural analysis. The "general assumption" that Leach attributes to Claude Lévi-Strauss—"society is a totality"—is the essence of structural analysis.[18] From this assumption of social consistency, it follows that society may be conceived of as elements comprising a system of relationships—the structure—held together by its own internal logic. The economy, the polity, the food, the family, the environment, the language, all fit together.

Structural analysis is by no means without rabbinic warrant, even in its lofty aspiration, except that the rabbis believe that no one gets to know it all. From the Torah as the embodiment or model of Jewish society follow all the other manifestations of culture; in it, the various elements form coherent teachings, which it is the interpreter's task to uncover. "Here I must emphasize," says Leach, "the very important distinction between structural contradiction (large-scale incompatibility of implication) and content contradiction (inconsistencies in the small-scale details of textual assertion)."[19] Contradiction (if it is not merely a trivial copying error or stray date) is a meaningful manifestation of a connecting structure that we, being fallible, have not yet had the wit or courage to discover. One of the rules for rabbinic interpretation states that if two passages appear to conflict, they can be made whole by a third.[20]

Leach recognizes that the relationship between the structural anthropologist and the theologian is close. Reading that two stories refer to individuals with similar sounding names, the historian, Leach observes, assumes simply that two different people are being mentioned; the structural analyst, on the other hand, considers whether the names may be used to link themes. The Middoth propose exactly this: "*Gezerah Shawah*, literally: similar injunction or regulation. 'Inference by Analogy,' by virtue of which, because in two Pentateuchal passages words occur which are similar or have the identical connotation, both laws, however different they may be in themselves, are subject to the same regulations and applications." As for historical chronology, it is stated in the Middoth that "many a biblical section refers to a later period than the one which precedes, and vice versa."[21] It is the associative logic of dreams, rather than the linear logic of our waking hours, that is followed in both structural analysis and in Middoth.

Historians are interested in why certain biblical events occurred. The structuralist, however, says Leach, "argues that the significance of individual items in any kind of story is to be found in their patterned arrangement. What attracts his attention is not the content... but the contrast of pattern as between one story and another."[22] Any number of rabbinic rules of interpretation run along the same lines. According to the Middoth of Rabbi Jose the Galilean, "Something important is compared with something trivial that a clear understanding may be facilitated." Others say simply: "A proposition serves to supplement a parallel proposition," or, "A specific case of a type of occurrences is mentioned, although the whole type is meant."[23] What the three rules have in common is precisely that they point to the pattern as distinguished from the content of a story.

The view that the remembered history of a people is significant because it is selected, so to speak, from alternative histories is a staple of both structuralists and sages. For the rabbis, every word, nay every letter of the Torah is significant, there for a purpose, which challenges them to ferret it out. Hence "A statement does not go well with the passage in which it occurs, but is in keeping with another passage and may then be applied to that passage."[24]

The unity of human experience, at least within a given cultural context, is also a cardinal tenet of structural analysis. In sharp contrast to the source critics, who speak of "a corrupt text" or of "inconsistency," Leach declares that the most distinctive feature of his structural method is that "this kind of analysis rests on a presumption that the whole of the text as we now have it *regardless of the varying historical origins of its component parts* may properly be treated as a unity."[25]

Now, to be sure, there is a difference: the rabbis believe their account to be true history, and Leach does not; or, rather, Leach does not care, because to him myth and history, being collective social products, serve the same function of justifying social relations. In rabbinic terms, however, the Torah is not a rationalization of social relations: it is the real thing, a didactic dictation of the social relations themselves.

If the terms "desired social relations" and "Torah" are equivalent as normative statements of how people should live, it is not surprising that rabbis and anthropologists who study a similar subject should have something in common. Going from the particular to the general pattern and deducing the particular from the general context are common to each of these scholarly enterprises. The key terms are generality, comparison, and context. "In contrast," Leach declares, "structural analysis leads to the recognition of relationships of a more abstract kind which may associate bodies of material which have little or no similarity of content."[26] By "abstract," he means general. Hence Leach speaks of comparisons among a variety of materials according to a general structure (or theoretical scheme) designed to get at patterns of social relationships. The same is true of the rabbinic Middoth.

One of the Middoth hits the structural nail on its conceptual head when it calls for "detailed determination of the General by means of the Particular, [and] of the Particular by means of the General."[27] Here we have parallel prescriptions—rabbinic interpretations and structural anthropology, separated essentially by vocabulary—for a method of analysis that is comparative and contextual, looking for analogies, generalizing in ever-larger dimensions until, it is hoped, the unity of the Torah and/or the structure of society stands revealed.

Listen to Leach on structural analysis of "precipitates," those unintended but meaningful residues of ways of life whose chance occurrence gives all the more guarantee that they contain the key to unlocking the culture codes: "The editorial amendments of various hands have become woven into an involuted network which can convey a 'message' which was not necessarily consciously intended by any particular editor." And, "What the myth then 'says' is not what the editors consciously intended to say but rather something which lies deeply embedded in Jewish traditional culture as a whole."[28] It follows that the endless editing of the Bible is the best guarantee that it still retains the most basic elements because these elements have survived editing. The more generations involved with a text, the longer the period of time, the greater its authenticity from the structural anthropological standpoint.

If the structural method and the rabbinic Middoth are, precept for precept, clear copies of one another, we know which came first. The best advice for fieldworkers in the Bible is similarly old-fashioned: Keep your feet on the ground, your eyes on the heavens, and do not accept any proposition that explains the one without the other—the institution without the ideas, or the God of Israel without His people.

THE STRUCTURAL METHOD VERSUS
SOURCE CRITICISM

Like any other method, structuralism has its drawbacks. The most serious of these, in my opinion, is the temptation it offers to subjectivity. One man's structure is another's incoherence. Consider, too, the trenchant criticism by Hyam Maccoby of a book that adopts the structural approach; the author, Maccoby writes, uses the method to give himself

> *carte blanche* to work within the structure of the tradition which he is examining.... In biblical studies, this means that we can jettison the critical programme of discerning sources and genres and the activity of editors, and concentrate on the Bible as a single literary work together with its leading exegeses.... Structuralist interpretation of the Bible has made some interesting advances, simply by taking the text as unitary instead of a haphazard collection made by scissors-and-paste methods. But at what point do we move from a new and welcome responsiveness to literary values to a self-indulgence that wilfully ignores the scientific work of two centuries?[29]

For me, however, the question is not whether the structural method has its faults, which it does, but whether source criticism, the recommended alternative, is superior for the purpose of studying leadership.

Let us suppose that one wanted to interpret political leadership in the Bible on the basis of source (or, as it is also called, documentary) criticism. In order to do this (as I know because I have tried), it is necessary to formulate hypotheses connecting the proposed sources to variations in leadership. What is troublesome is that the different sources are not connected to phenomena outside themselves. Interest in sources is almost entirely internal. Even if there were agreement on what parts of the Bible belong to which source, therefore, this would not usually aid in the interpretation of themes in the text. Until I learn of a better way of negotiating between the Bible and social science in regard to questions of leadership, I shall continue to rely on the structural method.

THE TORAH AS A TEACHING

That the Torah is a teaching, Jewish sages have maintained throughout the ages. Whatever else they are, its tales are meant to instruct. But they are not all-inclusive. The basis for their selection is their purpose in the life of the people the Torah was designed to serve. This view is set out by a modern sage, Samson Raphael Hirsch, in his celebrated commentaries on the Pentateuch: "The Torah does not narrate its stories for the purpose of teaching antiquities. Its aim is not to record history for its own sake.... Its goal... is... the religious and national education of the people of Israel, and to this end it employs traditional material. Only those tales were included from which religious or national instruction could be formed."[30]

My book intends to use ideas about leadership to interpret the Bible and to use biblical teachings about leadership to improve current understanding of that elusive yet essential activity. For these purposes, therefore, questions of origins—Who wrote the Bible? How was it written or rewritten? What ideological axes did the various hypothetical authors-cum-editors have to grind?—are subordinate to questions of content: Does the leadership perspective help us understand the Bible? What does the Torah teach about leadership? How valuable is this teaching? My emphasis is on the final form of the written Bible.[31]

I do not claim to depict the historical Moses, about whom nothing is known. It would be wonderful to have archaeological or other evidence relating to the period of the exodus from Egypt, but no such evidence is reliable enough to use.[32] All we have are the words. I do use the resources of traditional rabbinic interpretation and of current biblical criticism. The emphasis is on use, for my concern is with explicating the content of the Mosaic Bible as it bears on substantive issues of leadership. I use whatever interpretations help (whether by rabbis, churchmen, or secular scholars) and whichever methods work (semantic, structural, historical). The important limits are not the absence of eyewitnesses (or other corroborating data, which might tell us more about the actual events), but rather the limits of imagination and insight that can make the Bible speak in a meaningful voice.

How does one converse with the Bible? In the same way as with any rich body of ideas, by formulating and testing hypotheses about its meaning. But the rules for interpreting a text that expresses the collective experience of a people differ from those of ordinary history. Time sequence, for instance, is essential for narrative history; but for a book of instruction, chronology is merely a convenience. Thus, in interpreting the Bible, it is possible to group episodes without consideration of chronology. What matters is that the episodes be shown as comparable in terms of the meaning to be drawn from them.

We, you and I, reader and author, are the editor, translator, and interpreter of our teacher Moses.[33] What we learn depends on what questions we ask. For Jews, only Moses, through the Torah, can provide authoritative religious instruction. But this is not a book about religion, except insofar as it is necessary to illuminate the cultural context within which Moses acted. That is why the specifically sacerdotal, cultic, and sacrificial instructions are not discussed, unless they help us understand Moses as a political leader. Leadership is a subject on which no one is qualified to issue authoritative pronouncements and about which all of us are in need of instruction. Insofar as the secular subject of leadership is concerned, Moses is on his own.

The social science literature, as distinguished from biographies, seeks to generalize about leadership. It has sought to uncover the traits leaders have in common, the patterns of their relationship with followers, and the types of situations around which their interaction within groups occurs.[34]

Unfortunately, multiplying traits of leaders, times types of followers, times samples of situations, times group interactions has led to more variety than anyone can manage. Looked at in this light, leadership is an impossible subject for study, bogged down as it is in a confusing welter of personality and event. Are oversimplification (great man theories) or over-complexification (the interrelatedness of everything) the only alternatives? By showing that different kinds of political regimes produce different types of leaders, I hope to restore a semblance of order in the house of leadership studies.

Without relating leadership to regimes, the laudable efforts of social scientists to generalize leave them trapped in the very same prison of particularity from which they have striven so hard to escape. I therefore set out to develop abstract models of regimes, attaching to each a set of hypotheses about the behavior of leaders to be expected under each category. Evidence of the utility of these types of regimes depends on whether they enlighten us about the leadership of Moses, enabling us to interpret episodes hitherto regarded as obscure.

LEADERSHIP VARIES WITH REGIMES

Think of events in the Bible as a process of choosing among alternative ways of life. From a political viewpoint, the choice is among regimes, which relate rulers to the ruled. These political regimes are congruent with the social context from which they are derived. Each regime has its religious reflection up above; down below, each category of regime is accompanied by its style of leadership. The style stems from the way in which regimes are constituted. Leaders are shaped by (as they try to shape) particular regimes. Leaders like certain regimes and dislike others according to the fit between their proclivities and the prevailing patterns within which they have to operate. Most of us are born into regimes that we may modify but do not often change drastically. When we do change regimes, as Moses did, that is called a revolution; and its leaders, like Moses in his struggle against Pharaoh, are called revolutionaries.

Look at Moses as if he were the architect of an entire political regime. Sometimes Moses deliberately designs a regime to be compatible with his religion and his personality. At other times he blunders into a regime without fully understanding the consequences, either for his religion or for his style of leadership. Upon leaving Egypt, for instance, Moses is depressed by slavery and impressed by liberty. Like other revolutionaries, he vilifies the establishment and glorifies a free people whose future life is full of promise. How he (or any leader) will do without hierarchy, he cannot yet imagine. How this formerly enslaved population will ward off external attacks and resist foreign temptations to abandon its beliefs without accepting the authority of its leadership is too far ahead in emotional time to be envisaged. Moses and his people want to get out of slavery and they do. Only then does he realize that if all are free to choose what they will, some will choose Egypt, and others Israel—thus destroying not only the unity of the people but also any personality (Moses) torn between the two.

So Moses moves toward a regime of equity. Leaders gain consent by showing how bad others are, but they have no way of maintaining the support of their followers except by claiming divine inspiration. If leaders are to be pure and cannot be coercive, they will live short and unhappy lives.

Like many another leader, Moses was against the "establishment" until he realized that he was the establishment. This powerful personality then set up a regime of hierarchy, shoring up his leadership and simultaneously trying to stave off a return to the abuses the Hebrews had escaped by leaving Egypt. It would be terrible if the Promised Land turned out to be like the Egypt they had left. To revert to slavery of the spirit of their own free will would be worse than remaining in bondage by compulsion.

Just as Exodus and Numbers tell how the Hebrew people traveled from slavery in Egypt to self-government in the land of Canaan, so these models of regimes are a map of Moses' political wanderings. If Moses and his people discover there is no perfect regime, that each has its good and bad points (even slaves get fed), this, too, is part of their joint learning experience.

Considering these models as if Moses had constructed them should enable us to follow in his political footsteps. Moses' uniqueness is maintained because the models are made to fit his historical movements. The general applicability of the Torah as a teaching on leadership is enhanced, I think, by creating categories into which the experiences of others may also fit. These "ideal types," as Max Weber called them (or "extreme representations," as I do, to avoid suggesting desirability), range widely across experience. They vary from total equality to extreme regimentation and from groups that deal with everyone to those that traffic with no one. Most experience, no doubt, falls in between. Seeing Moses' difficulties with leadership as problems of political design encourages us, reader and author together, to view Moses' world from his point of view.

Slavery

Under the regime called slavery, outsiders manipulate the individual. The religion is narcissistic. The ruler is worshiped as a god, as was Pharaoh. The ruler alone receives revelation from on high. Leadership is despotic, involving continuous control of all aspects of life. The leadership problem in despotism is partly that of replacement—leaders are reluctant to let go—and partly overdependence—whether the leaders are foolish or insane, their orders are carried out, and there is hell to pay. This is the Egyptian regime in which the Hebrew people are living when Moses comes to tell them their God has said it is time to go.

What does Moses the designer do? Not much. Escaping from Pharaoh appears to be enough; subsequent events are left to take their own course. Instead of trying his best to design an appropriate regime, Moses passively lets the Lord provide. He has not yet learned, as he will, that even (or especially) after miracles—the division of the Sea of Reeds or the earth swallowing up Korah—nothing fundamental has changed. Moses does not know yet that the designer has to think about changing relationships among his people, not about magic rods or natural disasters.

One could try to rescue Moses from this error by making a retroactive virtue out of that contemporary necessity. As a political architect concerned with building a nation, one might say, Moses sees anarchy as a necessary transitional stage from slavery toward equity. Until the people themselves experience what anarchy does to them—observe the debauchery of the revelry before the Golden Calf, which (says the Bible) literally leaves the people naked before their enemies—they will not be prepared to take on the burdens of the Commandments. In my opinion, this hypothesis is implausible. No people would knowingly do this to themselves. And if Moses had known about all this in advance, he would have to be understood as divine, which would negate the most important distinction Moses tried to teach and would make a mockery of his life by turning him into an idol, just another self-worshiping Pharaoh.

Anarchy

Out of Egypt, the Israelites at once fall into anarchy. Each tribe has an equal chance to compete for political power, but group boundaries remain weak. The children of Israel are buffeted by outside influences; they will deal with anyone about anything. They have no permanent rulers, no permanent gods. Atheism or polytheism reigns. When they need a ruler or a god, the people go out and get one. The leadership problem for anarchies is to find a leader when one is needed, and yet be able to get rid of the fellow if he stays too long or exceeds his limited mandate.

Enter the complaining chorus. The people start threatening to choose new gods and appoint new leaders—it hardly matters in which order.

If Moses does not meet their demands, perhaps they will find a new leader who will.

What should they do? How can they design a new regime? Having so recently fled from Pharaoh, Moses is not about to jump into his shoes. Slavery is idolatrous as well as despotic. Nor did Moses think of himself as a temporary occupant of the role of leader—at least not until the people reached the Promised Land, a destination they would never approach if they vacillated. Anarchy—different gods for different purposes—is intolerable, as Moses showed at the incident of the Golden Calf. Equality among believers must remain. What the leader does is to shore up group boundaries to make the people resistant to outside forces. Lots more commandments! No more Golden Calves! But Moses still has much to learn. The equality designed into the new regime (*equity*, I call it) is going to cause havoc within the strong group Moses hopes to lead; the people will indeed resist outside intervention but will also resist leadership from within.

Equity

It is not true that equities have no rules; there are two: inside is equal and outside is awful. The truth, that there is only one God for this people, applies directly and equally to all members. All receive revelation and so all are entitled to interpret it. Leadership is sporadic but inclusive. There may be no leadership, but if there is, it must be charismatic—touched by the divine spirit and gifted with extraordinary personal abilities—or it would not be perfect and deserving of support. Leaders will be replaced, but while they rule, they are all-powerful. Whereas members of anarchies hedge leadership around with restrictions, hiring leaders only for specific and limited purposes, members of equities either reject or accept leadership wholeheartedly.

The leadership problem in equities is that such regimes are basically anti-leadership. As long as the leader is seen as pure and perfect, he gets unanimous consent. But if things go wrong or the slightest suspicion arises, leaders have no powers, such as exist in a hierarchy, by which to command consent; from being everything, they become nothing. How, then, do leaders hold on? The answer is to expel deviants and condemn the outside world. By showing how bad it is outside, charismatic leaders can hope to sustain support to rule inside. The sure sign of equity is a continuous need for leadership (how else to reach decisions when everyone is equal and divided?) accompanied by attacks on whatever leaders turn up.

As he liked the spontaneity of anarchy, so Moses cares for the participatory enthusiasm of equity. When things are good, they are very good indeed. But when they are bad, as the nursery rhyme says, they are horrid. Charges of being both too weak and too strong abound. No charge, including idolatry, was spared Moses. But that was not the worst. Lacking means of decision making—in the absence of unanimity, equities tend to split—disputes are resolved by one side leaving and forming its own equity. Thus, for Moses, equity turned out to block the desired unity of his God, his people, and himself.

By then, Moses realized that his Hebrew people had to be separated from others if they were to stick to the one God; strong group boundaries were essential. The idea of equality still appealed to Moses, so long as everyone came to the same conclusion on critical issues or leaders had sufficient authority to decide in cases of disagreement. Moses, the designer of regimes, in the end decided to make do with a little less equality in return for more hierarchy.

Hierarchy

Hierarchy is a pro-leadership regime. Revelation from God comes to the people only through its leadership. There is one universal God, just as there is one set of rules. Mediation is not occasional, depending on circumstance and inspiration; mediation between God and man (or between one man and another) is built into the regime. Hierarchy regularizes leadership. For each decision there is an authorized decision maker whose word goes. But, though leadership is continuous, it is not necessarily unlimited. People lower down may have rights against those higher up. The same laws apply to leaders and followers: within their spheres, leaders reign supreme; but outside them, they do not.

Hierarchy, too, has its difficulties with leadership. Obedience may begin to replace initiative; everyone may do the same foolish thing unquestioningly. The lack of criticism may prove stultifying. In practice, hierarchy could use a dash of equity. Criticism from the group is good for leaders, who easily grow used to being obeyed. How much hierarchy and how much equity works best? Moses struggled with this question. From that day to this, the political regime of Judaism has alternated between equity and hierarchy. If problems of leadership nowadays still rest on choices between hierarchy and equity, order and equality, then this is another difficulty about which the Bible can teach us.

The four regimes that occupy our attention, because they are the ones that matter in the Bible, may be thought of as the primary colors from which other combinations may be made.[35] Moses himself combines equity with hierarchy. Were we thinking about contemporary regimes, I would call that hybrid "social democracy," a regime in which equality modifies hierarchy and hierarchy stabilizes equity. Were I thinking about the Jacksonian era before the Civil War in the United States, the combination of anarchy and equity, based on the belief that equality of opportunity would lead to equality of result, would emerge as a regime of American individualism. Since this is a book about biblical regimes, however, it is the primary forms, not the hybrids, that are of chief concern.[36]

MOSES MAKES A U-TURN

Everyone knows that in the desert Moses led the Israelites on a path with many detours. The Book of Exodus states that God deliberately advised against a direct route, which we can take to mean that the children of Israel had a few things to learn along the way.

These political regimes constitute a map of Moses' political progress and, of course, retrogression. Nature has no straight lines and neither, needless to say, does politics. Learning about learning—learning from Moses how to learn about leadership—is not a straightforward process. As we know, a lot of backsliding takes place; it did then and does now. Movement is forward, but as the Bible shows us, roundabout. Piecing together Moses' political travels in a table, we can see that they constitute a U-turn from slavery to anarchy to equity to hierarchy. But the end result (until the next change occurs, of course) is not unalloyed hierarchy. Experience has led to an interpenetration of regimes. Slavery is impermissible. The state-worship that was Egypt is rooted out of Hebrew consciousness as the worst form of idolatry. The law applies not merely to ruler and ruled alike but with special severity to those who exercise public power. Anarchy remains a valuable element in social life, but it is relegated to the realm of private transactions, inappropriate for a religion or a regime with strong group boundaries in which decisions are taken for the people as a whole. Elements of equity exist, but the equality of believers is modified by established authority delegating power through hierarchy.

The instruction God gives Moses at the burning bush is that he cannot be a leader without followers. The dilemma Moses faces is whether he can be a leader with them. The incompatibilities in expectations about leadership, which we would call role conflict,[37] are illustrated in Moses. His greatness and his weakness are part and parcel of the same person. He worries about becoming so potent that God will strike him down as a rival or so impotent that he cannot carry out his instructions. His fears for the survival of his people, as well as his fear they will abandon him, and thus their God, by returning to Egypt, lead Moses to adopt fierce countermeasures. His desire to free his people from their tutelage to him, as well as to Pharaoh, leads him to devolve his powers. The rest that Deuteronomy promises those who do their duty—such as the happy medium between too much and too little power—is achieved only in the grave. In real life, the balance among personal needs is mediated by the never-ending search for a balance among regimes.

Before Moses goes anywhere, he must conquer his ambivalence and agree to lead. Chapter 1 takes Moses on an internal journey from the idolatry of Pharaoh's court, which worships a mere man as a god, to becoming a Jew by conviction as well as by birth. Without liberating himself from his doubts, Moses could not lead the Israelites out of slavery. We see in Chapter 2 how Moses learned what not to do by practicing on his inadvertent teacher, Pharaoh. Chapter 3 portrays Moses and his people under an anarchic regime. Once the revolution was successful, Moses had to decide whether to remain passive, thus letting the people slide back into polytheism, or to become active so as to save them as an entity, worshiping the same God and staying together on the journey to the Promised Land. Moses leads by overcoming the rebellions of the Golden Calf and the spies. Here he changes the political regime from anarchy to equity.

In Chapter 4, having experienced both the enthusiasm and the exhaustion of a regime of equity, Moses moves toward hierarchy. He simultaneously seeks to shore up leadership against endless attack and to guard the people against its excesses. Chapter 5 will show how—by not going to the land promised to him and his people—Moses exemplifies the greatest lesson he has to teach: the teacher must learn that his greatest accomplishment will be to have enabled his students to learn without him.

The Conclusion explores the social science literature on leadership and seeks to supersede it with a perspective in which leadership becomes a part of regimes. I appraise Moses' influence upon the regimes he led and consider how participation in different regimes affected his leadership. It does not come in a directly didactic form—do this, do that. It is self-exemplifying, not self-glorifying. Moses invokes the memory of the past so as to multiply and enrich the range of experiences relevant to solving the problems of succeeding ages. At his most successful, Moses teaches us that we can do without him by learning from his mistakes, as well as from our own. The Epilogue speculates about how the survival of the Jewish people, after their experience with judges and kings, may be traced to Moses' teachings about the variety of permissible political regimes.

1

SLAVERY
Passive People, Passive Leader

When Moses ascended onto the heights [to receive the Torah], he found the Holy One, blessed be He, sitting there tying wreaths [or crowns] to the letters. He said to Him: "Master of the Universe, who is holding You back?" [That is, why are You not satisfied with the letters as they are, so that You add crowns to them, that is, the little flourishes that occur on certain letters of the Torah scrolls?] He answered him: "There is a man who will arise after many generations by the name of Akiba ben Joseph; he will expound heaps and heaps of laws upon every tittle." Then he said to Him: "Master of the Universe, show him to me." He replies: "Turn around." Then Moses went and sat down behind eight rows [of the students of Akiba]. But he did not understand what they were talking about. Thereupon his strength left him [that is, he was perplexed because he was unable to follow discourses concerning the Torah he himself had written]. When Akiba came to a certain matter where his students asked him how he knew it, he said to them: "It is a teaching given to Moses at Sinai." Then he [Moses] was comforted and returned to the Holy One, blessed be He. He said to Him: "Master of the Universe, You have a man like that and You give the Torah by me?!" He replied: "Be silent, for this is the way I have determined it." Then Moses said: "Master of the Universe, You have shown me his knowledge of the Torah, show me also his reward." He answered: "Turn around." He turned around and saw that Akiba's flesh was being weighed at the market stalls [his flesh was torn by the tortures of the executioners]. Then he said to Him: "Master of the Universe, this is the Torah and this is its reward?" He replied: "Be silent, for this is the way I have determined it."

—Babylonian Talmud, Menahot 29b

The Garden of Eden sets the stage for human beings capable of accepting (because they are capable of rejecting) regulation of their relationships with other people and with God. There is a fundamental asymmetry: bowing down to God is one choice, bowing down to idols (that is, to the handiwork of men) is the other. Mankind is separated from God so that it can come together on some basis other than slavery.

There is no mystery to the main message. If God is good, the question is, how does evil come into the world? Genesis, Nahum Sarna tells us, "wishes to indicate very simply that evil is a human product, that God created the world good but that man, through the free exercise of his will in rebellion against God, corrupts the good and puts evil in its place."[1] Obedience to God is good, disobedience is bad. True so far as it goes, but not necessarily the whole truth.

Let us look more closely at the temptation of Eve and Adam's acquiescence. The subtle serpent is the scientist. Alouph Hareven, whose commentary has taught me much, observes that the Hebrew for serpent is *nahash*, from the same root as *nahesh*, to guess.[2] Where other people have certainties—Eve believes what God tells her, that if she eats the fruit "of the tree of the knowledge of good and evil" she "shalt surely die" (Gen. 2:17)—the serpent offers the hypothesis "Ye shall not surely die" (Gen. 3:4). Maybe she will and maybe she won't. If Eve does die, the serpent suggests, "your eyes shall be opened, and ye shall be as gods, knowing good and evil" (Gen. 3:5). The rest of the story we know: Adam goes along; he and Eve are punished by expulsion and condemned to earn their living instead of having it given to them. And the serpent is punished by being made to crawl and be crushed under foot. But is it obvious that the serpent is wrong and that the expulsion from Eden is entirely involuntary?

In fact, the Bible states that Adam and Eve do not die then. They do have to face up to mortality, which may or may not be the same thing. It is specifically stated that their eyes are opened, and they thus become ashamed of their nakedness. (Idols have no eyes and do not see.) In a word, they become human. In phrases remarkably similar to Aaron's mealy-mouthed excuse to Moses at the scene of the Golden Calf, Eve tries to escape responsibility, saying, "The serpent beguiled me, and I did eat" (Gen. 3:13).

Like most utopias, Eden appears to have been awfully dull. Adam and Eve are servants of the garden, guaranteed a living but in return forced "to dress it and to keep it" (Gen. 2:15). They do not even get to plant it because the Lord has done that. A boring bargain. Adam and Eve are no more aware of the differences among things than of distinctions between themselves.[3]

Expulsion, by contrast with the ennui of Eden, gave mankind the opportunity to test experience, to try and to fail. The story of Job's trials (why should the good man suffer?) ends not by God giving Job the answer he seeks but by God telling Job he was right to ask. In Eden, Adam and Eve can do no evil, but by the same token neither can they differentiate evil from good. Lack of opportunity is as poor a defense of morality as of virginity.

The Garden of Eden, in which all is provided and mankind has only to be obedient, can be seen as parallel to the regime of slavery in Egypt, a parallel made more powerful because the despot is benevolent.

The departure from the Garden of Eden is the first exodus. "Before they ate of the tree of knowledge," Umberto Cassuto tells us, "the man and his wife were like small children who knew nought of what exists around them.... He wished to enlarge the boundaries set for him... hence he fell prey to all the travails... outside these boundaries."[4] The boundary marker placed east of Eden—"a flaming sword which turned every way, to keep the way of the tree of life" (Gen. 3:24)—is equivalent, perhaps, to the "pillar of fire" through which "the Lord went before them" (Exod. 13:21-22) during the Hebrews' liberation from bondage in Egypt. The leadership of God is predicated on man's freedom to turn back. The gift of that leadership and this ability are owed to the time when mankind insisted on growing up and making its own mistakes.

SLAVERY AND IDENTITY

Under a regime of slavery, subjects become objects; the Hebrew people lose their identity. Pharaoh thinks he is a god, and the Hebrew people do not think at all. To the great cultural questions of identity—Who am I? To what group do I belong?—they can only give a negative non-answer—they are slaves of Pharaoh, which is to say they are not themselves. The other overriding question of life—What should I do?—does not arise because the people can only answer, "What we are told!" The rules of life are made by others, and slaves cannot change them. They are nonentities—bodies without brains—because they are idolaters, bowing down to men like themselves. The Hebrews are followers without leaders of their own; whether they will or not—the point is they have no will—Pharaoh and his overseers are their leaders.

How can change come about? Either slavery can become incorporated into hierarchy as leaders seek support from the lower orders, or leadership can be made entirely dependent on followers, in the form of an anarchy. Egyptian slaves might become, perhaps they were already part of, Egyptian hierarchy. For the Hebrews, however, lacking identity or even a place on the ladder of Egyptian life, anarchy—breaking their bonds—was the likely alternative. What they would become then, as in most revolutions, would have to be decided afterward.

The first dilemma is that the identity the Israelites hope to achieve by liberation also is its precondition. Without identity, there can be no action. They must be able to say something about who they are before there is a "they" to make a revolution. The second dilemma is that liberation from leadership under slavery also requires a restriction of liberty. Unless they act in concert, their course will be hopeless. Whether they wish to remain as they are or to make a revolutionary change, slaves need leadership.

But do leaders need slaves? Slavery is more likely to breed fear than fearlessness. It is not only hard to shake slaves out of lethargy, it is even more difficult to keep them going when things get tough. Not least is the fear of leaders that they will be killed by their followers, either because the leaders are unsuccessful or because they are too successful, thus threatening to enslave the people they have just liberated.

Identity creates a dual dilemma for leaders: they need one for themselves as well as for their followers. In Hebrew "to lead" means going out in front—being a driver, not a passenger. If leaders' identities are weak and their followers' are strong, leaders will be discarded at the first opportunity, the hoped-for hierarchy degenerating into anarchy. If leaders' identities are much stronger than their followers', leaders will be tempted to impose themselves on their followers, promising equity but practicing slavery.

Is the purpose of leadership to help followers realize a common conception of the good life? Or is the purpose to aggrandize the leader? Put in such blatant and unflattering contrast, the moral choice is evident. But virtue as well as vice has its excesses. When the Torah tells us that farmers must not harvest every bit of grain or collect every sheaf inadvertently left in the field, it is doing more than recommending social legislation to help the poor (as in the story of Ruth and Naomi). It is advocating moderation even in morality. Compulsiveness easily converts to fanaticism. The farmer who harvests not 99 percent of his crop but every last little bit becomes consumed by his compulsion. Soon enough excess—getting it all—becomes an overwhelming passion. His fellow man, the God in him, is squeezed out. This is why fanaticism is a form of idolatry—devoting one's life to one's own creations to the exclusion of others. The moral madman may murder millions—so long, of course, as it is in a good cause. Worshiping one's own virtue is the ultimate vice of leadership that Moses must renounce.

From the beginning, Moses, born a Hebrew and reared an Egyptian, has a split identity. Shall he choose Israel or Egypt; one God or many; independence or slavery? When he is chosen (or chooses) to lead, Moses also is healing the split inside of him. Choosing the one God makes Moses whole. Helping himself by helping his people, Moses becomes whole (holy, if you will), thereby elevating his personal drama to a profound religious and political level.[5]

A PASSIVE PEOPLE, A PASSIVE LEADER

Nothing about Moses can be understood without knowing that he began under a regime in which slavery was inside him as well as outside in the land of Egypt. Between the burning bush and Mount Sinai, Moses does not undertake a single independent act. He follows orders, even delegating implementation to his brother Aaron. Moses represents the people, voicing their complaints to God and adding one or two of his own. Nowhere does Moses seek to exert causal force, making outcomes different than they would have been without him.

Moses' passivity, as I shall demonstrate, stands in mute contrast to his activity before God revealed Himself. Moses had interceded to prevent the beating of a Hebrew (thereby killing an Egyptian) with more than ordinary deliberation. It was not a purely impulsive man of whom it was reported that "he looked this way and that way, and when he saw that there was no man, he slew the Egyptian, and hid him in the sand" (Exod. 2:12).[6] An imprudent man, fearing he had been discovered, would not flee "from the face of Pharaoh" (Exod. 2:15). Nor would a cowardly man, having nothing to gain, help the daughters of the priest of Midian when shepherds chased them away from the well. Moses drew out of this episode not only water but a wife, Zipporah, the priest's daughter, who—when doubts assailed Moses on the way to Egypt—saved Moses by reasserting his will to deliver the people. As he repeats Jacob's experience at the well, Moses also shares the patriarch's ambivalence about fulfilling divine destiny.

It was not as though God had not warned Moses, who is both repulsed and attracted. At the burning bush, the first words Moses hears (after his name) are "Draw not nigh hither" (Exod. 3:5). Moses is standing on holy ground. A boundary line separates man from God that he must not cross. And, as God warns, Moses hides "his face; for he was afraid to look upon God" (Exod. 3:6). In Egypt not long before, Moses had fled from the face of a smaller god.

At this early stage, Moses' passivity mirrors that of his people. Their bondage to Pharaoh parallels his subservience to his own doubts. Will Moses consent to make this self his self, this people his people, this God his God? Will his identity and action be fused into the common culture of Judaism?

What's in a Name?

When God first called his name from the burning bush, Moses, who
had spent his middle life in exile, cried out immediately, "Here am I."[7]
But, hearing what God demanded, he began to equivocate: "Who am I,"
he asked, "that I should go unto Pharaoh, and that I should bring forth
the children of Israel out of Egypt?" (Exod. 3:11). That gap between
the self-assured "Here am I" and the self-doubting "Who am I?" marks
a split within Moses. The "who" he is and the "what" he should do are
out of joint. On one hand, Moses is quick to admit frailty in light of
the awesome task to which he is called—to rescue an entire people from
bondage. On the other, even if Moses did rescue that nation, the danger that he might yet fail for lack of faith metamorphoses into another
danger: that he might overreact to his own success. From the first call
of Exodus to his farewell address in Deuteronomy, Moses continues to
question, "Who am I?"—a mere mortal charged with creating a nation
or a luminous leader, almost a god himself?

Moses also asks a second question—What should I do? Should he
become a permanent leader, risking idolatry, or a temporary teacher, risking disappointment? Dramatic unity is achieved because, given Moses'
upbringing in the Egyptian court, the two questions also spring from
his dual heritage, as Jew and as Egyptian.

Moses' essential qualities—the pride that will amplify and the humility that will restrict his potential as a leader—show forth in the first
dialogue with God. Moses' self-distrust is sympathetically portrayed; he
is understandably stunned by the part God summons him to play in
history. Moses continues to parade his own unworthiness despite God's
reassurance, "Certainly I will be with thee" (Exod. 3:12). It would seem
that Moses can take little solace from this assurance when he does not
know yet who this "I" is. Having begun by questioning his own identity,
Moses goes on to question the deity's: "Behold, when I come unto the
children of Israel, and shall say unto them, The God of your fathers hath
sent me unto you; and they shall say to me, What is his name? what
shall I say unto them?" (Exod. 3:13). No ordinary man, this Moses, who
presumes to question the Lord.

Before proceeding to the next passage—God's response, which begs
the question—it is worthwhile to look at Moses' style as interlocutor.

It seems surprising that the God who comes to call is not welcomed but interrogated. In reply to God's imperatives, Moses questions, "Who am I?" Then, "What shall I say?" If Moses seriously doubts his own adequacy in the first question, in the second he verges on doubting the divinity's. For though Moses asks God's name, he has already had an answer; when God first spoke He had announced His intention as well as His presence: "I am the God of thy father, the God of Abraham, the God of Isaac, and the God of Jacob.... I have surely seen the affliction of my people... and have heard their cry... for I know their sorrows; And I am come down to deliver them" (Exod. 3:6-8). God will give this same answer once again. What, then, motivated Moses' further quest for identification?

It will become clear that Moses is looking for what we all want—guarantees that things will turn out all right. If Moses can control the future by summoning the God who controls it, he will have what he wants when he wants it.

At this point, God grants the validity of Moses' protestations and remains patient, however ineffable in His response. Avoiding the direct appeal, God replies, "I am that I am" (Exod. 3:14) (implying "Mind your own business; it is not for you to limit the Lord"). Moses is saying, in effect, "Help me and I'll have faith"; and God is replying, "Have faith and I'll help you." These are two tough bargainers.

Moses does not press the issue here, but later (at Mount Sinai and in the wilderness of Kadesh) he will ask again for explicit assurances, only to receive the same idem per idem response.[8] At each point, God rejects the demand for a revelation, either of His name or of His glory—evading the question without unconditionally refusing the request. Since Moses, in this first dialogue, also wants to evade God's commission, what causes them simultaneously to hesitate? We have already noted why Moses might be ambivalent: a historical project is announced and, before having time even to consider its significance, he is called upon to enact it in all its magnitude. Why God might mistrust Moses is less easy to understand. Before we can explain the ambivalence of the chooser toward the chosen—why each dreads and desires the other—we must first ask: Who is this Moses that God has called?

From the few episodes related about Moses' life before the burning bush revelation, we know that he has a strong sense of justice. He has intervened three times on the side of the oppressed: first in a struggle between an Egyptian and a Hebrew, and then in a quarrel between two of his own Hebrew brethren. In the second instance, a Hebrew rebukes him: "intendest thou to kill me, as thou killedst the Egyptian?" (Exod. 2: 14). Of course, leaders do not intend to kill followers; it just sometimes turns out that way. Moses, realizing that the first deed is known, flees to exile in Midian. But despite this precautionary measure, he refuses a cover of anonymity. Once more he intervenes for the sake of the down-trodden, drawing water at a well for Jethro's daughters, who have been threatened by rival shepherds (Exod. 2:17). He marries one of them, Zipporah, and becomes a shepherd.

These three episodes help suggest why God would select Moses for his grandiose mission: high ideals and moral courage mark him equal to the task. Moses' identification with his own people is even more strik-ing, considering that he risked a comfortable life in the luxury of the Egyptian court for the sake of his beliefs. When we understand from the story of Joseph that "every shepherd is an abomination unto the Egyptians" (Gen. 46:34), who "might not eat bread with the Hebrews" (Gen. 43:32), we know that Moses had indeed put himself beyond the pale. God needs a zealous leader.

This capsule biography is equally instructive as to why Moses needs God. Moses' passion for justice, however admirable, results in violence that produces no significant result. The Hebrew who questions Moses' authority—"Who made thee a prince and a judge over us?" (Exod. 2:14)—has a good case. Impetuous slaughter and sporadic anger are no substitute for a well-conceived strategy. The fact that, after looking over both shoulders, Moses slays and then hastily buries the Egyptian sug-gests that he lacks legal authority. As a fugitive in Midian, what good can all his righteous indignation do? As Brevard S. Childs comments, "He has become indistinguishable from every other political fugitive."[9] A loose identification with the Hebrew people is not the same as their acknowledgment of his leadership. For the mission God has in mind, Moses must be invested with more authority than merely that provided by a personal sense of justice.

No doubt it was comforting for Moses to be instructed to tell Phar-aoh that the Lord said, "Israel is my son, even my first-born: and I say unto thee: Let my son go, that he may serve me: and if thou refuse to let him go, behold, I will slay thy son, even thy first-born" (Exod. 4:22-23). These are tough words, maybe too tough. If one first-born may be slain, why not another? For every affliction suffered by the Egyptians also threatens Hebrews, who are in Egypt not to learn about Pharaoh but about themselves. If the Egyptians do not seem to learn anything from one plague to another, neither do the Israelites from their experiences in the desert.

Later Moses would hear the Lord say that if the people followed Him and obeyed the law, "I will put none of these diseases upon thee, which I have brought upon the Egyptians" (Exod. 15:26). Comfort perhaps, but—for those strong or volatile enough to transgress—too close for comfort.

Will Moses be worshiped as divine if God invests him with divine authority? God has good reason to have reservations. A man capable of sudden rage, a man capable of killing, is also a man capable of taking matters into his own hands. Having slain an Egyptian in a good cause, might not Moses also kill in a bad one?

Nor, to extend the analogy, would this be a private enterprise. For the first time in history, God is choosing an agent for specific action in a political arena. The covenant He will make through Moses is not like the personal covenant God once made with Abraham, nor even the promise to a family that He offered the clan of Isaac and Jacob. Moses will be granted a power that no former covenant party enjoyed, as leader of an entire population, and could easily become the object of that people's faith rather than a vehicle for transmitting faith in God. After all, in the eyes of the world, Moses will (as God later tells him) be as "a god to Pharaoh" (Exod. 7:1). This injunction, however, cannot be taken too literally. To return to our point of departure, God's circular response ("I am that I am") does describe a boundary—paradoxically, a boundary that cannot be defined, but one that nevertheless limits Moses' ability to assume its powers.

If Moses wants control, the name of the divinity could provide it. To the ancient way of thinking, a name—which for us is more like a convenient label—represented the innermost identity of a being; consequently, knowing the name meant having access to the power such an identity implied. As Martin Buber points out in his *Moses*: "The 'true' name of a person, like that of any other object, is far more than a mere denotative designation for men who think in categories of magic; it is the essence of the person, distilled from his real being, so that he is present in it once again. What is more, he is present in it in such a form that anybody who knows the true name and can pronounce it in the correct way can gain control of him."[10]

Even if Moses does not calculate all that is thrown in the balance by his question—a leap from the magical belief system that had reigned for centuries to the new age of faith about to commence—God does. God has been asked this question before and will be asked it again. Two other passages in the Bible provide an illuminating context to Moses' request.[11] In Genesis we are told that a man "wrestled... until the breaking of day" with Jacob on his way home from exile (Gen. 32:24). In this nocturnal encounter (a parallel to one that Moses himself will soon face), it is clear that Jacob, wrestling with his own conscience, struggles with God as well. Presumption persists even in the face of fear and exhaustion. Jacob knows he is fortunate to be let off, "for I have seen God face to face, and my life is preserved." To Jacob's pleas, "Tell me, I pray thee, thy name," God has replied only, "Wherefore is it that thou dost ask after my name?" (Gen. 32:29-30).

In a second instance, that same question is more sharply rebuffed. Manoah, discovering that his wife has been visited by a divinity, is miffed that she passed up an opportunity to discover its name. When the angel of God pays a second visit, Manoah takes the initiative: "What is thy name, that when thy sayings come to pass we may do thee honor?" The angel this time returns an unmistakable rejection: "Why askest thou thus after my name, seeing it is secret?" (Judg. 13:17-18).

The very first man, Adam, was put to sleep to keep him from learning the secrets of creation. God is freedom. The best expression of this view I have been able to find comes from von Rad: "God condescends to men, He reveals Himself to men as the God who is there to help—the constant, active God. But at the same time He reveals that He is completely free in His own actions. He will always be the Lord, He never gives Himself up into the hands of men, and He will never put Himself at the service of their purposes."[12]

Manoah, like Moses, has a secondary motivation for his question. In order to worship God properly, Manoah reasons, it is necessary to know the name of the one whom one reveres. The logic appears convincing; man cannot honor an unknown. A finer distinction must be drawn, however, between positive invocation in prayer and the conjuring magicians practice. Is it necessary to possess His name in order to honor the one God, or in order to find out which god to honor? If the latter is true, a request for the deity's name represents return to a different faith through which many deities could be invoked. What is surprising is not that Moses gets no direct answer but rather the patience with which God entertains his appeal.

From the outset, even as the Lord urges Moses to lead, he is made aware of limitations to be observed.[13] Moses' solidarity with the people will make him an unparalleled leader, but the desire to overidentify with God must be continually circumscribed. This is the meaning of the literal *circum scription*, "I am that I am."[14] The very elasticity of the formula provides a direct, not a vague, response. *Ehyeh asher ehyeh* in Hebrew includes "I will be what I will be" and, if transposed into the causative mood (*Yahweh asher yihweh*), "He causes to be What Comes into Existence."[15] This meaning is particularly important for understanding what God wishes to tell Moses. God will intervene in history. He does not deny Moses knowledge of the future, but this is not the same as giving him an operational guide. God has begun an experiment with mankind, and man, not yet fully formed, can affect the outcome.

In this excursus on Moses' question and God's initial response, we have neglected the rest of God's reply. Refusing to give Moses a name in one verse, He appears to grant it in the next: "Thus shalt thou say unto the children of Israel, I AM hath sent me unto you" (Exod. 3:14); "Thus shalt thou say unto the children of Israel, the Lord [Heb., "Yahweh"] God of your fathers, the God of Abraham, the God of Isaac, and the God of Jacob, hath sent me unto you: this is my name for ever" (Exod. 3:15). The first verse emphasizes God's continual presence with no further qualification. What, then, are we to make of the name "Yahweh," which, were it not for this apparent interpolation, would seem to answer Moses' specific request?

God's "I am," or, here, "He is," includes past, present, and future.[16] The context only highlights this meaning. Coupling His plan for the future with the motivation of past history ("I have... seen that which is done to you"), God promises, "I will bring you up out of... Egypt... into a land flowing with milk and honey" (Exod. 3:16-17). In God's mode of argumentation, the past is always incorporated in a significant link to the future. God will reveal Himself only in the events of history, not in any specific name. The "token" of His presence, as He had told

Moses in their very first exchange, will be supplied only in the future: "When thou hast brought forth the people out of Egypt, ye shall serve God upon this mountain" (Exod. 3:12).

Actually Moses, not God, is being named. Moses' conscience already has an identity; it is his ego, his desire for self-esteem and self-preservation, that does not yet know who can call or make a claim on it.

Enough of hide-and-seek with names; it is time for the mission to be carried out. If naming cannot be used to control destiny, being named to leadership—captured by a role he does not wish to refuse but cannot quite accept—will be to Moses what he makes of it in history. The one thing God cannot do alone, because it is a contradiction in His terms, is to force faith. Like leaders everywhere, Moses will have to act without full understanding of the consequences for others and for himself. He is to be a faithful follower of a God whose power and will cannot be comprehended. Moses has his "name," but it is nothing without faith.[17]

At this juncture in their dialogue, Moses seems imbued with little faith. Though God reveals His long-range plan with a careful itinerary ("unto the place of the Canaanites, and the Hittites, and…" [Exod. 3:8]—a further concession to Moses' desire for details?), His "servant" balks at the very first clause. God has promised a future, but Moses cannot hear beyond the immediate instance. Stumbling over God's first assurance—"they shall hearken unto thy voice"—Moses continues to demur. "But, behold, they will not believe me, nor hearken unto my voice: for they will say, The Lord hath not appeared unto thee" (Exod. 4:1).

This objection seems doubly suspect. If Moses is so sure that the elders will not believe him, why did he need God's name? Was this name not to be the very proof Moses had requested to convince the people? If the people yet say, "So you mention a name, so what?" then the name is no substitute for faith, either for the Hebrews or for Moses. Is this excuse-making or a demand for yet more palpable signs? God interprets it as the latter. But God's concession of more visible proof for the skeptical is a compromise that compromises the mission as well. Having offered Moses the only meaningful mission (great work to do and faith that it can be done), God must now meet Moses at a lower level—not Moses the leader but Moses the magician.[18]

The Rod: Ambivalence about Power

Moses' staff—a valid symbolic attribute for one who is to shepherd a nation out of Egypt—becomes a rod, which in turn becomes a serpent. God then instructs Moses to place a hand on his midriff, which turns leprous until Moses withdraws it. The third and final concession—turning water into blood—is more than just a sign for Moses or the Israelites. With this "trick" we have moved beyond proof for the future faithful to the threat of plague for the disbeliever. God's first plague on Egypt will be to change rivers to blood: "And the fish that was in the river died; and the river stank, and the Egyptians could not drink of the water of the river; and there was blood throughout all the land of Egypt" (Exod. 7:21). Unlike the other two signs, the blood is not demonstrated directly to Moses. Though less frightening, this sign can be seen as more worrisome, alluding to a fate that was then (and could once again be) suffered by an entire people, including its leader. Moses is impressed and Moses is depressed; if this is to be a dangerous game, he will have to play his hand with care.

This confusion of plagues and signs is double-edged. The same powers God may wield against Pharaoh can equally be turned against His servant Moses. A sign showing God's faith in Israel simultaneously represents a threat for both Egypt and Israel. For instance, God's second sign, leprosy, is later used to rebuke the Israelite Miriam when she loses faith in God's enterprise; having questioned Moses' authority, Miriam is turned into a leper and ostracized from the camp for seven days.

Similarly, when God finally convinces Pharaoh to let his people go, the first-born sons of Egypt are slain for God's own first-born son, Israel. By telescoping sign and plague into one, God makes it clear that He brooks no questioning of authority. God may play favorites, but the prerogative of selection belongs to Him alone. Indeed, it is noteworthy that the first-born who are delivered from bondage will not be the generation that finally will enter Canaan.

The rod represents a power that may be wielded but, like the name, must not be abused; its power is qualified from the beginning. In the first round of the contest with Pharaoh, Moses throws down his rod and it becomes a snake. The Egyptian tricksters whom Pharaoh has summoned can do the same with their magic wands. What distinguishes God's rod from any sorcerer's paraphernalia is that it alone can subsume the others: "For they cast down every man his rod, and they became serpents: but Aaron's rod swallowed up their rods" (Exod. 7:12). Aaron's rod (or Moses'; versions vary as to who commands its use) effectively demonstrates God's power. It is no mere magician's wand. When confronted with magic, the rod literally consumes the magic symbols. Any magician can turn a shepherd's staff into a serpent, but God's power transcends that hocus-pocus.

The rod, then, carries a conditional clause; though it can work wonders, it must only be wielded in faith. Like the tree of life from which it comes,[19] the rod can live only so long as it is connected to its roots. As long as Aaron and Moses align their actions with God's greater purpose, the rod has full power. Throughout the plague sequence, the rod is an adequate symbol of the shepherd's mission: both a banner around which the people rally and the means to ward off Egypt's onslaught. A rod imbued with faith can divide the Reed Sea (Exod. 14:16), can turn bitter waters into sweet (Exod. 15:22-25), or can blossom forth in witness of Aaron's priestly authority (Num. 17:5-8). The rod, as at Meribah (Num. 20:8-12), can strike out in anger, attributing evil to the people, separating Moses from them and thus from the Lord.

With his rod as banner, Moses delivers the Israelites from bondage. As the biblical explanation of his name implies, Moses is the bucket that "draws out" the people in faith—as once before, while still only a shepherd, Moses drew water at a well for the oppressed daughters of Jethro. Throughout this sequence of imagery, Moses remains a shepherd; God's rod is his staff.

But what happens when the rod becomes a tool of destruction? The rod that turns into a snake can dazzle the unbeliever but, should Moses waver in his trust, the snake may bite its own master. A wand, which, as any sorcerer's apprentice learns, can work magicians' wonders, is a threat as well as a promise to the user: "and it became a serpent; and Moses fled from before it" (Exod. 4:3). Rabbinic writers understood: "Because he had acted like a snake," it says in Exodus Rabbah, referring to Moses' behavior at the burning bush, "therefore God showed him the snake."[20]

Just as people need rulers and yet fear them, just as leaders need followers and yet fear them, so Moses needed God and feared Him. Moses' experiences are suffused with ambivalence; he cannot be slave and free. How to marry the opposing qualities required for leadership—passion with patience, acceptance with renunciation, authority with sharing power—is Moses' perpetual problem.

Wrestling with God

Leadership must be accepted before it can be legitimized. The message of the serpent is that the snake who bites—or the rod that smites—would have been unnecessary if faith had prevailed. We now come close to suggesting that if Moses had had enough faith at the burning bush, the rod would have been superfluous. Was Moses stalling for time when he asked for further proof? It is clear that the mission is awesome and, as the dialogue progresses, that he will use any pretext to evade the task. All the ploys to find a loophole in God's plan have backfired. Moses has received all that he has requested so far—a name, a few magic tricks. No further probing will release him from the mission. Trying a completely new tack, then, Moses pleads lack of rhetorical skill: "O my Lord, I am not eloquent, neither heretofore, nor since thou hast spoken unto thy servant: but I am slow of speech, and of a slow tongue" (Exod. 4:10).

Commentators with a penchant for factual detail have concluded with some ingenuity that Moses must have had a speech impediment. God Himself provides a better answer. In lightning-like phrases, God answers Moses: "Who hath made man's mouth? or who maketh the dumb, or deaf, or the seeing, or the blind? have not I the Lord?" (Exod. 4:11).

The threats mount—blindness, deafness, dumbness. God knows that Moses has been anything but "slow of speech" and "of a slow tongue" in the present negotiations. And, in the future, this same stammerer Moses will deliver masterpieces of eloquence, his farewell speeches in Deuteronomy. But God refuses to point out Moses' error by simultaneously paying him a compliment. Instead, God emphasizes His own infinite design: if Moses wishes to insist he is a stutterer, well and good; God is patient. The God who first promised, "I will be with you" now promises, "I will be with thy mouth" (Exod. 4:12).

Moses, the one "of a slow tongue," tries one last objection, only to discover that even divine patience has its limits. In a last-ditch ploy to wriggle out of responsibility, he finally gives a more honest reason—the same reason behind all the rationalizations: "And he said, O my Lord, send, I pray thee, by the hand of him whom thou wilt send" (Exod. 4: 13). In the colloquial *New Translation*, Moses says, "Please, O Lord, make someone else your agent." Should Moses falter, no one will be able to say he asked for it. But the God of Israel is not one to be impressed by subtleties: "And the anger of the Lord was kindled against Moses, and He said, Is not Aaron the Levite thy brother? I know that he can speak well.... And thou shalt... put words in his mouth:... And... he shall be to thee instead of a mouth, and thou shalt be to him instead of God" (Exod. 4:14-16). Negotiations are closed. God makes Moses an offer he cannot refuse: "Now therefore go" (Exod. 4:12).

This last rebuff clearly separates the actors from the playwright. In the contest with Pharaoh, both Moses and Aaron will run messages between the parleying powers. But the institution of Aaron as "second in command" is significant. Is this not the same Aaron who later will lead the Israelites into their greatest apostasy? This "helpmate" won from God is to become the agent of Moses' own undoing. Thus God's compromise once again becomes a portentous double entendre. Aaron is well known as a soother and a mollifier—in relation to the people, definitely a man of peace. How could Aaron be forceful when he is a force twice removed, only a purveyor of the words God first gave Moses? No, whatever the appearances, Moses actually does the talking. For Moses, like Jacob, must prove he is strong enough to lead by first wrestling with God.

In contrast to other figures of "call" legends, Moses is more than a mere vehicle for God.[21] However stubborn his reluctance, it is more than simple quibbling. Because Moses is more than a slave to God's will, he can be the one to educate and to transmute the slave mentality of the Hebrews under Pharaoh into readiness for self-government. Though the land may have been promised, it will remain unfulfilled without human action. Moses, the human, will change God's promise into a perpetually renewable, hence perpetually valid, covenant.

A Close Call

The question of the perpetuation of God's covenant with the patriarchs is seen foreshadowed immediately after Moses' name is called at the burning bush. Here—an early parallel with the most dangerous moment in the future, when all ties between God and His chosen people threaten to break—God and Moses come near to an irrevocable parting of the ways.

To grasp its full import, we must backtrack to the end of the burning bush episode. God had concluded the elaborate negotiations with a simultaneous imperative and assurance: "Return into Egypt: for all the men are dead which sought thy life" (Exod. 4:19).[22]

But though Moses need not now fear retaliation for having slain the Egyptian, an unexpected attack comes: "And it came to pass by the way in the inn, that the Lord met him, and sought to kill him" (Exod. 4:24). This is a surprising reversal, and the interpretive problems are legion.[23] Why should God, who has just commissioned Moses, seek to kill him immediately thereafter?[24] To describe this passage as indicating God's "ambivalent" attitude toward Moses is an exercise in understatement.[25] God's reaction is not implausible. A Moses strong enough to justify the Lord's trust could also tempt His mistrust; might not the man who acts for God, act *as* a god? That is the way with leaders: they seek glory, often their own. How, then, should the Lord interpret Moses' extraordinary reluctance to carry the mantle of leadership: as genuine doubt or as genuine deception?

The agency for preventing Moses' death is his wife, Zipporah, whose intercession on Moses' behalf prefigures his own later intercession with Pharaoh for the Israelite nation—a foreigner for a foreigner. But the enigmatic compression of the verses that describe her deed have puzzled the most astute commentators: "Then Zipporah took a sharp stone, and cut off the foreskin of her son, and cast it at his feet, and said, Surely a bloody husband art thou to me" (Exod. 4:25).

Why did Zipporah cut off the foreskin of her son? Some commentators have maintained that God is angry that Moses' son is not circumcised, circumcision having been the accepted ritual to seal the covenant between God and His people. So important is circumcision, Rabbi Joshua ben Karha taught, that all Moses' merits could not make up for delaying the circumcision of his son.[26] This interpretation seems shaky. God surely would have known Moses' son was uncircumcised before He first approached Moses. Others have argued that God's wrath is incurred only because Moses delays in the circumcision, after having accepted the commission. This might help illuminate why God falls upon him in the night—Moses has delayed in more than circumcision—but it still does not explain why Zipporah's intercession succeeds.

It may be that a parallel to the Akedah, the binding of Isaac, is intended. As Abraham, at God's direction, substituted a ram for his son, so Zipporah may have succeeded by substituting the blood of the circumcision for that of her husband.[27] Better still, fulfillment of the covenant by circumcision is accepted for a covenant as yet unaccepted by Moses. But why does God accept this gesture from Zipporah?

Clearly, Zipporah "cut off the foreskin of her son," but, when she "cast it at his feet," are we to understand the son's feet, Moses' feet, or even the feet of the angel of God (as the Septuagint and Targum have it)?—all the time keeping in mind that "feet" is a euphemism for genitalia?[28] And, finally, when Zipporah exclaims, "Surely a bloody husband art thou to me," then—and, after God has let Moses go—repeats, "A bloody husband thou art, because of the circumcision" (Exod. 4:26), whom does she address?

These apparent contradictions may be explained by placing them within the context of the whole. Moses becomes a bloody husband on the literal plane when he marries Zipporah and on a symbolic one when she touches him with the foreskin. The blood reminds Moses that, though God's chosen intermediary, he is not above the law; Moses is mortal. Blood stands for life. "The life of the flesh is in the blood; and I have given it to you… to make an atonement for your souls" (Lev. 17:11). Just as Israel's first-born are saved by blood on the doorposts, the circumcision is a substitute sacrifice, a redemption. Blood is identified with life as in cleansing sin.

The angel of God—who stands for God at one remove and at whose "feet" Zipporah also casts the token of the covenant—is a "bloody husband" also. Zipporah asks God, in effect, "Having made a covenant with your servant Moses, will you kill him in cold blood? Have you married him in covenant only to bloody him with death?" Blood—the symbol of both circumcision and the covenant—stands for a contract God Himself must keep: "A bloody husband thou art because of the circumcision." Moses' first-born son becomes a bloody husband as well. Is not Israel the first-born of God and Moses the first in Israel? Thus Zipporah, in a tripartite ceremony, marries God and Moses to the people, God and the people to Moses, and the people and Moses to God.[29]

Moses was threatened because he remains uncommitted. "I sent you to go and redeem my children who are suffering," the *Torah Shlemah* has God say to Moses, "and you sit resting in peace and quiet."[30] His first-born, just like God's first-born, has remained uncircumcised in spirit as well as in the flesh. From this point on in the Bible, circumcision becomes a metaphor for a spiritual relationship as well as the outer sign of that relationship. The newly "circumcised" pact is increasingly internalized as the narrative progresses. When he is first sent to Pharaoh, Moses questions God in a familiar manner, "Behold, the children of Israel have not hearkened unto me; how then shall Pharaoh hear me, who am of uncircumcised lips?" (Exod. 6:12).[31] His relationship with God is still uncertain, so that the circumcision—the sign of the covenant with the children of Israel—is not yet manifest in Moses' voice. The literal genitalia have become a living voice, which in turn must be circumcised. In Deuteronomy, when Moses' lips have long since been sealed by this covenant, he exhorts the people: "Circumcise therefore the foreskin of your heart, and be no more stiffnecked" (Deut. 10:16). Obduracy must be tempered by faith, much as Zipporah once pleaded that violence must be stayed by faith. And Moses' staff—both rod and serpent, the positive and negative sides of leadership—must be circumcised, for it belongs to a "bloody husband."

Called to walk on the path of leadership, Moses hears it as an invitation to a dance of death. He might fail, and he gives voice to his possible inadequacies. Moses' faith is incomplete; he does not yet trust himself to lead the people without doing them in or being done in by them. Remaining split inside, he is still stepping on his own feet. Along the road to leadership in an independent regime, therefore, an implicit understanding is reached. If Moses will wed this people, God will temper justice with mercy. It will become apparent that until His people leave Pharaoh's slave regime behind, they cannot have real leaders. Even though Moses remains passive, so long as he links his fate with the Hebrew people, the Lord will protect him.

The burning bush promises that the flames of life may sear and singe, but the people will survive. A legend cited by Edmond Fleg captures the closeness of the call. In this dialogue, Moses says, "Lord, Thou sendest me unto Thine enemies: they have sought my life; they seek it yet." And God answers the only possible way for would-be leaders: "He with whom I go, My Fear goeth with him."[32]

Faith, in Judaism, means accepting the moral mission as one's own, not just following orders from above. Having ostensibly done so, Moses has not asked himself what is required of Jews, not even thinking to circumcise his son. Moses' uncircumcised son symbolizes his failure to commit himself to God or His people.

There are only two other episodes in the Torah in which God sends a man on a mission and then seeks to kill or stop him—those of Balaam's ass and of Jacob's wrestling match. (Jonah is not relevant because he does not claim to carry out his mission, fleeing instead.) We will see that both stories concern overcoming the ambivalence of would-be leaders.

BALAAM'S ASS

Let us consider a parable that tells any leader what is in store for him. The parallels to the episode of Moses' circumcision are striking even in the bare scheme of this narrative.

The story of Balaam's ass, told late in the Mosaic account, after Moses' followers have frequently turned against him, has two major themes: God's will and leadership. Only the former theme has been properly appreciated; the latter, except for David Daube's suggestion, has been ignored.[33] The interpretation that thrusts itself upon the reader is on the surface of the story. Balak, king of Moab, fearing that the Israelites will dispossess him, sends a message to Balaam, a priest and diviner of Midian, asking him to come and curse Israel so that it will be defeated. Presents are brought to seal the bargain. Balaam has the messengers wait while he consults the Lord, who tells him, "Thou shalt not go with them; thou shalt not curse the people: for they are blessed" (Num. 22:12). Balaam refuses Balak; more honorific messengers and more valuable presents arrive. Pushing his luck, perhaps because he would like to be rewarded, Balaam asks God again if he can go.[34] Eventually, God does tell Balaam to go to Balak. But as Balaam rides along to Moab on his faithful ass, an angel stands in the way with a sword drawn, apparently ready to kill him. Balaam is blind to what is happening, but his ass sees the angel and turns aside. Angered, Balaam "smote the ass" to bring her back to the path (Num. 22:23). When the Lord's angel moves into the path between two walls, the ass, in order to get Balaam out of the way, leans into the wall, thereby crushing his foot. Balaam hits his ass again. A third time, there being no place to turn, the ass goes down under Balaam, whose "anger was kindled, and he smote the ass with a staff" (Num. 22:27).

A rod is being misused to beat a poor brute. This rod should be used for a better purpose, as Balaam—like Moses—is about to learn:

> And the Lord opened the mouth of the ass, and she said unto Balaam, What have I done unto thee, that thou hast smitten me these three times?
>
> And Balaam said unto the ass, Because thou has mocked me: I would there were a sword in mine hand, for now would I kill thee.
>
> And the ass said unto Balaam, Am not I thine ass, upon which thou has ridden ever since I was thine unto this day? was I ever wont to do so unto thee? And he said, Nay.
>
> Then the Lord opened the eyes of Balaam, and he saw the angel of the Lord standing in the way, and his sword drawn in his hand: and he bowed down his head, and fell flat on his face.
>
> And the angel of the Lord said unto him, Wherefore has thou smitten thine ass these three times? Behold, I went out to withstand thee, because thy way is perverse before me:
>
> And the ass saw me, and turned from me these three times: unless she had turned from me, surely now also I had slain thee, and saved her alive. [Num. 22:28-33]

There it is: the ass that saves Balaam's life gets beaten in return. Had the Lord not opened Balaam's eyes, he would have tried to beat her to death. The ass is female—possibly in the same sense that Moses asked whether he was "a nursing father," carrying an ungrateful people in his bosom.

Aware that he has sinned, Balaam offers to return home. No, he is to go with Balak's envoys, but he is only to speak words given him by the Lord's angels. Though Balaam does not apologize to his faithful, long-suffering ass, he is not unmindful of his debt and seeks to repay it by bearing a similar burden himself.

Three times Balak asks Balaam to curse Israel. Three times, despite the promise of greater gifts, Balaam refuses. Three times Balak builds great altars laden with sacrifices in Moab so that Balaam should look over and curse Israel. Each time Balaam says, as he did at first, "How shall I curse, whom God hath not cursed? or how shall I defy, whom the Lord hath not defied?" (Num. 23:8). In the end, the moral is made clear; with his eyes open, but in a trance, Balaam the oracle pronounces the Lord's judgment on Israel's enemies, "Blessed is he that blesseth thee, and cursed is he that curseth thee" (Num. 24:9).

In the war against the Midianites, it is reported of the warriors of Israel that before entering the new land, "Balaam also the son of Beor they slew with the sword" (Num. 31:8) because he advised the indirect approach of enticing Israel into foreign practices (Num. 31:16). Is this the reward Balaam reaped for refusing to curse Israel?

Just as the she-ass three times refused to lead her master into disaster, so three times Balaam refused to curse Israel, thus saving his master from destruction and Israel from loss, receiving punishment from the one and death from the other. As Balaam would have killed his faithful servant, devoted but stubborn, so also he is done in. The parallel between the beast of burden and the prophet—for Balaam can speak only what God authorizes—is maintained in small things as in large: "Just so, the king was to infer," Daube concludes, "the prophet served him even when disobedient."[35]

The parallel reaches further. Balaam bears a message for Moses about the fate of leaders. Both Moses and Balaam are named to leadership. Both are ambivalent: they wish to go but are fearful. After negotiation suggesting they might refuse, they are commanded to go. Moses on the way to Egypt from the burning bush in Midian and Balaam on the way to his authorized appointment with Balak are waylaid by an angel of the Lord, who would kill them. After passing a test signifying obedience to God's will by identification with the people entrusted to their care, a test carried out by a female (Zipporah and the she-ass), each fulfills these obligations, only to be beaten in the process.

Now we are prepared to take a larger view of the Zipporah episode, and that of Balaam's ass, by asking what it signifies in the Bible to be named to leadership. Ambivalence—the burning desire to lead set against the fear of the consequences—is understandable. It is necessary to bind oneself to higher principles in advance; otherwise the temptation to sacrifice the followers to the leader's safety would be too great. Perfect obedience, however, is neither possible in human beings nor necessarily desirable. For the time being, Balaam is saved because his she-ass disregards his command in favor of his survival. Similarly, Israel is saved for God because Moses, on Mount Sinai, argues Him out of destroying the people and thus His relationship to it.

Balaam is not Moses; though a prophet, he is not a Hebrew prophet. In this respect, Balaam is a natural leader; with the relationship between

God and a particular people stripped away, it is possible to see what happens when the leader does his duty: he gets beaten by his followers.

Only one contradiction remains to be resolved; why is Balaam, like Moses, first commanded by God and then, in quick reversal, nearly rejected? Though Balaam is first told in no uncertain terms, "Thou shalt not go" (Num. 22:12), the second time he consults God, he is told to go with Balak's escort—but, of course, to do only as God tells him. Yet, as soon as Balaam departs, it is said that "God's anger was kindled because he went" (Num. 22:22).

What are we to make of this apparent anomaly—stop, go, stop—in the biblical account? Three main lines of interpretation have been developed. It is always possible to argue that there are errors in the text. Since the contradiction cannot have escaped the editors, however, we may ask why they did not smooth out the surface appearance of the story. A second line follows Maimonides and treats the parable as a dream. Once a literal interpretation is eschewed, it is a small step to view the entire episode as a hallucinatory vision, in which asses speak and ordinary logic no longer need apply. Apparent contradictions are dissolved by treating them as manifestations of Balaam's inner turmoil in choosing between God and gain. But this interpretation cannot explain the sequence of events and only restates the difficulty on another plane. Nor can it account for Balaam's protection of Balak, which is the point of the story. For it is one thing for Balaam—waking or sleeping—to give up gain and another to suffer pain at Balak's hands.

A more literal approach, following ibn Ezra and Rashi, is good as far as it goes: Balaam, driven by avarice, hopes he can importune God to let him go. The sages were certain that the moral man does not ask permission to do the impermissible. In the words of Isaac Arama: "Is it conceivable that when a man should propose to his friend that they should worship idols in secret, that he should answer, We'll go and ask the Sage if we may do it or not. Surely the prohibition is absolute and irrevocable! Should he ask, it is out of wickedness. How much more so if the seducer is a sage and prophet or near to God, that he should not say, Wait and I shall find out what my God has to say about it. But he should have said that such a thing was inconceivable and unheard of and even refused under threat of death."[36] The point is put succinctly in Bamidbar Rabbah, where it is said in regard to Balaam that "man is led down the path he chooses to tread."[37] But why, then, does God agree to the journey, when He could have forbidden it again? The Lord does not hesitate to deny Moses His name every time Moses asks. My own view is that interpretation should be guided by a general theory of what the Torah is trying to tell us and a particular theory of how this episode fits in. Moses and his people are being taught about leadership. The episode of Balaam's ass, in addition to reaffirming that human beings cannot contravene the will of God, instructs leaders both to submerge their individual interest for their people's welfare and to expect punishments instead of rewards for their pains, at least in this world.

Let us remind ourselves of a still larger theme of Mosaic leadership, which helps explain why the episode of Balaam's ass is included. Moses is named to leadership. He is chosen as much (or more) than he chooses. He wants to lead, yet he seeks to escape from it. He is, as it were, seized from behind ("Here I am") while worrying ("Who am I") whether he can fulfill the task or what will happen to him if he does make the attempt. The upshot is that Moses is sent on his way ("Now therefore go") by being named as leader whether he will lead or not. Throughout there is an ebb and flow to his ambivalence, but finally, in the desert, beset by domestic revolt and foreign aggression, forbidden to enter the land of promise yet longing to taste the fruits of his labors, Moses will again be in need of instruction. To reconcile him to his fate, to teach him so as to instruct others, the extraordinary story of Balaam's ass is told. Presumably the she-ass that talks to a man who speaks to God is near enough to principle and far enough removed in appearance for Moses to accept in allegory what he cannot accustom himself to by experience.

On the one hand, Balaam is told he must not go because God will not allow curses on those He blesses. On the other hand, if Balaam does not go, he will be able neither to prove himself nor to save Balak and his people. To prove the principle of leadership, Balaam must go; without his journey there is neither good nor evil. Though God Himself may lie in wait, as Moses learned on the way to Midian, leaders who are named must still set out to do their duty. If they can see God along the way, well and good; if they cannot, if, like Balaam, they rail against the seeming perversity of experience, then they have failed to understand that they are there to serve, being beaten, like Balaam's ass, for their faithful service.

There is more. Having heard the word of God, having been named and told to go, the leader is only at the beginning of his duties. Being named to begin is not being named to continue or to end. Completion, as Buber reminds us, belongs to God alone.[38] All along the way, the leader needs guidance and affirmation. As Moses went from Midian at God's command only to discover that death might separate him from the Israelites unless he joined his life to theirs, so "Balaam's contradiction" reaffirms the essence of Mosaic leadership—the going forth to serve people without knowing exactly where it will lead or how it will end. Balaam's ass retells Moses' story to him so that, thus clothed, he can come closer to accepting it.

There is a third episode in the Pentateuch—Jacob's wrestling with the angel—in which God seeks to prevent a man from carrying out a mission He has authorized. The reasons are the same—the leader is internally in conflict about his mission so that, as Balaam was told, "thy way is perverse before me." Jacob's struggle is an earlier manifestation of overcoming doubt.

THE DIVIDED SELF: JACOB AND MOSES

"Is he not rightly named Jacob?" his brother Esau muses, "for he hath supplanted me these two times: he took away my birthright; and, behold, now he hath taken away my blessing" (Gen. 27:36). In another word-name, Jacob signified not only "supplanter" but also "heel grabber" (for the hold he held on Esau's heel at birth)—hence, follower, reactor. Essentially, Jacob is passive. This seems a strange designation for a man so active in deceit, who dresses up as his brother to win his father's blessing, having already extorted that brother's birthright as a first-born—withholding a mess of pottage from a brother faint with hunger. In both situations, however, the context makes it clear that Jacob is reacting to opportunities created or instigated by others. It is said of Esau that he "despised his birthright" (Gen. 25:34), giving it up so readily for so little; of Jacob, that he feared being found out by his father "as a deceiver" and consequently bringing on himself "a curse... not a blessing" (Gen. 27:12). Rebekah, the first Jewish mother, offers to take the curse on herself if only Jacob will do as she tells him. Having learned Esau plans to kill Jacob, she sends Jacob away to her brother, Laban. "But the glaring contrast between the well-laden entourage that Abraham had sent [with Eliezer on behalf of Isaac] and Jacob's precipitate, lonely flight, on foot and empty-handed," Sarna tells us, "emphasizes the reprehensible nature of Jacob's actions which had led to his present plight."[39] Jacob flees with nothing to his credit, not even his own deceit.[40]

Jacob fears man, not God. Elsewhere the fear that comes from faithlessness is shown to be a form of idolatry. Thus when the people despair of Moses' returning from the mountain—saying in anxiety that they do not know what has become of him—they turn to the palpable presence of the Golden Calf. If all outcomes were certain, Franz Rosenzweig observes, then timid and fearful people would, ipso facto, be the most pious.[41] "Foxhole" piety is well known.[42]

When Laban kisses Jacob at their first meeting (a sign of similarity), Laban says, "Surely thou art my bone and my flesh" (Gen. 29:14), and speaks more truly than he knows. This pair is well matched in trickery. Laban cheats him as Jacob has cheated others. Laban tries to swindle Jacob out of the wife he has worked so hard for, requiring Jacob to labor seven more years for Rachel,[43] and another six for the flocks of sheep and cattle. Jacob, in turn, wins back his sheep and then some by using the Lord's power to trick Laban. As Sarna says, "It is not hard to see in the trickery Laban successfully practiced on Jacob in taking advantage of the darkness to substitute Leah for her sister, the retributive counterpart, measure for measure, of Jacob's exploitation of his father's perpetual darkness by masquerading as his own brother. The perpetrator of deception was now the victim, hoist with his own petard."[44] In addition to losing twenty years of his life, Jacob is deceived by his own children in regard to the death of Joseph; Jacob ends up in exile, dying in a foreign land even as in life he has been estranged from himself.

Deception does not necessarily doom Jacob, however; he is part of a divine plan. The question for Jacob is whether he will invest himself actively in this plan or remain a spectator, pulled through by someone else and barely holding onto life by the heel. The critical evidence is contained in the two episodes defining the boundaries of Jacob's life—at Beth-el on his flight from Esau; and at Peniel, when leaving Laban to confront again the brother who stands for the other self he has deceived.

Jacob's Ladder and Jacob's Angel

On his way from his father's house to Haran (where Laban lived) Jacob set up stones for pillows and lay down to sleep. "And he dreamed, and behold a ladder set up on the earth, and the top of it reached to heaven: and behold the angels of God ascending and descending on it" (Gen. 28:12). Above the ladder (whose import will be appraised later) stood the Lord, introducing Himself as the God of Abraham and Isaac, promising the land to Jacob and his descendants. The tone is unmistakably generous: "And, behold, I am with thee, and will keep thee in all places whither thou goest, and will bring thee again into this land; for I will not leave thee, until I have done that which I have spoken to thee of" (Gen. 28:15). Fearful before the holy place, Jacob vows less than wholeheartedly: "If God will be with me, and will keep me in this way that I go, and will give me bread to eat, and raiment to put on, So that I come again to my father's house in peace; then shall the Lord be my God" (Gen. 28:20-21). "If… then" is the familiar form of scientific propositions, expressing skepticism that is the opposite of faith. When Esau asks how his blessing can have been stolen by Jacob, Isaac uses the word "subtilty" (Gen. 27:35), earlier applied to the serpent who tempted Eve. Can Jacob possibly mean that he will test God and, if the deity does well by him, give God a house and a share in the family business? The sages raged back and forth over whether it was conceivable for a patriarch to treat God as if the two were haggling at a bazaar. But self-concern does fit in with what we know of Jacob's character; he was not exactly one to blaze a dangerous trail; wait and see was his motto.

By then, Jacob—having left Laban and hearing that his brother Esau approaches with an armed force—has assumed the responsibilities of two wives, two concubines, and eleven children. All his life, Jacob has avoided confronting the people who matter most—his father, whom he deceived; his mother, who controlled him; and his brother Esau, from whom he is still running. Now the question is whether Jacob will run again or will confront his brother and thus himself.

At the river Jabbok, boundary of the land promised to him and his people, Jacob sees his retinue safely across and is left alone to reconcile his inner conflicts. Will Jacob look after himself, bowing down in self-regard, remaining the passive person who deceives himself before he deceives others, or will he join himself actively to his people's past and future? (The same question was asked of Moses as he crossed the boundaries of Midian into Egypt.) The story, as usual, is told in few words:

> And Jacob was left alone; and there wrestled a man with him until the breaking of the day.
>
> And when he saw that he prevailed not against him, he touched the hollow of his thigh; and the hollow of Jacob's thigh was out of joint, as he wrestled with him.
>
> And he said, Let me go, for the day breaketh. And he said, I will not let thee go, except thou bless me.
>
> And he said unto him, What is thy name? And he said, Jacob.
>
> And he said, Thy name shall be called no more Jacob, but Israel: for as a prince hast thou power with God and with men, and hast prevailed.
>
> And Jacob asked him, and said, Tell me, I pray thee, thy name. And he said, Wherefore is it that thou dost ask after my name? And he blessed him there.
>
> And Jacob called the name of the place Peniel: for I have seen God face to face, and my life is preserved. [Gen. 32:24-30]

Clearly, the change of name—from Jacob to Israel, from "supplanter" to he who has met God and man and prevailed, from passive follower to active doer—legitimizes Jacob's birthright and blessing. At long last, he has won his blessing on his own, fair and square.

Beyond this, interpretive difficulties multiply. Who is the other man? If it is God, why does He wrestle with Jacob? Is Jacob crippled in the thigh, or is something else involved in the touching? How can Jacob be lamed and blessed at the same time? There are more questions, evidently, than answers. As before, looking upon these events as if they were lessons in leadership, viewing them as Mosaic, perhaps we can make some progress.

Like Moses on the way to Midian (and Balaam going to meet Balak), a mortal man who has been given a divine mission is waylaid in the borderlands, his life threatened by an angel standing for God. As in these other instances, if we want to understand why the mission and the messenger are threatened before they fairly start, we must go back to the beginning. Let us see if Jacob's ladder offers a broader perspective.

If there were borders to the realm of the spirit, they might well look like ladders. The stairway connecting heaven and earth, on which angels ascend and descend, appearing in Jacob's dream at Beth-el, is one that no man can climb. The ladder is in another world. But that world, according to the sages of the Hebrew people, speaks to human concerns. The "deeds of the patriarchs [their dreams, too, of course, in which their inner selves talk truth] are a sign to their descendants."[45] What do the dreams strive to say? Perhaps the angels go up to the ideal picture of man, as Hirsch suggests, and go down to see something worse.[46] So what? Everybody knows that heaven is better than the other place. To other interpreters, Nehama Leibowitz declares, "Jacob's ladder is taken to imply the ladder of history. The ascent of one nation on it implies the descent of its predecessor. The ladder is not an endless one, but the Lord stands at its top, as the master of history, assuring us that pride and despotism will be brought low, until His sovereignty alone is recognised at the end of days. This 'latter-day' vision is described to us by Isaiah."[47] No doubt; this will do as an introduction to God's glory, but the image is overly elaborate for that plain purpose. Best, as usual, is the French commentator, Rabbi Shelomo Yitzhaki (1040-1105), called Rashi, who asks, first, what is happening on the ground (Jacob fleeing from his brother, entering a foreign country) so as to relate it to what is happening above (angels going up and down). But why (since presumably they live in heaven), Rashi asks himself, are the angels doing the reverse—first ascending, later descending? Because, Rashi answers himself, Jacob is accompanied by the angels of his own country and these have to be changed in a strange land.[48] Deities in those days were thought to go with the place—David feared that exile from Canaan would lead him to worship foreign gods.[49] The dream of the ladder stakes a greater claim on behalf of the God of Israel.

Our own question is: What was God telling Jacob? The implication of Jacob's ladder was that wherever Jacob went, whatever the special spirit of the place, God, who stood above all, would stand with him. This was the image radiating in all directions—wherever Jacob was, whatever rung of life he climbed, his guardian angel would go along. Jacob's ladder is a dream of divine reassurance.

Let us briefly retrace the phases of God's contacts with Jacob. Seeing that no matter what they did, Jacob's efforts were far more successful than their own, Laban and his sons began to harass Jacob. It was time to go; Jacob tells Leah and Rachel that God has appeared in a dream, saying, "I am the God of Beth-el, where thou anointedst the pillar, and where thou vowedst a vow unto me: now arise, get thee out from this land, and return unto the land of thy kindred" (Gen. 31:13). When Laban labels it a surreptitious flight, Jacob, in a fit of righteousness, exclaims that, despite hard work and suffering, he would still have nothing, "Except the God of my father, the God of Abraham, and the fear of Isaac, had been with me, surely thou hadst sent me away now empty" (Gen. 31:42). However one-sided the bargain may have been at Beth-el, God has kept His part, and now it is Jacob's turn to do likewise.

From Jacob to Israel

By so circuitous a route, we come back to our questions about Jacob wrestling with the stranger. In Rashi's terms, those of medieval midrash, Jacob has been wrestling with the "prince" or angel of Esau, who, in the dream, is called a man. Before Jacob actually encountered Esau in the flesh, Nehama Leibowitz concludes, "his spirit struggled with Esau's, with his national genius. Only after the prince of Esau had acknowledged his title to the paternal blessing ('And he blessed him there') was Jacob, injured and limping, able to go forth to meet his brother and become reconciled with him."[50] Jacob is indeed wrestling with his fear of Esau, as manifested in lack of faith in God. Internally divided, Jacob is neither willing to let go of the God in him nor to accept God's promise.

What is the significance of the angel touching (therefore apparently dislocating) Jacob's thigh? The Rashbam, Shemuel ben Meir (1080-1158), Rashi's grandson, who often disagreed with his grandfather, comments that—seeing Jacob trying to flee his brother—the Lord sent an angel "from whom he could not flee, that he might see the fulfillment of the Almighty's promise that Esau would do him no hurt. 'When he saw that he could not prevail against him' i.e. the angel saw that Jacob wished to extricate himself and flee in spite of him—'and the hollow of Jacob's thigh became out of joint.' Jacob was hurt and lamed, because the Almighty had promised him safety and yet he had run away."[51] Lack of faith has been evident in Jacob's flight—from himself most of all—from the start. At the river Jabbok, boundary of the place first occupied by Israel in the conquest of Canaan, and therefore the place of Jacob's spiritual origins, Jacob is also forced to fight.

But why the thigh wound? Various commentators suggest that the injury is an exchange for the wrong Jacob has done; he pays the price, presumably, and is blessed, which reconciles him with his brother. Adopting a Mosaic perspective, I would urge a parallel to the Zipporah episode and suggest a complementary interpretation.

In his commentary, the Ramban, Rabbi Moshe ben Nahman (1194-1270), identifies the hollow of the thigh with circumcision.[52] "Now the thigh in biblical usage," Sarna informs us, "is symbolic of the reproductive process, the seat of the procreative power." Children are described as coming from the thigh. Making oaths by placing the hands between the thighs, as Abraham did in enjoining Eliezer to keep Isaac in Canaan, signifies the same source.[53]

I point up this detail to suggest either that Jacob is circumcised or that his existing circumcision is touched in order to show—physically, in the flesh, and symbolically, in the spirit—acceptance of the covenant.

One can limp from a circumcision as well as from a dislocated hip. Jacob's hip injury never again comes up, but his days of procreation are over. At long last, Jacob joins his people; his estrangement from them, from their God, and from himself, always fleeing, is overcome by acceptance of the everlasting covenant. And he who follows becomes he who leads,[54] Jacob's children becoming the progenitors of the twelve tribes of Israel.

Immediately before he lies down to sleep, Jacob divides his people and goods into two bands, thinking, "If Esau come to the one company, and smite it, then the other company which is left shall escape" (Gen. 32:8).

The two bands represent Jacob's divisions within himself. As he has now divided his people, signifying lack of faith, so Jacob is divided between sole reliance on his own strength and faith in the promise—one God, one land, one people—taken together as a whole. Will Jacob, in other words, worship the work of his own hands or seek something beyond himself? Having failed to heal this rift in his own heart, in conscious moments during the day, Jacob's internal action works itself out at night. "Every story of election," Hirsch reminds us, "is first the story of a setting apart,"[55] as Moses was separated at Mount Sinai. Jacob, Hirsch continues, is so isolated on the far side of the Jabbok that he cannot even call for help. He "was thrown back solely on what was innate in his own person."[56]

Jacob seeks to placate Esau with presents. It is not the gifts, however, but the blessing he had stolen from his brother—a blessing he has since won for himself from his heavenly father—that Jacob presses on Esau. The connection is made by a pun in which Jacob tells Esau to take back his blessing, using the "wrong" variant of the root BRKH, meaning both gift and blessing.[57]

At daybreak the scene changes. The time for dreams is over. Unable to overcome the faithless and fearful alter ego still sleeping within him, Jacob's suppressed self reaches for its ultimate weapon—the sign of the covenant committing him to his forefathers and his future. If not literally circumcised, Jacob is, as the Bible says, touched—circumcised in mind as well as body. He has become a responsible human being.

Who gets a new name? A king does when he is anointed; it signifies taking on a new corporate spirit in the royal person. The name of the river Jabbok is a synonym for struggle. Only at the very end, when he is named but cannot know the name of his adversary, does Jacob realize that he has been struggling with himself, as represented by the divine presence within him. Man cannot control God, but God can bless him. Though, as the name Peniel (turn to God) states, God prevails in the end, Jacob has indeed struggled with man and God; and the one has at long last overcome the other. Accepting the headship of his people, Jacob does manifest "power with God and with men."

The loud shenanigans of Jacob mirror the quieter struggle within Moses. Moses' resistance at the burning bush reflects the same passivity as does virtually all of Jacob's life. When Jacob changes from passivity to activity, so does his name, to Israel.

Jacob is not to be admired but observed. His life is a lesson in exile—psychological and geographical. Jacob's search for identity prefigures the search Moses undertakes to make of Jacob's descendants—of Israel—a nation. The meaning of Israel (*Yisreh im el*)—"will strive with God"— captures the teaching. No paragon is this Israel, no object of veneration. The best that can be said of these people and their leaders is that they will struggle for identity.

Moses began like Jacob—taking the law into his own hands, refusing to accept responsibility, passively following his fate—and goes on, as does Jacob/Israel, to identify with the people. But Moses wishes to end differently, leading his people into the Promised Land. Thus, in character as well as history, Moses' struggle begins where Jacob's ends.

JACOB AND MOSES: THE STRUGGLE FOR IDENTITY

What a marvelous compaction of images, each pressed within the other, is found in the tension between Beth-el and Peniel. Beth-el is childhood, dependence, self-deception, idolatry. The son wants to control the father. If the father will guarantee lifelong protection, the son will give obedience. Still a child, though adult in years, the son plays the same game with God—receive guarantees first, give faith afterward. Is this not idol worship, to worship a being one can control? It is as if the covenant were reversed so that God had to promise to be good before man would agree to accept Him. In terms of ego psychology, this is the childish craving for a security found only in the womb. Grown-ups take their chances. They work for what they want, never being certain either that they will get, or be allowed to keep, it. And grown-ups leave home to make their own way in the wide world.

Jacob's rite of passage from childhood to manhood—from self-deceit to self-awareness, from evasion to responsibility—runs parallel to the Garden of Eden and the exodus. The children of Israel in Egypt, like Adam and Eve, are safe so long as they tend to their business; they are permanently infantilized, except that Pharaoh is not benevolent. Adulthood begins when (whichever one prefers) either the Israelites break loose or they are driven out. Once they make choices, the people are accountable for their actions. They may fail and perish. The temptation is to return to the well-watered womb from which they came; God prevents this with His flaming sword on the borders of Eden, as Moses does with earthly weapons in the desert. Accountability—being held responsible for the possibility of failure, even unto death—is so frightening that some are willing to reverse their history by selling themselves back into slavery. Moses stands for accountability and responsibility, moving forward toward the unknown, fortified only by a promise, a covenant with the one God.

The signs of this covenant in the Bible are three—the rainbow, the Sabbath, and circumcision. Given to Noah, the rainbow is a universal sign that life will not be extinguished. Like a rainbow, the future is open and may be beautiful, but there are no guarantees as to where it will lead. What is guaranteed is what Moses sought after the Golden Calf episode—that man may continue to test his faith against God's promise.

The blood of the circumcision moves Moses twice, once on the way from Midian to Egypt, where he commits himself to the people, and once at the covenant ceremony by Mount Horeb. At Horeb the covenant is conditional on the people's good behavior and, in the aftermath of the Golden Calf, Moses renegotiates it. It is no longer a covenant conditioned on perfect human behavior. Nor is it the unconditional covenant of Genesis in which God binds Himself alone. It is a double bind, in which God maintains the promise, but His people remain responsible for their acts—a covenant for mature men.

"Jacob's struggle with the Almighty lasted one night," Andre Neher writes, "Moses' lasted 120 years."[58] One could quibble about whether Jacob, too, did not live a life of struggle, or whether Moses was not also passive some of the time. Jacob and Moses are closer in character than is comfortable. Yet to give Neher his due, once Moses has begun accepting responsibility, he perseveres; Moses begins where Jacob ends. By struggling to overcome his own ambivalence, Jacob is blessed, so as to become in his person the body of Israel. Moses has the harder task of wrestling with the body of the people of Israel. And, like Jacob, Moses is wounded in the thigh; he will neither found a people himself nor go with them to the Promised Land. Like Jacob, also, Moses will not let go until the people agree not to bless him—that would be idolatry—but to continue his struggle.

MOSES, THE MORAL MIDWIFE OF ISRAEL

We see in Exodus that "the children of Israel were fruitful, and increased abundantly.… But the more they [the Egyptians] afflicted them, the more they multiplied and grew" (Exod. 1:7, 12). No hard tasks inflicted by the Egyptians could stop this amazing fecundity. Biology overcomes policy. God is at one with nature as the rhythm of natural increase inexorably works its will.

Just as Israel was proverbially pregnant in Egypt, Israel would have to be delivered from the womb of Egypt, to be born again as a free people tied only (by covenant) to God. As Moshe Greenberg says, "Israel is a witless matrix, an infinitely fertile womb."[59] The analogy is by no means fanciful. It is evidently uppermost in Moses' mind when, trying to gauge the extent of God's commitment, he pointedly asks whether he is powerful enough to "go unto Pharaoh and... bring forth the children of Israel out of Egypt?" (Exod. 3:11).

Later, weary from warding off attacks on his leadership, sick of grumbling about the taste of food ("we remember the leeks, and the onions, and the garlic"), Moses returns to the same moral metaphor: "Have I conceived all this people? have I begotten them, that thou shouldest say unto me, Carry them in thy bosom, as a nursing father beareth the sucking child, unto the land which thou swarest unto their fathers?" (Num. 11:12).

Exactly. What else is a leader if not a "nursing father"? The Pharaoh is often pictured as androgynous; suckling his people as the Nile does. The more power leaders seem to have, the more people depend on them. The feminine principle that "beareth the sucking child" must also be an integral part of the male, if the children of Israel are not to perish as a people.

Moses—who delivers his people from the womb of bondage (from the watery source of life to the land for which they are destined), helped by nature as he helps it along—is the moral midwife of Israel. Greenberg refers to the refusal of the midwives to kill Hebrew babies—warding off Pharaoh with the claim that Hebrew women deliver before the midwives can get there—observing, "The first intelligent countermeasure... is taken by women, invokes the purported animal vitality of women, and succeeds by womanly wiles. At the next stage, Israelite actors appear, but the weakness of Israel is expressed by those who work on its behalf: a mother and sister moved by love—note it well! Neither Moses' father nor brother play any part in his preservation. The baby is saved by yet another woman, moved by feminine pity at the sight of his crying."[60] No doubt it is mere coincidence that Balaam's ass, who saves her master and gets beaten for it (the lot of the leader!), is also a foreign female.

Fearing that the Hebrew people will prove unreliable, Pharaoh seeks to prevent their further increase by instructing the midwives to keep the females but kill the males. "But the midwives feared God, and... saved the men children alive" (Exod. 1:17). Above all, this story says, Moses is to save the seed of Israel. Whatever happens, whenever Moses and his people face submersion in the watery abyss, he can keep faith only by helping God give birth to His chosen people.

"Because I drew him out of the water" (Exod. 2:10), the explanation for the name given Moses by his Egyptian mother—who should sense his destiny, having brought him into the world of royalty, where he might learn to lead instead of submitting as a slave—has been disputed by scholars on philological grounds. As far as anyone knows today, the name Moses is Egyptian, not Hebrew, and signifies "son of Egypt" or "born of Egypt,"[61] a name also given to Pharaoh and to the Nile. In this way, Moses is clearly marked off from his Hebrew brothers. As great leaders often are, Moses is a stranger, overidentifying with Hebrew possibilities, underidentifying with their necessities.

Moses' elevation to leadership stands in contrast to Joseph's call for continuity. When the question of retribution (for the evil done him) is raised, Joseph answers his brothers with a rhetorical question, replying, "Fear not: for am I in the place of God?" (Gen. 50:19). Ultimately, this is not an answer with which Moses can live. To act as a god may be the ultimate presumption, but to fail to act at all is the final abdication.

In the divine preference for intermediation, the survival of Israel is at stake. Teaching the people to take responsibility for themselves is Moses' task. But, before that can happen, before superseding, more than succeeding, Joseph, Moses must first take responsibility for his own actions.

PASSIVITY VERSUS RESPONSIBILITY

When Aaron and Moses request permission to leave the land so as to sacrifice to God in the desert,[62] Pharaoh retaliates by increasing the burdens of the Hebrew people; they will have to make the same number of bricks but without straw. The people complain that this privation does them no good. Moses does not urge faith or promise improvement. Instead, he figuratively lies on his back, kicks his feet in the air, and acts as if he were helpless. He adopts a whining manner, not only voicing the collective complaint—"Lord, wherefore has thou so evil entreated this people?" (Exod. 5:22)—but also indulging in self-pity—"why is it that thou has sent me?" (Exod. 5:22). Moreover, suggesting self-defeat rather than self-fulfillment, Moses doubts God's efficacy: "For since I came to Pharaoh to speak in thy name," he concludes, "he hath done evil to this people; neither hast thou delivered thy people at all" (Exod. 5:23). Moses' first intercession is recrimination against God (as if He were fate) for allowing the people to suffer. Moses, apparently, will have nothing to do with it. His passive, message-bearing approach is evidently making things worse for the Israelites and thus for Moses. It is not his God who is too passive, he is being taught, but Moses himself.

Here we have it all—bitterness, self-pity, derogation. Perhaps, after all, Moses is preparing to abandon the Lord, as he fled from Pharaoh. What is worse, Moses not so subtly separates himself from the people by speaking of them as "this," not as "his," people. At Mount Sinai, when he mends his ways, Moses will have to take some of his own medicine.

It is one thing for Pharaoh, himself a god, with other gods of his own, to deny the Lord: "Who is the Lord, that I should obey His voice to let Israel go?" (Exod. 5:2). It is quite another for Moses, who has already been satisfied about the Lord's identity at the burning bush, to doubt Him. Pharaoh's parody of Moses' earlier complaint ("Who are You?" "What is your name?" "Why should I do what you want?") reminds us that the difference between the two is not so great as it appears. Moses could well say Pharaoh's lines at the burning bush. Just as the desert is a way of taking the Egyptian out of the Israelites—including getting rid of their Egyptian jewelry, which Aaron uses to make the Golden Calf and Moses then makes the people eat—the Pharaoh-in-Moses (the regime of slavery) will have to be overcome before the Moses-in-Moses can prevail.

With a passivity bordering on aggression (Why me! Poor me! Woe is me!), Moses bargains for greater resources, commensurate with his task. The complaints of modern administrators about insufficient authority to fulfill their responsibilities receive a supporting echo. But it can never be. Authority has got to be less than responsibility or the task would be completed before it was begun. Closing that gap is what leadership is about. Under the circumstances, seeing that Moses is not ready to lead, the Lord allows what He can: a show of authority, a bit of magic, a semblance of control. Actually, Moses moves aside and God takes over.

"I have made thee a god to Pharaoh" (Exod. 7:1), the Lord tells Moses, in the next breath recommending a series of magic tricks, directing Moses as if he were a puppet. The Bible underlines the reality in a lovely construction that feeds on itself, a twice-told truth. "And Moses and Aaron did as the Lord commanded them, so did they" (Exod. 7:6). The effect of such phrasing is clearer if we think of it not as a text we read like a novel but as one that is read out loud to a group assembled for that purpose.

From there on, the pattern of the players is established. The Lord speaks to Moses, who does as he is told. The plagues progress, from the lice to the death of the first-born, until the exodus is engineered by the Lord, step by step. The entire escape—from the blood over the doorposts to the rituals of Passover to the route to be taken and the places to camp—is preorganized.

Evidently, Moses' invocation of the Lord displeased Him. For He says in no uncertain terms, "Wherefore criest thou unto me? speak unto the children of Israel, that they go forward" (Exod. 14:15).

If faith falters, try miracles; the Sea of Reeds is divided and the Egyptians perish. Whenever there is trouble, Moses stands back and waits for the Lord to move in. Evidence of Moses' passivity—he carries out orders but does not initiate them—abounds.

Moses displays only enough initiative to tell Pharaoh to choose the time for a plague to end, thus timing the display of the Lord's power. When Pharaoh begins to pursue the fleeing Hebrews, evidence of lack of initiative is plain. The first of a long litany of complaints comes chorusing from the people: Why did Moses lead them to the wilderness to die? Do not be afraid, Moses tells the people, for "The Lord shall fight for you" (Exod. 14:14). Not much room there for self-help.

Because he is human, Moses cannot always act. He needs passivity to be able to reflect by observing himself and others. Latency has to precede learning, so that Moses can, in effect, wind himself up for action. Judgment is, of course, retrospective, depending on whether passivity serves a purpose. It does, for it teaches Moses that he cannot be active in a regime of slavery. To change himself, he must also alter the power relationships between his followers and Pharaoh.

Whether Moses will remain passive, moving but not a mover, depends in part on whether, and what, he has learned from his joust with Pharaoh. In preparing Moses for leadership (by now it should be clear he was not prepared), God has given him the opportunity of practicing on a would-be deity, the minor leagues of the divine, the closest thing humanity has to offer.

2

FROM SLAVERY TO ANARCHY
Learning from Pharaoh What Not to Do

Now the two representatives of the children of Israel stepped before Pharaoh, and they spake, "The God of the Hebrews hath met with us; let us go, we pray thee, three days' journey into the wilderness, and sacrifice unto the Lord our God, lest He fall upon us with pestilence or with the sword." But Pharaoh answered, saying: "What is the name of your God? Wherein doth His strength consist, and His power? How many countries, how many provinces, how many cities hath He under His dominion? In how many campaigns was He victorious? How many lands did He make subject to Himself? How many cities did He capture? When He goeth to war, how many warriors, riders, chariots, and charioteers doth He lead forth?" Whereto Moses and Aaron replied: "His strength and His power fill the whole world."…Pharaoh answered and said: "I have no need of Him. I have created myself."

—Exodus Rabbah 5

By the time Moses meets them in Egypt, the people of Israel have only the bones of Joseph to remind them they have ever been anything but slaves. Regimes place their imprint on the people who live under them.

Moses discovers that good cannot come from an evil regime. But what of Joseph, the deliverer of his people? He chooses both to maintain his individual integrity and to serve Pharaoh in a slave regime. But are personal morality and collective immorality compatible? Perhaps it will help set the stage for understanding Moses' choice to lead a revolution to compare him with Joseph, who took a different path.

WISDOM VERSUS LEADERSHIP: JOSEPH AND MOSES

By contrast with Jacob, Joseph is a paragon, a product of what is called "wisdom literature" (of the kind found in the Book of Proverbs and preached in Egypt),[1] which specializes in how to get on. The story of Joseph is a Horatio Alger tale, down to the fact that Joseph's ultimate advancement comes about through the help of a high-ranking patron.

Without ever appearing on the scene, God guides Joseph's steps.[2] Joseph can let the guilty brothers off the hook, for instance, because he sees divine action as responsible for his near murder, actual kidnapping, and sale into slavery. God sent him before his brothers "to save your lives by a great deliverance," Joseph avers. "So now it was not you that sent me hither, but God" (Gen. 45:7-8). And when the brothers fear that their father's death will allow Joseph to take revenge on them, Joseph calms them in the words of one who understands the role of unanticipated consequences in the world: "Ye thought evil against me: but God meant it unto good" (Gen. 50:20).

Joseph is not usually thought of as the person who helped make Pharaoh's economic power absolute by turning farmers into tenants, but that is what the Bible tells us happened (Gen. 47:13-26). There is more to Joseph's relationship to Pharaoh, more in his dreams and their consequences, than meets the eye. Before Joseph, apparently, some Egyptians had owned their own land. After Joseph took land in exchange for food during the famine, only priests still held title to land; all else belonged to Pharaoh.

There is a story within a story; Joseph is able to make his own dreams come true (he does get to rule over his brothers) by successfully interpreting Pharaoh's dreams. The seven lean cows and thin ears of corn do turn out to mean lean years of famine, and they do figuratively eat up the seven years of plenty that came before. No doubt, also, it was prudent for Joseph to advise a policy of husbanding resources and smart of Pharaoh to choose such a man to do the job. Both men will be the better for this happy meeting. But the aura of self-congratulation surrounding Joseph's interpretation of Pharaoh's dreams has deflected inquiry away from the broader social significance of the story.

Who is this Pharaoh whom Joseph serves with such devotion? He is the same kind of despot and idolater against whom Moses fights—except that Moses' Pharaoh lives later and has added anti-Semitism to his crimes. Joseph's Pharaoh also is realistically portrayed. He sends his servants to prison, sometimes to death, for displeasing him. Pharaoh is not interested in his people. The only way to get to him is through his self-interest, his very own dreams.

What do we know about the purpose of presenting relationships between Egypt and Israel? The stories are not designed to teach us about Egyptians, or the moral would be about Egypt. Just as in Mosaic times, threats against Egyptians are warnings to Hebrews, so in this earlier story we must seek the moral for those Israelites and their leaders.

What happens to the Israelites in Egypt? They are enslaved. The fat years of the spiritual abundance of their patriarchs are indeed eaten up by the lean years of their moral servitude. Pharaohs come and go, but the regime of slavery carries on. The persecution of Israel in Egypt is no accident.

What has Joseph wrought in Egypt with his wondrous interpretations? Egyptians are made more subservient to their Pharaohs, who then proceed to enslave the Hebrews, who soon lose their faith. The famine is of the spirit as well as of the land. "Fear not," Joseph reassures his brothers, "for am I in the place of God?" (Gen. 50:19). These words of humility and comfort are the same in Hebrew as those with which Jacob, vexed by Rachel's lament that she must have children or die, wounded her: "Am I in God's stead, who hath withheld from thee the fruit of the womb?" (Gen. 30:2). Alluding to God's will may be a way to excuse evil.

What should Joseph have done? He should not have contributed to strengthening slavery; he should have tried to take his family/people out of Egypt into the Promised Land. Perhaps, as Joseph says, it was all meant to be. God is reported to have told Jacob that he need not fear Egypt, for he would be taken out again. But God did not say when.

Like Moses, Joseph begins his liberation by being rescued from water (in his case, a well). Unlike Moses, Joseph leads his people into, rather than out of, slavery. One difference between them apparently does not speak in Moses' favor: Joseph has a secure identity, Moses does not. Joseph always refers to himself as a Hebrew, taking the bad (prison) and the good (appointment as Pharaoh's chief administrator) as part of his heritage.

When Joseph's father Jacob died and was brought back to Canaan to be buried in the cave of Machpelah (which Abraham had bought for his posterity), Jacob's sons feared that Joseph would take revenge for the evil they had tried to do to him. But their fears were misplaced; Joseph was no Moses. Joseph was an administrator among the Egyptians, not a revolutionary among the Hebrews. He did not (as Rousseau would repeatedly say of Moses) create a people, taking them where they did not want to go, making them what they did not wish to become. Joseph's family needed only to escape from famine. Hunger attracted them to him; Joseph fed them but did not have to chastise them. It was not up to Joseph to let his people go, because he had no need to hold on to them. Nor was Joseph augmented or diminished by his people. Joseph is not an independent force, a creator, a first principle. He is, rather, a consequence—a creature not of human volition but of divine plan, a natural force, like the winds and the tides.

Out of travail comes creativity. Overcoming obstacles builds character. These platitudes apply to both Moses and Joseph. But Moses had a greater gap to close. Because Joseph was sold into slavery by his brothers—a story whose moral should not be lost on leaders who act too "uppity"—he had only to free himself. Moses had to deliver an entire people. From the first, Moses faces an imposing mission: not family but a "mixed multitude" must be moved, a multitude mixed in morality as well as origins, whose natural inclination is to be comfortable rather than heroic. Joseph had little difficulty getting his family to follow him to Egypt. First, he kept their brother Benjamin captive; he had the food; also, they were hungry. Moses had to lead, contrary to human inclination—away from home to the unknown, to manna instead of bread, to a strange land instead of a familiar one.

HARD HEARTS AND WEAK MEMORIES

The medium is Pharaoh, but the message is meant for Moses, that is, for Israel through its leader. Moses must learn to be a leader without being told directly what to do or how to do it. Since Pharaoh is the master in a slave regime, Moses is to learn from the bad example what not to do. What inferences about leadership, we may ask, is Moses intended to draw from Pharaoh's behavior? And, judging from Moses' subsequent behavior, what does he in fact learn from the king of the Egyptians?

One question implies another: How can Moses learn from a man without a will? "The mind manipulation of Pharaoh," Steven J. Brams tells us in his study of biblical conflict, "is one of the few instances... in the Old Testament in which a human character is robbed of his free will and, as such, his ability to make his own choices."[3] Over and over, we are told how God has hardened Pharaoh's heart so that he will not let go of the people of Israel. It begins at the burning bush, with God rehearsing the phrase. He will use it in the future (Exod. 4:21) to bring Pharaoh to a bad end. When Moses, sobered by the rebuffs administered to his people, reiterates his doubts, God speaks as though Pharaoh were solely an instrument to show off His greater glory: "And I will harden Pharaoh's heart, and multiply my signs and my wonders in the land of Egypt. But Pharaoh shall not hearken unto you, that I may lay my hand upon Egypt" (Exod. 7:3-4). The interpretation appears obvious enough to be uninteresting; God is making Pharaoh stubborn so that there will be more glory for Him in overcoming the resistance.

And it gets worse. Eleven times (once for each plague and once for good measure) Pharaoh's heart is hardened. The style varies only with the shift from active to passive voice. When Pharaoh sees a plague cease, it is said that "he hardened his heart" (Exod. 8:15, 9:34). When God wishes to express His authority, He speaks in the first person singular, as in the pursuit of Israel: "And I will harden Pharaoh's heart, that he shall follow after them; and I will be honored upon Pharaoh, and upon all his host; that the Egyptians may know that I am the Lord" (Exod. 14: 4). But when Pharaoh ignores the signs of the times—after his magicians fail to counter lice, or when God spares Israel's cattle—the passive voice, "Pharaoh's heart was hardened" (Exod. 8:19, 9:7), is used again.

This urging Pharaoh on, contrary to his best interests, has doubtless created difficulties for interpreters. Whether or not God or Pharaoh himself initiates the hardening, Egypt's king appears in the grip of compulsion. Anyone can outwit a wind-up toy. Where is the triumph in defeating a Pharaoh who is heedless of events around him?

Various interpreters have sought to clarify the situation. If God is the creator of all things from the beginning, then He must also have caused Pharaoh's obstinacy. According to Cassuto, for example, God is predicting, not controlling. Phrases like "but I will harden his heart," Cassuto writes, are ultimately the same as "but his heart will be hard."[4] Why, then, are these phrases repeated so often? And if events are preordained, why need anyone, including Moses, go through such a struggle for self-mastery?

Does evil stem from the same source as good? "One may also see in this concept of God's hardening Pharaoh's heart the same refusal (God organized history and at the same time was a responsible agent) to see a diabolical force of evil working against the divine intention," David Daiches tells us.[5] Yet demonstrating responsibility by denying it seems odd.

Saint Paul, by contrast, sees no apparent contradiction to explain away; "hardening" is but another manifestation of divine election. Unraveling the conundrum, Paul asks (and answers) the question: "What shall we say then? Is there injustice on God's part? By no means! For he says to Moses, 'I will have mercy on whom I will have mercy, and I will have compassion on whom I have compassion' (Exod. 33:19). So it depends not upon man's will or exertion, but upon God's mercy. For the scripture says to Pharaoh, 'I have raised you up for the very purpose of showing my power in you, so that my name may be proclaimed in all the earth' (Exod. 9:16). So then he has mercy upon whomever he wills, and he hardens the heart of whomever he wills" (Rom. 9:14-18).[6] Reason, as Luther said, cannot discover God.[7]

If Moses has been elected, the classic question continues, why did he undergo such a struggle to stay in office? God, as is made abundantly clear, has chosen Israel. If the march of history is inexorable, why is its direction emphasized by a negative—not Pharaoh—instead of a positive—yes, Moses?

To Childs, best of the modern commentators upon Exodus, the question is, "How can Pharaoh be made to discern the hand of God?"[8]

Pharaoh's behavior is rigidified, as the Bible says, so that "the Egyptians shall know that I am the Lord" (Exod. 7:5) and that "thou [Pharaoh] mayest know that there is none like me in all the earth" (Exod. 9:14). Undoubtedly, this means what it says—Pharaoh and Egypt, too, will recognize the greatness of God.

Yet Pharaoh does not recognize the Lord. And "dead men tell no tales," for of "all the host of Pharaoh… [in the Sea of Reeds] there remained not so much as one of them" (Exod. 14:28). Why would it be necessary to keep hardening Pharaoh's heart—even after the plagues and even after Pharaoh has asked Moses to bless him (Exod. 12:32)—if the presumed purpose had been achieved? If it is aimed at Egypt alone, the story makes no sense.[9]

Of what, then, does this hardening of the arteries of Pharaoh's leadership consist? To Pharaoh, after each plague is over, it is as if it had never happened. At first, the king thinks he need not pay attention because he, too, has magicians. But seeing that they cannot cure the boils or kill the lice or separate Egyptian cattle from those of the Hebrews, Pharaoh's less than all-powerful magicians ask the king to soften his resistance, saying, "This is the finger of God" (Exod. 8:19). Pharaoh practices deceit instead, seeking the appearance rather than the reality of letting the Hebrews leave. As soon as Moses intervenes to stop a plague[10]—frogs, lice, hail, and thunder—Pharaoh "sinned yet more, and hardened his heart, he and his servants" (Exod. 9:34). Eventually, Pharaoh's servants rebel, crying out, "How long shall this man be a snare unto us? let the men go, that they may serve the Lord their God: knowest thou not yet that Egypt is destroyed?" (Exod. 10:7). Acting as though he means to follow their advice, Pharaoh lets some go but not others, bringing upon his people locusts and darkness—until anger prevails and he drives Moses from him. After the first-born of Egypt die, Pharaoh finally expels Israel with the ambivalent message, "be gone; and bless me also" (Exod. 12:32). Pharaoh sees but does not understand. For, after Israel flees, the king and his advisers regret the departure, asking (in the light of all that has transpired) an incredible question: "*Why have we done this*, that we have let Israel go from serving us?" (Exod. 14:5; emphasis added). Pharaoh and his servants have no future because they can remember no past.

By hardening the ruler's heart, God is showing that Pharaoh lacks memory; he has reacted to each plague as if it had been the only one. Yet without memory, there can be no learning: scientific man sums up past episodes that are relevant to the future in order to make present decisions. Psychological man seeks to deal with the issue before him in its own terms, without allowing inner compulsions to dictate a decision out of touch with the external world of action. Pharaoh either cannot or will not do this.

Like his memory, the language Pharaoh uses is frozen—static and stilted. Each incident is a final and permanent monument—inscribed, elaborated, then forgotten. There is no hesitation, no doubt, no error. There is also no learning from language.

How different is Moses, who brings to the Hebrew people a flow of language to go with his dynamic view of history. For Moses, truth is no longer established by definition; even the definitions he does devise are circumlocutions, around which one must still struggle to learn what is going on. Pharaoh, by contrast, has no need to remember; his words become deeds and make history only because he believes himself to be divine. No matter how often Pharaoh is surprised, he does not revamp his hypotheses about the world; because what he says is true by his definition, there is no need to check on what has happened.

How can Pharaoh let the Hebrew people go, or keep them for that matter, when he cannot remember anything? Lack of memory is not a random occurrence; it is a characteristic feature of slave regimes, for slaves and masters alike. Having no need to take account of others, masters ape the mentality of their slaves; without responsibility, masters have no need to remember or to teach. The concern is not limited to Pharaoh. Forgetting the signs God has already revealed, Israel (like Egypt before it) murmurs in the wilderness each time something goes wrong. So as not to do what Pharaoh has done, Israel is advised to remember.

After the Lord has again told Moses that He has hardened Pharaoh's heart, He goes on to reveal His method: "And that thou mayest tell in the ears of thy son, and of thy son's son, what things I have wrought in Egypt, and my signs which I have done among them; that ye may know how that I am the Lord" (Exod. 10:2). Israel is endlessly exhorted to remember, to make present choices in awareness of past experiences, so as not to enslave itself by paying attention only to momentary passions. Though the present world of action deserves attention, it must be considered against a background of past experience.[11]

Faith is the willingness to act in the absence of things seen; but faith in the future requires knowledge of the past, from which stems the fortitude to overcome seemingly insurmountable obstacles. The faith of leaders should thus be retrospective as well as prospective: they leap into the void of the present, illuminated by past memory of promise for the future. Israel is taught to be historically minded, to speak of and interpret its history.

Without memory there is no learning; without learning there can be no teaching; and without teaching no one else will be able to remember. This social circle of remembrance is God's gift to Israel, without which its people would long since have perished.

It is as if Moses is making up for what he missed as a child. By giving himself a hard-won tradition, and by reminding himself to remember it, Moses (re)creates a past on which to base a future for his people. From then on, actions may be justified on the grounds that things have always been that way. History is (re)written by selective attention.

Hence the signs of remembrance abound. On the Passover, the Hebrew people are exhorted: "And thou shalt show thy son in that day, saying, This is done because of that which the Lord did unto me when I came forth out of Egypt" (Exod. 13:8). This line is elaborated at home in the Passover service, in that each individual partakes in the deliverance as if it has happened to him. "And this day," the Lord says to Moses and Aaron, "shall be unto you for a memorial; and ye shall keep it a feast to the Lord throughout your generations… for ever" (Exod. 12:14).[12]

If the exodus is not a unique episode but a generalization of revolt against slavery, the present must creatively reinterpret the past as if it were relevant to today's concerns. By reliving the exodus as if it actually had happened to them, future generations maintain the tradition of change by interpretation in their own time.

"Much social legislation in the Pentateuch," David Daube points out, "is reinforced by reminders of the exodus or even represented as a consequence." Slaves held by Hebrews in Israel are to be well treated "for they are my slaves whom I brought out of the land of Egypt."[13] As it is said, "Love ye therefore the stranger: for ye were strangers in the land of Egypt" (Deut. 10:19).

Especially interesting is this prohibition: "Thou shalt not abhor an Egyptian; because thou wast a stranger in his land" (Deut. 23:7). Other examples of social legislation urge identification with the unfortunate or oppressed on the analogy of Israel's similar position in Egypt. Applying this principle to the oppressor requires further explanation. Plenty of reason exists for eternal enmity against a people whose rulers sought to kill every male child of Israel; yet the entire text (not just this passage) is remarkably free of rancor against Egypt.

Without erasing the memory of these events (quite the contrary!), responsibility for the harsh treatment of the Hebrews has been shifted from a particular people to a divine intention manifested in history. In the beginning, biology accounts for the natural increase of Israel, setting off an inexorable train of events. In the middle, Pharaoh, held in the grip of impersonal historical forces, has his heart hardened. In the end, Egypt is the womb in which the memory of a nation and its discovery of history are formed.

EGYPT AS A SCHOOL FOR ISRAEL

It is hardly an exaggeration to say that without Egypt there could hardly have been an Israel. Passover is the prime Hebrew holiday precisely because it concerns the forging of a people. Not only the future of Israel but its past genesis would not have figured in history without the exodus of the Hebrews from Egypt.

But we anticipate; there was perhaps a people—by biology but not yet by cosmology. A common core of values, beliefs, and practices, reflecting and justifying a way of life, had not yet emerged.

Moses has to make a revolution, knowing where it is supposed to lead (the Promised Land) and who is supposed to lead it (himself), but not knowing what regime will best enable him to lead. Hierarchy might help, but (a) it is too much like the regime he is rejecting and (b) the people, being taught to break their bonds, will not accept it. So Moses is, willy-nilly, moving toward anarchy—no restraint but also no group boundaries. At the start, that is all right. Leaders of anarchies get full war powers so long as the emergency lasts. After the revolution, however, anarchy—in which coalitions are continuously reformulated and past leaders are replaced or ignored—may prove trying. The leader Moses will find the rule of "What have you done for me lately?" more than he can bear.

The children of Israel had to engage in that most human quality of "observing-while-doing" to school themselves for the life to come.

For no man is this more important than for Moses, who must learn to lead. Indeed, his task, in common with all founders, is to act, to err, to learn, and then to teach. Moses is simultaneously the formulator and reformulator of Israel's becoming (the eternal editor, so to speak, in whose name his and his people's history is written). By no mere happenstance is Moses the first and greatest Jewish author.

It is not just what has happened but what Moses chooses to make of events that will be actualized in the collective consciousness of Israel. Before Moses can learn from history, he must engage in it. His school is the negotiations with Pharaoh, king and god of the Egyptians. The two leaders are contending for the future of a people, Moses to acquire legitimacy as their leader and Pharaoh to retain his omnipotence over them.

The long-lasting memory we call writing is not only recall but review. Events are altered as they are written up from this or that perspective. That is why it is important to Moses that he not only be good but also appear—to himself and to others—to do good. Whatever he does becomes history, once by the doing and a second time by the writing. If memory, being selective, is a form of interpretation, Moses must be able to remember actions worthy of being considered.

What might a weak, would-be leader learn from negotiation with a strong man of acknowledged leadership?—how to convert weakness into strength; how to turn the apparent strength of an opponent into weakness. The pyramidal shape of a slave regime may prove its undoing. Unlike Pharaoh, for instance, Moses need not worry about orders being carried out immediately, with all the attendant consequences.

Pharaoh thinks he does not have to consider the preferences of his followers when deciding whether to give in or to resist, whether to accept or reject a concession; his followership is assured. Not so for Moses, who must persuade his people. Pharaoh has the power to enforce commands; Moses must learn how to formulate an agreement to cover contingencies so he will know whether agreements are kept or broken; this may well call for learning how to detect and deal with duplicity. Moses has to consider carefully what ruses to try, for he must justify the consequences of his actions to his followers. By contrast, until he starts to lose his grip, Pharaoh need not use guile.

These are the early events: God instructs Moses and the elders of Israel to ask Pharaoh to let the Hebrew people go for three days into the wilds so as to sacrifice to the Lord. Pharaoh refuses; moreover, he decreases the resources of the Hebrews for making bricks while demanding maintenance of their former level of production. The people complain bitterly to Moses, who complains to God, who initiates the plagues. The bare bones of this account contain instruction for Moses and the people of Israel that they can disregard only at their peril.

Allegiance

To whom do the Hebrew people owe allegiance? This is the crucial question because neither the identity nor the identification of the people is yet settled. Pharaoh either does not think he needs allegiance or assumes he already has it because he separates himself from the Israelites even before they have an opportunity to choose between him and Moses. After Pharaoh increased the Hebrew people's work load, they could not keep up the same output, so "the officers of the children of Israel, which the Pharaoh's taskmasters had set over them, were beaten" (Exod. 5:14). Apparently there existed a cadre of Hebrews who had been appointed by Pharaoh; might not those men be beholden to the king or concerned about keeping their offices? Because of what happens next, we see that indeed they might; the Hebrew officers (not Moses or Aaron or the elders) themselves go to see Pharaoh, adopting a mode of address that suggests they belong to him: "Wherefore dealest thou thus with thy servants?" (Exod. 5:15).[14] As Moses is a servant of God, they are servants of Pharaoh. Instead of taking this opportunity to split his opposition, however, Pharaoh drives them away, saying, "Ye are idle, ye are idle.... Go therefore now, and work.... And the officers of the children of Israel did see that they were in evil case" (Exod. 5:17-19). Thus Pharaoh imposes on the Hebrews something they have been unable to attain on their own—a group identity.

The purpose of Pharaoh's maneuver, other than to vent his spleen, is to detach the Hebrew people from their new potential leaders, by showing that Moses' intervention only makes things worse for them. And, for the moment, it appears to work; the officers criticize Moses and Aaron "because ye have made our savor to be abhorred in the eyes of Pharaoh, and in the eyes of his servants, to put a sword in their hand to slay us" (Exod. 5:21). And Moses passes on this accusation to God, saying, "Lord, wherefore has thou so evil entreated this people?" (Exod. 5:22). Pressed between the people and the Lord, Moses appears ready to abandon leadership, asking, "Why is it that thou hast sent me? For since I came to Pharaoh to speak in thy name, he hath done evil to this people; neither hast thou delivered thy people at all" (Exod. 5:22-23). Despite the Lord's reassurances to Moses—"Now shalt thou see what I will do to Pharaoh" (Exod. 6:1)—and the winged words Moses carries from God to the people—"I will bring you out.... I will redeem you.... and I will bring you in" (Exod. 6:6-8)—"they hearkened not unto Moses for anguish of spirit, and for cruel bondage" (Exod. 6:9).

Immediately thereafter, Moses asks the Lord why Pharaoh should take his words seriously, seeing that Moses' own people pay him no heed. All Moses gets in return is another charge—to tell Pharaoh the same things as before. The answer as to how a leader should behave—identifying with, not separating himself from, his people—has been given earlier, in counterpoint to Pharaoh's rejection of the officers, when the Lord leaped into action by inclusion: "I will take you to me for a people" (Exod. 6:7).

Duplicity

Leaving nothing to chance, the Lord tells Moses to gather the elders of Israel to see Pharaoh and say, "The Lord God of the Hebrews hath met with us: and now let us go, we beseech thee, three days' journey into the wilderness, that we may sacrifice to the Lord our God" (Exod. 3:18). These words, as commentators throughout the ages have noted, implicate God in an apparent duplicity.[15] Evidently, as other episodes in the Bible testify (from Jacob and Laban to Sarah and another king of Egypt), it is all right for Moses to dissemble in the face of superior force.[16] Perhaps also, though there is nothing specific in the text, the context suggests that Pharaoh might have destroyed the Hebrews, or at least their leaders, had they revealed outright to him their real intent. Possibly, as many commentators have observed, Pharaoh is given a limited demand to handle (politely phrased), the more to show the unreasonableness of his refusal. Because our interest is in leadership, and dealing with demands is one important component, we will probe further.

As usual, God's orders are not aimed at Pharaoh alone but also at Moses, who is being taught that his people can stand only so much. To be turned down on such a small request does not yet require them to risk all. It is important for the Hebrews to observe these modest requests being refused; it will then be easier for denial of the larger ones to justify counteraction on their part.

To think about prior preparation of followers is essential; as we are told, "And it came to pass, when Pharaoh had let the people go, that God led them not through the way of the land of the Philistines, although that was near; for God said, Lest peradventure the people repent when they see war, and they return to Egypt" (Exod. 13:17). A leader needs to learn about his people's weaknesses.

Consider the contrary situation: when should seemingly small demands be refused? Learning to accede to smaller demands so as not to have to grant larger ones is part of the art of leadership. The difficulty is that narrow concessions may also spread into wider ones. The distinction depends on whether a concession can be confined, or whether it is of such significance that the consequences could not be managed. By his action in welcoming, rather than repressing, the independent prophesying of Eldad and Medad, to mention a future episode, Moses shows that long years of wandering have not made him forget this lesson. Since he then hopes to establish a hierarchical regime, Moses wishes to encourage those who act to do so in accord with authority.

Were he to accept this proposal to allow a sacrifice in the desert, Pharaoh might be unable to justify refusing other such requests in the future. Such permission would, moreover, imply acceptance of a new leadership independent of Pharaoh's; a leadership without which the Hebrews would not have won respite from their labors; a leadership whose very purpose sets up a rival deity. So Pharaoh rejects the leaders: "Wherefore do ye, Moses and Aaron, let the people from their works? get you unto your burdens" (Exod. 5:4). To punish the Hebrews for their presumption, the king of Egypt increases the very burdens those illegitimate leaders sought to diminish. Yet, at this early stage, there were alternatives. Pharaoh might have invited the Hebrews to a feast of his own, for example, compelling them to choose: respect for Pharaoh and an easier life versus a hard life and obedience to upstart leaders. Once he has given away the contest for leadership of the officers of the people of Israel, however, Pharaoh has nothing left except force. The less the legitimacy, the more the force.

Taken at face value, Moses and Aaron's request to Pharaoh is true as far as it goes; they do want to take their people out to sacrifice to the Lord. Indeed, the leaders embellish the Lord's instructions so as to soften and stiffen their position simultaneously, maintaining the need to go lest God "fall upon us with pestilence, or with the sword" (Exod. 5:3). It is not just that they want to go, the leaders imply, but someone else is breathing down their necks. Since Moses and Aaron will be damned if they do and damned if they don't, they suggest that Pharaoh's threats cannot be the only consideration. Building a fire behind one, Thomas C. Schelling points out, strengthens a stand against retreat.[17]

Contingency

Moses' insistence and Pharaoh's refusal involve the two in negotiations that illustrate the classic contours of bargaining—evasion, obfuscation, escalation. Moses is a beginner, but he will learn. As the plagues begin to have their effect, Pharaoh switches from threats to evasion—from overt to covert resistance—offering to let the people go but never quite doing so. It seems there are unspecified conditions—such as where (in the land of Egypt or outside), who (all the people or only some), and with what (the people with or without their possessions)—that have yet to be met. In future negotiations with others, Moses will be more careful to tie down the conditions that alter positions.

Long afterward, toward the end of Moses' life, as the people approached the Promised Land, he showed he had not forgotten the necessity of dotting the i's and crossing the t's of agreements, even with his own people. Briefly, the tribes of Gad and Reuben, seeing that Jazer and Gilead had good lands for raising cattle, asked Moses for permission to settle there, instead of crossing over the Jordan into Canaan with the other tribes. Moses was reluctant, for fear others would be discouraged from taking possession of the land of promise. To Moses' question, almost a rebuke, "Shall your brethren go to war, and shall ye sit here?" (Num. 32:6), the two tribes promised they would fight with the rest: "We will not return unto our houses, until the children of Israel have inherited every man his inheritance" (Num. 32:18). In contrast to his early experience with Pharaoh, Moses here sets out precise stipulations:

If ye...
will go all of you armed over Jordan before the Lord, until he hath driven out his enemies from before him.
And the land be subdued before the Lord: then afterward ye shall return, and be guiltless before the Lord, and before Israel; and this land shall be your possession before the Lord.
But if ye will not do so, behold, ye have sinned against the Lord: and be sure your sin will find you out. [Num. 32:20-23]

By the time he was finished, Moses was able to anticipate many more contingencies than when he started.

Time

Making time an ally instead of an enemy is part of leadership. The plagues do not merely happen. After the first two, the time when plagues will start or stop is announced in advance—tomorrow; the next day; about this time; as soon as Moses is out of the city; around midnight. There can be no doubt about the source of power (who causes things to be other than they would, against opposition, as social scientists say)[18] when Moses offers to let Pharaoh name the day—"Be it according to thy word" (Exod. 8:10)—when the frogs return from the land to the river,[19] so that the natural order of things be restored.

As time runs out on Pharaoh, he also loses the physical sight that symbolizes foresight. There was a "darkness which may be felt" (Exod. 10:21). The Egyptians were unable to take care of one another, the worst weakness in a social structure. At the appointed midnight, the first-born of Egypt die (impartially afflicted, from Pharaoh's son to the prisoner in the dungeon, which meant communal responsibility for their leadership). "In the night" (Exod. 12:30), Pharaoh arose. "By night" (Exod. 12:31), Pharaoh calls upon Moses and Aaron, whom he had previously banished, and Pharaoh's curses turn into a request for blessings.[20]

Nor is this new. Pharaoh blew hot and cold all along, changing as soon as he got into trouble. "Entreat the Lord," he tells Moses and

Aaron, "that he may take away the frogs from me, and from my people" (Exod. 8:8). Had Pharaoh meant what he said, there would have been no need to go further. Apparently Pharaoh deluded himself more than he deceived Moses, who, on the next go-around, agreed to ask the Lord to remove the lice, "but let not Pharaoh deal deceitfully any more" (Exod. 8:29). Then new plagues come, and Pharaoh is more contrite: "Entreat the Lord (for it is enough) that there be no more mighty thunderings and hail; and I will let you go, and ye shall stay no longer" (Exod. 9: 28). But again Pharaoh reneges; and, after the devouring locusts, "Then Pharaoh called for Moses and Aaron in haste; and he said, I have sinned against the Lord your God, and against you. Now therefore forgive, I pray thee, my sin only this once, and entreat the Lord your God, that he may take away from me this death only" (Exod. 10:16-17). Time is not on the side of those who temporize when fundamental choices must be made.

Pharaoh's backsliding from earlier agreements is but a pale foretaste of what Moses will face from the Israelites. Not once or twice but many times, the Hebrew people go back on their decision to leave (as they wish to go back to) Egypt. Thus they also renege on their history and their language, which will not be known or spoken if Israel becomes indistinguishable from Egypt.

Mixing

Moses was most fierce against other peoples: they entangled Israel in their own customs, blurring the distinctiveness of Israelite beliefs so as to weaken the Hebrews' special relationship to the Lord. A pointed example comes in Moses' last commission from God, to make war on Midian. The war that God had commanded was fierce enough; all the males were slain, all the cities were burned, and Midianite women, children, and goods were taken. Yet still "Moses was wroth" (Num. 31:14) with the men of war. His words wound us still, reflecting the vengeance the Lord had told Moses to take against Midian. "Have ye," says the implacable leader, "saved all the women alive?" (Num. 31:15).

The explanation that follows helps us understand why Moses would not relent. These women, he says, had caused the men of Israel to sin against the Lord; they were the source of impurity. The Bible leaves little to the imagination: "And the people began to commit whoredom with the daughters of Moab. And they called the people unto the sacrifices of their gods: and the people did eat, and bowed down to their gods" (Num. 25:1-2). The moral of the times was that mixing led to murder: "Now therefore," Moses commands, "kill every male among the little ones, and kill every woman that hath known man by lying with him" (Num. 31:17). First the people mixed, body into body, then the worship mixed, false god for true, then the killing mixed, women with men, children with adults.

Slavery and anarchy, because their boundaries are weak, are incompatible with membership in what afterward was appropriately called the Mosaic community. Innumerable prescriptions are imposed on slaves because they lack defenses against external rule. Trying new things, converting risks into opportunities, is the leitmotif of anarchies that encourage each individual or clan to transact with whomever it wishes. Jews may order themselves into hierarchies and equities, making decisions collectively for the group as a whole, because these regimes have strong boundaries, but not into regimes that make them vulnerable to outside influences. Jews must remain a community with strong boundaries so that they can worship the one God. From this prohibition against idolatry (slaves worship masters and anarchists contract with whom they will) stems the Judaic abhorrence of mixing and Judaism's conceptual concern about keeping like categories together.

Separation

Moses' task is to create a people by leading them intact out of Egypt. They may go earlier or later, this way or that, but they must go as a whole. If the wiles of the women of Midian, known so briefly by the Israelites, were a snare, then how much greater was the allure of Egypt? All the habits of a lifetime, of a home town—food, clothing, customs— worked against making slaves, especially slaves to creature comforts, into a fully formed people who would follow a rigorous way of life all their own. Compromises were possible—but not those that would move Israel toward, instead of away from, contact with other cultures.

Moses will wait: Moses will be patient even as Pharaoh breaks promises. But Moses will not accept Pharaoh's offer for Hebrews to worship the

Lord in the land of Egypt. Moses uses the argument he believes—do not mix cultures—except that he turns it around to apply to the Egyptians, who, he tells Pharaoh, would be angry to witness worship of a foreign deity. "And will they not stone us?" (Exod. 8:26), Moses asks, adverting to the Hebrew form of punishment, as if the Hebrew people had to leave because the Egyptians would insist.

It takes several plagues before Pharaoh suggests, in effect, that the Israelites go—but only the men, leaving the women and children behind. Moses will have none of it—all must go, including the animals. The Hebrew people must be kept whole. Pharaoh refuses. The locusts come. Pharaoh appears repentant; the children can go but not the cattle. Moses is adamant: "There shall not a hoof be left behind" (Exod. 10:26). What is a sacrifice without animals? Besides, Moses continues, you never know what you might need. It is no wonder Pharaoh threatens to kill Moses if he shows up again.

The plagues themselves make clear the principle of separation designed to keep the Hebrew people pure and, therefore, apart. As usual, the Lord gives Moses advice ostensibly addressed to Pharaoh, ordering Moses to tell Pharaoh, "I will put a division between my people and thy people" (Exod. 8:23).

The sign of separation is behavioral; Goshen, where the Hebrews lived apart from the rest of Egypt, because raising animals was considered an abomination, would not be affected by the plagues afflicting the Egyptians. First came the lice, then "the cattle of Egypt died: but of the cattle of the children of Israel died not one" (Exod. 9:6). To drive home the thesis that safety lies in separation (Hebrews from Egyptians, the people of God from idolaters), the Lord let it hail everywhere with one exception: "Only in the land of Goshen," the account continues, "where the children of Israel were, was there no hail" (Exod. 9:26). It was dark in Egypt during the three days of the ninth plague, "but all the children of Israel had light in their dwellings" (Exod. 10:23).

The final plague, the death of the first-born children, which causes an outcry "such as there was none like it, nor shall be like it any more" (Exod. 11:6), is the ultimate exemplification of the separation that will redeem Israel. The first-born of Egypt die. "But," God promises through Moses, "against any of the children of Israel shall not a dog move his tongue, against man or beast: that ye may know how that the Lord doth put a difference between the Egyptians and Israel" (Exod. 11:7).

As the Passover celebrates the departure from Egypt, it also solemnifies the ritual differences between Israel and other nations. Like the blood of circumcision, which unites the people and separates them from others, "The blood [of the lamb upon the doorposts] shall be to you for a token upon the houses where ye are: and when I see the blood, I will pass over you, and the plague shall not be upon you to destroy you, when I smite the land of Egypt" (Exod. 12:13).

The Passover ritual itself parcels out what is permitted and what is not by arranging two classes of goods, the pure and the impure. The lamb used must be (like those who wish to worship the Lord) without blemish. The unleavened bread, symbolizing the haste of the departure—the people being thrust out suddenly as in a breech birth—is to be sharply distinguished from the leaven, which is forbidden during the Passover week lest "that soul shall be cut off from Israel" (Exod. 12:15).

It is this social separation, as Mary Douglas proposes, that is behind the "kosher–non-kosher, permitted-impermissible dichotomies of Jewish dietary provision." The rationale for keeping kosher is not to be found in illnesses to be suffered from eating pork or shellfish or in the allegedly unnatural nature of beasts that chew this way or that but in the maintenance of a social system threatened by insidious external forces.[21] "Don't mix disparate categories" is not far from "don't mix with the Midianites."

The essence of Leviticus is found in the tenth verse of the tenth chapter: "And that ye may put difference between holy and unholy, and between unclean and clean" (Lev. 10:10). Equitable social laws are equated with fair measures, holiness with wholeness, for "Ye shall not offer unto the Lord that which is bruised, or crushed, or broken, or cut" (Lev. 22: 24). Israel is separated from other people so it can be kept together in worship. As we are told,

> I am the Lord your God, who have separated you from other people.
>
> Ye shall therefore put difference between clean beasts and unclean, and between unclean fowls and clean: and ye shall not make your souls abominable....
>
> And ye shall be holy unto me: for I the Lord am holy, and have severed you from other people, that ye should be mine. [Lev. 20: 24-26]

The injunction to differentiate the clean from the unclean is directly tied to the unity of the people, the differentiation of objects serving to reinforce their differences from other peoples.

Why always separation of the pure from the impure? Death for both is the penalty for intercourse between a man and his daughter-in-law because "they have wrought confusion" (Lev. 20:12). Just as no man must covet his neighbor's wife, and no father-in-law take his daughter-in-law, no tribe must occupy the place allotted to another. Confusion of categories, of that which may and may not be done, spells the end of a common culture under which men are able to regulate their lives. In short, cultural confusion could turn Israelites into Egyptians.

Social impurity leads to pollution of the land. The Hebrew people are warned not to transgress God's law lest "the land spew not you out also, when ye defile it" (Lev. 18:28). When the people pursue abominations, the land dries up and its produce withers. As Nehama Leibowitz sums up the commentary, "The soil, the ecology is put out of joint by any kind of human misconduct."[22] When Deuteronomy warns its listeners, "Thou shalt not cause the land to sin" (Deut. 24:4), it is talking about proper conditions for divorce. Though its effects may be physical, sin is social.[23]

Is this talk about the significance of separation in Hebrew life made up out of whole cloth? No, it has been there literally from the beginning. The Book of Genesis (in Hebrew, *Bereshit,* "In the beginning") is a Mosaic teaching. Mosaic doctrine begins at the beginning—like Israel, mankind is first separated from other creatures.

The first sentence of Genesis ("In the beginning God created the heaven and the earth") sets up the most fundamental separation of all—between God and man. The Creator is not the created. And man can never cross that boundary to become God. The significance of the Sabbath is that the day on which God rested, when the Creation was over, is devoted to observing the unbridgeable divide; man worships the Creator, not himself. In the beginning, in the first sentence, idolatry is proscribed. No humans must be able to say that they, with their own idolatrous hands, made the earth or named the active and willful creatures in it.

The Tower of Babel is testimony that in the time when all men spoke a single tongue nothing was "restrained from them, which they have imagined to do" (Gen. 11:6). What might they do? Worship not

God but the work of their own hands. For this reason, God separated men, by geography and by language. Thus they would be prevented from acting together to do the worst. The severe judgment against mankind's mixing of cultural categories in the Tower of Babel prepares the way for the separation and selection of Israel. According to political philosopher Leo Strauss, "The sequence of creation… can be stated as follows: from the principle of separation, light; via something which separates, heaven; to something which is separated, earth and sea; to things which are productive of separated things, trees, for example; then things which can separate themselves from their course, brutes; and finally a being which can separate itself from its way, the right way."[24]

What is the purpose of this separation? The French commentator Rashi gives us Rabbi Isaac's social explanation. It is "in order that He might give them the heritage of the nations. For should the peoples of the world say to Israel, 'You are robbers, because you took by force the lands of the seven nations of Canaan', Israel may reply to them 'All the earth belongs to the Holy One, blessed be He; He created it and gave it to whom He pleased. When He willed He gave it to them, and when He willed He took it from them and gave it to us.'"[25] The Creation is not about, or for, just anybody. It rationalizes one of the most important claims Moses made for this people—the land of Israel is theirs by right because the Owner gave it to them.

If the children of Israel had any doubts about the mixing of people (as well as categories), the Lord's instructions for entering their home-land-to-be (Num. 33:52-55) should dispel them. The people are to "drive out all the inhabitants," "destroy all their pictures, and… molten images… and high places" and divide the land among themselves. If they fail to do so, "those which ye let remain… shall be pricks in your eyes, and thorns in your sides"—altogether disagreeable. And, if that were not enough, there is the discomfort of knowing that "Moreover it shall come to pass, that I shall do unto you, as I thought to do unto them" (Num. 33:56). Israel is being warned to leave Egypt morally as well as physically, lest it share the same fate.

Spoiling and Separation

Though Israel is expelled from Egypt, the people do not leave empty-handed. Nor does Israel amass goods by accident or without permission. From the first, after previewing how He would overcome Pharaoh's resistance, the Lord promised Moses that, "When ye go, ye shall not go empty: But every woman shall borrow of her neighbor, and of her that sojourneth in her house, jewels of silver, and jewels of gold, and raiment: and ye shall put them upon your sons, and upon your daughters; and ye shall spoil the Egyptians" (Exod. 3:21-22). The people followed orders.

Taking spoil from the Egyptians has caused some difficulty and no little dismay to commentators down the centuries. It does not seem like a nice thing to do. And why would Egyptians trust Hebrews with gold and silver and other fine things? It is true that to avoid further trouble "the Egyptians were urgent upon the people, that they might send them out of the land in haste" (Exod. 12:33). And it may also be, as we are told, that Moses had won a great reputation in Egypt. Still, the element of divine magic ("And the Lord gave the people favor in the sight of the Egyptians, so that they lent unto them such things as they required" [Exod. 12:36])—though the plagues themselves, frogs and hail and such, generally work with nature—has given cause for disquiet.[26]

Is it possible that the attention given to looting the Egyptians is an awkward effort to rationalize an unsavory act, or even to explain why Hebrew former slaves in the desert had enough gold to make a Golden Calf? Of course it is possible. But such an interpretation, which sees the spoiling as running contrary to the content of other events, can be challenged.

From a theological point of view, the looting of the Egyptians signifies something straightforward: God commanded it; any effort to resist Him would prove counterproductive. As the diviner Balaam explains to King Balak, in terms applicable to Pharaoh, "God is not a man, that he should lie; neither the son of man, that he should repent: hath he said, and shall he not do it? or hath he spoken, and shall he not make it good?" (Num. 23:19). What good has it done Pharaoh to humble Israel, the spoiling implies, if the children of Israel can leave richer than when they lived in Egypt?

Deuteronomy recapitulates these events, recounting the time when "the children of Israel went out with an high hand in the sight of all the Egyptians" (Num. 33:3). This, if one were going to create a people, is how one would like them to go—head high. This, if the Hebrews were going to build a new life, is how one would like to send them off—with a shower of gifts. The people who come before the Lord to make their covenant are to be suitably attired.

From the standpoint of social legislation, the spoiling speaks to permanent provisions. The laborer is worthy of his hire and must be paid his due. "One law shall be to him that is homeborn"—according to the ordinances of the Passover given by the Lord to Moses and Aaron before the exodus—"and unto the stranger that sojourneth among you" (Exod. 12:49). Indeed, in Deuteronomy the same expression is used, harking back to the memory of Egypt, in reference to freeing Hebrews who have served as slaves: "And when thou sendest him out free from thee, thou shalt not let him go away empty: Thou shalt furnish him liberally out of thy flock, and out of thy floor, and out of thy winepress: of that wherewith the Lord thy God hath blessed thee thou shalt give unto him" (Deut. 15:13-14).

Basing his interpretation on the Deuteronomic requirement that a slave who departs at the end of six years be well supplied, Daube writes that "Pharaoh is requested to behave as a decent master should." The provision by Pharaoh of beasts of his own (which others find impertinent, if not absurd), Daube likens to the relationship between Jacob and Laban, who ends his efforts to impoverish his son-in-law with farewell gifts. According to Daube:

> No doubt the general scheme, God helping his protégé out of danger and distress, is independently common to both. So is a good deal else. The falling into slavery or a sort of slavery abroad; the falling into it owing to an arbitrary change of attitude on the part of a host; the ambiguity in the conduct of the master who wishes at once to be rid of the dangerous subject and to keep him for the benefit he derives, and who tries to recapture him when finally he runs away with considerable wealth; the interposition of God by force or threat of force; the defeat of the masters' gods.[27]

In the end, God's plan prevails, despite the wiles of the most devious of men, whether Laban or Pharaoh.[28] The spoiling, far from establishing an evil practice against Egypt, sets a worthy standard for Jews. It sets the stage for the foreigner and the laborer to receive social justice. It acts to ward off the intrusion of exploitative practices common to a slave regime into the new life the Hebrews hope to live.

Israel's separation from others is not a mark of superiority. Moses is aghast at the thought: "Not for thy righteousness, or for the uprightness of thine heart, dost thou go to possess their land" (Deut. 9:5). Nor does separation mean condemnation of others' customs. Indeed, when strangers come into Israel, their very differences are used to argue for justice for the stranger. Israel alone risks contamination by foreign practices.

The spoils of Egypt point not only forward to victory but also back to defeat. Escaping from Egypt physically is not the same as leaving it emotionally; to cut that umbilical cord will not be easy for the Hebrew people.

From Rebellion Against Pharaoh to Retreat from Moses

At the fateful moment, as the Hebrew people are moving out of Egypt, both peoples regret what they have done—the Hebrews in going and the Egyptians in allowing them to leave. Only Moses stands firm. To judge the depths of his dilemma, only the biblical account will do:

> And when Pharaoh drew nigh, the children of Israel lifted up their eyes, and, behold, the Egyptians marched after them; and they were sore afraid: and the children of Israel cried out unto the Lord.
>
> And they said unto Moses, Because there were no graves in Egypt, hast thou taken us away to die in the wilderness? wherefore hast thou dealt thus with us, to carry us forth out of Egypt?
>
> Is not this the word that we did tell thee in Egypt, saying, Let us alone, that we may serve the Egyptians? For it had been better for us to serve the Egyptians, than that we should die in the wilderness. [Exod. 14:10-13]

Moses can say only, "hold your peace" (Exod. 14:14). Faced with internal insurrection, he confronted conflicting criteria. A fair translation of God's retort to Moses when the people threaten to turn back is, "Don't cry to me! Lead the people!"[29] The Babylonian Talmud imagines God telling

Moses, "My beloved ones are drowning in the sea and thou prolongest prayer before Me!"[30]

With Pharaoh behind and the sea in front, Moses' advice to "stand still, and see the salvation of the Lord" (Exod. 14:13) has a certain cogency. Suppose, on the contrary, that in future circumstances the people were not trapped between fire and water and wished to "go back," either to Egypt or to foreign customs? Would Moses, then, have to coerce consent? What kind of mediator would he be if he punished, instead of persuaded, his people? And what kind of leader would he become if he destroyed his disobedient people in order to save them?

There follows the division of the Sea of Reeds and the Lord's victory over Pharaoh. Temporarily, the breach between Moses and his people has been healed. But fresh in his mind is the experience with a Pharaoh who kept changing his mind, who committed himself only with reservations. How much more changeable might Moses' own fearful followers be? Conditions encouraging the Hebrews' consent are, moreover, not auspicious. How long will the Lord continue to fight their battles? If leadership is up to Moses, and if his followers threaten to desert him—morally as well as geographically—every time there is trouble, will he then have to do to the children of Israel what the Lord did to Pharaoh's Egyptians?

With Pharaoh and his forces vanquished, the Israelites sang songs of victory, "saying, I will sing unto the Lord, for he hath triumphed gloriously: the horse and his rider hath he thrown into the sea" (Exod. 15: 1). Three days later, hardly long enough for memory to dim, the people were without water. Then began the refrain that continued through the years until the death of the leader: "And the people murmured against Moses, saying, What shall we drink?" (Exod. 15:24). And Moses "cried unto the Lord" (Exod. 15:25), who showed him a tree that when dipped into the water made it sweet. Bittersweet is the motif.

A few weeks later, in the wilderness of Sin, the grumbling (as the *New Translation* calls the King James' "murmuring") escalates. "And the whole congregation of the children of Israel murmured against Moses and Aaron in the wilderness:... Would to God we had died by the hand of the Lord in the land of Egypt, when we sat by the flesh pots, and when we did eat bread to the full: for ye have brought us forth into this wilderness, to kill this whole assembly with hunger" (Exod. 16:2-3). Hyperbole hurts.

"Then said the Lord unto Moses, Behold, I will rain bread from heaven for you; and the people shall go out and gather a certain rate every day, that I may prove them, whether they will walk in my law, or no" (Exod. 16:4). The people's material needs were met in a way that would test their future faith. They were to collect the manna for six days but leave it on the seventh, which was the Sabbath.

It was not the bread to which the Hebrews were accustomed; this was the bread of faith, abundant no matter how little or how much was picked from the ground. It stank if kept over the seventh day. Nevertheless, some people did gather it on the Sabbath, leading the Lord to complain, not to the people but to Moses, "How long refuse ye to keep my commandments and my laws?" (Exod. 16:28).

Much later, Moses rationalized those events in retrospect, explaining that the Lord "humbled thee, and suffered thee to hunger, and fed thee with manna, which thou knewest not, neither did thy fathers know; that he might make thee know that man doth not live by bread only, but by every word that proceedeth out of the mouth of the Lord doth man live" (Deut. 8:3). Would it were so! Moses does not denigrate the material world. He understands that leaders must see to creature comforts. There was no suggestion that man could live without bread, only that bread is not enough. The people could not live without faith, but they were not yet ready to live on it.

Yet there was no punishment, only an injunction to preserve a jar of manna that future generations might see how the Lord fed the people in the wilderness. One moral was clear: faith would feed the people. Another was only slightly oblique: material provision had been made before spiritual salvation had been demanded. Moses alone was told ("How long refuse ye...") that this situation was temporary.

Observing that the jar was to be placed before the ark of testimony, which had not yet been built, Childs believes that the inverted sequence makes a theological point: "A jar of manna which is the sign of God's sustaining mercy is kept alongside the tablets of the law. Indeed, the sign of divine grace preceded the giving of the law of Sinai! Rather, the point of the text focuses on the testimony that the manna and the tablets belong together before God. In New Testament terminology, the gospel and the law cannot be separated."[31] This suggests that the outcome was preordained, in that the people were given a sign that they were there to be saved—not, I think, the stuff of the Torah. The struggles that were to come and the subsequent fierce punishments matter, because in human-life outcomes always are (and have to be) open and success (similarly) problematical.

Moses still maintains his passive stance. It was only half-true that, as he told the people, their "murmurings are not against us [Moses and Aaron] but against the Lord." For if lack of trust in the leaders meant lack of faith in the Lord, the contrary condition, no God, no Moses—or "no Bishop, no King" as the English once put it—was equally salient. No doubt, the people might have learned that God provides, but they were also lulled into a false sense of security in accepting the food of His displeasure.

In Rephidim the people again complain about lack of water, more vigorously than before. It is said they "chided" with Moses, which we may take to mean that they went at him. And he went at them; Moses warns the people not to "tempt the Lord" (Exod. 17:2) by acting as if He would not provide. Nevertheless, "Wherefore is this," the people murmur, "that thou hast brought us up out of Egypt, to kill us and our children and our cattle with thirst? And Moses cried unto the Lord, saying, What shall I do unto this people? they be almost ready to stone me" (Exod. 17:3-4). This time Moses receives an unusual response. He is to take his rod, the same one used in the Sea of Reeds, and strike a rock from which water will flow. It seems an easy way out. (Later, Moses will come to grief when he attempts to repeat his earlier success.) What is most unusual, however, is that the Lord stood upon the rock as Moses struck it.

The place of the rock is called Massah ("strife"), because the people "tempted the Lord, saying, Is the Lord among us, or not?" (Exod. 17: 7). We should accept the plain meaning. There can be no more direct answer than the divine presence atop that rock. Is God's presence manifested so that the people will assume He is at their beck and call? From all we know, that seems unlikely. Rocks are constantly used to symbolize bastions of faith, as when Psalm 89:26 speaks of God as "the rock of my salvation." We might think God was wildly waving His arms, trying to gain attention, indicating, as Moses first did at the burning bush, "Here I am!" If that was not enough, what would be?

Perhaps the prior passivity of Moses reflects God's rule; He is to lead and Moses to follow. Lacking the faith in the future that depends on being able to remember the past, the people grumble as if for the first

time about each new round of adversity, and Moses carries their complaints to God, who then comes through with the goods. Clearly this
cannot go on; otherwise the people will convert the God of Israel into a
caricature of Pharaoh, and Moses into their memory of what an overseer
had been. Moses must accept that political leadership is subservient to
ultimate moral imperatives. That is what Exodus teaches.

The Hebrew people's lack of faith parallels Pharaoh's absence of
memory. Until Pharaoh himself had to share his people's fate, he could
afford to ignore them. Moses had both memory and need; he had to
remain dependent on his people so that Israel's suffering would not go
unheeded. The plagues against Egypt prefigure the rebellions against God.
There are (more or less) ten plagues and (soon enough) ten rebellions.
Each adversity appears to be met by the Hebrews as if it were new. Each
gracious provision by God was apparently taken not as a sign that faith
leads to fulfillment, but rather to signify temporary good fortune that
could not continue. What is to be done?

Whether Moses will at long last don the mantle of leadership—with
the pain as well as the privileges this implies—is about to be decided.
What Moses has learned has by no means disposed him to view leadership
as an unalloyed pleasure. If the "greasy pole" of leadership (as English
politicians call it) is hard to shinny up, it is all too easy to slide down.
Is it utterly incongruous for him to be passive? Are there leaders who,
when faced with similar challenges, never waver in their faith? If anyone
deserves the appellation of faithful, it is Abraham, but we will see that
he also was assailed by doubt.

MOSES AND ABRAM

The history of the Hebrew people begins when Terah, father of Abram
(whose name is changed later), journeys to Canaan from the land of Ur.
On the way, Abram is overtaken by a divine mission. Without warning or
preparation, at the age of seventy-five, Abram (like Moses after him) was
seized from behind, as it were, by a command to separate himself from
all he knew and go he knew not where: "Get thee out of thy country,
and from thy kindred, and from thy father's house, unto a land that I
will show thee: And I will make of thee a great nation" (Gen. 12:1-2).

Note that the promise is to make of Abram "a great nation" (*goy*), not a people (*am*); the difference, E.A. Speiser says, is that nation is a territorial and political concept,[32] which would be out of place in ethnic beginnings but appropriate for a later leader seeking to establish a state.

At a similar crisis in his life, at the burning bush, Moses is informed of a divine mission. Moses asks many questions, Abram does not. Is Abram's faith formed perfectly from the beginning?

We have ample evidence (besides the binding of Isaac) of Abram's faith.[33] After a dashing raid to recover his brother-in-law, Lot, from captivity at the hands of five kings, Abram refuses Melchizedek's offer to share the booty, saying, "I will not take from a thread even to a shoelatchet, and that I will not take any thing that is thine, lest thou shouldest say, I have made Abram rich" (Gen. 14:23); Abram is offering instead to praise God from whom good fortune comes. Again, when there was strife between Abram's and his brother-in-law's retainers, Abram asked Lot to "separate thyself... from me" (Gen. 13:9) and to choose to go either to the right or to the left; Abram knew that even though Lot chose the seemingly better place (Sodom, as it turned out!), the Lord would bless Abram's efforts.

Is it "impossible," then, as Hirsch says, in view of all that has happened, that Abram lacked "confidence in God's guidance"?[34] Quite the contrary. The evidence is overwhelming. Why else does God give Abram so many (apparently unasked-for) reassurances? After decisive victory in battle, for instance, "the word of the Lord came unto Abram in a vision, saying, Fear not, Abram: I am thy shield, and thy exceeding great reward" (Gen. 15:1). Abram's immediate response exudes doubt: "Lord God, what wilt thou give me, seeing I go childless, and... to me thou hast given no seed" (Gen. 15:2-3). In return the Lord seeks to soothe Abram by assuring him he will have an heir "out of thine own bowels" (Gen. 15:4). How does Abram react to this bounty? "And he said, Lord God,"—again adopting the supplicating form—"whereby shall I know that I shall inherit it?" (Gen. 15:8). In answer, the future of Abram's people is revealed in a dream.

Nevertheless, Abram's wife, Sarai, being childless, suggested he take her maid as a concubine; Abram agreed and Ishmael is born to them. But, as von Rad says, Ishmael "conceived in defiance or in little faith cannot be the heir of promise."[35] That is, if Abram had the faith to believe that God begins where human capability ends—for Sarai had long since passed the age of childbearing—he would not have needed expedients. When Sarai later does bear Abram a son, the child's name, Isaac (in Hebrew, Yitzhak, or "one who laughs," because Sarai doubted she could conceive), is an intended irony.

As soon as Abraham received God's confidence about the destruction of Sodom and Gomorrah ("Shall I hide from Abraham that thing which I do?" Gen. 18:17), he hastened to raise critical questions, of interest to his successors.

"Shall not the Judge of all the earth do right?" asks Abraham (Gen. 18:25). Surely, men have seldom spoken to deities in this way! Before the dust has settled on this cry for justice, Abraham goes on to raise the asking price; if there are fifty righteous men in the city "wilt thou also destroy and not spare the place?" (Gen. 18:24).[36] That all should be saved for the sake of a few is more like mercy than justice.[37] Moses, who, after the idolatrous behavior before the Golden Calf, requested that judgment be made individual, not collective, could not ask for more.

God agrees. Humbly, to be sure, but persistently, Abraham drives down the critical number from forty to thirty to twenty to ten. But there the bidding stops. If you cannot find ten religious men, the minyan necessary for religious services, the rabbis advised, move to another city.[38] Judaism is a communal religion. Moses also must stop when the survival of his community is at stake.

The similarities between Abraham and Moses extend to the kind of covenant created. His name changed to signify "father of nations," Abraham is promised "an everlasting covenant" (Gen. 17:7) extending to future generations. The sign God gives is circumcision: "My covenant shall be in your flesh" (Gen. 17:13)[39]—even as Jacob was wounded at the Jabbok and as Moses was reminded on the road from Midian to Egypt.[40]

Yet there was a qualification: Abraham "will command his children and household after him, and they shall keep the way of the Lord, to do justice and judgment; that the Lord may bring upon Abraham that which he hath spoken of him" (Gen. 18:19). Apparently Abraham must remain the kind of person for whom God would want to make the promise come true. In this respect, as in so many others, Moses (the second Abraham, as he is sometimes called), like his great predecessor, abounds with the infirmities he finds in his people.[41]

GOD AND MOSES

I suggested earlier why Moses needs God; now I can conjecture why God should need Moses. For God to enter history, He needs more than a megaphone to broadcast His message, least of all an echo chamber that merely bounces His wisdom back to Himself. The boundless circle of "I am that I am" or "I will be what I will be" is still unbroken unless He engages human nature.

Moses' task will be to mediate between the ferocious power of absolute law and the weakness of human nature, to show that conscience should be limited by capacity. It is as if God had instituted an earthly force to check Himself, like empathy reining in rationality. For if all who break the law deserve to die, no man (including Moses) could stay alive.

If the moral law is to be observed to the letter, survival of the people is at peril. Some agency must exist to assuage the law's ferocity. Moses, this agency, must be more than a servant but less than a god. If Moses only parrots God's words, neither gains. Moses is giving up one form of slavery for another; and God gets a pawn instead of a forceful agent. Moses must lead; he must exert independent causal force, taking chances with a history that may be the product of human intention (as Hume put it), but cannot be a product of human design.

If God wants a capable human intermediary, He must risk human defiance. It is human defiance that saves Israel; human defiance ensures that His plan will remain historically effective when Moses, on Mount Sinai, disobeys God's command (of a kind, admittedly, made by One who wishes to be held back): "Now therefore let me alone, that my wrath may wax hot against them, and that I may consume them" (Exod. 32:10). Because Moses implores God to "repent of this evil against thy people" (Exod. 32:12), God and Israel are not severed forever. Moses' intervention gives meaning to God's promise. When Israel finally does worship God at Mount Sinai, the people do not receive a unilateral covenant; they make a bilateral one. God—as Moses then shows he understands—did not deliver a people from one bondage to subjugate them to a new one. God's will would be empty if He had not (through Moses) provided for free will in human nature.

A struggle for the soul of the Hebrew people is in the making. Will they worship one God, for better or worse, or many, according to their needs at the moment? Will they live under an anarchic political regime, changing allegiance the way they change clothing, according to the climate? Or will they live under a regime of equity, following a charismatic leader who is imbued with the spirit of God and who therefore deserves allegiance in all things?

The failure of anarchy would leave the people defenseless against a return to slavery; order would have to be reimposed from the outside. The success of anarchy would leave the people divided, forming and reforming different coalitions. There would be no one god, any more than there would be a permanent coalition. Anarchies sign temporary contracts; they do not make permanent covenants. They have no permanent leaders, but they may have many gods, bargaining with each for better favors.

3

FROM ANARCHY TO EQUITY
Leadership in the Golden Calf, the Spies, and the Akedah

"I have said: The idolater shall die; upon My life, he shall, surely." "Where hast Thou said it," Moses asked Him; "in Thy Torah? And to whom hast Thou given Thy Torah? To them or to me?" "Upon the mount I commanded: 'Thou shalt have no other gods before Me,' and at the foot of the mount they sware saying: 'All that God shall command we will do and hear.'" "But knew they the punishment, the death of the idolater, that Thy hand wrote in Thy Torah after? Thou didst spare Cain, because he killed, not knowing the punishment for killing, and Thou wouldst punish them by a law that they knew not?" "I will consume them from the face of the earth; and I will make My people come forth from thee alone." "Blot me rather from Thy Torah, King of the World; or, rather, let me blot from the world Thy Torah. I alone knew it, I alone shall have sinned, if I alone shatter it."

—Edmond Fleg, *The Life of Moses*

Finding the earth full of evil deeds and worse imaginings, the Lord grieved and repented of His creation and decided to do away with the human race, except for Noah, whom God found good. "But with thee," God tells Noah, "will I establish my covenant" (Gen. 6:18), including Noah's family and an ark full of living creatures. Because "Noah was a just man... and... walked with God" (Gen. 6:9), human and animal life was saved. (Observe that the covenant was one-sided: it came unasked-for at God's initiative.) After the deluge stops: "the Lord said in his heart, I will not again curse the ground any more for man's sake; for the imagination of man's heart is evil from his youth: neither will I again smite any more every thing living, as I have done" (Gen. 8:21). The tendency to human corruption is recognized. Man will be punished—"Whoso sheddeth man's blood, by man shall his blood be shed: for in the image of God made he man" (Gen. 9:6)—but he will not be destroyed. There will be no more final floods.

Taking the initiative again, God establishes a covenant with Noah and his descendants and with every living creature, "for perpetual generations" (Gen. 9:12). This is what Moses was to work for on behalf of the Hebrew people. The sign for which Moses searches is one to signify that the slate of his people has also been wiped clean. Before that can happen, however, there must first be a separation and differentiation of peoples, so that those allotted to Israel may receive special treatment.

Just as the waters below and above were parted during the Creation—life begins with differentiation—so the waters were combined in the flood,[1] that confusion of categories making for destruction. The token or sign of renewal is the rainbow: "And I will look upon it," the Lord says, "that I may remember the everlasting covenant" (Gen. 9:16).[2] As the rainbow spans the skies, refracting light into its primal colors, so God reminds Himself of the different qualities—the spectrum, if you will—of living creatures. The rainbow is God's ark.

As the first generation of the exodus was to fail at Sinai, so the first human race had been lost in the deluge. Noah has aptly been called the second Adam, only with a clearer conception of the differences among living creatures. He is also the first Moses, the chosen instrument for perpetuating life when it deserves to die.

The dialogue between God and Moses atop Mount Sinai about whether Israel will live or die is the climactic episode in Hebrew history. As the exodus from Egypt had determined that there could be a free nation able to act independently, the debate on Mount Sinai would determine whether this people could survive to make history. Though the Hebrews would be held to high standards—the risks being commensurate with the rewards of a higher moral code—Israel's human limitations would be taken into account. The Hebrew people would be able to transgress, to suffer for their sins, and, when capable, to triumph over them. Having Moses as mediator made it possible for Israel to accept falling short of God's ideals while still striving to achieve them. So long as the covenant was made perpetual by Moses' mediation, it was possible for the people to keep trying to live up to the Commandments.

Seeing the children of Israel threatened with genocide, Moses finally chooses leadership. In what appears foreshortened into a single, breathless action, he identifies with his people, refuses to be separated from them, offers to die with them, rejects the opportunity to found his own line, and, by punishing Israel, accepts the responsibility of self-government. Bearing the burden of revolt, Moses overcomes his ambivalence by fusing into his personality a series of unitary conceptions—one God, one land, one people, tied together in an eternal covenant.

COVENANTS AS ELEMENTS OF CULTURES

Covenants specify a sort of superconstitutional leadership; relationships between God and man prefigure the proper positions of ruler and ruled. Covenants are not so much constitutions as the conditions of rule on which subordinate propositions are based.

Thus the two questions raised earlier about leadership—its scope and duration—can also appropriately be asked of covenants. Is the biblical covenant perpetual—broken, perhaps, but always renewed—or does it ultimately fail? Does it depend on performance? By the scope of the covenant, the Bible understands the character of the commitment made. When members of an equity break a commandment, they are expelled. Or, if they believe the leader to be imperfect, group members may leave and form their own equity. Slaves, on the other hand, exist without covenants; human rulers are their gods. Anarchies either have no covenants or many; they value the right to form covenants but also to reformulate them. Easiest is a covenant that is unconditional and perpetual. It lasts forever, no matter how one behaves. But is it for this world? Such a covenant would be totally one-sided, God giving protection and man responding with disobedience.

The Mosaic alternative is a covenant that is perpetual but conditional; the Lord's commitment lasts, but the people will pay when they violate the laws that are the conditions. The price of perpetuity is to have some degree of hierarchy—a set of laws that are to be obeyed, coupled with a mechanism for enforcement.

Covenants are constituent elements of cultures. They answer both the question of identity—the Hebrews are the children of the God of Israel; and that of action—follow His Commandments. Not surprisingly, the choice of covenants is also a choice of regimes and of the patterns of leadership within regimes.[3]

In the first flush of liberation, Moses is reluctant to restrain spontaneity. Would that every man were imbued with the holy spirit! But the people are easily disheartened; they complain a lot; their memories are short. Moses initially vacillates between the ecstatic ideology of equity and the more orderly and restrained world-view of hierarchy. He does not yet have to choose. He can wait and see. If he is to lead an equity, he will need more charisma than he has—substituting his personality for the authority he lacks. God builds him up. "And the Lord said unto Moses, Lo, I come unto thee in a thick cloud, that the people may hear when I speak with thee, and believe thee for ever" (Exod. 19:9).

Playing it safe, however, Moses introduces the first significant elements of hierarchy. The revelation alternates between having the covenant come directly to all the people and having it come through the elders and Moses. There is, if you wish, confusion. But it is a muddle with a meaning. The government of Israel is at stake.

Freedom as Responsibility

What should be the nature of the relationship between the God of Israel and the people He liberated from Egypt? If the covenant were dependent on possession of the land of Israel and attendant obedience to the laws, the question of whether that promise would be fulfilled for these people would be prejudged. And those whom history placed outside Israel's borders would not belong. If the covenant were the people's, entirely apart from the Commandments, it would look as if the people were to be protected regardless of their behavior. God, the moral imperative, would be getting the short end of the stick. If the Commandments belong with the covenant, one faces the question of whether the violation of one necessarily leads to abrogation of the other. And if there are to be violations, as there must be, who is to judge between the spirit and the letter of the law or to decide between rival interpretations? George E. Mendenhall, who is unusually sensitive to this profound political issue, realizes that "a question had been raised which is just as relevant today as it was in pharaonic Egypt: what is the ultimate authority for the exercise of force when the authorities themselves engage in clandestine murder?... The authority of the peacemaker must be based on something other than his superior ability to commit murder."[4] Was Moses justified, I will ask, in the killing to which he was ineluctably, however reluctantly, being drawn?

This story begins three months after the exodus, when the children of Israel reach Sinai, the sacred mountain. There the Lord reminds Moses that the covenant is based on the liberation in which "I bare you on eagles' wings, and brought you unto myself" (Exod. 19:4).[5]

The covenant is evidently conditional: "Now therefore, if ye will obey my voice indeed, and keep my covenant, then ye shall be a peculiar treasure unto me above all people: for all the earth is mine: And ye shall be unto me a kingdom of priests, and an holy nation" (Exod. 19: 5-6). Who will have authority to interpret this conditional covenant? Is Moses supposed to be believed forever?

Forever, as we say, is a long time. The people may believe that God speaks to Moses. But does God not also speak to the people? Why should the Israelites take Moses' word as authoritative if they can hear God for themselves? At first, it appears that God will do just this, "com[ing] down in the sight of all the people upon mount Sinai" (Exod. 19:11). But it turns out that this is not what happens. Either there is confusion in the account, as critics are quick to charge, or there is a conflict of principles that leaves the issue open.

After Moses calls together the elders, "laid before their faces" the words of the Lord, and received their assent, God tells him how to sanctify the people for a holy occasion—having them wash their clothes and refrain from sex: "come not at your wives" (Exod. 19:15). But then the people are suddenly enjoined to wall themselves off from God's presence: "And thou shalt set bounds unto the people round about, saying, Take heed to yourselves, that ye go not up into the mount, or touch the border of it: whosoever toucheth the mount shall be surely put to death" (Exod.

19:12). Who would want to touch a mountain? And who would care? After all, weren't they all invited, even commanded to come to this place?

Against what disturbances of the social order, we may ask, are these boundaries designed to guard? It cannot be contact with strange people following foreign customs. If that were so, the insulation would be directed outward, not inward toward the people themselves. Indeed, as if to reemphasize the point about excluding the people, "The Lord said unto Moses, Go down, charge the people, lest they break through unto the Lord to gaze, and many of them perish" (Exod. 19:21). Understandably perplexed, Moses retorts, "The people cannot come up to mount Sinai: for thou chargedst us, saying, Set bounds about the mount, and sanctify it" (Exod. 19:23). Undeterred—so imperious as to be thought by commentators to be like an irascible old man—the Lord repeats Himself in no uncertain terms, "Away, get thee down, and thou shalt come up, thou, and Aaron with thee: but let not the priests and the people break through to come up unto the Lord, lest he break forth upon them" (Exod. 19: 24). Apparently Moses is to go down from conversing with the Lord so that he can come up again without the priests and the people.

The confusion about the comings up and goings down (it is hard to say exactly how many there are) is a product of trying to say something about the separation of the people from God; any effort to profane the holy will be punished. Having offered the people a conditional covenant (if they do as commanded, they will benefit), God is fending off in advance any presumption on their part to partake—by touch, sight, or speech, all of which are now ruled out—of the divine.

The covenant is its own concern, warning against the temptation of a chosen people to make inordinate claims. No one, the people and priests alike are told, however sanctified, can have a direct line to God. No one, that is, except Moses. Moses' exclusiveness is a protection against false prophecy, whether then or afterward, for tradition authenticates the Torah as the words that God gave Moses to write down.

As eager as Moses may have been in the beginning to share authority (and hence responsibility), he is warned—more than once and in more than one way—that this is not to be. The people are put off: "And it came to pass on the third day in the morning, that there were thunders and lightnings, and a thick cloud upon the mount, and the voice of the trumpet exceeding loud; so that all the people that was in the camp trembled" (Exod. 19:16). But that is by no means all. Moses brought the people near the mountain a second time: "And mount Sinai was altogether on a smoke, because the Lord descended upon it in fire: and the smoke thereof ascended as the smoke of a furnace, and the whole mount quaked greatly" (Exod. 19:18). Nor was that enough. It took a third display—after the Commandments of the covenant had been spoken to Moses and he had presented them to the people—for God's actions on the mountain to have the intended effect. Learning the intended lesson, the people back off, "And they said unto Moses, Speak thou with us, and we will hear: but let not God speak with us, lest we die" (Exod. 20:19).

It would be hard to claim that the people voluntarily give up a claim on God; they are frightened out of it. Is this a form of protection for their own good, God knowing they will transgress and need Moses to intercede for them? Or is all this trumped up by Moses alone, to cow the people into submission to his (not divine) authority?

Can the covenant itself (Exod. 20:1-17) explain to us its great concern with internal boundaries? God is identified as the one who liberated Israel from "the house of bondage." "Thou shalt have no other gods before me" (Exod. 20:2-3). His name must not be taken in vain, nor images made like "any thing that is in heaven above, or that is in the earth beneath, or that is in the water under the earth" (Exod. 20:4). The Lord is the ultimate authority; no one must serve or bow down before any other. The terms of the covenant include regulation of interpersonal relationships, by separating the real from the apparent, the holy from the unwholesome—lying, stealing, coveting, and adultery. Murder is prohibited as usurpation of the divine prerogative. Honoring "thy father and thy mother" is also a sublimated statement about the fealty due to the Creator, who made the earth and the people in it. The unbridgeable boundary, and thus the model of all boundaries, is between God and man.

The order of the Commandments, and the short space devoted to the purely interpersonal, suggest that the later ones depend on those at the beginning. The (utterly unremarkable) conclusion is that obedience to God is the prerequisite for orderly social relations. The boundary between God and man is His supreme safeguard against social chaos. For what would men not do to one another if they were to claim ultimate authority?

The social legislation that follows—laws protecting property, strangers, widows, the poor, on and on—is also predicated on acceptance of an authority that cannot be disobeyed. These boundaries, which emphasize keeping relationships whole, each partaking only of what properly belongs to its class, are of special social significance in a tribal society. Each tribe is to be kept whole. No tribe is to transgress against another. What better guarantee that tribal borders (so carefully demarcated before entry to Israel) will be sacrosanct is there than a system of classification—from food to clothing to marriage—that stresses wholeness and separation from top to bottom?

Moses' own interpretation of the fireworks—"fear not: for God is come to prove you, and that his fear may be before your faces, that ye sin not" (Exod. 20:20)—is elusive. How can the Lord test the people when they have not had a chance to do anything yet? And wouldn't the fear of God be greater if they saw divinity "face to face"?

The second story Moses tells, long after these events, is more instructive. In Deuteronomy we learn that heads of all the tribes, as well as elders, had come to Moses asking him to assume their risks. They observe "that God doth talk with man, and he liveth"—that is, that Moses may know how to coexist with the absolute. Why, indeed, should all the people fear death from exposure to divinity if Moses is there to take risks for them? It looks like a fair exchange: Moses will listen to the Lord, pass the words on to the people, "and we will hear it, and do it" (Deut. 5:27). These words echo acceptance of the covenant. Under the twelve pillars standing for the twelve tribes, Moses repeats the laws, sacrifices are made, the book of the covenant is read to the assembled audience, and the people promise to do as the Lord says (speaking through Moses). "And Moses took the blood, and sprinkled it on the people, and said, Behold the blood of the covenant, which the Lord hath made with you concerning all these words" (Exod. 24:8). Soon enough the blood will be theirs. The bloody bridegroom has warned his people.

What does the promise signify? Evidently, the Israelites think it does not mean quite as much as it would have if they had heard the Lord and promised Him directly. Otherwise they would not have asked Moses to stand between them and the Almighty—a mediation that signifies protection to the Israelites. If something goes wrong, or if they do wrong, they hope to escape the full fury of the Lord. They want the truth but not the consequences. The theophany at Mount Sinai appears to have conditioned people to expect a steady stream of revelation and reassurance.

But however gradual is the movement toward holiness, its demands are evidently too great. The people are never portrayed as happier or more willing to act than when crafting the tabernacle, whose life-size dimensions represent all their minds can encompass. This limited perception of the divine contributes to their sense of estrangement—the Lord no longer leads the people in person, and Moses puts up his tent outside the camp—that surrounds the community both before and after its renewal.

How the Israelites came to this pass (what they got and what they gave up) can be understood only against the background of the covenantal relationship established before the apostasy and the punishment for the Golden Calf. The people want to keep a good thing going, to have God always at their service in time of need. Yet the people also fear God and want to keep Him at a distance: as the medieval adage had it, one king far away is preferable to many princes close by. God wants to loan the Hebrews liberty so they can come to Him of their own free will; there is no point in putting the people to the test unless they are free to fail. If they fail too frequently, however, the future of their relationship will remain in doubt; so God needs a mediator in charge of the covenant.

Moses is evidently a man in the middle. The kingdom of God will come when, in modern parlance, freedom and necessity are joined, so that individuals want to do what they should do. So long as the public interest (as we would say now)—the accepted basis of collective action—does not diverge from the sum of private interests, there is no problem. But until that millennium is reached when mankind does not wish to act against itself, politics remains the way to resolve conflicting interests. If Moses were inclined to take comfort from the Lord's words, he might think again of the lover's lament that follows: "O that there were such an heart in them, that they would fear me, and keep all my commandments always, that it might be well with them, and with their children for ever!" (Deut. 5:29).

By that time Moses may have been sufficiently sophisticated to worry, in the words of Psalm 78, that no matter what the people said, "Nevertheless they did flatter him with their mouth, and they lied unto him with their tongues" (Ps. 78:36). No wonder Jeremiah wants the Commandments engraved on the heart! The implications of another verse—"When he slew them, then they sought him" (Ps. 78:34)—were soon enough to trouble Moses.

Generations of commentators have sought unsuccessfully to keep the door shut on issues that the Bible, reflecting the live history of the people of Israel, insists on keeping open: Is the covenant conditional on Israel's keeping its Commandments? What happens if they are broken? If God is not to enforce them, who will? How? With what authority? If Moses the mediator interprets the covenant, does he, by virtue of that role, also become its enforcer? Have the people come full circle, exchanging the yoke of Pharaoh for one of their own making?[6]

A Dialogue Against Death

The events at Mount Sinai are so terrible and so wonderful that even now it is difficult to absorb them. Moses spends forty days and nights on the mountain to receive the law. The people worship the Golden Calf; Moses shatters the Ten Commandments and orders thousands killed. By what right does Moses deal out death? Why is Aaron, the main culprit, spared? Next, Moses has the Golden Calf ground down and mixed with water from a nearby stream and compels the children of Israel to drink of their iniquity. Why does Moses have the people eat evil when he could as well have ground up the Ten Commandments and had them taste good? Why, having dreadfully dispatched his enemies, does Moses not, in modern terms, engage in a permanent purge and rule forever after by fear?

The trouble begins when the people (fearing Moses had abandoned them) demand of Aaron, "Up, make us gods, which shall go before us; for as for this Moses, the man that brought us up out of the land of Egypt, we wot not what is become of him" (Exod. 32:1). Thus the people distanced themselves from "this Moses," treating their leader as a stranger, as Moses himself had earlier done to his God and to them.

"And the Lord," seeing all, "said unto Moses, Go, get thee down; for thy people, which thou broughtest out of the land of Egypt, have corrupted themselves: They have turned aside quickly out of the way which I commanded them: they have made them a molten calf, and have worshipped it, and have sacrificed thereunto, and said, These be thy gods, O Israel, which have brought thee up out of the land of Egypt" (Exod. 32:7-8). As one parent says to another about a misbehaving child, See what your daughter has done! The Lord will distance Himself from the Hebrew people until they become "thy people," for which Moses alone is responsible.

Two peremptory commands clash here: "get thee down!" says the Lord, telling Moses it is time to deal with his corrupted people; "Up, make us gods!" the people cry to Aaron, denying that their destiny lies in Moses, God, and themselves and affirming it to be found only in a multiplicity of deities—hedging their bets, if you will. Apparently, the people have had too little, rather than too much, leadership. If a god is to make impossible demands, they want to play that one off against others.

"Now therefore let me alone," the Lord continues, "that my wrath may wax hot against them, and that I may consume them" (Exod. 32:10). The penalty for idolatry is, after all, death. The meaning is made clear when Moses, in his later recapitulation of these events, attributes to God the intention to "destroy them, and blot out their name from under heaven" (Deut. 9:14).

In almost the same breath as the threat to wipe out Israel, God tempts Moses by offering to "make of thee a great nation" (Exod. 32:10). Embellishing these words in his farewell address, Moses adds that the Lord proposed to make of him "a nation mightier and greater" than the Hebrew people (Deut. 9:14). Moses refuses. It is as if Moses counters with "If you take me, you must take them!"

In intercession Moses is inspired to use God's arguments, including His very phrases, recalling the Lord's life-giving promise to His people's patriarchs, Abraham, Isaac, and Jacob. Moses is not above invoking vainglory—"Wherefore should the Egyptians speak, and say, For mischief did he bring them out, to slay them in the mountains, and to consume them from the face of the earth?" (Exod. 32:12). Nor is he afraid of plain talk—"Turn from thy fierce wrath," he tells the Lord, "and repent of this evil against thy people" (Exod. 32:12).

It is tempting to take these words at face value because they do have some surface validity. Moses, imputing to God a less-than-divine inconsistency, reminds the Lord of past promises: had He not said that the seed of Israel would inherit the Promised Land "for ever" (Exod. 32:13)? To save the Hebrews from being sacrificed to the justifiable wrath of God, Moses must show that he has learned the lessons of leadership sufficiently well to be entrusted with this "stiffnecked people" (Exod. 32:9), who have corrupted the covenant almost as soon as they made it.

Moses makes three arguments. The first is that the people are the Lord's; He can no more be severed from them and their history than can Moses. The narrative is careful to specify that "Moses besought the Lord *his* God," making it clear whose side he was on before interceding for "*thy* people, which *thou* has brought forth out of the land of Egypt with great power, and with a mighty hand" (Exod. 32:11; emphases added). If keeping whole things whole, like with like, is the cultural principle of Israel, God must exemplify it as well by making perpetual His unity with the people.[7] The ultimate rationale for Hebrew culture as a seamless web of whole social relations is the hope of unity and the fear of separation from their God and hence from one another. Yet if the Lord has infinite freedom (first and last cause combined), He can drop this people as easily as He adopted them. No wonder Moses is nervous about being abandoned. Even after the Golden Calf episode is over (historically, if not spiritually)—with Moses having punished, and God having plagued, the people—Moses pleads for reassurance "that this nation is thy people" (Exod. 33:13). The Lord replies, "My presence shall go with thee, and I will give thee rest" (Exod. 33:14). This personal preference is precisely what Moses had asked for at the burning bush, but, though reassured there, he wanted more at Mount Sinai. True, Moses wanted the Lord to go with him, but also with the people. "For wherein shall it be known here," Moses replied, "that I and thy people have found grace in thy sight? is it not in that thou goest with us? So shall we be separated, I and thy people, from all the people that are upon the face of the earth" (Exod. 33:16). A people must survive before it can be separated.

The second argument Moses makes is that God's reputation is at stake. The Egyptians will think badly of One who brought the people out of Egypt "for mischief [malice or harm]... to slay them" (Exod. 32: 12). Going back on a promise is not mere inconsistency but would be a violation of God's own prescription against confusion (or mixing) of categories. Moses hints that God would be contradicting Himself not only in particular but also in principle.

Moses' third argument brings up the same lack of memory that the Lord had invoked against the Pharaoh of the hardened heart. "Remember," Moses reminds the Lord (who once had reminded Moses of the same allegiance), "Abraham, Isaac, and Israel, thy servants, to whom thou swarest by thine own self" (Exod. 32:13). By invoking the lineage of leaders, thus implying those yet to come, Moses is suggesting "remember the future." God has long-range plans, Moses suggests, too important to be thrown away in a moment of anger. By asking the coy question, "What will Egyptians think?" Moses adopts God's earlier logic (that to reveal His glory He will not destroy Pharaoh but allow him to experience God's wonders). Invocation of the past—"Remember thy servants, Abraham, Isaac, and Jacob"—is joined to a present plea—"look not unto the stubbornness of this people, nor to their wickedness, nor to their sin" (Deut. 9:27).

The American community organizer Saul Alinsky used these negotiations to exemplify his main principle of persuasion: "getting a fix on his [another person's] main value or goal and holding your course on that target." From the negotiations between God and Moses, Alinsky infers "That God wanted to be No. 1."[8] But this cannot be for the Lord is already preeminent. No, the Lord's aim is the more difficult one of getting Moses to lead the people while recognizing that he can never be "No. 1."

As leader of the Israelites, Moses' task is to convince God to accept human nature. Where there is freedom, there is sure to be transgression. The people will err; hence there can be no covenant if, the moment it is broken, the people are destroyed. To give them the law and the punishment, knowing the law will be broken, would be equivalent to a sentence of death. Yet Moses has learned that the law must not be violated with impunity. If God agrees not to enforce it wholesale (without distinction, so that the people as a whole are punished), another agency is needed, able to punish and also to preserve. Moses must show Him therefore, that there is a body of humans able to repair the covenant even as it is broken. Somehow a sin shared by the entire people had to be interpreted so that not all would have to die. Irrevocably binding himself to his people, in the hope of binding the Lord to them, Moses turned and went down from the mount, "and the two tables of the testimony," beginning with the prohibitions against idolatry, "were in his hand" (Exod. 32:15).

Breaking the Law

The Ten Commandments as we know them today are not the original ones, which were dashed down by Moses, but a later set, rewritten to symbolize restoration of God's relationship to the Hebrew people. What matters is that they were given anew, even after it was obvious that the people had sinned before and would sin again. We are in little doubt about the matter because Moses, in a marvelous conflation of sentiments, says, "go among us; for it is a stiffnecked people; and pardon our iniquity and our sin" (Exod. 34:9). The reply is also unmistakable—"Behold, I make a covenant" (Exod. 34:10)—after which the Lord reiterates the main provisions. These are not identical with the originals, just as the understanding about the covenant is not the same.

The story is simplicity itself. Moses descends from Mount Sinai with two tables of testimony, written on both sides. Specifically, it is stated that the writing and the tables were God's work. "And it came to pass," the account continues, "as soon as he came nigh unto the camp, that he saw the calf, and the dancing: and Moses' anger waxed hot, and he cast the tables out of his hands, and brake them beneath the mount" (Exod. 32: 19). Why, we ask along with countless others, does Moses break the very tablets that signify the covenant upon which he and his people depend for their lives? Von Rad states that "Moses (in his office as mediator of the covenant?) regards as broken the covenant which has only just been made, so that the tables handed to him have become meaningless."[9] "Indeed," Moshe Weinfeld informs us, "the term for cancelling a contract in Babylonian legal literature is to 'break the tablet.'"[10] The *Jewish Encyclopedia* holds that "the calf and the 10 words [or Commandments] could not exist in juxtaposition."[11] Early Christian commentators, too, eager to justify subordinate status for Judaism, claimed Moses as their authority for holding that the covenant was shattered almost before it was entered into.[12] In this view, either Moses gave up before he had fairly begun, or he saw some advantage in suspending the law until it could be resumed on a better basis.

Rabbinical commentators were no less ingenious in answering the charge that the Golden Calf showed Israel in league with the devil. Early rabbis argued that the people could not be held responsible for their actions unless and until all the law had been taught to them in the Tent of Meeting.[13] Surely, by that time the people knew idolatry was forbidden to them and that it carried the ultimate penalty. If they did not know that, what did they know?

There is a certain appeal to the theory that Moses thought he could let the people off lightly by breaking the tablets (and hence the covenant) before the people had become aware of the consequences. This view can be encapsulated neatly in a rabbinic comparison: "To what may this be likened? asks Rabbi Samuel bar Nahman. To that envoy whom a king sent to espouse his bride in his name. When the envoy came to seek her, he found that she had defiled her flesh with another. What did he? He tore up the contract of marriage, saying: 'It were better for her to be judged as a maid than as a bride.' In the same way Moses thought: 'It were better for the congregation of Israel, since the Torah condemneth them, not to be united to God by the Torah.' And he shattered the Torah."[14]

Caught between a rock and a hard place, Moses has to draw a fine line. Is maintaining the law his responsibility alone because the tablets were broken before the people knew about them? For letting people off the hook, this works well; but by keeping Moses dangling on the hook, it is not so good. Without the authority of the law—having broken the tablets—what right does Moses have to punish the people? The last time Moses killed without authority, his own people had rejected him and he had spent long years of exile in this very wilderness. What can Moses do if he does not wish the people to be destroyed (as they deserve) and yet cannot allow them to continue (as they desire)?

He chooses to lead, taking, as the gesture symbolizes, the law into his own hands. Yet he does more. By cracking the Commandments, Moses literally breaks the law, signifying both determination to root out evil and his own participation in it.[15] For, when it reaches epidemic proportions, evil begets evil even (perhaps especially, since the temptation is greater) among those who seek to suppress it.

The splintering of the tables has a special significance in Hebrew culture. Imperfect objects are unholy—unkosher in more ways than one. Thus physically imperfect persons cannot approach the house of the Lord until they have been purified, often by fire, and made whole, their blemishes healed. Hoping to be whole also is a reasonable

aspiration for a federation of tribes and for a leader who hopes to overcome his ambivalence.

After Moses had judged the people—taking a terrible toll in order
to join together that which had been rent asunder, an episode to which
we shall return—he received a special sign that the covenant had been
renewed on the basis of a new understanding. The Bible relates, "And
the Lord said unto Moses, Hew thee two tables of stone like unto the
first: and I will write upon these tables the words that were in the first
tables, which thou brakest" (Exod. 34:1). The tables that were tried out
at first were entirely the work of the Lord, handed down intact to Moses
as a mere receptacle: "And he gave unto Moses, when he had made an
end of communing with him upon mount Sinai, two tables of testimony,
tables of stone, written with the finger of God" (Exod. 31:18). The second set, however, was made by Moses, with the Lord writing the same
words on them.

That a human intermediary has participated is a sign showing the
Commandments have been humanized. The ideals are identical, but
the expectations have altered. The burning bush has been merged with
Mount Sinai. The mercy of the Lord—the people burn but are not
consumed—has been restored by the mediation of Moses, who does his
earthly duty so that the Israelites will not perish.

The Lord understands that the people literally cannot live with Him,
with the ideal, in their midst. Recalling His earlier promises, the Lord
will send an angel to guide them to the land of milk and honey. But,
He continues, abruptly changing emphasis, "I will not go up in the
midst of thee; for thou art a stiffnecked people: lest I consume thee in
the way" (Exod. 33:3).

When Moses came down from Mount Sinai the second time, again
with tables of testimony in his hand, "And when Aaron and all the children of Israel saw Moses, behold, the skin of his face shone; and they
were afraid to come nigh him" (Exod. 34:30). This "reflected glory," as
it has been called, shows the asymmetry in the situation. Moses' entreaty
to see the glory of God (His attributes) is met by what appears to be a
put-down: all the goodness of the Lord will be shown Moses, but presumably he will be unable to fathom it. Instead of letting Moses in on
the secret of good and evil, the Lord responds "I… will be gracious to
whom I will be gracious, and will show mercy on whom I will show
mercy" (Exod. 33:19). Moses has to accept human limitation—never

being entirely sure his acts are right rather than wrong—as the condition of everyday human life. For to know the difference and to choose evil, as men do, is to die. Hence the Lord said to Moses, "Thou canst not see my face: for there shall no man see me, and live" (Exod. 33:20).

Now we know how it is possible to interpret the otherwise unthinkable idea that, in response to Moses' arguments against genocide, "The Lord repented [thought better] of the evil he thought to do unto his people" (Exod. 32:14). (In Hebrew the word for repent, *naham*, means a change of mind or purpose.)[16] Before the covenant embodied the law, there could be no concept of deadly sin. Once the law was known, however, earthly justice had to be joined with divine dispensation, else no one would be allowed to live. Moses' problem was how to break and repair the covenant simultaneously. His solution—the covenant may be conditional on good behavior but is nevertheless perpetual—still endures.

Inoculation Against Idolatry

As soon as Moses saw for himself the frenzy before the altar, where sacrifices were being made to an animal, "He took the calf which they had made, and burnt it in the fire, and ground it to powder, and strewed it upon the water, and made the children of Israel drink of it" (Exod. 32:20)—an immediate demonstration of the impotence of the idol, so quickly reduced to ashes. Aside from that, the idea of ingesting evil calls for inquiry.

The usual explanation, as far as it goes, has much to commend it. Numbers describes a procedure called "the law of jealousies" for putting to the proof a woman accused of adultery. She is given a liquid, mixed with dust, which is supposed to bring bad effects—"thy thigh to rot, and thy belly to swell" (Num. 5:21)—unless she is innocent, in which case "be thou free from this bitter water that causeth the curse" (Num. 5:19).[17] Perhaps those who felt guilty would react differently than those who were innocent. Looked at another way, it was not inappropriate for a people drunk with drink to be purged with the dregs of their own doings.

Yet Moses, as the continual shifting of perspectives from the valley to the mountain and back suggests, has to look up to God as well as down to the people—transmit the message both ways. And what better way to say that sin is inseparable from human life than to have each person (having ingested the evil) carry a part of the transgression forever?

The foreshortening of history, writing as if what happened had been preordained, is a besetting vice of the craft. Moses had alternatives. He could, for instance, have ground down the tables containing the Commandments, testing his people against the good. Such a situation would, however, have been contrary to Moses' experience. The good is transitory, achieved briefly, from one renewal to the next. The bad is permanent, overcome from time to time but ever-present.

Aaron: Representative Leadership for a Representative Event

The Hebrews' impatience and lack of faith in Moses is also a lack of faith in God. If they had presumed that Moses died while on the mountain, they would have had to conclude as well that God would not, or could not, help him and, therefore, them. Thus the people appeal for a new religion and a new leader. It may appear that the people want only a more comprehensible leadership, but Moses knows that the Calf cannot coexist with the covenant. Without their distinctive religious practices, the people will lose their Lord and hence their life—their very reason for being together as a nation.

Before Moses undertakes his fiercest act of leadership—punishing his own people—a kind of comic relief, designed to demonstrate non- or negative leadership, is provided by Aaron's effort to evade Moses' anger. The exchange, which shows how differently Aaron and Moses see leadership, deserves to be quoted in full:

> And Aaron said, Let not the anger of my Lord wax hot: thou knowest the people, that they are set on mischief.
> For they said unto me, Make us gods, which shall go before us: for as for this Moses, the man that brought us up out of the land of Egypt, we wot not what is become of him.
> And I said unto them, Whosoever hath any gold, let them break it off. So they gave it me: then I cast it into the fire, and there came out this calf. [Exod. 32:22-24]

In an apparent parody of Moses' intervention to cool things down by questioning the Lord's anger ("Lord, why doth thy wrath wax hot against thy people?" [Exod. 32:11]), Aaron works on Moses so as to separate himself from the common fate. Whereas Moses reiterates his and the Lord's identification with the people, Aaron speaks of them as a "they" who are inclined to evil. It is not only the fact that Aaron has a "low estimate" of the people that "is striking," as Childs writes,[18] for Moses is of the same opinion: "Ye have been rebellious against the Lord," Moses concludes in his last speech, "from the day that I knew you" (Deut. 9: 24). Rather, what is damaging is Aaron's abdication of responsibility as a leader—accepting the probable as permanent without struggling against it. He excuses his own idolatrous behavior by using the passive voice, saying, "There came out this calf"—untouched, apparently, by human hands. Aaron is (as Moses was) the representative leader. He works with, not against, the tendencies of the people. Because he takes the people only where they would have gone anyway, Aaron wields no power.

Aaron knows he is in trouble. The very salutation he uses to Moses— "my lord"—is akin to the one used by Jacob to mollify Esau, whose birthright he had taken.[19] And if we use the more direct *New Translation* of the sentence about the people being naked and frenzied before the Calf ("Moses saw that the people were out of control—since Aaron had let them get out of control" [Exod. 32:25]), it is clear that Aaron knew he was being held responsible.

From Moses' later account we learn that "the Lord was very angry with Aaron to have destroyed him" (Deut. 9:20). With good reason: to sin is one thing; to commit idolatry another; to give it all the gloss of godliness by calling it a religious ceremony, all the while invoking the Lord's name, and building "an altar before it" (Exod. 32:5), is still more heinous. And, should there be any mistake, the biblical account ends with a plague on the people who "made the calf, which Aaron made" (Exod. 32:35), Leivy Smolar and Moshe Aberbach state:

> Of all the sins committed by the Israelites in the wilderness, none proved to be so embarrassing to later generations as the making of the golden calf. With the growth of pagan anti-Semitism and, even more, with the emergence of the anti-Jewish polemics of the early Church, the whole episode of the golden calf became highly disconcerting. The participation of Aaron in the construction of the golden calf was an additional source of deep concern. This inevitably led to the emergence of an apologetic literature, the basic tendency of which was to minimize the guilt of Israel in general, and of Aaron in particular.[20]

Since Aaron was to become the head of the priesthood, a strenuous search has been made over the centuries to blame the Golden Calf on other people or to find extenuating circumstances. Anyone possible who might be blamed in Aaron's stead was considered a likely candidate, not excluding the Almighty. Rabbis blamed God for tempting the people by having given them too much silver and gold when they had despoiled the Egyptians. How could a son avoid sin, asked the rabbis by analogy, if he were left at the door of a brothel? "Did you not bring them forth from Egypt where all worshipped idols," Moses was reported to have rebuked the Lord, "and from whom your children learned to worship the Golden Calf?" Since God knew, even as He delivered them, that the people were going to worship the Calf, we hear a taunting Moses ask, "Why do You seek to slay them now that they have made it?"[21]

Often Aaron is portrayed as trying to gain time until Moses comes to save the day. In one fanciful version, for example, two Egyptian magicians—presumably part of the "mixed multitudes" in the exodus[22]—were supposed to have made the Calf move as if it were a living creature. In another—so tall a tale that one can hardly see over it, but with a charm of its own—Hur (said to be the son of Caleb and Miriam) was allegedly killed in his effort to stop the sin; after that, Aaron (nothing if not a man of peace) thought it better to ride with events rather than let the people commit the unforgivable sin of murdering two leaders in one day.[23] Even Rashi views the people as making a mistake—they included the day of Moses' ascent in their figuring, whereas he did not, thus confusing the calculation of the day of his return. Rather than committing a terrible sin, Aaron is made blameless by the implication that he is helpless.[24]

The most interesting modern defense of Aaron comes from Cassuto, who argues that "Aaron, who was not as resolute as Moses, was unable to withstand the rebellious people, and seeing that after all they did not demand a substitute for the God of Israel, but only a surrogate for Moses, he did not reject their request completely, but gave them a non-committal answer that could gain him time.... Although Aaron intended only to present the people with a palpable symbol, a kind of empty throne,... the Israelites went astray after the concrete representation, and treated it as an actual deity." As Cassuto conceives it, Aaron's error was not idolatry—for then he could not have been allowed to found the priesthood—but that he did not realize that the people would confuse the Calf with God.[25]

In support of this hypothesis, it may be noted that on the next day
Aaron proclaimed a feast to the Lord, indicating that he did not see the
Calf as contradictory to allegiance to the Lord.[26] And we may follow
Elias Auerbach in imagining that animal cults were familiar to the people but that a single, imageless God was not.[27] Hence Aaron's passivity
is compatible with an attempt to appease the people so that they would
not, at least not right then, leave the Lord. Aaron's behavior, however,
is also compatible with enticement to evil—seeking to save himself at
the people's expense by suggesting the means (the golden earrings) that
became their undoing, without having directly involved himself. This,
at least, is Moses' interpretation when he asks Aaron accusingly, "What
did this people unto thee, that thou hast brought so great a sin upon
them?" (Exod. 32:21).

The account of I Kings 12:28 of Jeroboam's construction of "two
calves of gold" saying, "Behold thy gods, O Israel, which brought thee
up out of the land of Egypt," has naturally led to theories about which
is the earlier and which the later account. We may take as authoritative
the conclusion of the *Encyclopaedia Judaica* that "scholars are divided on
the question of the chronological relationship of the two accounts."[28] Thus
it is possible to argue that Aaron is the victim of later efforts to project
back into history attacks on Jeroboam's apostasy by giving them an early
and dishonorable lineage.[29] The parallels are many,[30] including Jeroboam's
offering of incense, an offer of a kind that was reported in Leviticus (10:
12) as the cause of the untimely death of two of Aaron's sons.

Christian critics in the early centuries, as Saint Stephen had before
them, considered Israel condemned for having rejected the true prophet,
Moses, for the false and devouring Moloch, who was likened to the
Golden Calf (Acts 7:40-43). The implication that Jews rejected Jesus as
they had Moses ("ye do always resist the Holy Ghost: as your fathers
did, so do ye" [Acts 7:51]) was picked up by Saint Augustine. He saw
the pulverizing and drinking of the Golden Calf as a sinful sacrament
whereby those who worshiped the Calf were in analogy to the Christian
Eucharist, spiritually transmuted into the body of this devil.[31] Had the
Jews not been ungrateful as well as stubborn, Christian commentary
continued, they would not have exchanged the glory of God for (the
image of) a creature that eats grass.[32] Josephus was so embarrassed that
he omitted the Golden Calf episode from his history of the Jews. Apparently he feared lending credence to the then-current allegation (found,

for example, in Tacitus and Apion) that Jews worshiped an ass' head in their temple.[33]

When not defending themselves against threats from the outside, rabbinic commentators concurred in assessing the extremity of the situation. "There is not a misfortune that Israel has suffered," said the Sanhedrin, "which is not partly a retribution for the sin of the calf."[34] The rabbis argued that the people lost their purity, thereby bringing on themselves, beyond the immediate punishments suffered, a loss of wholeness. Whereas before Mount Sinai the people had been fearless, afterward they were afraid. Rabbi Jose the Galilean, early in the second century, even claimed that before that time there had been no venereal disease. Going him one better, Rabbi Simeon ben Yohai stated that "when Israel stood at Mount Sinai, there was none among them with an issue, or leprous, or lame, or blind, or dumb, or deaf; nor were there any fools or imbeciles among them."[35]

The Golden Calf incident is portrayed in the Bible as not isolated but representative. The law and its violation virtually coexist. If everything is allowed and all is forgiven, however, the earth will descend into bestiality. Therefore, there must also be punishment.

If there is an arbitrary element in the punishment, it is surely Moses' intercession for Aaron, who, as we are told more than once, made the Calf. If Aaron deserved to die (And who deserved death more? Had he died, no one would have thought it odd), why is he saved? So far as I can tell, Aaron neither repents nor (aside from sharing in Moses' sin, which also denies Aaron entry to Israel) is punished. Perhaps understanding why Aaron lives will help us understand why so many others died.

Aaron is the brother of Moses; Moses is told that he is to be as a god to Aaron, who is to learn from Moses as Moses learns from the Lord. The passivity that proved so pernicious in Aaron—for example, the Calf that virtually made itself—had been picked up from Moses. The Golden Calf is a consequence of purely passive leadership. The Calf is, therefore, a retrospective condemnation of Moses, embodying, as it were, the implications of his behavior from the burning bush to Mount Sinai: passivity becomes apostasy. When Moses prays for Aaron, he also asks forgiveness for himself—that is, for what he might have become had he remained at Aaron's level.

Saving Aaron also preserves a form of leadership. Perhaps studying the usual naive view of the contrast between Aaron and Moses will give us a clue as to the types of leadership represented. As *The Interpreter's Bible* has it, they are "Aaron, the ecclesiastical politician, the apostle of the second best, the feeble excuser of supine subservience to popular clamor; and Moses, the real leader of men with his white-hot indignation against sin and his tender intercession for sinners."[36]

Are we to understand from this, as from other such interpretations, that nothing can be said for representative leadership? What would become of people if the repertoire of leadership alternated only between "white-hot indignation" and "tender intercession"? Aaron's survival tells us that the people need representation as well as exhortation; otherwise they will be unable to express themselves or, when necessary, to restrain their leaders, as Moses restrained the anger of the Lord.

The people cannot continually live at an exalted level; every day cannot be a holy day. The virtues of the common man—almost everyone, almost all the time—lie in craftsmanship: in doing well, and with integrity, the ordinary tasks of life. In the skill, even the purity, of the completed object lies the holiness of everyday life. This conception of craftsmanship comes across in the lengthy biblical instructions for building the tabernacle, full of advice about the best materials and minute considerations of how the work is to be performed. Several sages see in this detail a kind of creation. The tabernacle signifies man's "making of a house for God"; a modern sage sums it up as "paralleling God's making of a world for man."[37] The best parallel I know in literature is the carving of the whale in Herman Melville's *Moby Dick*, another process whose purpose is to divide the aspirations of the common man (represented by the motley crew) from the demonic possession of Captain Ahab (named after a particularly unpleasant king of Israel), who kills his crew by seeking to penetrate the malevolence that is also part of the secret of creation. Just as the people need a Moses for great occasions, they need an Aaron for the time in between.

The Golden Calf episode is not only about the apostasy of a people but also about the connivance of a leader. Even if Aaron has not instigated the evil, he who orders the gold collected and shapes the Calf certainly is an accomplice. So the question of leadership is whether leaders are obliged to head off, or put an end to, an evil act, or whether, once begun, the evil should be tolerated—the leaders hoping, perhaps, to moderate the people's behavior when evil's passion is spent. Which would exemplify the Mosaic ideal of leadership, reaction or resignation?

The passivity of resignation, we will see, passes out of Moses when he destroys the Golden Calf and its adherents, seeking, in effect, to inoculate his people against it. Our puzzle remains Aaron, who acts with resignation but is not punished.

Yet the Bible itself provides as direct a response to the question about the role of the high priest—active or passive—as one can imagine. As the people approach Canaan, on the borders of Moab, after the Calf episode, Zimri, a prince of the Israelites, asserts the right to have and to hold Cozbi, daughter of a leading house of Midian. Whereupon "Phinehas, the son of Eleazar, the son of Aaron the priest" (Num. 25: 7) spears the couple through. As a reward, as if to accentuate the lesson, the Lord tells Moses that Phinehas

> hath turned my wrath away from the children of Israel, while he was zealous for my sake among them, that I consumed not the children of Israel in my jealousy.
>
> Wherefore say, Behold, I give unto him my covenant of peace:
>
> And he shall have it, and his seed after him, even the covenant of an everlasting priesthood; because he was zealous for his God, and made an atonement for the children of Israel. [Num. 25:11-13]

By conveying the connection between the initiative of leaders and the mercy of God, Phinehas' initiative helps us put the final element of the puzzle into place. Whether or not to destroy Aaron presents problems both for Moses and for the institution of the priesthood. Aaron is kept alive, and the priesthood passes on to Phinehas. Thus the line is maintained, but its rationale rests on Phinehas' action, not on Aaron's passivity. Aaron is reprimanded in retrospect by being shown how a leader should have behaved.

"Slay Every Man His Brother"

We are back to our beginning: Can Moses be justified in having the people killed? Now that we know more about what faced Moses at Mount Sinai, we are in a better position to ask whether such fanaticism—killing people for a cause—can be comprehended or condoned.

When Moses comes down from the mountain, he correctly sizes up the situation, having had enough experience with the impatience of the people. "It is not the voice of them that shout for mastery," Moses discerns, "neither is it the voice of them that cry for being overcome: but the noise of them that sing do I hear" (Exod. 32:18). The dilemma facing Moses was how to combine punishment of the people with the survival of their species. There can be no repentance without renewal and no renewal without survival. He therefore seeks signs through which to separate the less sinful, or at least the more visibly rebellious, from the rest, so that the suffering does not appear to be wholly arbitrary.

Moses' strategy was to divide the Israelites to keep them whole. Treating the people as a collective unit exposed them to collective punishment. If Moses had not shown that he would punish at least some of the people, the Lord, in whose eyes all were equally guilty, would have done them all in. So Moses had to separate some to save others. The old cannot coexist with the new, the cult of the Calf with the worship of the God of Israel; the people will have to choose for or against God, but not in between.

"Then," we are told, "Moses stood in the gate of the camp, and said, Who is on the Lord's side? let him come unto me. And all the sons of Levi gathered themselves together unto him" (Exod. 32:26). Only the sons of Levi stood by Moses at the side of the Lord.[38] The falling away, we are thus led to understand, is not that of a small minority, which might be exiled or exorcised from the body politic, but eleven of the twelve tribes, a mighty majority. The disorder into which the Israelites have fallen, the nakedness that leaves them exposed, stands in contrast to the orderly existence they have so quickly abandoned.

Moses now uses a rare form of address, reserved for the most solemn occasions because it invokes divine authority: "Thus saith the Lord God of Israel" (Exod. 32:27). Yet there is no mention of any such instruction from God, either then or in the future, when Moses might have justified excusing himself in this way.[39] All he has to go on are the injunctions to go down and to let the Lord alone in His anger. Moses has argued the Lord out of slaying the people after Sinai, but this commitment remains conditional on what he will do to enforce obedience. He must bring back from the brink of extinction not only the people as a whole but the relationship with God upon which the survival of their social structure depends.

Speaking words like knives, Moses exclaims, "Put every man his sword by his side, and go in and out from gate to gate throughout the camp, and slay every man his brother, and every man his companion, and every man his neighbor" (Exod. 32:27). Who can read these words even today and not shudder? Brother is pitted against brother. No consideration of family or friendship or proximity is to prevail; there is no compromise and no pity.

"And the children of Levi did according to the word of Moses: and there fell of the people that day about three thousand men" (Exod. 32:28). The exact number is less important than the principles the act pursues. Yehezkel Kaufmann may be correct when he concludes, "With Moses the sin of idolatry—particularly as a national sin—comes into existence. Before, idolatry was nowhere interdicted and punished. The stories depicting idolatry as a national sin presuppose the existence of a monotheistic people. Since such stories begin only with Moses, we infer that it was in his time that the great transformation took place. By making Israel enter a covenant with the one God, he made it a monotheistic people that alone among men was punishable for the sin of idolatry."[40]

Moses returns to the Lord heavy not only with self-criticism ("Oh, this people have sinned a great sin" [Exod. 32:31]) but also with self-sacrifice: if the Lord will not forgive their sin, "blot me, I pray thee out of thy book" (Exod. 32:32). He has no purpose apart from his people. Moses is not, it should be stressed, offering to substitute for his people but rather to share their destiny. Having broken Holy Writ,[41] he joins his sin to the people's apostasy.

In the sense that divine criteria forged the law, it can be said that Moses carries out a divine punishment. The fact that God's wrath continues means, however, that concurrent human action (Moses') cannot substitute for divine punishment, which stands in its own right. As the term "blotting out" suggests, Moses is well aware that his action, however justified, has to be judged separately. Just as David, knowing he has sinned, throws himself on God's mercy, choosing punishment by the pestilence that comes from the Lord,[42] Moses is subject to a higher judgment.

The justice Moses metes out—drawing a line that pulls some to the saving side—establishes a principle from which he also benefits. Moses' offer to die with his people is rejected. Abraham's admonition not to "destroy the righteous with the wicked" (Gen. 18:23) has become permanent. Henceforth justice will be made individual and particular.

Moses has been justified. His actions in the name of the Lord have been accepted. Their purpose is accomplished—the people survive, the covenant is renewed, sin is individualized so that the community can continue. As usual, however, the story is not so straightforward. Individuals are part of the community; when they sin, those associated with them suffer. Guilt may be individual, but (speaking in secular terms) experience warns that consequences often are collective.

THE 'SPIES' AS A PARALLEL TO THE GOLDEN CALF

The themes of the Pentateuch are these: the God who possesses the people; the law they are supposed to obey; the land they are promised; the leader who is to take them there. All these—God, people, law, land, and leader—are at issue in the Golden Calf. That episode is too encapsulated, however, to carry the entire burden of instruction or to stand as a metaphor for all the trials and errors on the long way between Egypt and Israel. A more varied picture, subject to finer distinctions, emerges from parallel consideration of the episodes of the spies and the binding of Isaac. The structure of all three stories involving tests of faith is strikingly similar.

As Exodus (in Hebrew, "Names") is about selection, Numbers (in Hebrew, "Wilderness") is about testing of leadership. The account in Numbers has the Lord instructing Moses to send spies to search out the land of Canaan. But in Deuteronomy, Moses will write that the people came to ask him to send out an advance party so that they would know how best to go into the new land. Moses is pleased at this commendable commitment, suggesting the initiative and prudence appropriate to a people able to govern themselves.[43] Combining the meaning of both accounts, we see several tests of leadership established—God tests the people's willingness to be led, to overcome adversity in order to take the land promised them; the people test both the promise of the land (hence also testing God, whose promise it is) and Moses who is to lead them there.

The men to be chosen as advance scouts, the Lord says, should be leaders from every tribe. Moses tells these scouts to report about the people of Canaan—few or many, strong or weak—and about the land—good or bad, fat or lean—and to bring back its fruits. After forty days (the same amount of time Moses spent on Sinai), the spies return carrying figs, pomegranates, and a cluster of grapes so heavily laden it has to be carried between two men on a staff (Num. 13:23). Presumably this is the ample, tasty, and diverse food whose lack until then has occasioned so many sighs and murmurs. Nevertheless, the spies also "brought up an evil report of the land... saying... it is a land that eateth up the inhabitants thereof; and all the people that we saw in it are men of a great stature. And there we saw the giants, the sons of Anak,... and we were in our own sight as grasshoppers, and so we were in their sight" (Num. 13:32-33).[44]

Was this intelligence estimate (as we would call it today) "a slander upon the land" (Num. 14:36), as the narrative has it, or was it an honest report? How this question is answered matters. If the spies lied, deliberately misrepresenting what they saw, we would have to conclude that these tribal leaders never had intended to fulfill their promise to "take the land." They had merely found a convenient opportunity to discredit the entire enterprise, making the people fearful enough to want to return to Egypt. With this interpretation, there is no test of faith, only confirmation of conspiracy.

Though the narrative is presented in a jerky style, befitting disputation and indecision in which many voices compete for attention, there is agreement on essentials.[45] The spies do not try to deny the bounty of the land. The people of Canaan are described as numerous, strong, and well fortified. What is in dispute is not the evidence but how to interpret the import that the spies give to their findings.

Facts cannot speak for themselves; it takes people with theories to order data, which can then informatively relate to the issues at hand. As any study of intelligence estimates will show, it is the inferences made from data that are decisive. The spies give away their negative frame of reference when they say that the tall people of Anak saw the Hebrews as grasshoppers. Having already decided upon a conclusion ("We be not able to go up against the people [of Canaan]; for they are stonger than we" [Num. 13:31]), the report is tailored to suit. Caleb, by contrast, does not deny the data, only the conclusion: "Let us go up at once, and possess it [the land]; for we are well able to overcome it" (Num. 13:30).

If the inhabitants of Canaan actually were small and weak (even normal), faith would neither be required to conquer them nor God to provide. But if the reports were essentially accurate—so that, in a fair fight, man to man, the Hebrew people would face defeat, possibly destruction—

their faith would be tested. What is being decided now is whose interpretation will prevail—Caleb's or the others'; forward or back.

That night "all the congregation lifted up their voice" (Num. 14:1), crying and weeping, saying they had been better off dying in Egypt or in the wilderness than in Canaan. It sounds as though the people feel that each place they leave would have been a better place to die than the next one, which they have not reached.

The truth is out. It is not Canaan but God himself the people reject. What was implied by the Golden Calf comes to pass in the wilderness of Paran. "And wherefore," the people protest, "hath the Lord brought us unto this land, to fall by the sword, that our wives and our children should be a prey? were it not better for us to return into Egypt? And they said one to another, Let us make a captain, and let us return into Egypt" (Num. 14:3-4). A new captain to take the people back to the gods of Egypt implies a new religion. It is man, after all, whom Isaiah likens to grasshoppers (Isa. 40:22), not the inhabitants of Canaan whom the spies lacked the faith to overcome.[46]

"Then Moses and Aaron fell on their faces before all the assembly of the congregation of the children of Israel" (Num. 14:5). What a gesture! The leaders of Israel signify by this submission that they are helpless, that the action of the people in returning to slavery in Egypt is beyond their help, but yet that they continue to supplicate the Lord.[47]

Interposing themselves before it is too late, Caleb and Joshua (two of the twelve spies) "rent their clothes" (Num. 14:6) as Jacob had when he believed his son Joseph was dead. This ancient expression of mourning warns that the death of faith is the death of the Hebrew people. Caleb and Joshua get their reply as "all the congregation" (not just some or most) bid to "stone them with stones" (Num. 14:10). The die is cast, and the Lord appears to pronounce judgment.

What angers God is that the people continue to test ("provoke") Him after He had given them so many proofs. For their part, the Hebrews have given few proofs of fidelity. The divine leader recalls "all those men which have seen my glory, and my miracles, which I did in Egypt and in the wilderness, and have tempted me now these ten times, and have not hearkened to my voice" (Num. 14:22).[48]

"How long shall I bear with this evil congregation, which murmur against me?" cries the Lord (Num. 14:27). The inexorable conclusion follows: "I will smite them with the pestilence, and disinherit them, and will make of thee a greater nation and mightier than they" (Num. 14:12). The principle of correspondence is maintained with a vengeance. The people want a new leader; God offers Moses a new people. As John Sturdy says, interpreting the offer as a reference to Moses and his descendants, "As a whole nation had been made of the descendants of Abraham, so a new nation would be made of the descendants of Moses alone."[49]

The intercession of Moses is based on the fear, to use his chilling image, that God will "*kill all this people as one man*" (Num. 14:15, emphasis added). Therefore, invoking the formula of Exodus that balances retribution with mercy, Moses pleads once again for pardon of the people, as they have been forgiven all along. "And the Lord said, I have pardoned according to thy word" (Num. 14:20).

Pardon, as we know now, need not mean the absence of punishment. God acts in history but does not displace it. The decision is finely proportioned. The people, conceived of as a social entity, will survive. But this generation, save Caleb and Joshua, who kept the faith, will wander forty years—a year for each day the spies spent on their mission.

It is hard to improve upon the pungent phrasing of God's judgment: "But your little ones, which ye said would be a prey, them will I bring in, and they shall know the land which ye have despised. But as for you, your carcasses, they shall fall in this wilderness. And your children shall wander in the wilderness forty years, and bear your whoredoms, until your carcasses be wasted in the wilderness" (Num. 14:31-33). The spies themselves, all except Caleb and Joshua, die on the spot of plague.

In the episode of the spies, Moses makes another fateful choice, reconfirming and modifying his direction at the time of the Golden Calf. He will not separate himself from his people, either by their death or by taking on perpetual life himself, through foundation of his own line. Moses rejects that kind of immortality. He is unwilling to abandon either his God or his leadership. Concluding that this generation is too tied to the past, Moses decides, though not without opposition, to spend his life teaching a new generation to profit from the mistakes of the old.

The people now seek to pass the test by doing what they should have done before. The narrative states that the people "presumed to go on the hill top," a presumption that can be variously translated as reckless and headstrong, though I prefer Rashi's "insolence."[50] "What they would not trust God to give them," von Rad comments, "they are now going to take by their own efforts."[51] Alas, it is not possible to rewind the reel of history. "Wherefore now," Moses responds, "do ye transgress the commandment of the Lord? but it shall not prosper" (Num. 14: 41). Moses and the ark of the covenant stay where they are. Refusing to wait for God's permission, and bereft of spiritual support, the Hebrew army is defeated at Hormah by the Amalekites and the Canaanites (Num. 14:45).

The identification of Moses with the Hebrew people is never more complete than when he deliberately chooses to share their wandering, suspended for so long between the home that was and the homeland yet to be. We cannot know whether Moses sensed that his own purgatory was permanent—that the desert is life and wandering the condition of man. Already old, Moses must have realized that, without divine dispensation, forty years for him was tantamount to a life sentence. He, too, was close to killing what he loved most.

THE AKEDAH: THE BINDING OF ISAAC

"God did tempt [the *New Translation* has "test"] Abraham," the Bible relates, by telling him, "Take now thy son, thine only son Isaac, who thou lovest... and offer him... for a burnt offering" (Gen. 22:1-2). Abraham takes Isaac with him to the required place, Mount Moriah. When Isaac understandably asks, "but where is the lamb for a burnt offering?" the father replies, "My son, God will provide" (Gen. 22:7-8). Abraham builds an altar, places the wood on it, binds Isaac to both, "and took the knife to slay his son" (Gen. 22:9-10). Instantaneously, the angel of the Lord calls Abraham's name and Abraham replies—even as Moses will at the burning bush—"Here am I" (Gen. 22:11). He is told that he need not harm his boy but instead should substitute a ram caught in a nearby thicket.

The angel, standing for God, has Abraham stay his hand for "now I know that thou fearest God, seeing thou hast not withheld thy son, thine only son, from me" (Gen. 22:12).

The stated moral is self-evident—by offering to sacrifice what he most cares for, his only son, Abraham shows perfect faith. This much Maimonides affirms in his *Guide to the Perplexed*:

> The sole object of all the trials mentioned in Scripture is to teach man
> what he ought to do... so that the event which forms the actual trial is not
> the end desired; it is but an example for our instruction and guidance....
> For Abraham did not hasten to kill Isaac out of fear that God might slay
> him or make him poor, but solely because it is man's duty to love and
> to fear God, even without hope of reward or fear of punishment. The
> angel, therefore, says to him, "For now I know," etc., that is, from this
> action, for which you deserve to be truly called a God-fearing man, all
> people shall learn how far we must go in the fear of God.[52]

To take a modern affirmation, Speiser concludes that the purpose
of Abraham's "ordeal, then, was to discover how firm was the patriarch's
faith in the ultimate divine purpose. It was one thing to start out reso-
lutely for the Promised Land, but it was a very different thing to maintain confidence in the promise when all appeared lost."[53]

The idea of a man being about to kill his son has set off endless
debate about whether such a sacrifice could ever be justified. Does anyone
have a right to take life, especially an innocent life? Could Abraham be
sure he had heard a guardian angel and not a devilish impulse? Child
sacrifice is condemned elsewhere in the Bible, to show the superiority of
Judaic morality.[54] How, then, can one reconcile the goodness of God, the
foundation of the laws of Judaism, with this request for an unthinkable
act? Indeed, medieval commentators, concerned that the binding of Isaac
not be interpreted to mean that God thus gained new information, say
that God, already knowing Abraham would meet the test, had no intention of allowing him to proceed. According to Elimelech of Lyzansk,
Abraham and Isaac went through the motions of sacrifice to show they
would have done it.[55]

The most influential commentary of the last two centuries is undoubtedly Sören Kierkegaard's *Fear and Trembling*, in which Abraham is
portrayed as a "knight of faith" who suspends the ethical imperative to
love the son better than himself by preparing to kill Isaac because of the
higher obligation of faith in God. Kierkegaard imagines how Abraham
would be remembered if he had refused God's command: "For his retreat
would have been a flight, his salvation an accident, his reward dishonor,
his future perhaps perdition. Then he would have borne witness neither
to his faith nor to God's grace, but would have testified only how dread-
ful it is to march out to Mount Moriah."[56]

With characteristic force, Kierkegaard asks and answers his own question about the morality of the impending sacrifice: "If faith does not make it a holy act to be willing to murder one's son, then let the same condemnation be pronounced upon Abraham as upon every other man. If a man perhaps lacks courage to carry his thought through, and to say that Abraham was a murderer, then it is surely better to acquire this courage, rather than waste time upon undeserved eulogies."[57] Compared to denying that there was a dilemma, Kierkegaard's views have much merit. Whatever we imagine about them, Abraham and Isaac cannot have been certain of the outcome, for then they would have taken the place of God.

Without denying Kierkegaard's passionate insight, I think he has missed the other, social (and, for Judaism, the most important) part of the story. "The knight of faith," Kierkegaard writes, "is obliged to rely on himself alone."[58] He stands isolated throughout *Fear and Trembling* without even a minyan (the minimum ten men required to hold a prayer service) between him and his God. By suffusing his account with this radical individualism, by failing even to ask who Isaac is and what he represents in Hebrew history, Kierkegaard misses the social significance of the Akedah, the binding of Isaac.

Isaac is the people and the promise. If Isaac dies, the people of the future die with him, unborn, for he is Abraham's "sole heir,"[59] the only link between Abraham and posterity. "Isaac is the child of the promise," writes von Rad, meaning that God confronts Abraham with the question of whether Abraham could give up God's gift of promise. These words come closer to the essence,[60] but the emphasis is still too individualistic, for von Rad implies that the main result of an unfavorable outcome will be Abraham's disappointment. Yet what is at stake is the future, not only the present—the very existence of a people to be.

In discussing the Akedah, it is usual to regard Abraham as practically powerless. God is putting him to the test; Abraham is seen as having no control over the terms of the interaction. Once it is recognized that Abraham has his knife at the throat of the entire Jewish people, however, this encounter may not seem so unequal.

The life of God's promise is also at stake. It is God's first-born, Israel, who will die along with Abraham's only son. They, the man of faith and his God, are in this together, for the one gives life to the other.

This social test examines whether the Hebrew people have sufficient common belief to stick together. The beliefs and practices incorporating them are their God, or as much of Him as they will ever ascertain. The chief principle of the Hebrew God is exclusiveness—one God. Anything or anyone that takes precedence, even an only son or an only people, is idolatry.

Abraham's stature stems from his willingness to put his faith on the sharp edge of God's promise. This is exactly what Moses does at the Golden Calf, when he places his life on the line to assure the fulfillment of God's promise by a perpetual covenant.

The Akedah is an earlier version of the Golden Calf. As far as may be understood, it is a justification for the sacrifice of an entire generation in order to create a people able to fulfill its promise. The entire people—that is, Isaac—is to be offered to the God who stands for unity of the people.[61] The risk, the Akedah instructs us, is worth taking. Dramatizing a situation in which not just one generation but all future generations are at stake—bound to their faith, risking all—makes the larger-scale activity at Sinai more comprehensible.

The Mosaic perspective of the Akedah comes clear in the substitution of an animal for the child sacrifice; God thus redeems the first-born who belongs to Him. Various rabbinic interpretations, Geza Vermes informs us, hold "that this religious rite was founded on the vicarious offering of Isaac's ram, an example reflected in the Passover in Egypt."[62] Ram to ram, sacrifice to sacrifice, renewal to renewal, blood to blood, from the denial of man's right to take life, as if he were a god, to the worship of the pseudo-god, the idolater, Pharaoh, the exodus is encapsulated in the Akedah.[63]

PREVIEW

If Moses alone can cross the boundaries separating Israel from God, then he is both Israel's deliverer and its threat. Because only Moses talks to God face to face, only Moses can assuage divine wrath and intercede to deliver Israel. That is a powerful position, perhaps too powerful. The danger is that he who is given the right to dispense life can also dispense death.

Presumably the people had exchanged government by Egyptian kings for the rule of God, who, in return for their allegiance, gave them a past (being the God of their fathers), a future (a land of promise), and a present full of abundance. Had God delivered them out of the hands of Pharaoh in Egypt, however, only to hand them over to Moses in the desert? To see Moses as a more monstrous (because more powerful) Pharaoh, using the power of the Lord to enslave his followers, would be to make a mockery out of Moses' life. The question raised at the beginning (appropriately by an ungrateful Hebrew, whom Moses had saved from oppression)—"Who made thee a prince and a judge over us?" (Exod. 2: 14)—reappears in all its poignancy.

Ezekiel spoke of the Lord's everlasting search for leadership: "And I sought for a man among them, that should make up the hedge, and stand in the gap before me for the land, that I should not destroy it: but I found none" (Ezek. 22:30). In the preceding verses, Israel's leaders—her prophets, priests, and princes—are likened to lions or wolves who devour their prey, the people, who are like sheep. God needs a shepherd who will build a wall enclosing a sheepfold and will stand in the gap (the break in the wall that serves as a door) to prevent wild beasts and thieves from coming in to steal and kill the sheep. In the verse above, God Himself is seen as a lion or wolf seeking to destroy Israel in His wrath. Moses stands in the gap Godward. Moses protects the people against their own excesses, that is, against the just wrath of the God who encapsulates their conscience. But always there is a price to pay for leadership; the guardian may steal the sheep; the shepherd, in an excess of zeal, may even slay the sheep. Leadership may turn on itself, setting in motion a series of events that can be countered only by ever greater administration of violence. What first was good now feeds on itself to become grotesque. The good leader uses force when necessary; the great leader seeks to make force unnecessary.

4

FROM EQUITY TO HIERARCHY
The Institutionalization of Leadership

"Art thou," replied Korah, "the only one to know the will of God? Thou pretendest that He speaketh to thee secretly, when none can hear His voice nor behold His countenance. But hath He not spoken to us all before the eyes of the whole world? Wast thou alone upon Sinai, when resounded His Ten Words? Wast thou alone when His face appeared amidst the flame and the thunder? We have all seen Him, we have all heard Him. Wherefore shouldst thou alone speak in His name? Doth Abraham's blessing rest upon thee alone? Are we not all children of Israel? Children old enough to choose a leader, and not to choose one if we do not desire one?"

"Yea, yea," cried the multitude; "we are all equal! We desire a leader no longer! Thou, who art our leader, hast flouted the Ten Words of Sinai that we all heard. Thou hast stolen from us the joys of Egypt, the fleshpots, the sure bread!... Thou hast lied to us, with thy Land of Promise that exists nowhere, that we shall never see!... Thou has desired to become all-powerful through our slavery!... Thou hast committed adultery with the souls of our wives!... By taking away all rest from our days and our nights, thou has broken the Sabbath rest. Thou hast killed us by hunger and thirst and pestilence in the desert, and thou desirest to kill us, through forty years, by repentance!... Thou hast profaned the

Name of the Lord, by forcing it to work miracles against us!... Thou hast graven

an idol out of flesh, by making of thyself an idol!... And the One God, Him thou

hast blasphemed, for thou hast said: 'I am Moses, your God.'" A Legend.

—Edmond Fleg, *The Life of Moses*

Even divine selection of leadership cannot guarantee satisfactory performance. Leaders have to be proved in the crucible of conflict before anyone, including the leaders themselves (Abraham until the Akedah, Jacob until the Jabbok, Moses until Mount Sinai), can know whether they will fulfill their obligations. Leaders must be tested contrary to their strongest inclinations: Abraham to save the life of Isaac, Jacob's temptation to flee from responsibility, and Moses' desire to enter the Promised Land.

Throughout the Bible, conflict plays a creative as well as a destructive role. Opposition—whether between Egyptian masters and Hebrew slaves or Moses' commandments versus Aaron's license—is necessary to test the mettle of leaders and to work out the coming sharing of power with followers.

Conflict is creative (in other, more contemporary words) when it enables leaders and followers to choose between competing hypotheses—different leaders and the different regimes for which they stand—Pharaoh for slavery, the worshipers of the Golden Calf for anarchy, Korah for equity, and Moses for each at different times, but in the end for hierarchy, however weak.

Internal conflict becomes destructive when it leaves the populace helpless in the face of attack, whether from foreign military forces or from domestic corruption. Where the people become slaves to their passions, even as they were once bodily enslaved by the Egyptians, they are unable to test any hypothesis of their own.

TESTING MAKES CONFLICT CREATIVE

A test of ideas is also a test of force. The one, the potency of ideas, is seen as inseparable from the other, the virility of fighting forces. Military

react, the one because he cannot know without doing, and the other because He has limited his foreknowledge so as to make the virtue of man meaningful.[3]

The two types of testing show a certain symmetry: just as God tests man because He doubts his ability to perform, so man tries God because he doubts His saving power. Faith, Moses argues on Mount Sinai, is a two-way street. Either way, the one who tests demands that the other perform an act that is not strictly essential—Abraham's binding of Isaac, say, or God's producing food and water in the desert.

Being tested provides an opportunity for man to show his faith and for God to perform His miracles. Were God to do things alone, events could always be argued away on the grounds that they would have happened anyway. The difficulty in attributing causality is ancient. But if man asks for a sign—show me You are whole, real, powerful—God can be more dramatic and more persuasive.

To test God instead of relying on faith is a sin—but not always and in the same degree. For those without experience (the Hebrew people just after leaving Egypt, or those, like Gideon, newly approached by God, so that their demands have an air of innocence), there are wonders—water from rocks, bread on the ground, and meat from the sky. Those who should know better—for example, the Hebrew people after the Golden Calf, who have tested God once too often, or Moses at Meribah, who fails the test offered him—must face the consequences of faithlessness. Among the many exhortations to remembrance is Moses' summation of testing: "And thou shalt remember all the way which the Lord thy God led thee these forty years in the wilderness, to humble thee, and to prove thee, to know what was in thine heart, whether thou wouldest keep his commandments, or no" (Deut. 8:2).

Ultimately, the people were testing themselves and, in accordance with common experience, found slavery easier to deal with than liberty. Pharaoh's foreign rules were easier to disobey (when possible or convenient) than self- (or God-) imposed laws of their own. A legend long ago caught the tone better than I can:

In each case he [Moses] consulted the Holy One, blessed be He, who answered him: "Assemble the people, and let the sinners be stoned [to death] before the face of the multitude." "Punish them Thyself, Lord," Moses besought Him; "as Thou Thyself didst punish idolatry and lust,

Thyself punish blasphemy and the violation of the Sabbath; but command not me to punish." Thus did the Prophet implore Him, and his soul trembled in his flesh, for, for the first time, he must ordain death. But God replied: "I have entrusted to thee My Torah; what will become of it if its guardian dare not guard it? Wishest thou that I take it back from the world, and that, deprived of it through thy fault, the world remain unperfected?"

And the two men were stoned. Then a clamour rose from the Israelites: "What have we done? Why have we accepted the Torah? It promised us joy, but it bringeth malediction. Take back thy Torah, Moses. Give it back to the Eternal, for it will kill us all. We desire a Torah to live, not to die."[4]

Moses first experiences wilderness as an escape from history, a temporary detour on the way to the Promised Land, where Israel's real life as a people will begin; he is about to learn that for him, as for most of mankind, wilderness is history.

Moses, or any leader, is in a "no win" situation. Under the thumb of Pharaoh, the question of leadership among the Hebrews hardly arose. Whatever local jurisdiction was left was apparently exercised by the elders of tribes or clans. There was only oppressive external leadership.

During the exodus, Moses unites the tribes temporarily against the external enemy. Leadership under this anarchic regime is meteoric—it blazes brightly for a time but fizzles out. The people bargain about leadership as they haggle about goods, seeking the most—food, water, protection—they can get. The question of who will lead whom is hardly raised, except when the people threaten to desert their leader if he does not offer enough.

Because Moses finds this minimum unity disintegrating, he secures, as best he can, agreement on a covenant written around religious practices that emphasize unity as purity. The regime is one of equity; practices within the system are perceived as pure and those outside as polluted. Social relations are egalitarian; lack of differentiation defines internal purity. The only internal rule is one of diminishing differences. Leadership, which implies inequality in influence, belongs to central authorities from which equities wish to escape. Leadership can retain purity only by charisma—successfully claiming to speak with divine authority. The slightest speck of suspicion, therefore, is sufficient to produce attacks on the leader. Either equities claim that human nature is perfect, needing

no institutions to perfect it or they claim that it is corrupted by institutions, so that it can only be saved by separation from authority. Either
way equities attack established authority. And if there are disputes, equities resolve them by splitting apart, each new unit remaining pure in
its own conception.

What, then, are leaders to do if hierarchies appear oppressive and
equities unstable? Rebellion, as the Bible tells us more than once, is the
natural condition of the Hebrew people. In order to understand Mosaic
leadership, let us look at the problems the people had with him; then
we will turn to how Moses tried to solve his problems with them.

Of the adult generation that left Egypt in the exodus, only Caleb
and Joshua survived to enter the Promised Land. Had the people known
the odds, they might never have left. Revolutions, it is said, devour their
children, and the children of Israel were no exception. They can hardly
be said to have gone willingly; their kicking and screaming takes up the
longest part of the narrative. If Moses felt he had dragged them most
of the way, he was not far from wrong. The Israelites never stopped
complaining and, so far as I can see, have not stopped to this day—in
or out of Israel.

LEADERSHIP FROM THE FOLLOWERS' VIEWPOINT

Appreciation of the position of this people, empathic understanding of
their situation, appears to be the one consistent element lacking in the
commentaries. The children of Israel rejected their God; hassled their
Moses; were tried and found wanting. They had, Buber says of a people virtually without survivors and plagued at every point, a permanent
passion for success.[5]

It is, in fact, precisely the rebellion of the Israelites that gives dig-
nity and meaning to their lives. The very qualities for which Moses is
praised—the guts to disagree directly with the divine and perseverance
(a euphemism for stubbornness)—are the same as those for which the
"stiffnecked" people are condemned. If only in this respect, the Israelites
were truly a Mosaic community.

After all, why must a people born out of rebellion against Egypt
learn to love deprivation in this desert? When the Hebrews' deference

to the Egyptians—like any group's to any authority—had been undermined, obedience to future leaders could not be taken for granted but
had to be earned. Without rebellion against leadership, the children of
Israel could not have acquired an identity. Without leaders who argued
with the Lord, the Hebrew people would not have survived divine wrath.
And without people to challenge those leaders, there would have been
no test of basic principles on which to base knowledge that could be
passed on to future generations.

Because it is so seldom done, let us look at their complaints and
rebellions from the point of view of the populace. When the Hebrews
groaned under the yoke of Egyptian oppression, they were undoubtedly
thinking more of getting relief than of fomenting revolution. Indeed,
there is no suggestion that the Israelites appealed to the God of their
fathers; rather it was the other way around. "God heard their groaning,
and God remembered his covenant with Abraham, with Isaac, and with
Jacob" (Exod. 2:24). It is all the Lord's doing: "I will bring you out…
and I will bring you in unto the land" (Exod. 6:6-8).

It is one thing to hope to get more than you had; another to give
up what you have. Whatever their difficulties in Egypt, the children of
Israel had enjoyed their creature comforts. Suddenly, everything long
taken for granted was to be swept away, replaced with promises about
a better future (but one that was to keep receding into the distance).
The rigors of past servitude paled in memory by contrast with a new,
unrecognizable universe. In Egypt oppression had been predictable and
for that reason perhaps endurable.

That the Torah might be too heavy has been a consistent element
in Jewish thought; it is understandable that people might wish to escape
from its innumerable impositions. But can we find defenders of the mass
of Israelites? And on what grounds? Perhaps among Marxists who seek
to unmask relations of dominance. A perusal of their literature, however,
soon suggests approval of elitism rather than of popular rule. For instance,
Wilfried Diam's discussion of the Korah episode (Num. 16:1-40), which
stands as a prototype of rebellion, concludes that Moses was right to put
his preferences before those of his followers. Diam writes:

> The shortsightedness of Korah's rebellion is typical of left-wing devia-
> tionists—sectarians and adventurers as they are called in the current
> Communist vocabulary. Everything written by Mao Tse-tung (in his
> essay "On Protracted War"), all his arguments against deviation to the

right or the left, can be applied just as well to the deviations from the Mosaic revolution.

In addition, though Moses held firmly to the principle that all men are equal before the Lord, he had to delay democratization. Moreoever, he had to keep the reins in his own hands until such a time as the nation's re-education was completed. He had to remain as the central force of equilibrium and reason until the nation achieved inner stability.

This was the explanation of Moses' drastic action against Korah's rebellion. He liquidated Korah and his men, just as he had liquidated the counter-revolution of the Golden Calf. Again, the objectives of the Mosaic revolution were the justification for his actions.[6]

In the Marxist ideology, hierarchy becomes the handmaiden of equality—but that, as we know, is a contradiction in terms.

If possible, the children of Israel fare even worse at the hands of Lincoln Steffens, the American journalist and "muckraker," who sought to defend Lenin and the Bolshevik revolution against charges of cruel excess by arguing that they had done no worse than Moses. It is not the dictatorship of the proletariat that interests Steffens but the dictatorship of Moses (read, Lenin). Steffens' thesis in *Moses in Red* is that "this is what Moses seems not to have understood till almost the end: that slaves will not free themselves, but must be freed; that a people will not take their liberty, but have to have it forced upon them."[7] If many people die, as they did in the Bolshevik revolution, that is the price that must be paid. If an entire generation had to die, this sacrifice was justified because

the Lord showed from the beginning that the old people who had known the conditions of slavery and the culture of Egypt were not fit to live in the wilderness; He had fought their battles, provided them food and drink, till He saw that they would be of no use in the land flowing with milk and honey. He went on with them only for the sake of Moses, the faithful, and even to Moses He had said, when He pardoned the people and waited, He would do—what He would do. He knew then what He had to do. He knew what the Russians have learned. He knew that old people, who have lived and been formed on the earth as it is yet, are not fit for the kingdom of heaven; they must be put to death; and the children, the unspoiled, the untaught, the unformed—they alone can go over—and even they must first pass through the purifying experience of the natural conditions of the desert.[8]

The doctrine that the end justifies the means, I should think, is precisely what the moral law is designed to prevent. Otherwise, the law itself would specify only what, not how, things should be done. This is not the realm of instrumental rationality in which one might ask, "If not the means, what else would justify the ends?" Rather, this is the realm of substantive rationality, in which the ends themselves are (or ought to be) the objects of attention. Reformation of character, as slavery shows, is hardly a likely outcome of a despotic regime.

QUESTIONS WITHOUT ANSWERS: DILEMMAS OF LEADERSHIP IN EQUITIES

All leaders like to be loved, but leaders in some regimes need love more than leaders in others. Despotic leaders in slave societies, if they have to, can get along without affection. Autocratic leaders in hierarchies can rely on obedience to laws and their executors. Meteoric leaders in anarchies need substantial support only for short periods while doing the deeds they have been selected to perform. But charismatic leaders of equities, who would represent purity and who really rule by affection, need a steady diet of adoration. Indeed, if they were chosen for their purity, why should charismatic leaders not be abandoned when they fail to achieve perfection? So long as it lasts, their rule is subject to complete popular support. Lacking other modes of gaining support—by suppression, bargaining, or secrecy—charismatic leaders must be most reluctant to punish the people on whose love everything depends. But punish they must for if they fail to expel their accusers, charismatic leaders are suggesting that the spirit has departed from them and thus that their rule is illegitimate.

For any political entity, the great questions are how its regime should be organized, what it should do, who should take action, and what they should do. Of course, the questions are interconnected. Organization may determine authority: Who has the power may decide what is done, how, and by whom. Who acts may determine how (or whether) things are done. In the history of the Hebrews, all these questions are raised and given answers—some permanent, others tentative—by challenges to the

authority of Moses. Instead of speeches, we get stories; instead of pat solutions, we are offered outcomes that in turn become future problems.

What more fundamental challenge to Moses could there have been
than the people's demand to appoint new leaders and return to Egypt?
Only, perhaps, a revolutionary threat that would lead to immediate occu-
pation of Canaan without adequate preparation—cashing in the promise,
so to speak, before there was moral money in the bank.

In order to connect the spies to the Golden Calf, because they
are different versions of the same dilemma, I departed, in the previous chapter, from a chronological presentation. Here we go back to the
period immediately after the Calf and reconstitution of the covenant.
From slavery the Israelites now have gone through anarchy to equity,
but they are not yet prepared to accept a regime of hierarchy. Catharsis
did not take place until the desert because leaving Egypt did not solve
everything. The Israelites were free, but for what they knew not. Perhaps
if the people had participated in their own liberation, they might have
valued it more. They might also have become more inured to adversity
and less dependent on divine intervention.

The call for self-reliance sounded by the Lord as soon as the people
leave Egypt is met instead by fear of pursuit, coupled with an urge to
return home. When the Lord serves up another miracle at the Sea of
Reeds, however, a perverse pattern is seen to be established; the people
protest, the Lord provides. Neither Moses nor the Lord but anarchy
reigns. It is too much.

Breathlessly (not a spare word, nothing to indicate context, except
the place-name "Taberah," which means "burning") a typical story is
told: "And when the people complained, it displeased the Lord: and the
Lord heard it; and his anger was kindled; and the fire of the Lord burnt
among them, and consumed them that were in the uttermost parts of
the camp. And the people cried unto Moses; and when Moses prayed
unto the Lord, the fire was quenched" (Num. 11:1-2). Often the Lord's
presence is signaled by fire.[9] Here the metaphor is extended to mean
burning out memories of the old ways in Egypt.

But the murmuring chorus continues without a moment's pause. "And
the mixed multitude that was among them fell a lusting: and the children of Israel also wept again, and said, Who shall give us flesh to eat?
We remember the fish, which we did eat in Egypt freely; the cucumbers,

and the melons, and the leeks, and the onions, and the garlic: But now our soul is dried away: there is nothing at all, besides this manna, before our eyes" (Num. 11:4-6). The people wept, Moses was displeased, and the Lord was angry.

God will provide meat for the people to eat, not for a day, "But even a whole month, until it come out at your nostrils, and it be loathsome unto you: because that ye have despised the Lord which is among you, and have wept before him, saying, Why came we forth out of Egypt?" (Num. 11:20). Moses wonders where meat for so many people can possibly come from. "And the Lord said unto Moses, Is the Lord's hand waxed short? thou shalt see now whether my word shall come to pass unto thee or not" (Num. 11:23). The Lord sends forth a wind that brings innumerable quail.

This ill wind also brought death at the place called Kibroth Hattaavah (meaning "the graves of lust"): "And while the flesh was yet between their teeth, ere it was chewed, the wrath of the Lord was kindled against the people, and the Lord smote the people with a very great plague" (Num. 11:33). The events at Taberah and Kibroth Hattaavah signal a new situation. Though basic needs are met, the Israelites are being punished for lack of faith.

Moses goes to some trouble to avoid being suspected of imposing harsh penalties. After the episode of the spies, but before Korah's rebellion, for example, God announces laws to be observed in "the land of your habitations" (Num. 15:2). Distinctions are made between sinning through ignorance or inadvertence, and sinning "presumptuously"—that is, willfully and defiantly. Such a "soul," the Lord tells Moses, "shall be cut off from among his people" (Num. 15:30). At that very moment a man is found gathering sticks on the Sabbath and brought to Moses for judgment. Presumably the matter is cut-and-dried. "Ye shall keep the sabbath therefore; for it is holy unto you. Every one that defileth it shall surely be put to death," the Lord had declared (Exod. 31:14). Yet instead of carrying out the prescribed punishment, the entire congregation, including Aaron and Moses, "put him in ward, because it was not declared what should be done to him" (Num. 15:34). It has been suggested, notably by Rashi, that the nature of the punishment was not clear.[10] Yet the existing ordinance leaves little doubt—gathering sticks definitely comes under the prohibition of work on the Sabbath.

It might be maintained that the text has been tampered with to the extent that laws of a later era, like those about the Sabbath, have been interpolated into earlier times. Whatever the historical relationships, however, the punishment remains to be interpreted. Viewing these events through the lens of leadership, the story does speak to Moses' current concerns. The atmosphere is heavy with suspicion. The reiterated theme that the people might have done better to die in Egypt reeks of the universal fear of sudden demise—not least of all at the hand of Moses, who has, after all, done it before.

Is all this for God or for the self-glorification of Moses? Exercising power while seeming to renounce it is not an easy stance, either in action or in logic. Buber puts the Mosaic position: "Power lies in the hands of the 'charismatic' leader who is led by God; and, for that very reason, this wielder of power must not engage in any transformation to dominion, which is kept for the God alone."[11]

Here we have the dilemma of acting in this world while claiming the authority of another. "I didn't do it," Moses is made to say, "God did it." Like many another leader, he longs to combine the advantages of opposition with the perquisites of power. To avoid the imputation of abusing power, Moses should not be the one to carry out the death penalty. Better the people should do it together—"And all the congregation brought him without the camp, and stoned him with stones, and he died; as the Lord commanded Moses" (Num. 15:36)—and be implicated in the act.

In another case, in which a young Israelite is found guilty of blasphemy, the Lord commands that he be taken outside the camp to separate the people from this source of pollution, adding, "let all that heard him lay their hands upon his head, and let all the congregation stone him" (Lev. 24:14). The laying on of hands, signifying collective responsibility for enforcing the Commandments, expresses communal, not individual, judgment.

When a leader's authority depends on his presumed ability to exemplify beliefs in action, to attack that assumption can undermine his credibility. People who answer questions they have not been asked offer a convenient clue to what bothers them. In the midst of a particularly noxious series of accusations by "certain of the children of Israel," in which Egypt (Egypt!) is recalled as the land of milk and honey, Moses (accused by Dathan and Abiram of misusing power) reacts by urging the

Lord, "Respect not thou their offering"—choose between us, that is. "I have not taken one ass from them, neither have I hurt one of them," he asserts (Num. 16:15). From this we may conclude that Moses (who doth protest too much) was worried that others would think he had profited personally from his leadership.[12]

It would be difficult to think of a sin closer to the heart of a religion based on clean categories than wrongful marriage, with its imputation of impure sexual relations. Just such a charge was leveled at Moses by his own brother and sister, Aaron and Miriam, who "spake against Moses because of the Ethiopian woman he had married" (Num. 12:1). We are not told anything about the surrounding circumstances. What matters is the accusation, for if Moses is defiled, he is not fit to lead. Pharaoh, we recall, was overcome by a member (Moses) of his own family.

Aaron and Miriam do not have to claim a personal channel to God. They need only say that they, too, have access to the Almighty. "And they said, Hath the Lord indeed spoken only by Moses? hath he not spoken also by us?" (Num. 12:2). Such a claim is understandable only in a regime of equity. Under slavery, masters are gods; anarchies have different gods for different purposes; in hierarchies, the Supreme Being speaks through the system, from the top down. Only in a regime without authority would each person have direct access to the one truth. If everyone is a leader, no one can dominate, for all would have an equal right to set their own, or the group's, direction.

The voluntary organization of equities raises the stakes in internal differences. Disagreement cannot be bargained out, as in anarchies, or compromised, as in hierarchies, which seek to subdivide responsibility so as to mitigate envy. Either the charismatic leader must expel his rivals or they will expel him.

With Moses' authority at stake, the Lord bids Moses, Aaron, and Miriam to come to the door of the tabernacle, where He appears in a cloud, saying,

> Hear now my words: If there be a prophet among you, I the Lord will make myself known unto him in a vision, and will speak unto him in a dream.
>
> My servant Moses is not so, who is faithful in all mine house.
>
> With him will I speak mouth to mouth, even apparently, and not in dark speeches; and the similitude of the Lord shall he behold: wherefore then were ye not afraid to speak against my servant Moses? [Num. 12:6-8]

This is to say that the Lord appears only indirectly to other spokesmen, in dreams and visions, but to Moses he speaks "face to face." Here indeed is preferment, marking Moses as not *a* but *the* servant of the Lord. Now that is charisma!

Suffering the Lord's anger for her challenge to Moses as God's chosen leader, Miriam is made leprous—a condition the Bible treats as a paradigm of blemish, unwholesomeness, lack of holiness. Aaron quickly admits that he, too, has sinned (or at least acted foolishly) and acknowledges Moses' authority ("my lord," he calls Moses, as in the Golden Calf episode). Pleading for Miriam, Aaron asks God to "Let her not be as one dead, of whom the flesh is half consumed when he cometh out of his mother's womb" (Num. 12:12). Miriam's sin has literally made her into an abortion, one who should not have been born.

Moses, too, asks for intercession—"Heal her now, O God, I beseech thee" (Num. 12:13)—and his prayer is answered. But the Lord insists that Miriam first be publicly shamed for having rent the social fabric. The locution used is interesting in itself: "And the Lord said unto Moses, If her father had but spit in her face, should she not be ashamed seven days? let her be shut out from the camp seven days, and after that let her be received in again" (Num. 12:14). The connection to social categories is made explicit by analogy with the law of Levirate marriage in Deuteronomy that lays down the duty of a brother to marry his brother's widow. The clear conception is to keep families, like tribes and the nation, whole. Should a brother refuse this moral obligation, the spurned woman, in the presence of the elders, shall lift off his shoe "and spit in his face, and shall answer and say, So shall it be done unto that man that will not build up his brother's house. And his name shall be called in Israel, The house of him that hath his shoe loosed" (Deut. 25:9-10). Miriam, too, had failed to build up the house of her people; indeed, she had shamed its leader—and was publicly shamed.

Like those marvelous movie blow-ups in which frames of a scene are successively enlarged, the Bible provides additional opportunities, under varying conditions, to work out the application of general principles. Who has the right to interpret the word of God? Should anyone, even Moses, have the exclusive right? How may it be known that words come from God, that is, are right and righteous, therefore to be obeyed? These issues, raised by Aaron and Miriam, are worked out in succeeding episodes.

ABUSE OF POWER: KORAH, ABIRAM, AND DATHAN

Then Korah betook himself to the people to incite them to rebellion against Moses, and particularly against the tributes to the priests imposed upon the people by him. That the people might now be in a position to form a proper conception of the oppressive burden of these tasks, Korah told them the following tale that he had invented: "There lived in my vicinity a widow with two daughters, who owned for their support a field whose yield was just sufficient for them to keep body and soul together. When this woman set out to plow her field, Moses appeared and said: 'Thou shalt not plow with an ox and an ass together.' When she began to sow, Moses appeared and said: 'Thou shalt not sow with divers seeds.' When the first fruits showed in the poor widow's field, Moses appeared and bade her bring it to the priests, for to them are due 'the first of all the fruit of the earth'; and when at length the time came for her to cut it down, Moses appeared and ordered her 'not wholly to reap the corners of the field, nor to gather the gleanings of the harvest, but to leave them for the poor.' When she had done all that Moses had bidden her, and was about to thrash the grain, Moses appeared once more, and said: 'Give me the heave offering, the first and the second tithes to the priests.' When at last the poor woman became aware of the fact that she could not now possibly maintain herself from the yield of the field after the deduction of all the tributes that Moses had imposed upon her, she sold the field and with the proceeds purchased ewes, in the hope that she might now undisturbed have the benefit of the wool as well as of the younglings of the sheep. She was, however, mistaken. When the firstling of the sheep was born, Aaron appeared and demanded it, for the firstborn belongs to the priest. She had a similar experience with the wool. At shearing time Aaron reappeared and demanded 'the first of the fleece of the sheep,' which, according to Moses' law, was his. But not content with this, he reappeared later and demanded one sheep out of every ten as a tithe, to which again, according to the law, he had a claim. This, however, was too much for the long-suffering woman, and she slaughtered the sheep, supposing that she might now feel herself secure, in full possession of the meat. But wide of the mark! Aaron appeared, and, basing his claim on the Torah, demanded the shoulder, the two cheeks, and the maw. 'Alas!' exclaimed the woman, 'The slaughtering of the sheep did not deliver me out of thy hands! Let the meat then be consecrated to the sanctuary.' Aaron said, 'Everything devoted in Israel is mine. It shall then be all mine.' He departed, taking with him the meat of the sheep, and leaving behind him the widow and her daughters weeping bitterly. Such men," said Korah, concluding his tale, "are Moses and Aaron, who pass their cruel measures as Divine laws."[13]

Clearly, in this legend, hierarchy had replaced equity as the ruling regime of Israel. Instead of serving the people, Korah claimed, Moses had made them serve him. Moses had corrupted earthly rule by usurping divine prerogatives.

A rebellion broke out among the Israelites. A large group led by Korah, and joined by 250 princes of their assembly, "famous in the congregation, men of renown... gathered themselves together against Moses and against Aaron, and said unto them, Ye take too much upon you, seeing all the congregation are holy, every one of them, and the Lord is among them: wherefore then lift ye up yourselves above the congregation of the Lord?" (Num. 16:2-3). Like Aaron and Miriam before them, Korah's men accused Moses of abusing personal power, upsetting the equality of believers.

But this accusation, important as it is, hardly does justice to the immense importance of the claim made by Korah. If all Israelites receive revelation equally, without the necessity of mediation, they need neither leaders nor priesthood. Bid Moses and Aaron goodbye. If the people are good in the sight of God by virtue of the revelation, they do not have to strive to become good. Bid the Commandments goodbye. If every man is a judge of revelation, bid the law and the community goodbye. This is heresy. This is the end of Israel.

Flinging the accusation back in the faces of Korah and the others, Moses says that they, not he, are the ungrateful ones presumptuously seeking power.[14] "Seemeth it but a small thing unto you," Moses retorts, "that the God of Israel hath separated you from the congregation of Israel, to bring you near to himself to do the service of the tabernacle of the Lord, and to stand before the congregation to minister unto them?... Seek ye the priesthood also?"—Moses taunts those who have accused him of exactly what they now are doing (Num. 16:9-10). To settle the matter that these principles come from God and not from a man called Moses, he calls on Korah and his company to burn incense before the Lord so that God may choose among the factions.

Equality in belief is a principle with which Moses does not argue; rather, he opposes to it the principle of separation (that is, purity or holiness) that distinguishes the functions of the Levites from those of the priests led by Aaron. The logic of separation, Moses argues, suggests that if the division of labor between higher- and lower-level priests were to be set aside, other divisions would be, too, such as Israel versus Egypt; Sabbath versus working day; and, ultimately, one familiar God versus many strange ones. That is why Moses says the murmurs are not directed at Aaron but rather at the Lord—which is to say, at the principle of separating functions He has established to govern relations among the children of Israel.

By invoking a series of separations, Moses converts equity into hierarchy. Both regimes are collectives. Both protect their boundaries by pollution taboos. But the taboos of a hierarchy defend its minute functional divisions; in equities, by contrast, a single wall of virtue upholds equality of result.

Interwoven with the religious rebellion of Korah is the civic strife initiated by Dathan and Abiram. Whereas the Korah affair concerns the right of any man—especially, perhaps, the brother of Moses—to monopolize the priesthood, Dathan and Abiram protest against poor leadership. To Korah, there is excessive leadership; to Dathan and Abiram, the leadership is incompetent.

The Israelites' criminal code distinguished between inadvertence and deliberation. The worse punishment, however, was reserved for outright defiance. When Moses sends for Dathan and Abiram in connection with the Korah affair, they refuse to appear. They charge that Egypt was the good land abandoned by Moses, who has failed to replace it with anything except tyranny and promises. "Is it a small thing," they say, "that thou hast brought us up out of a land that floweth with milk and honey, to kill us in the wilderness, except thou make thyself altogether a prince over us? Moreover, thou hast not brought us into a land that floweth with milk and honey, or given us inheritance of fields and vineyards: wilt thou put out the eyes of these men? we will not come up" (Num. 16: 13-14). "Putting out the eyes" may be meant both literally—killing them so they cannot see—or figuratively—throwing dust in their eyes.[15] Either way, Moses is accused of sowing confusion (promising to take the people one way and actually taking them another) and showing incompetence by failing to provide the promised inheritance.

Dathan and Abiram charge that Moses is neither interested in nor capable of fulfilling his promises and is seeking to hide his failings. Because they do not accept Moses' authority,[16] they will not heed his call. No wonder Moses is reported to have been "very wroth" (Num. 16:15). His reply to the charge of tyranny is that he has taken nothing from them. But this did not answer the complaint that Dathan and Abiram (and the others) had not come with him just to wander endlessly in the wilderness.

There are three expressions for ruling, Hirsch tells us, which sound alike in Hebrew but have different meanings—superior power, moral influence, and capricious tyranny—the third of which led to the reproach Dathan and Abiram brought against Moses. The essence of such tyranny is that there are no laws to restrain it. Immediate proof of abuse, according to Abiram and Dathan, is found in Moses' attempt to call them to account, when he himself is actually the one who should have had to answer for his deeds.[17] In an equitable regime the very existence of authority is an abuse.

Showing that personal status is not at stake, Moses does not stand on ceremony; he goes to Dathan and Abiram. But the message he bears can hardly be considered conciliatory. Following the Lord's instructions on separation, Moses warns the people to "Depart, I pray you, from the tents of these wicked men, and touch nothing of theirs, lest ye be consumed in all their sins" (Num. 16:26). Disobedience is apparently catching.

Above all, Moses wishes to demonstrate that the acts of which he is accused, that would be abuses in a human being, belong to God. "And Moses said, Hereby ye shall know that the Lord hath sent me to do all these works; for I have not done them of mine own mind" (Num. 16:28).[18] A scientist could hardly set up a stricter hypothesis. If Korah, Dathan, Abiram, and their ilk die a normal death, "then the Lord hath not sent me. But if the Lord make a new thing," Moses hypothesizes, "and the earth open her mouth, and swallow them up, with all that appertain unto them, and they go down quick into the pit; then ye shall understand that these men have provoked the Lord" (Num. 16:29-30). This "new thing" is used in the sense of (pro)creation—that is, an act of God similar to the creation of the earth itself.[19] The pit is called *sheol*, the nether world of the dead, another boundary that can be crossed only by divine permission.[20]

When Moses finishes speaking, the ground opens up and the company around Korah, including their families and tents, falls into the earth, which, remarkably, covers them over.[21] The desire to return to Egypt is thus equated with the destruction of the Hebrew people as if the earth had swallowed them up and left no trace.

Seeking a social basis for dealing with this affair, Frederick V. Winnett concludes that the revolt stood for "traditional privilege against upstart nobility."[22] Dathan and Abiram were leaders of the tribe of Reuben; the two had held, and lost, senior status in the tribe. They might well have regarded the tribe of Levi, including Moses and Aaron, who were Levites, as upstarts. How one regards a complex arrangement in which social categories are hierarchical and insulated depends on whether one's own group is on top or bottom. Rearranging these relationships, as Moses did, was bound to raise hackles.

Though Korah was a Levite, the 250 princes were not; they came from all the tribes. What, then, made them so interested in the Levite cause? Those princes who pursued the cause of the first-born might, for instance, have had interests opposed to those of the Levites. Moreover, critics say, the meaning is confused because the narrative itself is not understandable. My preference (as the reader knows by now) is to try to interpret by fitting incidents into general themes.

What, we should ask, does the inclusion of these "men of renown" add to what we know about the Mosaic view of leadership? Many expressions are used to convey the sense that all Israel was involved in the rebellion. The participation of so many princes reinforces that point. To involve all the tribes tends also to heighten the importance of the issues in contention. If it concerned only the priesthood, the matter, though important, might be considered a limited struggle. The very inclusion of tribal notables with diverse interests suggests, however, a general struggle over authority, civil as well as religious.

Depending on how one chooses to slice into the substance of the material, there may be as many as four rebellions—the people, led by Korah, versus Moses and Aaron; the Levites, led by Korah, against Aaron; Abiram and Dathan against Moses; and the chieftains, with Korah, against Aaron and possibly Moses.[23] The important point for us, however, is not exactly how many revolts there are but what the confusion signifies. Each successive rebellion appears wider in scope than the one that preceded or accompanied it. First Korah, then Dathan and Abiram, then

250 princes; at last the entire community is involved. Similarly, Aaron
and Moses' religious and secular authority is attacked—each singly and
then both together. Despite its chronological inconveniences, the inter-
twining of accounts does serve the purpose of pointing to the cascading
consequences of rebellion.

That the message might not be lost on future generations, "The
censers of these sinners against their own souls" (Num. 16:38)—censers
within which the incense had been burned—were hammered into broad
plates to cover the altar. This was "To be a memorial unto the children
of Israel, that no stranger, which is not of the seed of Aaron, come near
to offer incense before the Lord; that he be not as Korah" (Num. 16:
40).[24] The struggle for power over the priesthood was settled by the demise of one side.

Though fear of the Lord evidently had been put into the people, they
could not accept the carnage, blaming Aaron and Moses for the death
of Korah and his followers. "Ye have killed the people of the Lord," the
congregation cries (Num. 16:41). Neither is this the first or last time
that miracles, however impressive, seem not to solve anything (cf. the Sea
of Reeds). "Miracles cannot change men's minds and hearts," Nehama
Leibowitz asserts, "they can always be explained away."[25] The next day
the complaints continued.

While the masses are mobilizing against Moses and Aaron, the cloud
containing the presence of the Lord grows more intense. A final, awful separation is about to take place. "Separate yourselves from among
this congregation," the Lord tells Moses, "that I may consume them in a
moment" (Num. 16:21). Genocide again. And again Moses acts to ward
off the worst. He instructs Aaron to take the familiar fire from the altar,
burn incense in the censers, "and make an atonement for them: for there
is wrath gone out from the Lord; the plague is begun" (Num. 16:46).
Aaron, representing the permanent priesthood, "stood between the dead
and the living; and the plague was stayed" (Num. 16:48). The narrative
notes, however, that in addition to those who were killed in the Korah
affair, 14,700 died in the plague.

Enough? Evidently not. Death and destruction should not stand
as the only way to maintain the priesthood. In A.S. Yahuda's view,
"Moses had therefore to discover some way out of the difficulty in order
to avoid further dispute on either side, and to keep all parties within
their limits."[26] The Lord suggests to Moses that the people choose a rod

for each tribe, inscribed with the name of its house, and leave it in the tabernacle. God will then choose leaders among the tribes so as to end this incessant strife. "And it shall come to pass, that the man's rod, whom I shall choose, shall blossom: and I will make to cease from me the murmurings of the children of Israel, whereby they murmur against you" (Num. 17:5).[27]

Case closed. Or maybe not. For the Hebrews still fear to live with the holy in their midst. "Behold, we die, we perish, we all perish" (Num. 17:12), the people cry. How can they approach the tabernacle of the Lord and yet live? The answer given is that Aaron's house (the Levites) "shall bear the iniquity of the sanctuary" but that only Aaron and his sons "shall bear the iniquity of your priesthood" (Num. 18:1). There follows a detailed specification of who—all Levites or only Aaron's sons—will be allowed to do what, just as in a hierarchy. Use of the word "iniquity" suggests that responsibility goes with power. That those who hold powerful positions (subjecting them to temptations) bear an iniquity will become apparent from God's denial of the Promised Land to Moses.

The people say that only Aaron's rod had "buds, and bloomed blossoms, and yielded almonds" (Num. 17:8). Aaron's rod was "to be kept for a token against the rebels; and thou shalt quite take away their murmurings from me, that they die not" (Num. 17:10). According to Yahuda, the Egyptians kept holy rods inscribed with the names of deities, priests, and kings. Aaron's rod was placed before the sanctuary, Yahuda writes, in order "to prevent any priest from using the rod for himself, and calling himself priest of the rod of God after the fashion of the Egyptian priests."[28] And, as we know, it is not Aaron himself but his rod (figuratively, his son Phinehas) who inherits, because Phinehas deserves the priesthood.

Everybody with power wants more. Korah and company are but extreme examples of a universal tendency, which includes Moses' own family (Korah is a first cousin) and people he has personally appointed. The "lack of localization," Martin Noth notes about the episode of Dathan and Abiram, which yields no clue as to where it occurred,[29] expresses the ubiquity of the phenomenon. Do not the Levites themselves try to take over Aaron's position?

Why, then, should Moses be different? He, too, is mortal. He also uses extreme measures to protect his position. If Moses is convinced that he acts rightly in the interests of others, no less so are his opponents.

That God is on his side is recognized only because Moses uses force more successfully. In the Dathan and Abiram episode, for instance, no mention is made of any test introduced by God. Rather, testing in this violent way is Moses' idea, for which he then summons God's support. In what way, then—except for being on the winning side, if that is so—is Moses different from, and superior to, those who oppose him?

His special status certainly sets Moses apart from the people. It is so special, however, as to create additional difficulties. If Moses alone can speak for the Lord, what, in the long run, will happen to the people? Is Moses to be with them forever? Lack of faith at Mount Sinai led the people to believe Moses had abandoned them. Lack of faith at Kadesh (on the plains of Paran, near the borders of Canaan, where the episode of the spies took place) moves the Israelites to abandon Moses—and the Lord to threaten to abandon the people. Does the problem rest with the people or with their dependence on Moses—that is, on charismatic leadership?

Moses' chief claim is that he pleads for the people even though they have turned against him. Moses acts most independently (and is least selfish) precisely when he himself is attacked. Instead of taking revenge on an entire people, he singles out the worst offenders. Because he does not lose control, Moses' people live to fight another day—even against him.

Selflessness and superior understanding are not, however, sufficient to save this first generation. It can hardly be said that Moses is totally persuasive, for otherwise so many would not have to perish. Viewed as struggles over obedience to the law, or faith in God, or commitment to the Promised Land, or acceptance of leadership, these episodes represent failure. Can Moses win if his people lose? Unless what follows justifies what came before, unless rebellion and the reaction of the leader are hedged with mutual restraint, Israel will have instituted a system of permanent purge. A regime of equity becomes intolerable to Moses, partly because it is incapable of ruling for more than short periods, but mostly because a charismatic leader—the alternative to hierarchic authority—has to use extreme methods to put down dissent. Like other leaders, Moses would prefer that the people do what is good for them (that is, what he wants). But, remembering failure, he balks at coercion. Anarchy has given way to equity, and the ideal of equity has in turn become insupportable. What now?

The people lack memory; each murmuring is a complaint of the moment. Moses' emphasis on remembering—remember to remember, remind your children to remind theirs—reflects his commitment to learn from the past. Remembering is the opposite pole to murmuring. Ability to learn from their failures is a measure of the greatness of leaders. Remembering the difficulties of a regime of equity, Moses seeks to supplement it with a dose of hierarchy.

Another line of development parallels the long series of rebellions with which we have been concerned. Instead of confronting force with force, the force of rebellion with the force of suppression, Moses seeks to divide power so as to control it. Hierarchy is about to replace equity.

BROADENING THE PYRAMID OF POWER

After the Lord "took of the spirit that was upon him [Moses], and gave it unto the seventy elders" (Num. 11:25), the elders began prophesying, accompanied by wild gestures. But presently they ceased, never to begin again.[30] Ecstatic prophecy was given a place under controlled conditions, a short and circumscribed place.

Authorized prophecy, however, was another matter. Here the question was not whether speaking with the voice of God was permissible but whether Moses had a monopoly on that wavelength. The story is short enough to be quoted in full:

> But there remained two of the men in the camp, the name of the one was Eldad, and the name of the other Medad: and the spirit rested upon them... and they prophesied in the camp.
>
> And there ran a young man, and told Moses, and said, Eldad and Medad do prophesy in the camp.
>
> And Joshua the son of Nun, the servant of Moses, one of his young men, answered and said, My lord Moses, forbid them.
>
> And Moses said unto him, Enviest thou for my sake? would God that all the Lord's people were prophets, and that the Lord would put his Spirit upon them. [Num. 11:26-29]

Note that it is Joshua, Moses' successor, who is afraid of Medad and Eldad. Moses teaches Joshua one lesson—leaders ought not to fear sharing authority. In the revolts that follow, Moses also teaches Joshua another—don't give away the store; you can't share what you haven't got.

If each person has the right to interpret the law to suit himself, he also has the right to make the laws. A direct pipeline to God would let every man set up his own shop. To maintain the unity of the faith, the center has to be shored up, not subverted.

THE KISS OF OFFICE:
INSTITUTIONALIZATION OF AUTHORITY

From the moment Moses is invested with authority at the burning bush, he shares it symbolically with Aaron, the brother who is to speak for him. Aaron, who founds the priestly order, is more than a mouthpiece; he takes part of the Mosaic authority upon himself. This division of authority, like all the other good things, is two-sided: it shores up the center of the established order—absorbing by channeling shocks and disturbances—while at the same time providing an alternative to the central leadership. While defending Aaron's authority, Moses is also attacked by it. The kiss with which they greet when Moses meets Aaron in the desert on the way from Midian is, to be sure, the kiss of obedience that Aaron owes the brother he is to serve. It is also a kiss that marks Moses as a victim of the passive leadership for which Aaron stands. Aaron will acquiesce in the apostasy of the Golden Calf, challenge Moses' authority, and share with him the disobedience that is punished by being forbidden entry into the Promised Land. The humanity they share—for Moses and Aaron are facets cut on the same stone[31]—results in a common fate. Except for one thing: Aaron's seed will be perpetuated in the priesthood; Moses will receive no tangible perpetuation other than in the Bible.

The kiss of Moses goes also to his father-in-law, Jethro, who meets Moses soon after the exodus, to prepare for another division of authority. The "polite formality" that Childs says is produced by "repetition of his [Jethro's] kinship with Moses seven times in twelve verses,"[32] I ascribe to recognition that another aspect of Mosaic authority is about to be transferred. The almost accidental character of the encounter—Jethro just happens to be there when Moses is hearing cases—is negated by the prior statement that "all the elders of Israel [came] to eat bread with Moses' father-in-law before God" (Exod. 18:12). "Accidentally on purpose" the elders are consecrating, by taking into themselves, the bread of a new life among the Israelites. Only its institutional embodiment remains to be established.

All along, Moses continues to divest himself of facets of his authority. The personal power Moses gives up is traded for institutional immortality.

"How can I myself alone," the Deuteronomic Moses tells the people, "bear your cumbrance, and your burden, and your strife?" (Deut. 1:12). Just before Jethro advises a necessary division of labor, Moses has related to him how "for Israel's sake… the Lord delivered them" out of Egypt (Exod. 18:8). For Israel's sake, too, the burden of leadership is to be made lighter by being shared among more men. Thus there is a point in attributing to Jethro the idea of bureaucracy. Wisdom is not confined to the chosen people. Besides, Moses can discard or adopt practical advice from outside without being bound by it. The scene between Moses and Jethro is a mnemonic link, extending from past to future—from Moses as a man with a family, who gives his father-in-law due deference, to Moses as the embodiment of authority, who must eventually decide how to pass it on even as he himself passes on.

Before Moses meets Jethro, Israel fights with Amalek on the way to Sinai, at Rephidim. With the "rod of God" in his hand, Moses goes to the top of the hill. Whereupon:

> And it came to pass, when Moses held up his hand, that Israel prevailed: and when he let down his hand, Amalek prevailed.
> But Moses' hands were heavy; and they took a stone, and put it under him, and he sat thereon; and Aaron and Hur stayed up his hands, the one on the one side and the other on the other side; and his hands were steady until the going down of the sun. [Exod. 17:11-12]

When Moses looks up to God, in sum, his people triumph. The power of the Lord flows through Moses, but evidently it is too heavy for him to bear alone. Moses needs his people to uphold his power.

Nor is Moses slow to act on this sign. Immediately thereafter, he is visited by his father-in-law, Jethro, from whom Moses hears the echo of his own voice, for Jethro represents another aspect of Mosaic leadership. The Bible tells us that Moses sat to judge the people....

And when Moses' father-in-law saw all that he did to the people, he said, ...Why sittest thou thyself alone, and all the people stand by thee from morning unto even?

And Moses said unto his father-in-law, Because the people come unto me to inquire of God....

And Moses' father-in-law said unto him, The thing that thou doest is not good.

Thou wilt surely wear away, both thou, and this people that is with thee: for this thing is too heavy for thee; thou art not able to perform it thyself alone....

Moreover thou shalt provide out of all the people able men, such as fear God, men of truth, hating covetousness; and place such over them, to be rulers of thousands, and rulers of hundreds, rulers of fifties, and rulers of tens:

And let them judge the people at all seasons: and it shall be, that every great matter they shall bring unto thee, but every small matter they shall judge: so shall it be easier for thyself, and they shall bear the burden with thee....

So Moses hearkened to the voice of his father-in-law, and did all that he had said. [Exod. 18:13-24]

Jethro's advice to Moses, which he implements, comprises what in our time have become classical principles of public administration. There is "management by exception" under which routine matters are covered by standard operating procedures, leaving the difficult cases for special attention by higher authority. There are job qualifications established in the selection criteria set out by Moses: employees should be capable, God-fearing, truthful, honest, unswayed by prospects of material gain. Specialization was there before Moses' time as indicated by the numerous references to craftsmen. Division of governmental labor, however, Moses owes to Jethro in the persons of the captains of tens, hundreds, and thousands. Were it not so jarring to a biblical consciousness, we could say that by following these principles of administration, Moses was able "to devote his time planning, directing and coordinating the activities of those in his command."[33]

As he himself is an intermediary, Moses appoints others to share his rule. The administrative division of *labor* is established. But is it also to be a division of *authority*? Moses keeps for himself not merely the harder cases but also all that go "Godward." What would happen if his authority as intercessor, as sole link to God, were challenged? What, indeed, if the very people he appoints to help "bear the burden" add to it by trying to change the direction (back to Egypt rather than forward to Israel) and question the desirability of Moses' leadership?

Moses reserved to himself the power to appoint and, if Korah and company are included, the power to dismiss as well. Korah claims that Moses assumes too much authority, and Moses cries that the people are too much for him. Moses needs help in moving the people in his direction; Korah claims Moses has no right by himself to move them in any direction. There is sufficient symmetry in their attitudes to suggest that both see something similar. Moses is attempting too much. The solution to this problem, other than abandoning leadership, involves either increasing his control or decreasing the mass he has to move. Hierarchy does both.

The Mosaic Division of Authority

Gradations of authority are in evidence even before Jethro gives this advice. Hebrew officers who had been appointed by Pharaoh's taskmasters disappear; henceforth, short of conquest, no foreigners will be allowed to rule; Deuteronomy explicitly places this prohibition on future kings. Elders existed under slavery. The elders, now numbering seventy, appear again at the covenant ceremony before Mount Sinai. They go up to the Lord with Moses, Aaron, and two of Aaron's sons. Together all "saw God and did eat and drink" (Exod. 24:11). Since authority was not centralized but dispersed among the tribes, it could not be decentralized. At that time, authority was, properly speaking, noncentralized. Let us briefly review what the Bible tells us about who should have what authority.

In the second year after leaving Egypt, after the Golden Calf but before the episode of the spies, while murmuring about this and that, the people again complained about the lack of variety in their diet. Moses felt much put upon, asking why God makes him bear the burden of this entire people. God, not Moses, created this people and promised them a land. Presumably, therefore, God should feed and lead them. Tired of incessant demands, Moses says that unless God lightens his burdens, he would as soon die as be so wretched. Avoiding the hyperbole, but getting to the heart of Moses' plea, the Lord acts directly by dividing the responsibility:

> Gather unto me seventy men of the elders of Israel, whom thou knowest to be the elders of the people, and officers over them; and bring them unto the tabernacle of the congregation, that they may stand there with thee.
>
> And I will come down and talk with thee there: and I will take of the spirit which is upon thee, and will put it upon them; and they shall bear the burden of the people with thee, that thou bear it not thyself alone. [Num. 11:16-17]

The seventy elders represent a division and a delegation but not a devolution of authority. Buber understood that authority was to be exercised "from above downwards," not "from below upwards."[34] A new structure is to be superimposed on top of the clans and tribes and houses that make up the traditional authority of the people. Like French prefects, rather than American governors, such elders are appointed from above. Like members of the British House of Lords, but unlike the United States Senate, these councillors are from localities but are not chosen by people in them—they are co-opted from above, not chosen from below.

The division into captains is attributed to Jethro, but appointing the council of elders is reserved to God. God keeps the sum of established central authority whole by taking some of the spirit that is in Moses and transferring it to the elders. Being too much for one person, that authority, for convenience, may be parceled out. But it belongs together. How does one know, then, whether any proposed division of authority is legitimate? Because it is proposed by the central authority—loaning it to others, shall we say, without reducing the principal. Division down is all right, because it keeps the center intact, but final choice from below (as Korah, Abiram, and Dathan discovered) is not. This is the principle of hierarchy.

Toward Hierarchy

The God of Israel, Max Weber wrote, "remained the god of political destinies."[35] One God stands as an aspiration for one people. Morality and community are intertwined. It is the covenant that is primary, not the specific forms that leadership takes at a particular time. For there to be central leadership at all, however, Moses must create a regime that is hospitable to it.

Moses faces two fundamental challenges, linked by the Hebrews' desire to return to Egypt, which would have destroyed the people. There are two apostasies (flights from God, so to speak). At first, the frightened and frenzied people try to replace God with the Golden Calf. In handling this direct assault, the difficulty for Moses lies in having to pass from passivity to activity, to identify with his people strongly enough to save them. The spies incident is a variant, in which rejection of the Promised Land substitutes for rejection of the promiser.

Coping with Korah's rebellion is more complex, however, because it has the appearance of an excess of virtue. Equity does appear equitable on the surface. The splits it generates, the accusations of hidden contamination, the destruction of those believed to be impure, become apparent only from experience. Hence Moses' behavior is more defensive and more metaphorical—the swallowing up of the rebels stands for the internal implosion they have caused in Israel. For the rebels propose, in effect, to swallow up the Lord. Remember that Korah claimed the people were already holy. Thus interpreted, law and leadership had become obstacles to holiness, restraining the natural spontaneity of the people. A rebellion that assumes holiness is obviously harder to put down than the one that rejects it, though the consequences would be identical—namely, a return to spiritual, as well as physical, slavery in Egypt.

Once it has been decided that Moses will not only take the populace out of Egypt but will also try to transform them into a community with new moral-political precepts, his problems with purity begin. The equality of believers, the principle of purity that was used to justify the initial separation, serves just as well to justify any number of new ones.

Splits and disunion, tolerated for a time, are eventually challenged by a new principle—hierarchy. Order is enforced. Social purity is to be protected from confusion by hierarchies of rules enforced by hierarchies of rulers. As the initial rebellion becomes the rallying point for revolutionary principles—the permanent revolution of purism—a new establishment seeks to impose order. On one side, the revolution is identified with freedom—every man his own theologian. On the other, it is identified with order—a place for everyone and everyone in his place.

Moses' leadership dilemma is rooted in these contradictory demands: a revolutionary in regard to the Egyptians, he is a reactionary in regard to the Israelites. His initial task is to root out the Egypt in Israel—material, habitual, spiritual; he is a social critic denouncing the wrongdoing of those in authority. Moses makes Pharaoh look foolish, vain, contradictory, and, worst of all, weak.

The critical spirit thus engendered in the people was to plague Moses' authority as it had plagued Pharaoh's. Against Pharaoh, Moses called upon his people's ancient rights—to their God, their laws. Barely remembered (Joseph's bones were about all that was left), the memory of time immemorial was to be written down in a covenant, broad enough to cover future eventualities. What, then, was to stop anyone from claiming that this same covenant supported their opposition to the current interpretation and interpreter?

More than one can make a claim on tradition. Jewish history (ca. Josephus' *Jewish Wars*, and after) seethes with internal conflict over the meaning of the covenant. The first step is always to undermine the establishment. But Moses has to administer, as well as found, a state. How, then, can he justify being both a critic *and* a conserver?

How, we may well ask, may leaders uphold a conception of the purely equitable life in a murky social situation? What happens without bargaining and compromise? Who decides what rule applies? How are differences to be settled? How can there be unanimity when circumstances change and application of general principles must be left to those at the scene? One need not envisage great affairs of state; even ordinary families find pure principle stultifying.

Religion aims at a unity of experience. Basing social legislation on the experience of the exodus—setting similar boundaries around tribal as around religious functions—is meant to bring coherence into the world. To say that there should be a single law for the stranger as well as the citizen and that he who causes a blemish shall, in the well-known words, have it done to him "breach for breach, eye for eye, tooth for tooth" (Lev. 24:20) is to extend rules so that social balance and symmetry are made equivalent to religious holiness.[36]

When we first meet Moses, he is taken out of the waters of chaos into the order of land. He leads his people out of the watery womb of Egypt into the dry desert. The wall of water in the Sea of Reeds—water only temporarily held back by God lest it engulf the Israelites as it already had the Egyptians—is a reverse threat: to return to Egypt, to turn one's back on God, is to be submerged forever.

The land that is God's eternal promise to Israel is a land that tames water to serve man. This taming of nature is a gift from God, with the various injunctions to share in the fruits of the land that Henry George, the secular prophet of the land tax, later found so appealing:[37] "For the poor shall never cease out of the land: therefore I command thee, saying, Thou shalt open thine hand wide unto thy brother, to thy poor, and to thy needy, in thy land" (Deut. 15:11). The land by itself, however, provides only the opportunity for unity in experience, by no means the guarantee.

What is this land that, along with the law and covenant, sets the stage for the future life of the Israelites? It is lush with abundance and ripe with temptation. It is, in a phrase, the real world. Canaan is not a free gift but must be taken, and those who take it, like all men, must build on the ruins of others who came before. When they do, they will have to confront themselves as a nation, not just as a sect. The land is a promise, not a fulfillment.

The promise of the land is also a sine qua non for Mosaic leadership. Without the land, and the power that goes with it, politics is an empty exercise; neither for good nor for evil can the mettle of the people be tested. As spectators of other people's problems or as appendages of other countries' regimes, the Israelites make history no longer. Hebrews once more would become, as they were in Egypt, political children in an evil Garden of Eden.

Moses has put down a series of revolts that sprang from demands for equality in the matter of interpreting God's will (Korah), which soon enough (Dathan and Abiram) turn into a call for replacing leaders—no Moses, no God, no Judaism. The children of Israel and their Moses wander for forty years while waiting for the new generation, born and educated outside of Egypt, to begin a new life in a new land. Will Moses, their perpetual teacher, go to guide them, as if in this respect they would always be his children?

Moses' reply to Joshua, allowing Eldad and Medad to continue prophesying, according to S.R. Hirsch, "remains for all teachers and leaders as the brilliant example they should keep before their eyes as the highest ideal aim of their work, viz., to make themselves superfluous, that the people of all classes and ranks reach such a spiritual level that they no longer require teachers and leaders."[38] This lack of jealousy extends, indeed, to Moses' teaching, which he willingly shares. Does the generosity extend also to his person? Is he willing to efface himself in the sense of not trying to perpetuate his personality or his position? Can his pupils do without him? Or must he be around continuously to tutor new generations?

5

THE LEADER DISAPPEARS INTO THE BOOK
Why Moses Does Not Get to the Promised Land

"If I must not lead them as Prophet into the Land of Promise, let me enter in as the disciple of another." "Thou shalt not enter it." "Let me enter it like whomsoever amongst them." "Thou shalt not enter it." "If I enter it not alive, let me enter it dead. Let my bones rest there." "Thou shalt not enter it. I have said that the whole generation of sin shall die without entering in. All are dead. Miriam is dead, Aaron is dead; like them, without entering in, thou shalt die."

"Have I not walked in Thy ways, Lord, all the days of my life? Have I not fled iniquity and deceit and forsworn all delight to be Thine alone? What sin have I sinned to deserve Thy wrath?" "Seek thy sin." "By the burning bush, when Thou didst wish to send me to save Israel, I said to Thee, 'Send another.'" "That sin was the son of a greater sin." "By the rock of Meribah I refused in my anger Thy miracle for Thy people." "That sin was the son of a greater." "By the idol of Moab I commanded that all the Canaanites, with the women and the children, the young and the old, should be put to the edge of the sword." "That sin was the son of a greater sin." "Lord, Lord, what is this greater sin?"

Then God said: "Thou hast doubted Me: I forgive thee. Thou hast doubted thyself: I forgive thee. But thou hast doubted Israel, thou has doubted mankind, wherefore thou shalt not enter into this Land of My Promise. Israel is laden with defilements; but whence comest thou if it be not from Israel? My prophet is, My people; My people is, My prophet. Men are cowardly, perverse, envious, lustful, lying, thieving, murderous, and blaspheming; but what art thou if not a man? What thou hast comprehended of Me, wherefore should not the others one day comprehend it also?" A Legend.

—Edmond Fleg, *The Life of Moses*

Think of Moab, the thin slice of land between the wilderness and Canaan, as a spatial metaphor. Moab is between the wilderness and the conquest, parallel to the Sea of Reeds crossing, which is situated at a moment between Egypt and the desert. In time, the Sea of Reeds is a crossing between past and present, while Moab is a thin line between present and future. Lest the lessons of the past be lost to the detriment of the future, Moses must make the past come alive in the present.

Moses' speeches in Deuteronomy are a recollection of the past for the sake of the future. When God threatens to destroy the people and offers to make of Moses a great nation, his immediate response is "Remember thy servants, Abraham, Isaac, and Jacob." Moses does not make claim that universal laws of history exist to work themselves out regardless of man. History to Moses is revelation of the will of God,[1] especially worthy of study so that men can learn from it.

What is the Book of Deuteronomy (called "These Be the Words" in Hebrew) but an eloquent effort to make memory live for a new generation that we may say "knew not Pharaoh."[2] Moses tells the sons of the generation that witnessed the covenant to take care "lest thou forget the things which thine eyes have seen, and lest they depart from thy heart all the days of thy life: but teach them thy sons, and thy sons' sons" (Deut. 4:9). If not kept current in the memories of the people, the covenant would become a mere historical curiosity, chewed over by antiquarians. "The Lord made not this covenant with our fathers," Moses teaches, "but with us, even us, who are all of us here alive this day" (Deut. 5:3). Forward and back, in and out, this way and that, Moses expounds his message—remember. Do not forget! As a memorial of the Commandments, "thou shalt write them upon the door posts of thine house, and upon thy gates" (Deut. 11:20) and "ye shall teach them your children, speaking of them when thou sittest in thine house, and when thou walkest by the way, when thou liest down, and when thou risest up" (Deut. 11:19). Moses as rhetorician and Moses as lawgiver reinforce one another; his style is complemented by the Commandments, so that word and deed are one.

Oral tradition alone is not enough. Memory is not only to be "in their mouths" (Deut. 31:19) but also to be written "on your hand." The Lord instructs Moses directly to "Write this for a memorial in a book" (Exod. 17:14). Along the way, "Moses wrote all the words of the Lord" on the mountain (Exod. 24:4), inscribed "the words of this law in a book" (Deut. 31:24), and not only wrote down the words of a song but "taught it the children of Israel" (Deut. 31:22). To his long list of roles, Moses can, then, add "song leader" and "social director."

History is open-ended; what there is to be learned depends on the needs and circumstances of future generations. "Theological dialectic" is not just a fancy way of comprehending Jewish history as a dynamic that can encompass discrepancy or even contradiction. The notion that each new generation must reinterpret its history in light of the history of the covenant is already evoked by Moses himself in his last speech. In retelling a selective version of the past, we see Moses emphasizing the illustrative side of events rather than the particular details of any one historical situation. Deuteronomy is the first commentary (or midrash) on the Bible.

For the Hebrews, history is an activization of memory, not one smooth, chronological line of events. Moses' recollections in Deuteronomy differ from the descriptions of events in Exodus. Reinterpretation is renewal of the covenant, a present-time renewal, not an imitated allegiance to a rote code. Just as in the modern legal system, cases serve as precedents (not as exact parallels) for decision making, form and content are mutually interdependent in the Bible.

Moses is his own first interpreter. God is his Torah, which he continually rereads, changing from passive reader to active shaper of the text of Israel's history. Moses is the first individual to recount the history of the covenant; and henceforth, part of the renewal of the covenant becomes a recounting of his history.

At that very moment, Moses faces the task of making history. He is speaking to a generation that did not itself witness these events and that would yet have to apply an understanding of that past to the conquest and settlement of a land about which these younger children of Israel can know only as past promises.

Moses has passed from acting as the mediator between God and his people (as von Rad sums up) and now is to act "as the mediator of Yahweh's great revelation. His personal service as a mediator has, in fact, come to an end. Thus care must be taken to provide for another form in which to preserve and to mediate Yahweh's revelation. What Moses had till then carried in his mind and handed on by word of mouth is now transmitted to the priests in the form of a book, which they must read out from time to time to the assembled community."[3] The books of Moses are the permanent embodiment of the past that Moses is instructed to write down for the sake of the future. The law becomes a book, which is to be placed next to the ark of the covenant and to be read regularly to the people. "Indeed," Childs concludes, "the original role of Moses as the unique prophet of God who proclaims the word of God as a witness will be performed by the book of the law in the future. Moses will shortly die, but his formulation of the will of God will continue. Throughout the rest of the Old Testament the identification of the divine law with Moses' writing of it in a book is continued."[4] Moses has become a book, but Moses cannot be both book and reader; he will have to be satisfied with the inscribed word. Thus it is wholly appropriate that Moses dies talking. Only the words are left.

Nothing is more important for understanding Moses (including his lessons on leadership) than the meaning of the one thing he does not do—go to the Promised Land. His history, Hebrew history, would be entirely different if Moses had gone to Canaan but left his words behind, rather than staying behind and sending the words ahead. If his pupils, the people, are to become teachers in their own right, they must have their own experiences from which to learn. There comes a time when students can learn only if their teacher is not there to tell them what to do. The story of how the Hebrews became an independent people, able to make their own history, is the other side of why Moses does not go with them to the Promised Land.

MERIBAH: GIVING UP ON THE FUTURE

Back in Kadesh, after the spies had been severed from the body of Israel
and the rebellious swallowed up, everything was supposed to be settled,
but in fact the situation was no different than before. Enter the murmuring chorus: there is no water to drink, the cattle and people will
die—unless, of course, they have already been so fortunate as to perish
with their brethren in Korah's rebellion. The place is "evil" (Num. 20:5).
There are no figs or pomegranates or vines—just those few things, it
happens, that the spies have brought back from Canaan.

Once more, in response to the chorus of complaints, Moses is to
draw water from the rocks. God instructs him: "Take the rod, and gather
thou the assembly together, thou and Aaron thy brother, and speak ye
unto the rock before their eyes; and it shall give forth his water, and
thou shalt bring forth to them water out of the rock: so thou shalt give
the congregation and their beasts drink" (Num. 20:8).

The command is explicit. Moses is to take the rod (symbol of power)
with him, but to *speak* to the rock to draw forth water. Instead, "Moses
lifted up his hand, and with his rod he smote the rock twice" (Num.
20:11).[5] Water flows; God will not put Moses down before his followers
now, but threat of punishment follows immediately. "Because ye believed
me not, to sanctify me in the eyes of the children of Israel," the Lord
declares, "therefore ye shall not bring this congregation into the land
which I have given them" (Num. 20:12).

After Moses' momentous sacrifices—has he not jeopardized his own
life for the sake of the people?—why does God refuse him his most ar-
dent wish? Striking a rock, or momentary anger, or fleeting callousness
seem justifications too slim to deny Moses entry to the Promised Land.
There must be a better reason. "Citing Rabbenu Hananel, Nahmanides
[Rabbi Moshe ben Nahman, 1194-1270] cuts close to the heart of the
matter: Moses made the fatal mistake of saying, 'Shall *we* bring you
forth water,' instead of saying 'Shall *God* bring you forth water,' as in
all the other miracles where the authorship of God is always explicitly
stressed (cf. Ex. 16, 8 'when the Lord giveth you meat in the evening
to eat'). The people might have been misled into thinking that Moses
and Aaron had extracted the water for them, by their own skill. Thus
they failed to 'sanctify Me in the midst of the children of Israel.'"[6] If

that "mistake" were willful, it would be apparent immediately that Moses was guilty of idolatry.

At Meribah, Moses substitutes force for faith. In his hands, the rod reduces a divinely ordered act to a trickster's shenanigans. But the import runs deeper. If Moses' strongest leadership quality has been his ability to identify with the people, then the lack of faith at Meribah is a double one. Moses not only distances himself from God by doubting the adequacy of His work but also distances himself from the people by assuming power that was God's. Tired of the incessant murmurings, Moses taunts the people just before he strikes the rock: "Hear now, ye rebels; must we fetch you water out of this rock?" (Num. 20:10).

Instead of exhorting a stiffnecked people to greater faith, Moses condescends to their plea with an arrogant jeer. His words imply acceptance of the people's evil (separating himself from it) rather than hope of overcoming it. "Ye rebels" assumes very much what Aaron had presumed in trying to rationalize fashioning the Golden Calf. At that point, Aaron had lamely pleaded for Moses' sympathy: "thou knowest the people, that they are set on mischief" (Exod. 32:22). Like Aaron's defense then, Moses' "Hear now, ye rebels" now becomes its own accusation. Similarly, Moses taunts the people with rebelliousness, yet is himself rebelling when he smites the rock without authority—the authority God alone can provide. Perhaps, after all, Moses does have more authority than he, or any man, can handle.

Korah, in rebelling, had turned Moses' own words about the equality of believers against him. In the rebellion at Meribah, Moses does usurp divine authority. A key consideration turns on the meaning of the plural "we" in "must we fetch you water out of this rock?" At first blush, the plural seemingly refers to Moses and Aaron. But M. Margaliot has other ideas. He believes that, seeing in Moses' hand the very rod through which God had worked His miracles, the people "would have understood Moses to mean by 'we' 'God and I.'" In this interpretation, Moses strikes the rock twice to show that water will not come. If this interpretation be granted, the nature of Moses' sin—denying God's willingness to help—is evident.[7] To this Eugene Arden adds that, in his anger, Moses assumes that God is angry, too, although there is nothing in the text to justify that assumption.[8]

A better explanation, because it is more powerful and more consistent, is that Moses was guilty of the worst form of idolatry—self-worship.

Spiritually, he has gone back to slavery, as if to replace Pharaoh. Jacob Milgrom has forged an interpretation that does not require bending the text—the "we" does refer consistently to Aaron and Moses but nonetheless "indicates that Moses and Aaron publicly usurped the role of God."[9] For if it is clear that "we" means Moses and Aaron, the words that suggest they have the power to perform miracles are the essence of idolatry—worshiping the work of one's own hands, as exemplified by the rod. Noting the lengths to which the Bible goes to distinguish between the magic of Egypt and the faith of Israel, Milgrom concludes that

> thus, the nature of Moses' sin far from being obscure or unjustified is now projected with startling clarity. Moses' sin was not an ordinary transgression. His defiance of God was not merely a countermanding of His order but a denial of His essence. In the sight of the assembled throngs of Israel Moses and Aaron muffed the opportunity to "sanctify" God "before the eyes of the children of Israel" (Num. 20:12, 27:24; Deut. 32:51). Instead they showed no trust, acting treacherously, rebelling against God (Num. 20:24, 27:14; "you changed My words"—Ramban's rendering), setting themselves up in His place, arrogating to themselves the divine power to draw forth water miraculously from the rock.
>
> Thus all prior incidents of Moses' petulance and doubt pale before the magnitude of this sin. For now, in a direct address to his people, Moses ascribes miraculous powers to himself and Aaron. Indeed, by broadcasting one word, "we shall bring forth," Moses and Aaron have made themselves into God....
>
> One final observation. If correct, we have uncovered the true pathos in the personal tragedy of Moses. Israel's teacher is condemned for revealing the very failing which he tried to rectify in his charges. There was a promised land also of the spirit to which he successfully brought his people, but which he himself failed to reach.[10]

What had previously seemed a minor matter—why does God instruct Moses to bring his rod if he is not supposed to use it?—now becomes more important. An easy way out is to say that this version is edited from the earlier Massah incident, when Moses strikes the rock with God's approval and water flows. I am not in favor of eliminating profound problems by attributing them to editorial errors. More consistent interpretations would be either that Moses is being tested or that Moses would loom greater in the eyes of God if the rod of authority were available but need not be used by him who would instead rely on faith.

How do Moses' actions at Meribah differ from those at the other times when the people complained? Elsewhere, Moses punished the people either to keep them together in acknowledging a single divine authority or to avoid the greater evil of their total destruction. In the other episodes, Moses accepted that evil would take place and that evildoers must be punished. But at Meribah, driven back to his original impulsive behavior, Moses displaces the intent of divine punishment—that is, from exemplifying better behavior, he reverts to demonstrating his own personal power. At Meribah, Moses, like Aaron at the Golden Calf, becomes an accomplice of the people. He neither punishes the Hebrews for doing the wrong thing nor exhorts them to do good. Moses acts as if he expected (wanted?) them to rebel against the Lord. To give up on the future possibilities of the people (as the legend recounted in the epigraph to this section indicates) makes Moses unfit for future leadership. Leaders who do not identify with their people, as Zipporah understood, do not even get as far as Egypt; they get buried along the way.

Loosely translated, the word Massah, where the earlier water episode took place, means "strife." Meribah means "contention."[11] The question is, who is striving or contending with whom?

Rods and Serpents

The physical expression of acting without thinking (remembering) is Moses' rod. Striking the rock of faith (be it faith in the people or in the God who once stood on it) is Moses' sin.

Throughout the Pentateuch, the rod of Moses represents both the power faith can provide and the consequences that result from lack of faith. The rod that heals can also kill. From the very beginning, when God bids Moses use it, the rod is both a shepherd's staff and a serpent that, like the archserpent of Genesis, can become an agent of temptation. The final link in this chain of imagery merges rod and serpent into one.

On the borders of Edom, once more, "the people spake against God, and against Moses, Wherefore have ye brought us up out of Egypt to die in the wilderness? for there is no bread, neither is there any water; and our soul loatheth this light bread" (Num. 21:5). What bread they have is apparently not good enough for them. So the Lord sends fiery serpents to kill many people. "Therefore the people came to Moses, and said, We have sinned, for we have spoken against the Lord, and against thee: pray unto the Lord, that he take away the serpents from us" (Num. 21:7). After Moses prayed for the people, the Lord said, "Make thee a fiery serpent, and set it upon a pole: and it shall come to pass, that every one that is bitten, when he looketh upon it, shall live" (Num. 21: 8). Is God tempting Moses—suggesting that the brass serpent (an idol) can save the people? If people believed in God enough to walk past the serpent, they would not need it in the first place.

In a sequence of episodes that share the verbal cognates *smite, smote, smitten,* the rod has changed from an instrument of authorized violence at the Sea of Reeds to a means of transgressing God's work at Meribah. Now, with snake and rod fused into the brazen serpent, the image functions as a permanent spiritual reminder: "Every one that is bitten, when he looketh upon it, shall live" (Num. 21:8). But of what, exactly, is this passage supposed to remind the reader?

During his reign, King Hezekiah of Judah, who, we are informed, "trusted in the Lord God of Israel" (II Kings 18:5, 7), destroyed places and symbols of unauthorized worship. Among other things, Hezekiah "brake in pieces the brazen serpent that Moses had made: for unto those days the children of Israel did burn incense to it: and he called it Nehushtan" (II Kings 18:4). At a later time, at least, the brazen serpent Nehushtan was recognized as an idol. Needless to say, interpretations abound.[12] N.H. Snaith says that the story in Numbers is "designed to justify the continuance of the cult during the kingdoms by associating the serpent with Moses."[13] Hugo Gressmann's seminal study *Mose und seine Zeit* (Moses and his time) incorporates the earlier and the later uses. Roughly translated, Gressmann says that "since the brazen serpent, like Moses' staff had a cult, and since with respect to its form, it is nothing else but a serpent staff, there can be no doubt—after all this—that the two are identical."[14] We are being told something about Moses and his rod. But what?

I shall follow the rabbis in the Mishnah, who do not interpret verses such as these as describing magical events but as teachings about the responsibility of Israel. That the position of Moses' hands at Rephidim should make for victory or defeat is not considered possible. Similarly, conceiving of a snake as a life-giving being is out of the question. It is Israel's relationship to these symbols that interests the rabbis. In both instances, the Babylonian Talmud comments that when the Israelites look upward, bending "their hearts to their father in heaven," they win in war or are healed in body.[15]

In many ways, Christians have been more interested than have Jews in the brazen serpent. Saint John cites Jesus as saying, "And as Moses lifted up the serpent in the wilderness, even so must the Son of man be lifted up" (John 3:14). In this view, by looking to heaven, man is healed. The serpent stands for resurrection.

In the context of Mosaic lore, the brazen serpent is a caricature—strength become weakness. If you can name it, embrace it, control it, summon it up for your own personal purposes, it is not worth having. If the people had faith, if they looked to the Lord rather than to their own strength, as this instance of divine irony is designed to remind them, they would not have ended up worshiping a snake.

A spear also is a staff and a serpent. The episode of Phinehas, who spears defiant pollution through its private parts, occurs after the scene with the brazen serpent. This time I shall call not upon the biblical account, but on a more graphic reenactment in a rabbinic legend that leaves little to the imagination.

> Now Zimri, son of Salu, Prince of Simeon, sought out Cozbi, the daughter of Balak the king, and said to her: "Be mine!" She answered: "My father reserveth me for Moses, in order that through his sin ye shall all be lost." "I will show thee that I am greater than Moses." And, taking her by her hair, he dragged her to the feet of the Prophet, and cried: "Son of Amram, is this woman permitted to me?" "Thou knowest my reply," said the Prophet. "Where, then," retorted Zimri, "didst thou go to find Zipporah, the daughter of Jethro? Cometh she from the Patriarchs, the Midianites whom thou didst take to wife in the time of thy delights? Wherefore dost thou forbid us that which thou didst permit to thyself?"
>
> Moses paled, and was silent. The Elders wept around him, and Zimri cried: "Live, if it seem good to thee, according to the laws that thou hast made, but by what right would ye bend down others to them? Shall we be thy slaves rather than Pharaoh's?"… Stripping her veils from Cozbi, and stripping from himself his cloak, he threw himself upon the naked girl, and knew her, beneath the eyes of the Prophet and of Israel.
>
> Then Phinehas, son of Eleazar, son of Aaron, the High Priest, cried out: "Moses, Moses, our master, hast thou, then, forgotten thy Torah? Will God's chastisement suffice His justice if men themselves do not

do His justice?" And beneath the eyes of Israel and the Prophet, thrusting into the bodies of the two clasped sinners his sharp and shining lance, he made of them a single corpse, that he raised on high, like a standard, towards the Lord. The pestilence ceased: they ceased from their sins. Twenty-four thousand Israelites were dead.[16]

Cozbi stands for the forbidden fruit that Moses has once tasted but later denies himself (he has no wife during the wanderings) and that the law denies to the people. Flesh is put upon the bare bones of that phrase about "whoring after" strange gods. In Mendenhall's view, "We do not, in fact, have any historically plausible narrative which would indicate that the covenant community before this time conferred upon anyone the authority to put persons to death for violation of the covenant. Phinehas represents the transition from covenant to law: from the enforcement by Yahweh to the enforcement by human action."[17] Substance is given to this supposition by the graded distinction between the instructions given by God and Moses, as compared to Phinehas' direct action. The Lord wants the leaders hung in sight of the people; Moses wants those who have had intercourse with the women of Moab to be killed; but Phinehas spears those most culpable, in the very act. Spearing the sin is an individual act against an individual offense, unlike stoning—participated in by all—for deliberate desecration of the Sabbath. The saving spear is an extension of Moses' rod. It is not a symbol of the lack of desire—quite the contrary—but of its extinction, because its fulfillment is contrary to God's law.

In relation to Moses' continuing to wield the rod of God, what does Phinehas teach? Patently, that others among the Israelites are capable of leading, and their direct action may be more appropriate. Moses is no longer indispensable.

RENUNCIATION

For Moses thought that if his life were spared, he should be able everlastingly to restrain Israel from sin and to hold them forever in faith to the one God. But God said: "'Let it suffice thee.' If thy life were to be spared, men should mistake thee, and make a god of thee, and worship thee." "Lord of the world!"

replied Moses, "Thou didst already test me at the time when the Golden Calf was made and I destroyed it. Why then should I die?" God: "Whose son art thou?" Moses: "Amram's son." God: "And whose son was Amram?" Moses: "Kohath's son." God: "And whose son was he?" Moses: "Levi's son." God: "And from whom did all of these descend?" Moses: "From Adam." God: "Was the life of any one of these spared?" Moses: "They all died." God: "And thou wishest to live on?"

—Louis Ginzberg, *The Legends of the Jews*

The question of why Moses (who had sacrificed so much) was denied entrance to the Promised Land, so that he would be unable to experience everything he had worked for, has properly fascinated interpreters over the centuries. That this should happen to the greatest men among them—that it is precisely Moses' unique status that justifies his humbling—has been appreciated but not entirely accepted. In a way, this explanation gets by; but deep down, it does not satisfy. So let us look again at the hero whose renunciation becomes the ultimate affirmation that one lifelong self-struggle has not been in vain.

Interpretations of why Moses does not get to the Promised Land are less important than the fact that he does not go. The situation is its own statement. Leaders are not gods. The Hebrew people must not deify their leaders. Though the temptation to do so is understandable, it is also impermissible.

Retrospectively, as well as prospectively, the verdict is approved. Noth observes, "It is noteworthy that in the whole of pre-exile prophecy the name of Moses is mentioned with certainty only in a single passage, namely in Jer. 15:1. Here Moses and Samuel are designated as great intercessors for their people, so that indeed reference is made to these historical figures only in a very general way. And even in later prophecy Moses is mentioned only one more time, namely in Is. 63:11, 12, in connection with a retrospective view of God's acts of guidance in history—specifically the miracle at the Reed Sea."[18] Until this very day, the Passover Hagada, read in the home to recall and retell the story of the exodus from Egypt, contains, remarkably, no reference to Moses. The rabbis would countenance no cult of personality.[19]

Teaching is storytelling. In Murray Baumgarten's eloquent words, "Moses, the stutterer, makes the Hebrews into Jews by teaching them to tell their own story."[20] It is not only the knowledge Moses possessed that makes him significant but his ability to pass it on to future generations. By persuading others to retell his story in their own way, Moses enters their lives (and ours, too) but does not replace our experience with his.

Two different explanations for keeping Moses out of Canaan are offered. One is that Moses must pay for the sins of his followers. The other (which I take up first) is stated at the time of Aaron's death: "because ye rebelled against my word at the water of Meribah" (Num. 20: 24), the Lord tells Moses, Aaron shall not enter the land. Then God instructs Moses to "strip Aaron of his garments, and put them upon Eleazar his son" (Num. 20:26).[21] Whereupon Aaron dies. While he was still alive, the vestments of the priestly office were passed on to Aaron's successor. Aaron is to live on through the institutionalization of his office. Surrounded with safeguards, the symbol of his headship, his rod of leadership, can be transferred.

When Moses' time comes, the Lord instructs him to go to a mountaintop to "be gathered unto thy people; as Aaron thy brother died" (Deut. 32:50). Moses is to merge into the body of the people, ending up physically indistinguishable from the least of them. No one strips him of any office—possibly because he has none, possibly because his role is not to be reassigned. At the very end, after Moses is gone, it is declared in Deuteronomy that "there arose not a prophet since in Israel like unto Moses, whom the Lord knew face to face" (Deut. 34:10). It is but a short step to saying that there not only was not, but should not be, a successor to Moses.

At the time of the covenant (when Moses is invested with authority), much is made of reinforcing this interpretation—about death being the inevitable consequence of having seen the divine. The people ask Moses to intercede precisely because he can see the Lord "face to face" and live and they fear they cannot. Except in one blinding moment, to be sure, Moses, at best, sees only His back parts, an enormous concession now put into a different perspective. A man called Moses may have been on familiar terms with the Lord, but it will not happen to any other Israelite. Future fanaticism will be limited because henceforth no other man can presume, with divine authority, to speak for the Lord.

The Deuteronomic account goes on to specify the charges against Moses with which we are familiar, adding a slightly different emphasis.

The trespass against the Lord of which Moses is accused is said to occur "because ye sanctified me not in the midst of the children of Israel" (Deut. 32:51). Moses has struck the rock of faith on which the Lord once stood. So far, much the same as before.

But what about the reference to the act (or failure to act properly) taking place in "the midst" of the people? A puzzling element of prior invocation of people watching ("What will the Egyptians say?") was why anyone, especially the Lord, would worry about the opinions of others. The Egyptians were not there in the desert; they would hear of it only secondhand. As for the Hebrew people, why does it appear that God has somehow been shamed by Moses' behavior, as we might say, "in front of the children"?

Apparently appearances matter. Leaders are objects of attention. For good or for ill, their deeds (perhaps more than their words) speak for them. Leaders are also teachers in that their behavior inevitably constitutes an example that followers observe and from which, willy-nilly, followers will learn. The Lord is angry because Moses has taught the wrong lesson—anger over deliberation, force over persuasion, division over unity, rebellion over faith.

Why has Moses sought collective responsibility for punishment if he is not also to uphold a collective sense of right and wrong? If there is no common sense of shame, especially in a culture created around perceptions of purity, how can good conduct be enforced? The slave leader who always rules his people has no need of shame because his will alone matters, and he will always be there to enforce it. Anarchists need show shame only if they cannot compete by making new transactions. In equities, shame implies inequality. Leaders may be shamed by showing that they usurp more than their share of power. In hierarchies, shame is a result of violations of rules. Since a hierarchical regime depends on everyone, leader and led, following rules, it is most fearful of a public contagion of disobedience.

The leader who wants his people to follow cultural norms must be especially careful not only to command but also to exemplify those same standards. A generation like ours—from which shame appears to be fast disappearing, in which the very word has an almost quaint connotation, as if each person were to be the sole judge of his or her own behavior—may well find this verdict on Moses unconscionable (its basis being barely recognizable). Genesis Rabbah states that God sees a significant distinction between the "private" anger of Moses and his public display of anger. Being human, leaders may have private doubts and weaknesses. But to display them in public is unforgivable. After all, this midrash continues, Moses did worse things than striking the rock at Meribah; he showed even less faith when he doubted God's ability to provide in the incident of the quails. Seeking an analogy, the midrash compares God "to a king who had a beloved subject and there was an argument between him and the king where he showed disrespect and the king didn't discipline him. Days passed and once again an argument erupted between the king and his subject. But this time it was in front of the king's legions and the king had him put to death. And thus God said to Moses first, it was between us, now that it has been done before the public this is not tolerable. As it is written: 'To sanctify me before the eyes of Israel.'"[22]

The other explanation for denying Moses entry to the Promised Land is based on words attributed to Moses himself. Referring to his recollection of the spies (who refused to take the land and were punished by death in the desert), Moses adds, "Also the Lord was angry with me for your sakes, saying, Thou also shalt not go in thither" (Deut. 1:37). Translating the term "angry" to "furious"[23] makes the indictment still stronger. The great question is what is to be made of the phrase "for your sakes"?

There are many possibilities. Use of the phrase in connection with the spies might imply, as Winnett has it, that "Moses' guilt arose solely out of the fact that he was the leader of the people and not out of anything that he personally had done or failed to do."[24] This interpretation might be strengthened by the moral consideration that leaders should share the fate of their people. It is, in fact, true that leaders are often punished for the sins of their followers (and vice versa). Still, this interpretation contradicts efforts throughout the exodus to assign individual responsibility for sin—let alone the statements in Numbers blaming Moses personally for misuse of the rod of leadership at Meribah.

"We must not think here of the pattern of the great prophets of judgement," von Rad writes, "but of the way in which Moses himself discharged the duties of his office in accordance with the Deuteronomic conception: interceding, suffering as the representative, actually dying, and therefore this portrait of a prophet is in harmony with that of the suffering servant of God in Deutero-Isaiah."[25] As a Christian conception, this interpretation has merit; as a Jewish view, certainly in the Torah, it does not. Jews may be expected to suffer, to undergo privation, to take their chances, but not directly to do themselves in.[26] Whenever, as in the negotiations with Pharaoh, a life is directly threatened, evasive action may be taken. God alone has the right to take life.[27]

It is not as if dying in the wilderness is Moses' first or favorite idea. Quite the contrary! He holds onto life and to the promise of the land with all the tenacity for which he is famous. After all, he is, by biblical account, 120 years old and might be expected to die. Just as Moses tries at the burning bush to know God's name and, after the Golden Calf to see God's face, he is nothing if not persistent in trying to reach the Promised Land. If Moses achieves only a glimpse of Canaan, as he gets only a glimpse of God, something other than unvarnished self-sacrifice by his own will is at work.

Listen to the imploring words Moses ascribes to himself as he tries once more to bend the will of God. The form of address used, "Lord God," appears only twice in Deuteronomy, both times in a personal plea:[28]

> O Lord God... I pray thee, let me go over, and see the good land that is beyond Jordan, that goodly mountain, and Lebanon.
>
> But the Lord was wroth with me for your sakes, and would not hear me: and the Lord said unto me, Let it suffice thee; speak no more unto me of this matter.
>
> Get thee up into the top of Pisgah, and lift up thine eyes westward, and northward, and southward, and eastward, and behold it with thine eyes: for thou shalt not go over this Jordan. [Deut. 3:24-27]

"Speak no more" is a tough line for God to take after Moses' lifetime of service.

I make no claim to have a better interpretation than anyone else, either here or elsewhere in this book. Too many possibilities remain unexplored. If there is merit in the interpretation I am about to venture, it lies, as with those that have gone before, in the value of the questions I am asking about leadership. Supposing that Moses (and through him, his people) are being taught lessons in leadership, what does denying Moses the right to enter Canaan signify?

Starting from the firmest ground, the Torah teaches that even God's chosen mediator, with whom He speaks directly, must be set limits. No man is blameless in the sense that he will not attempt, if allowed, to become more powerful than is good for himself or for others. With-holding Canaan from Moses is meant to show the necessity of limits, categories that cannot be crossed—even as limits exist in the principles of the religion Moses helped found. That Moses constantly strives to cross over Jordan—implying that he could lead the people in perpetuity, for there would always be new challenges for which they were unprepared without him—shows how much Moses, like his people, needs bounda-ries. Despite his subservience to the Lord, even Moses, were his power unlimited, might choose to be a god or godlike.

Moses is never physically or psychologically described. We see him only in action, his personality totally embedded in reactions to historical events, and with no status outside of the history in which he himself is an actor. Moses is presented as unique precisely in order to guard against any codification of godlike status for future leaders.

There are other protections against a Moses cult as well. He is buried in a valley near Moab, the narrative stating that "no man knoweth of his sepulchre unto this day" (Deut. 34:6). If no one knows (read "should know") where Moses is buried, no one can organize a cult around his grave.

There is no one "like unto Moses" (Deut. 34:10), the last line of Deuteronomy says, because there is not supposed to be. Why not? A new Moses would present the danger of a religion and a people permanently organized around one personality. A new Moses might also make new laws. Of course, the prohibition against adding to, or subtracting from, the laws cannot be taken literally, or it would make future development impossible; its purpose is to prevent new lawgivers from introducing practices that violate essential tenets of the religion. Without change, no continuity is possible. Incessant change makes continuity impossible.

Only the greatest leader is able to inculcate principles so profound that other people can successfully implement them well into the future. God is trying to teach Moses that the greater accomplishment is to have done this without going into Canaan. Moses is by now an old man. Physical death cannot be of great importance to him. The hard thing for Moses is not death, but rather his absence at the culmination of all his plans.

When Moses says that he does not get to go to Canaan because "the Lord was angry with me for your sakes," he is saying that it would not be good for the people if the leader who had taught them how to assume self-government were to deny it to them by his perpetual presence. Moses the eternal teacher would then instead be Moses the permanent master. What Moses teaches in Deuteronomy is not just law but institutions for the transmission of law, continuity of leadership to make the law effective. It is better for the people that Moses die physically than that his character be assassinated morally.

In his final phase of leadership, Moses includes provisions to help future leaders avoid the danger to which he has almost succumbed. Having learned that no leader is indispensable, Moses relinquishes his own role, while simultaneously guaranteeing that the people will not be "as sheep without a shepherd" (Num. 27:17). Moses inaugurates a system of checks by institutionalizing forms of leadership and by delegating authority to numerous others, who are themselves further subdivided in function and limited in power. His own paramount achievement, perhaps—achieved only by continuous inner struggle—is that he subscribes to the limitations on leadership he seeks to impose upon others. In Deuteronomy, by then teacher as well as leader, Moses continually exhorts the people to remember the great events of Israel's history, rather than his personal role; in order to avoid the danger of a new personality cult, Moses effaces himself. Still, left to his own devices, without external constraint, Moses might not have let his people go.

The final events in Moses' life suggest that he who teaches must continue to learn. Meribah, as we have seen, represents Moses' own supreme moment of forgetfulness. Backsliding even more than the people, Moses forgot that he was to inspire them to learn and teach them to aim at a higher goal than slavery. Since after the apostasy of the spies, the generation that left Egypt is doomed to wander in the desert, Moses must reaffirm his bond by sharing their fate. Learning to accept this responsibility is Moses' last challenge. The fact that his self-renunciation coincides with his farewell address tells us that leaders must make themselves redundant; and that the best teacher, or leader, leaves a living tradition that others can continue to shape. By reactivating the events of history in the light of present and future significance, Moses inaugurates a tradition of interpretation, a model of self-scrutiny, and critical, historical consciousness.

Moses eventually understands that the chief virtue in leaders is to make themselves unnecessary. To be a "nursing father"—knowing that the child may die, will probably rebel, and must be allowed to make history on its own—is the essence of Mosaic leadership. Teaching that leads to learning that creates new teachers is a circular process of renewal, not a linear model of leadership.

TEACHING THROUGH TALKING

When Moses dies in Moab, he is spoken of as "the servant of the Lord" (Deut. 34:5), not the master of the people. Moses is subject to the same law as all the people—more rigorously, actually, because his punishment for failing in faith at Meribah is greater in proportion to the offense than such consequences would be for other people, expectations about whom are lower.

It is said that Moses died "according to the word of the Lord" (Deut. 34:5). A more literal translation would be that Moses died "mouth-to-mouth" or "by the kiss" of God. This fond farewell is also a kiss of death. That Moses goes with the Lord's blessing is evident. The kiss signifies that it is right for Moses to die, that the kiss seals his lips outside the Promised Land, into which only the written words of the Lord's prophet can go.

In Deuteronomy Moses seeks to pass on what he has learned about leadership and followership—who should be obeyed, what should be done, and how change should come about. Deuteronomy is not Greek philosophy; it is a self-exemplifying book, not a theoretical system. History is the teacher, and the lessons are in the deeds; the applications are explicitly intended to be inferred anew in each generation. "It is characteristic of the rationalizing trend in Deuteronomy," von Rad writes, "that the story of God's actions is regarded principally from its educational aspect."[29] Moses teaches that the people need leaders through whose examples they can learn to become teachers themselves. Memory is the gene of the community through which parents teach children the law. As an aid to remembrance, a warning against disobedience, and a text for learning, the Torah is passed from teacher to student to teacher.[30] What could be a more persuasive point about teaching than the Lord's indication that He, too, needs instruction? Moses would not have been made a mediator between God and man if the Lord had not wished to learn about the limits of human nature. The two crucial scenes of intercession—the episodes of the Golden Calf and the spies—also are examples of teaching, through which God learns from Moses about keeping the covenant in a condition of constant repair. God, as well as Moses and Israel, is a "bloody bridegroom" who has married for better or for worse. The role of intercessor exists precisely to renew the faith on which the covenant is based when one party or another threatens to renege.

Covenants are broader than constitutions. The structure of relationships under which the covenant operates and is enforced must be perpetual. Without such continuity, the everyday expectations on which social life is based would be disrupted. Though the covenant is permanent, its constitution is not, alterations being subject to experience. As Israel is conceived to be the "first-born" of God, with the penalties as well as the preference this provides, it was expected that the first-born after the exodus would be Israel's chief protectors.[31] The Golden Calf episode showed Moses that this was not going to work. The first-born were perhaps too like the people to be able to restrain them(selves). By answering Moses' call to stand on the Lord's side to help enforce the covenantal injunction against idolatry, the Levites (a tribe apart, sufficiently separate to give special support) took the place of the first-born. The Levites, in turn, were then made dependent on the support of the other tribes. Leaders must learn that important relationships have to be continuously reestablished—the covenant being a preeminent example—without their personal presence.

THE BOOK

"Moses the man of God" (Deut. 33:1) blesses the people, tells them how fortunate they are, looks over toward the Holy Land, and then dies. The narrative tells us that the people wept and mourned for thirty days but then, as must be, went on their way. "Joshua...," it is said at the end, "was full of the spirit of wisdom; for Moses had laid his hands upon him" (Deut. 34:9). Who can say whether the rest of the sentence is intended to be ironical: "and the children of Israel hearkened unto him, and did as the Lord commanded Moses" (Deut. 34:9). If the people were to treat him as they had his predecessor, Joshua had his work cut out for him.

Moses had few illusions about the future performance of his people. Whether written in afterwards or predicting forward, Moses' words fit his philosophy:

> For I know thy rebellion, and thy stiff neck: behold, while I am yet alive with you this day, ye have been rebellious against the Lord; and how much more after my death?
>
> Gather unto me all the elders of your tribes, and your officers, that I may speak these words in their ears, and call heaven and earth to record against them.
>
> For I know that after my death ye will utterly corrupt yourselves, and turn aside from the way which I have commanded you; and evil will befall you in the latter days; because ye will do evil in the sight of the Lord, to provoke him to anger through the work of your hands. [Deut. 31:27-29]

But not content to end with negativism, Moses makes the people a gift, the book of the law. Their few triumphs, but also their many transgressions, are recorded there. The book will be a testimony against wrongdoing: it is to be placed "in the side of the ark of the covenant of the Lord your God, that it may be there for a witness against thee" (Deut. 31:26).

Enlightened self-interest is not to be despised, but neither is it to be depended upon. Charity is demanded, for example, not only because one understands having been poor (and might be so again) but also because helping the poor is an unconditional obligation imposed by God. "He is the Rock," Moses says (Deut. 32:4). This grounding of obligation in divine command may appear arbitrary but, in the Mosaic conception, it serves as an essential counterweight to the usual human proclivities. When, out of self-interest or self-absorption, men will not act as they should, there remains the divine imperative, "Thou shalt not oppress..." or else "it be sin unto thee" (Deut. 24:14-15).

Safeguards against official abuse were doubtless necessary, but there was also the evil of the people to consider. Worst among these was a tendency to confuse selection by God to be His people with election to the divine. To have been named the Lord's people too easily could become the right to the Name. Moses must make the people understand that Israel's election is a burden, not a reward for elevated moral character: "Not for thy righteousness," Moses teaches, "or for the uprightness of thine heart, dost thou go to possess their land: but for the wickedness of these nations the Lord thy God doth drive them out from before thee, and that he may perform the word which the Lord sware unto thy fathers, Abraham, Isaac, and Jacob" (Deut. 9:5).

Self-renunciation and self-teaching coincide in the Mosaic tradition. When Moses reshapes the events in Deuteronomy, we find a multiple layering. Moses teaches now in a new way with a renewed emphasis on both what he was taught and what he taught. As the first commentator on the events of Israel's history, he reinterprets his own role with a two-fold result: the law and Commandments must be passed on to the future, but Moses himself has no ultimate authority; he is neither a paradigmatic leader nor the only writer in Israel's history.

The absorption of Moses into the book means that the book must be reread, reinterpreted; it is open to each generation. Just as leaders are historically contingent, the meaning of the Pentateuch is to be continually informed by new historical contexts. Commentary has an equal authority with the original authorship. On earth, the majority should rule.

This is a book about a writer; in the spirit of the self-exemplification of Mosaic leadership in the Bible, Moses the stutterer has become a teacher of language. Moses wants the reader to invest himself in the words, changing himself as he interprets them. Memory should guide interpretation so that the past can inform the present.

Is Moses finally blotted out of the Lord's book?—physically, yes; spiritually, no. Above all, the book abides. The gift of the book remains precious because it is a guide to (not a personal replacement for) self-government. Moses needs all his self-control to pass on to the children of Israel the greatest gift: self-confidence that, though setbacks will occur, the people can make it on their own. The right to make their own mistakes is all any people can ask.

ABUSE OF LEADERSHIP

Books are public property. The written Torah, once it is "published," so to speak, is two-edged. It can be used against the leader as well as by him. Once the Torah has come down to the people, anyone can quote it. Thus begins the oral tradition. The existence of a Torah to be talked about prefigures Moses' highest principle of leadership—to send ahead his teaching rather than himself.

To show that the change to hierarchy is not merely a cover for personal aggrandizement, Moses acts out the limits on leadership in hierarchies by denying himself (or being denied) entry to the Promised Land. When Moses institutionalizes various leadership roles—when he separates his own acts of leadership and makes divisions among judges, priests, and national leaders—he disperses the power he was tempted to withhold for himself. His own self-effacement ensures both that the tradition will be carried on and that it will continually emphasize scrutiny of one's own objectives.

The Mosaic teaching on leadership begins (with the first Hebrew Moses helps) and ends (by keeping him outside the Promised Land) with warnings against its abuses. For followers, the classical dilemma of leadership is that a regime or leader strong enough to get them through enormous difficulties may prove too great a threat to their future liberties. Abuse of power is always a temptation. And, as Moses shows, the greatest temptation—to usurp divine prerogatives, to think mere man can dispense life and death—afflicts the greatest leaders. In discussing atonements for inadvertent transgressions, for instance, the Torah tells Jews what to do "*if*" a soul errs, but refers, by contrast, to situations "*when* a ruler hath sinned" (Lev. 4:2, 22; emphasis added).

A dilemma described by Kenneth Boulding sums up the universal experience with leadership: "The dismal theory of political science is that the skills which lead to the rise to power all too frequently unfit people to exercise it."[32] Is Moses different?

Moses is a founder. Does that entail additional rights, heavier responsibilities, or both? Sometimes the fact of founding a community of believers seems enough to justify almost any behavior. Knowing what Moses could not have known—that this community would last for thousands of years—some commentators see simple solutions to dilemmas whose outcome must have been in doubt at the time. They kill Moses with kindness, in a perverse way, by trying to minimize the element of force, and thus denigrate Moses' efforts to mitigate the terror. Moses' struggle to find ways of leading, without losing the moral stature he sought to attain with his people, is the leitmotif of the wanderings in the desert.

Moses travels a long distance from his early self-doubt as well as from his later self-assurance. He comes to realize that ambition must be

controlled, that—as Alexander Hamilton and James Madison were to argue so much later in defense of the U.S. Constitution—"ambition must
be made to counteract ambition." Recognizing that abuse of leadership is
as great a threat to a governmental system as no leadership at all, Moses
has to accept, more literally than the Federalists intended, that men are
no angels: "If men were angels, no government would be necessary. If
angels were to govern men, neither external nor internal controls would
be necessary. In framing a government which is to be administered by
men over men, the great difficulty lies in this: you must first enable the
government to control the governed; and in the next place oblige it to
control itself."[33]

Moses' encounter with God at the burning bush epitomizes this "great
difficulty." How is Moses to be "enabled" to lead a people; how is he to
be "obliged" at the same time to control himself? How can Moses be summoned to fulfill a unique historical role and simultaneously be reminded
that this unique position belongs not to him but to his people?

It is easy enough to lead when followers already are headed in the
same direction (for example, like Joseph). It is not so easy when the goal,
as the leader himself conceives it, suggests a different destination, or when
sacrifices must be imposed for a greater good. Selection of leaders is a
matter of finding those who will not refuse to use power yet also will
not abuse it for personal purposes. Risks are, however, most likely to be
undertaken by leaders who expect to be around to gather the rewards. In
Number 72 of *The Federalist*, Hamilton warns, "An ambitious man, too,
when he found himself seated on the summit of his country's honors,
when he looked forward to the time at which he must descend from the
exalted eminence for ever, and reflected that no exertion of merit on his
part could save him from the unwelcome reverse; such a man, in such
a situation, would be much more violently tempted to embrace a favo-
rable conjuncture for attempting the prolongation of his power, at every
personal hazard, than if he had the probability of answering the same
end by doing his duty." What about prolongation of leadership beyond
a single lifetime? Would not hereditary leadership provide incentives for
still better behavior? If so, George III should have been a model monarch.
Hence the authors of *The Federalist* thought it wise to rely on more than
the motives of individuals: "The desire of reward is one of the strongest incentives of human conduct;... the best security for the fidelity of
mankind is to make their interest coincide with their duty."[34]

Spinoza, who was sensitive to structural incentives for good behavior, wrote in approval of such a system of social safeguards:

> When those who govern... do anything wicked they always try to cover it up with a show of legality, and to persuade the people that they acted virtuously; which is easily done when they alone control the whole interpretation of the law. This in itself undoubtedly gives them the utmost freedom to indulge their desires and do everything they wish; but such freedom is largely removed if the right to interpret the laws is vested in another, and if, at the same time, their true meaning is so obvious to all that no one can be in any doubt about it.... Thus if the captains wished to be held in high honour by the people, they had—simply in their own interests—to be very careful to govern entirely by the written laws which were familiar to all. [35]

When Moses shares his authority with others, when he encourages the development of diverse institutions, he is also appealing to rival motives as a safeguard.

Moses himself instigates the plan of passing on the leadership under official auspices:

> And Moses spake unto the Lord, saying,
> Let the Lord, the God of the spirits of all flesh, set a man over the congregation,
> Which may go out before them, and which may go in before them, and which may lead them out, and which may bring them in; that the congregation of the Lord be not as sheep which have no shepherd.
> And the Lord said unto Moses, Take thee Joshua the son of Nun, a man in whom is the spirit, and lay thine hand upon him;
> And set him before Eleazar the priest, and before all the congregation; and give him a charge in their sight.
> And thou shalt put some of thine honor upon him, that all the congregation of the children of Israel may be obedient. [Num. 27:15-20]

In the Mosaic conception, leadership literally does mean going out in front, as in battle—figuratively, sticking your neck out. No nonsense about the leader bringing up the rear is countenanced. Cautious as in all things, the Lord has Moses put only "some of thine honor" on Joshua. One Moses is evidently enough.

Moses' most independent act of leadership is to ask God to set up a new leader. Whatever his fears for the future, Moses has overcome the fear of death and the longing for immortality—the ubiquitous human fear that the world will go to hell without us.

Moses teaches his people by leaving them. Were he to go with them to the Promised Land, he would no longer be a leader but a god, always knowing the difference between good and evil, therefore without need of hope or hope of improvement. By being denied their Moses, the Hebrew people were instructed to seek their own salvation anew in each generation. Just as the covenant is constantly broken and mended, so leadership cannot be exercised once or by one for all but only continuously by all together.

I argued earlier that Egypt was a school for Israel; messages sent to Egypt, so to speak, were meant to be received by Israel. The major message addressed to Pharaoh has come down to us in story and song as "Let my people go!" Only now we know that all along it was intended for Moses.

BARGAINING AND COMPROMISE

Ahad Ha-am, the Hebrew essayist, has his own ideas about why Moses does not go to the Promised Land. Apparently, Moses' ideals are too high. According to Ahad Ha-am, "Moses' vision is of the perfect society, of the what ought to be rather than the what is.... Because his vision is unqualified Moses must die without entering the Promised Land. The prophet is too uncompromising to be the leader of the people in the stark realities of the actual human situation. The leadership must pass to another more capable of coming to terms with life as it is, even though this involves a diminution of the dream. Thus Moses is the symbol of Israel's divine discontent with the present."[36] I disagree with the view that Moses was a perfectionist; except when operating under rules of equity, he constantly bargains and compromises.

From the first, Moses is a mediator, not an executioner. Born between two cultures, torn between a desire to learn the truth and fear of the consequences, an ambivalent Moses bargains at every turn. Compromises with the community are legion. The people will not leave Egypt on his word alone, so Moses offers signs. They will not leave at once, so Moses delays, using that time to escalate the demands being made of Pharaoh. Moses makes progress through compromise.

Moses may expect gratitude; but what little he gets does not get him very far. Each appeasing act—water, food, whatever—is met by demands for more. What appears to Moses to be ingratitude based on insatiable appetite seems to the Hebrews a result of insatiable demands on them made by Moses (and his God). If, indeed, the Torah were too heavy, if (as in one image) Mount Sinai were being held over the heads of the Israelites to coerce compliance,[37] failure would be entirely excusable. Here, too, we find compromise. Only direct, defiant, and knowledgeable disobedience is punished, and this only if judges can agree and if the entire community will carry out the sentence.

Wherever he can, Moses goes along with popular sentiment. As long as the tribes of Gad and Reuben will first fight for Canaan, Moses will let them settle east of the Jordan, outside the borders of the Promised Land. Moses will share his authority many times over as long as it accords with the law given by the Lord.

Implacability is not the only, or the dominant, Mosaic strategy. There is resort to force only when destruction of the people is threatened. The death penalty is invoked only when the core values—God, land, law—are at stake. Compromise, rather than implacability, is the common Mosaic mode of resolving conflict. We can with confidence describe Moses' leadership as an endless adjustment, a tissue of evasions and compromises; Moses always prefers persuasion.

The exception that proves the rule occurs within the regime of equity. Unable to maintain leadership (and hence the unity of his people with their God) without demonstrating that the spirit is in him, Moses does in his opponents before they can do the same to him. He cannot make concessions because, in an equity, compromise would be its own accusation of corruption.

In sum, Moses compromises most in anarchy, taking almost any bargain he can get, and in hierarchy, where he avoids confrontation by obfuscating differences. Only in his charismatic phase, as the leader of an equity, does Moses put his principles above the people.

Not only Moses but the heavenly hosts themselves are subject to suspicion. The Book of Job tells us that the Lord "putteth no trust in His servants and His angels He chargeth with folly."[38] If we were to ask about

Moses' indispensability (the mental experiment of the "actor-dispensability" test urged by students of leadership), the answer would have to be an emphatic "No!" There can be no indispensable leader. When Moses accepted his God, he simultaneously accepted his human boundaries.

This is why Moses is denied perfection—his Promised Land. Or, to take up a parallel, David is denied the building of the temple, which must be turned over to Solomon.[39] The ordinary man is enjoined to complete the everyday activities that make up life—planting, marrying, building (Deut. 20:5-7)—but the great man is forbidden to do so, lest he come to worship his own work. Only the Almighty begins and ends revolutions; human beings have to take their place in the evolution of consciousness, taking their chances by passing along unfinished work to others. Even at the end, when God digs Moses' grave (so that no man will know where it is), completeness—to end as well as to begin, to control final consequences as well as initial causes—is denied to Moses. And to whom is it more necessary to deny this godliness than to those who have come the closest?

THE CHARACTER OF MOSES

A certain king, having heard of Moses' fame, sent a renowned painter to portray Moses' features. On the painter's return with the portrait the king showed it to his sages, who unanimously proclaimed that the features portrayed were those of a degenerate. The astonished king journeyed to the camp of Moses and observed for himself that the portrait did not lie. Moses admitted that the sages were right and that he had been given from birth many evil traits of character but that he had held them under control and succeeded in conquering them. This, the narrative concludes, was Moses' greatness, that in spite of his tremendous handicaps, he managed to become the man of God. Various attempts have, in fact, been made by some rabbis to ban the further publication of this legend as a denigration of Moses' character.

—'Tiferet Yisrael,' legend recorded by Lipschuetz b. Gedaliah

Father Zossima in Dostoevsky's *The Brothers Karamazov*, whose horrible odor at death reeks of his possession of all the human qualities, is reminiscent of Moses in the legend "Tiferet Yisrael."[40] Only the word is holy; not so the body of Moses, which is not to be venerated.

The few direct characterizations of Moses in the Bible are elusive. That he is the servant of God who spoke with him face to face tells us only of Moses' importance, while simultaneously stressing his subordinate status. The closest approach to delineating the man himself—"(Now the man Moses was very meek, above all the men which were upon the face of the earth)" (Num. 12:3)—is the most elusive of all. It occurs as a parenthetic remark in the midst of the accusations of unholy marriage leveled against Moses by Miriam and Aaron. Does this meekness, however translated (humility?), mean that Moses is mild-mannered? Hardly. Does it suggest that Moses wanted nothing for himself? No; he may covet less in some ways, such as material rewards, but in others Moses wants much more than any man can, or should, have: to know the name and see the glory of God. Moses' attributes are proverbial, that is, opposites.[41] Long-suffering, no doubt, but also quick to anger; patient, yes, but also rash; wise, to be sure, yet often wrong. Unless we are to make of Moses a Uriah Heep, too 'umble by 'alf, we have to take another tack.

Moses has reason to be modest. If meek means much imposed upon, Moses (like Balaam's ass) certainly qualifies. If meek means admitting mistakes, Moses does. Coming closer to the matter at issue, there is a meekness born of recognizing one's own faults sufficiently to intercede for others who also are weak. Indeed, Moses almost goes too far in his intercessions, saving those who will one day return to plague him.

Moses never entirely overcomes error. That is the meaning of being human. No man lives forever or gets to complete the work of history. Divinity lies beyond a barrier, which no man can pass. When Moses is shown the land of Canaan from a great height, as if the boundaries of his property are being pointed out to him,[42] the two aspects of his limitations merge: he is given a share in the land even as he is kept from occupying it. Moses is not the Creator, and he has rejected becoming the second father of his people. He is to remain their teacher, who saw more clearly than other men, but nevertheless at a distance.

Moses' teaching on failure is splendidly stated by David C. Rapoport:

The most profound consequence of the mediation is a radical transformation of the community's understanding of the proof and meaning of its mission. Originally, proof was always associated with success:
setback created panic for fear that God, the sole architect of their successes, could be tiring of the enterprise. The renewed Covenant is final
proof that God is irrevocably bound, and ironically, the commitment
is strengthened and made more intelligible by Israel's provocations. Because it knows Him to be entirely faithful, setbacks or misfortunes now
signify Israel's inadequacies or failures—which may delay but can never
annul fulfillment of the divine promise. As the locus of responsibility
shifts so must the response. Misfortunes no longer dissolve confidence;
now they can intensify or renew it, generating greater community efforts. Israel learns the secret that any community whose life is based
on a promise to be fulfilled in the indefinite future must learn—how
to interpret failure to fortify faith.[43]

Moses' course is not upward and onward. His fortunes wax and wane
more than most. From abandonment and near-death at birth to becoming a prince of Egypt; from being a shepherd of sheep to becoming a
leader of men; from the status of a would-be ruler with a land of his
own to that of a wanderer in the desert; from proud exodus to wearying
mutiny, Moses goes as much in circles as in a straight line. Until Moses
understands that the "medium is the message," that the ups and downs
are his destination, his disappointment is understandable and he may be
excused for doubting the potential illumination. In this respect, those
who come after are more fortunate; they can see that Moses' life is not
to be imitated but rather to be understood. Would-be imitators cannot
say that they, too, are Mosaic merely because they are long-suffering or
quick to anger.

The Bible hardly offers us an exemplary Moses. Indeed, the narrative emphasizes the nonexemplary leader on two separate counts. On the
one hand, though he alone can converse directly with God, it is made
clear that Moses is mortal. The leader who delivers a people from slavery
does not, for example, become the guarantor of their ultimate freedom.
The requirements of freedom and slavery differ. This is the prescriptive
conclusion, one that Moses must learn and that we may draw: leaders
of free men should not be cult figures.

On the other hand, neither is Moses' leadership a model for imitation. Desiring hard-and-fast guidelines for his leadership, Moses instead receives God's Commandments and the Law. The Commandments stipulate basic moral precepts for individual behavior, but their import is so general as to demand continual reinterpretation. The laws offer precise prescriptions for individual observance, but they are too specific to cover the broader issues of leadership. Without learning, the Law and the Commandments remain but dead letters.

LEADING AS LEARNING

The tension between leading and learning and teaching is at the heart of Moses' career as a political leader. Were I to offer a synopsis of his development in terms of these three themes, these would be the bare outlines. Moses is called to leadership, but he must first learn how to lead—hence he practices with a small god, Pharaoh. At this learning stage, Moses undertakes little independent action. Yet if God gives no directives beyond "Go unto Pharaoh," how do we explain Moses' passive role here? Why should Moses be sent to Pharaoh if he is only to pass on God's command? The point of the Pharaoh interlude, I argue, is a lesson for Moses in negative leadership. Pharaoh, a leader who is unable to learn from mistakes, teaches Moses by bad example. Slavery is bad because it corrupts master as well as slave. If the slave has no need to learn, because he has no need to make decisions for himself, the master loses the capacity to learn from the experience of teaching.

In the second phase of his leadership, following the escape from Egypt, Moses demonstrates that he has indeed learned. At Mount Sinai, Moses engages in his first independent action; he has realized that one who is to lead cannot always expect to be led. The people, however—still overly dependent on their leader, having forgotten the meaning of the exodus and fearing that Moses may have abandoned them—return to idol worship. Moses' intercession does save the people from total destruction; but it is the argument he makes on Israel's behalf that marks this act as a monumental moment of leadership. Moses not only convinces God that there is a human agency that can punish evil but also prevents annihilation by reminding God not to forget His promise to deliver this people. Moses not only gets God to accept human error, even while punishing it, but also ties God to an errant people by a perpetual covenant. Moses teaches, then, what he himself has learned: the ultimate act of leadership is to bind oneself to a people who cannot be expected to reciprocate.

By this act of binding, as with Abraham before him, Moses makes himself whole. The split in himself, which he shares with Jacob, is healed when Moses attaches himself to Israel, first physically by Zipporah's circumcision, the sign of the covenant, and then morally, when he refuses to usurp Abraham's place as father of the people, choosing instead to share his followers' fate. The unity of God with the people of Israel is Moses' own completeness. One God, one people, one land, and now one Moses. Just as the Akedah, the binding of Isaac—by allowing nothing and no one to be worshiped for itself—provided the faith to preserve the children of Israel, so, too, the rejection of the Golden Calf—by making Israel into an idol-destroying people—unites them with their God in a perpetual covenant. By binding himself, Moses frees his people to act in history—to err, to learn, and to live with his teaching, but without his presence.

Moses' interrogation of his own experience as a leader and as a teacher leaves us with the challenge of learning for ourselves. In learning how to make sense of the past as part of an effort to create an intelligible present, past instances and present problems merge to become a common body of evidence. As a rabbinic legend tells it (see the epigraph to Chapter 1), Moses himself goes on learning about the teaching he first imparted. The tradition has become autonomous. Once it is out of his hands, once his teaching becomes Torah, Moses has to learn from it like everyone else.

GOD AND MOSES

When it is observed that the God of Moses performs miracles for him, the first implication drawn is that Mosaic leadership must be either irrelevant or unique. If Moses is more than mortal, he is irrelevant to the study of leadership; if he is unique, he cannot be copied. Either way,

Moses and his God appear as impediments to our understanding; if we cannot learn from them, they cannot teach us about leadership.

If, unlike other leaders, Moses had God on his side, the Torah would be teaching a lesson about leadership that only those who communicate with God can follow. If there is not only a deus ex machina, but a deus in machina, a god on whom Moses alone can call, his experience would be part of a private cult into which we cannot enter.

In the revolt against Egypt, the people obey Moses and not God. The Supreme Being, who is far away, cannot capture their allegiance—at least not yet. Not until their human leader is cut down to size can they see their God. The Hebrews, as a passive collectivity, do nothing except worry; they do not so much leave Egypt as get expelled. The Hebrew people play follow the leader; and their leader in the desert is not the transcendent God but the ascendent Moses.

There is nothing new in transformation being the work of the few who constitute a revolutionary vanguard (even a vanguard of one, though Moses obviously had helpers). What is unusual is the rapidity with which the hollowness of this leadership principle is exposed. The people fall apart the first time the leader fails to fill Pharaoh's previous role as provider. And, as soon as Moses is out of sight on Mount Sinai, he is also, as the proverb warns, out of mind.

When he does not provide immediate gratification, Moses is replaced by what he has always been to his followers—a golden cow for whom they have no use once he, the nursing father, stops giving milk. All the people want is a more benevolent master. Could Moses have achieved a revolution without God?

Moses transforms the collective consciousness of a people so that they can live on without him. To say that he could not have done this without God is true but insufficient. Alone, Moses could not have succeeded in his revolutions, but neither would he have tried. Without his ideals, he is just another gifted man. If Moses had been a prince of Egypt, for example, we would know nothing of him. God is the ground of Moses' existence, his axiom, and he is as entitled to test its working out in history as any other leader is to try out a different (and more profane) perspective.

What about the miracles? Wars, natural calamities, internal divisions within enemy ranks have frequently enabled leaders to do things they otherwise could not have done. Such opportunism (the dependence of

Bolsheviks on the weakening of czarism during World War I, for example, without which their revolution could hardly have begun) may not exactly be what we have in mind when we think of miracles. It is the ability of Moses to wield his wand at his own discretion—so as, say, to time a plague—that other leaders cannot imitate.

But what did Moses get for invoking God's miracles? A liberation of body but not of spirit. The crutches he won—the magic rod of leadership and the voice of Aaron to speak for him—became elements of self-delusion, almost self-destruction. Reliance on direct divine intervention is a mistake. Nehushtan, the brazen serpent, to cite but one instance, tells a tale of divine irony: God orders an idol made, only to show that it is unnecessary. Korah disappears into the earth, to mention another episode, but his conception of equity lives on.

The importance of divine intervention diminishes throughout the Bible. Only when Moses frees himself from it and accepts the human need to wrestle with history can he begin to free his people from the moral and mental fetters of slavery. The Egypt of those days was a specific place. But the slavery it symbolizes is a permanent condition, from which men must continually struggle to liberate themselves. It is not physical miracles for which Moses deserves praise—running contrary to nature, like the death of the first-born—but rather the miracle of moral rebirth, through which mankind occasionally can overcome the slavery of its self-absorption.

CONCLUSION
Leadership as a Function of Regime

This book makes two claims: one is that the biblical sense of leadership as a function of regime is more satisfactory than current conceptions in the social sciences; the other is that viewing the Bible as a teaching about leadership enhances its interpretation. The first claim involves learning from the Bible in order to improve understanding of leadership. The second claim uses the perspective of leadership to advance interpretation of the Bible. The two claims are connected by viewing leadership in the context of political regimes. In this concluding chapter, I begin by showing how social scientists have attempted to grapple with leadership as a general phenomenon. I then go on to elaborate a different conception in keeping with the biblical view, and conclude by applying this perspective to Moses' transformation of political regimes.

STUDIES OF LEADERSHIP IN THE SOCIAL SCIENCES

"The concept of leadership," writes Cecil A. Gibb in the *Encyclopedia of the Social Sciences*, "has largely lost its value for the social sciences, although it remains indispensable to general discourse."[1] But if all of us (including social scientists) find this term indispensable, why has it been

so unsatisfactory in social research? Some say the concept is so general
that researchers cannot tell to what leadership refers; others say the term
is too specific to cover the vast range of possibilities. What makes leadership too vast a subject to be encompassed?

Despite Gibb's claim, the topic spawns extensive studies. If leadership is an endangered species, it is not extinction that threatens. Rather,
the very tendency of the concept to engulf those factors supposed to
distinguish it makes the subject amorphous and indefinable. An analytic
history of the leadership debate will help us understand.

Early on in leadership studies, scholars assumed that leaders were
self-evident agents with certain physical or psychological traits that explained their rise to power.[2] It must have been disconcerting to discover
that the correct number of essential traits could vary from two to somewhere between nineteen and thirty,[3] and that universal traits stubbornly
refused to reveal themselves. Worse, people supplied with those hypothetical traits often did not assume leadership positions, however broadly
defined. For example: did leaders exhibit a drive to dominance? At the
most frequently reported correlation of .20, this would mean that only 4
percent of total variance could be attributed to dominance.[4] Score one
for the Bible, which does not play the "trait" game at all, but, rather,
tests the capacity for leadership through action.

Dominance, recognized as a critical trait, led to the question of leadership styles. Was there no difference between leaders who used brutality
and others who dominated through persuasion? As a trait, "dominance"
suggested dangerous ideological overtones. Alfred R. Lindersmith and
Anselm L. Strauss—writing not long after the struggle against Nazism—attributed fascination with traits to "current popular conceptions of leaders
as... objects capable of being transformed into the 'magical helpers' sought
by those whose need for security is resolved by finding some powerful
authority upon whom they can become dependent."[5] Similarly, Daniel
Bell found that almost all the literature, based on Aristotle and Machi-
avelli, conveyed the "image of the mindless masses and... the strong-willed
leader."[6] Robert Tannenbaum added that "classical models of bureaucracy
share with these elite conceptions an authoritarian bias in their emphasis
on the exclusive prerogative of leaders to command the unquestioning
obligation of subordinates to obey."[7] The contrast with Moses could not
be clearer; from the time he offers to liberate the Israelites through the

exodus to the wanderings in the desert, his people constantly chastise him, several times revolting against his leadership.

The dominance approach, moreover, came to seem ill-conceived. Since one could not imagine leaders without considering followers, scholars posited, perhaps there was something about followers—some ineffable clue—that led leaders to them. Exit the "hero in history" and enter group dynamics—more prosaic but perhaps more profound. It turned out, of course, that there were almost as many dynamics as groups. Sometimes group members were led; sometimes they did the leading; often, in the midst of exponentially increasing interactions, the observer could not tell which.

Perhaps there had been an oversight? Leaders and followers, embedded in history, interacted in regard to something called "the situation." "Situationists" entertained a variety of opinions. Ralph Stogdill concluded that the "qualities, characteristics and skills required in a leader are determined to a large extent by the demands of the situation in which he is to function as a leader."[8] Since separate situations make different demands on leaders, Alex Bavelas suggested that we must instead try to "define the leadership functions that must be performed in these situations and regard as leadership those acts which perform them."[9] Thus there could be as many leaders as there were different situations. Situations, then, were even more varied than followers, who in turn were more diverse than leaders.

What, indeed, is a situation? William Thomas and Florian Znanieck's famous "definition of the situation" is composed of kitchen-sink variables, beliefs, values, groups, the physical environment, tasks, perception of all the above, and, for good measure, the surrounding culture.[10] Not surprisingly, A. Paul Hare concludes that "the major finding of this research is that there are more differences between situations than between the two leader styles" tested in his research.[11]

If (to follow the logic of the literature on leadership) the slavery of the Hebrews under Pharaoh was a "situation," was Moses' effort to beg off from his mission to lead the people out of slavery also a situation? And if one characterized as a situation Moses' efforts to placate his complaining people in the desert, would that designation also hold for Moses' use of force to put down the effort of dissidents to return to Egypt after the spies reported that Canaan would be difficult to conquer? Sometimes "situation" appears to designate one event, such as Moses fleeing from Pharaoh, sometimes a series of similar events, such as the periodic discontent of the people with the leadership of Moses. Does the concept include both events (such as the Israelites crossing the Sea of Reeds) and patterns of power relations—slavery as a system of rule, or the Israelites' bazaar-like bidding and bargaining for favors after the exodus? Apparently, the answer is "all of the above." Yet a single episode may have different implications than does a series; and a pattern of rule is not necessarily the same as a series of situations. Theorizing depends on seeing patterns in what may originally have appeared to be disparate happenings. Treating situations as discrete events would make theoretical interpretation impossible, for history then would be reduced to narrative.

What is the alternative? To consider situations as patterns of events calls for a prior interpretative scheme (a theory) according to which events will be classified and given some order of priority. Thus in this chapter, the categories of regimes proposed are designed to give meaning to the events that take place within each regime. Moses' passivity—from the burning bush episode up to (but not including) Mount Sinai—may be attributed, for instance, to his being part of a pattern of master-slave relationships, in which there is no room for leadership.

As ontology was once said to recapitulate phylogeny, the individual passing through all stages of the species, so each approach to leadership ends up, willy-nilly, by incorporating the others. If anything is evident, it is that individuals do not act alone. "A group," according to Gibb, "is characterized by the interaction of its members, in such a way that each unit is changed by its group membership and each would be likely to undergo a change as a result of changes in the group. In this case there is a dependence of each member upon the entire group, and the relation between any two members is a function of the relation between other members."[12] Leaders are nothing if they cannot attract followers. Thus begins the blurring; as leaders merge into followers, social life becomes a seamless web. With increasing sophistication, scholars succeed only in making leadership indistinguishable from other phenomena.[13]

Once leadership depends on acceptability within a group, group members are seen to lead as well as follow. "Clearly," Kenneth F. Janda concludes, "a member cannot be salient unless he can be differentiated from other group members on one or more criteria, and, of course, almost every group member can be differentiated from other group members on the basis of one or more of these criteria. From this realization, it is just a short step to conclude that every group member can be, and often is, a leader."[14] Is there, then, no difference between groups that mandate inequality and those that reject authority? The thesis that every man was his own authority was the major challenge to Mosaic leadership posed by the rebellion of Korah.

"The individual who engages in leadership events becomes a sometimes leader," say Abraham Zaleznik and David Moment. Leaders no longer tell followers where to go, but rather help followers get to where they want to be. "Leadership," Dorwin Cartwright and Alvin Zander assert, "is viewed as the performance of those acts which help the group achieve its preferred outcomes."[15] "Group norms" become social science code for "democracy." In these terms, Moses would not be judged a leader because (at the Golden Calf and again just outside the Promised Land) he prevented his followers from going where they wanted to go—back to slavery in Egypt.

Leadership also is represented as part of the "general process of role differentiation, by which a group develops 'specialists' in the performance of recurring functions."[16] If some people are specialized to "leadership roles" and others to followership, however, this division of labor will reintroduce all the old differences that the group interaction approach is supposed to obliterate. "Let George do it" is qualified by "if he can."

Most studies seem to show some sensitivity on the part of leaders to group concerns. Is it true, therefore, that members of a group (another euphemism for followers) approve of leaders who show "consideration" and who side with the group in disputes with outsiders or higher-ups? Would Aaron, on these grounds, be preferred to Moses? This reverse-twist trait approach, however, is undermined by situational findings. D.C. Pelz discovered that most white-collar workers—aware of the need for someone to run interference outside the work group—preferred a supervisor who was well-connected in the hierarchy, even if that meant the supervisor was not close to them.[17] These findings were rationalized by positing a difference between task and emotional leadership; sensitive leadership makes the group happy, it seems, but not necessarily effective. And then there are circumstances. Colonel Nicholson of the movie *Bridge Over the River Kwai* is superb in circumstances calling for sticking to the rules but rigid when he should be flexible. So, too, the group-centered leadership of Aaron made his people happy at the time of the Golden Calf, but without the task-centered leadership of Moses none would ever have reached the Promised Land.

In a creative construction called "idiosyncrasy credit," E.P. Hollander suggests that leaders first perform a series of services for their followers, thus building up credit, then trade in those credits for permission. (This, of course, assumes that the people involved will remember!) Moses did indeed build up credit for the exodus—credit that lasted somewhere between three days and three months—before his erstwhile followers demanded immediate gratifications. Storing up credit requires a regime that values contributions over time, not an anarchy, focused on current rewards, or an equity, which insists leaders be perennially perfect.

Simply saying that life is a social activity is a truism. To specify forms of social organization and to relate each to different types of leadership would reduce, instead of expand, the realm of relevant leadership behavior.

We are indebted to Gibb's invaluable surveys of the literature on leadership for the ultimate synthesis, which he calls "interaction theory," possibly because it covers all conceivable relations. A comprehensive theory of leadership, in Gibb's words, must include not only the personality of leaders, followers, groups, and situations, but also "must recognize that it is not these variables per se that enter into the leadership relation, but rather the perception of the leader by himself and by others, the leader's perception of those others, and the shared perception by leader and others of the group and the situation."[18] Viewing leadership as all-encompassing provides no perspective on perception; considering leadership as a function of regime explains why people adhering to different ways of life would perceive leadership differently.

Enter charismatic leadership. Max Weber—desiring to distinguish between small, repetitive choices that reinforce existing institutions and large, unusual ones that create new designs—decided to classify political systems by the kinds of authority that legitimate leadership. Weber saw traditional authority repeating itself; a rational-legal authority making minor adjustments; and charismatic authority introducing new patterns of action, new values, and new institutions. Weber's charismatic leader is distinguished by a divine call to duty (or, at least, so the leader thinks and followers accept) that is transmitted to, and shared by, followers because of a certain glow radiating from the source.

Observing charismatic traits attributed to people performing ordinary secular roles, Edward Shils suggests that "charisma not only disrupts social order, it also maintains or conserves it." It is not the concentration of charisma, however, but its "dispersion" in society that interests Shils. A society in which people are civil to one another, he says, "entails not only the imputation of charisma to the mass of the population by itself; it also requires that the established and effective elite impute charisma to the mass as well, that the elite regard itself, despite all its differences as sharing some of the charisma that resides in it with the rest of its society."[19] The more equally traits are distributed, to be sure, the more they characterize entire populations rather than particular people within them.

Charisma is thus both democratized, becoming a mass as well as an elite trait, and deradicalized, supporting stability as well as its opposite. It has, however, been removed from its essential mooring in some particular political regime. If charisma is a substitute for authority, one might ask, what sort of regime is it that tries to organize itself without a binding source of rules?

Leadership as 'Cause'

With interdependency so rampant, there might be lots of leadership, but how could researchers isolate specific leaders? If leadership is everything in general, can it be anything in particular?

Leaders have been variously defined as those who occupy high-level positions; who have been elected by a group; who are most influential in setting goals (or helping achieve them); who influence others, whether or not goals get accomplished; who try hard, or often, to exert influence but do not succeed; or who do succeed more often than anyone else.[20] Alternatively, Robert T. Morris and Melvin Seeman assert that "leader behavior may be defined as any behavior that makes a difference in the behavior of the group."[21] Thus attention shifts from leader as cause to leader as effect. Is leadership, one wonders, a tower of power or the Tower of Babel?[22]

Recently, leadership has been defined as "cause."[23] Leaders are those who make things happen that otherwise would not come about. The criterion can be strengthened by adding that power-wielders get their way against the opposition of followers over whom the powerful exercise control.[24] The definition can be made more precise by converting it into a statement of probabilities or alternatives foregone.[25] The probability of exerting influence would thus vary with what had to be given up in order to achieve that sway. Influence would vary also with the difficulty of the attempt or the importance of the issue.

Conceiving of leadership as a causal relationship is an advance; but its proponents immediately fall victim to the same difficulties suffered by those who study power, influence, control, and other synonyms for "cause."[26] There are as many leaders as there are causes, and there is much trouble distinguishing one from the other or assigning them relative weights. Clearly, some things must be held constant so as to be able to observe variations in leadership.

The most imaginative attempt to link leadership to power, influence, and cause is by Andrew S. McFarland, who proposes the following setup for research:

> Let us outline some important considerations for the study of leadership, defined as influence. First, we must establish the limits of a person's action in terms of general social forces, although this is obviously difficult. Second, we "think away" the existence of the particular leader, and consider what might have happened if the leader had not lived. Third, we compare the more probable "might-have-been's" with the actuality in order to assess the magnitude and significance of the influence (causality) the leader has exercised on human events. Finally, such judgmental-probabilistic reasoning need not be restricted to past events but can be applied to future possibilities.[27]

Without Moses, I surmise, there would have been no Hebrew people; they would have remained slaves to Pharaoh, either because they could not liberate themselves or because, even having done so, they would have decided to give up freedom and return to Egypt.

In a valiant effort to rehabilitate the utility of personality in political analyses, Fred I. Greenstein tries to break the big question into more precise and answerable units, speaking of "action dispensability" (would it matter if an action were different?) or "actor dispensability" (would it matter if the individual actor were different?):

> The objection to studies of personality and politics that emphasizes the limited capacity of single actors to shape events does not differ in its essentials from the nineteenth and early twentieth century debates over social determinism—that is, over the role of individual actors (Great Men or otherwise) in history.... Questions are asked such as, "What impact could Napoleon have had on history if he had been born in the Middle Ages?" Possibly because of the parlor game aura of the issues that arise in connection with it, the problem of the impact of individuals on events has not had... much disciplined attention.... The impact of an individual's actions varies with (1) the degree to which the actions take place in an environment which admits of restructuring, (2) the location of the actor in that environment, and (3) the actor's peculiar strengths or weaknesses.[28]

It is exactly these environments admitting of restructuring that I try to supply with the classification of regimes.[29] So long as the emphasis is on the individual and not on the regime in which action takes place, variety in personal behavior will always overcome our ability to generalize about leadership. Moses matters because the changes he helped bring about culminated in permanent differences in how rule was exercised among the Israelites.

If leadership is equivalent to cause, the greatness of the cause determines the importance of the leadership. Should we attribute great leadership, then, to anyone who drastically changes the lives of other people, whether for good or ill? Do the moral ends or objectives not matter? "To differentiate the leadership of a Luther from the leadership of a Hitler is crucial for a political science that is to 'make sense'; if a political science is incapable of that," Carl J. Friedrich declares, "it is pseudo-science, because the knowledge it imparts is corrupting and not guiding."[30] Alas, leaders may both guide and corrupt, as with a Hitler or a Mussolini. And they may both lead and coerce, as, from time to time, Moses did.

"Coercive strategies need not detain us here," James M. Burns swiftly asserts, like many other authors, thus disposing of an ancient issue by fiat, "since we exclude coercion from the definition of leadership."[31] Are dictators not leaders, then? What about those mixed cases in which leaders use force and yet appear to gain consent? If follower-response is to determine who or what is legitimate, we are back to square one—in which influence is determined by interaction.

The identification of leadership with legitimate moral purpose would tie organizational objectives to the consent for carrying them out. Philip Selznick maintains that the purpose of leadership is to imbue administrators with a vision of the ultimate importance of their work by evoking objectives that relate what they are asked to do to what is desirable. "The problem," in Philip Selznick's view, "is always *to choose key values and to create* a *social structure that embodies them.*" Whose values, however, are to be judged key ones? If values are articulated and rejected, does the failure to adopt them lie in the leader or in potential followers? "Our dilemma... is not an absence of leaders," Benjamin Barber observes, "but a paucity of values that might sustain leaders; not a failure of leadership but a failure of followership, a failure of popular will from which leadership might draw strength."[32]

Observing that "some frustrated political scientists have tended to throw up their hands and settle for tracing circular patterns of influence between leaders and followers, without coming any closer to determining the nature of leadership," Lewis J. Edinger expands the problem:

> If it is difficult, if not impossible, to discover what causes people to follow a leader, it is equally difficult to ascertain the motives which determine the leader's behavior.... The individual may deliberately conceal his "real and true motives," he may rationalize them and accept them himself as "real and true," or he may not even know what they are because they are "unconscious motives." The complexity of motivations and the difficulty of discovering, identifying, and attributing motives makes it practically impossible to satisfy the requirements.[33]

If Edinger is right, we need an approach to leadership that either does not require attribution of motives or that infers them from the regimes within which leadership is exercised. Leadership has to be made part of politics.

Leadership Without Politics

The most remarkable feature of the literature on leadership is the near total neglect of large-scale politics. Analyses of political situations proliferate. But there is almost no discussion of types of political systems as productive of different kinds of leadership.

"Why," John A. Miller inquires in his exhaustive review, "has no amount of data massaging been capable of establishing consistent relationships between leader behavior and organizational outcomes?" A plausible answer is that neglect of regimes attenuates the perceived relationships between leaders and the organizational imperatives they face. "Why is it," Miller continues, "that well-planned and well-executed attempts to change leadership styles by various training procedures have such unpredictable—even dysfunctional—outcomes?" Because detaching leadership from regime separates the requirements of the organizational context from personal performance, I would reply. Miller comes close to answering his own question with another, which reveals an anomaly: "If the effectiveness of leadership behavior is situationally contingent," he writes, "and prescriptive models call for leader flexibility, why are observed leadership styles so stable?"[34] If leadership is a function of regime, as I claim, leadership should vary more with regime than with situation.[35] Examining the events themselves cannot determine whether the Hebrew people worshiping the Golden Calf is a momentary aberration—a final parting of the ways between God and man—or an opportunity to reshape the understandings between men by transforming the regime expressing their relationships.

That blending of description with prescription found in the study of leadership cannot be eliminated without doing violence to the subject itself. The leadership literature asks, "Who shall lead?" as if it did not matter where. "Perhaps," Gabriel Almond writes, "the confusion [between types of leadership] arises because... the focus is on the leader as the 'causer,' and not what is being caused."[36] Just so. From a strictly descriptive standpoint, as Arthur F. Bentley argued, the actor and the activity must always be kept together because the significance lies in the process of which they are a part.[37] From a Mosaic perspective, leader and follower are always in the act of choosing among regimes as well as among leaders. The Bible does not ask only, "What is the proper purpose of leadership?" but also (and simultaneously), "What is the proper choice of regimes?" It thus places the consequences of leadership in different regimes at the forefront of political consciousness.

In the small politics of everyday activity, leadership means getting people to do things they otherwise would not do. In this sense, leadership is equivalent to power, influence, control, in that all these terms are synonyms of cause. But if we ask what causes cause—what way of life, or what general theory, makes sense out of politics—we get no answer. In large-scale politics "cause" involves the transformation of regimes from one set of social relations, values, and beliefs to another. Micropolitics has to be seen in the context of macropolitics—those regimes from which the small maneuvers of everyday politics take on their meaning.

Philosophers have no more found an all-purpose definition of cause than psychologists have constructed a secure typology of personality. Leadership analysis is as situational as the leaders it studies. But suppose we see this stultifying symmetry as reflecting perennially valid elements of a protean subject? Our task then would be to embrace the difficulties without obliterating the elementary scaffolding necessary to any intellectual edifice. The Mosaic conception of leadership recognizes that just as there are no leaders good for all seasons, no single concept of leadership can serve every purpose.

If leadership varies with the regime in which it is being exercised, the various definitions commonly in use can find their places without being forced. There is no a priori need, for example, to eliminate coercion or rule by persuasion. A special merit of the Mosaic approach is that it deals with a variety of perspectives—not only the difficulties of leaders but also those of followers, depending on what is demanded of them in different regimes. Surely the same qualities are not called for in slavery as in anarchy. By conceiving of leadership as contingent on context, we are at least warned that it is futile to search for single types. And this will make us more receptive to the biblical effort to teach us how to learn from our own cultural context—to act as best we can, to reformulate our hypotheses, and to go at it again.

DIMENSIONS OF VIABLE REGIMES

The social science literature on leadership either ignores regimes or jumbles them together in a woefully wide definition of situation. If "situations" are used to describe both patterns of power relationship (as in regimes) and particular events (as in bargaining between Pharaoh and Moses), an important sense of discrimination is lost.

In this section, I will try to unpack "situation" by deriving, from their cultural contexts, four political regimes. The Epilogue contains a detailed discussion of the two of these regimes—equities and hierarchies—most important to Moses.

The Bible is about what matters most to people: living with themselves and with others. Human life poses two great questions: the question of identity—Who am I?—and the question of action—What should I do? Identity involves recognizing the boundaries that separate some people so that others can be together; the Ten Commandments illustrate both boundaries (God/man, your neighbor's goods/your own, his wife/yours) and actions (stealing, coveting, honoring). Thus the Bible answers fundamental questions about relationships among people. Who regulates these relationships in the Torah? Moses, the mediator, the servant of God. Is there danger of confusion between servant and master? Yes, and that is why idolatry—making man into God—is prohibited.

Can there be order without omnipotent leaders? Yes, within a viable regime the people who matter most do believe in the rules and do not need to be coerced. For those who live together, the accepted rules of action (that we call institutions) are justified by their shared values and are made credible by widespread agreement about what will happen if a rule is violated. Individuals try to operate their institutions so as to make sense out of life: if they behave according to the rules, they expect the results to be predictable and desirable. If their expectations are upset, they will, if they can, seek to transform their way of life so as to make it supportable.

But there are great leaders; and great leaders alter regimes. Indeed, the ability to do so is a measure by which we determine force of personality. Without understanding what type of leadership goes with what type of regime, however, one cannot judge the degree to which a regime has been changed by the impact of a dynamic person. By placing personality within a context of political regime, it should be possible to do justice to both.

Model I classifies regimes in the abstract so as to facilitate the study of Mosaic leadership. The dimensions of political regime, corresponding to identity and action, respectively, are the source and distribution of power. Is the source of reward and punishment (or identity) inside or outside the group of which the individual is a part? If it is inside the group, the fortunes of the individual are tied to it, and he will be discouraged from contact with the outside. If the individual is given incentives to engage in transactions outside his group, his fortune will depend on such external interaction. Within his group, the question is whether political actions are undertaken among equals or unequals. Do some people have the right to make decisions for others (unequal distribution of power), or do all participate equally in decision making? Who, we ask, is manipulating or being manipulated by whom?

As shown here (Box 1), the combination of unequal distribution of power within the group and external allocation of reward defines the regime commonly called slavery, about which it is said that individuals cannot control the decisions that affect their lives. Instead, these decisions are made by others, as the Pharaohs did for the Hebrew people for over four hundred years.

Model I. **Political Regimes**

		Source of Power	
		External	Internal
Division of Power	Unequal	(1) Slavery	(4) Hierarchy
	Equal	(2) Anarchy	(3) Equity

As far as it is possible to get politically from slavery, we find anarchic regimes (Box 2). Rewards are external—everyone can deal with anyone about anything. Boundaries are weak in that people in the anarchy are encouraged to make deals with people outside of it. Alliances shift as advantage or whim suggests. Internal relationships are egalitarian; there is an equal right to engage in transactions, but both gains and losses belong to the individuals who risk their resources in competition. No one in the anarchic regime can tell anyone else what to do. There is no authority, only mutual advantage. How, then, could an anarchy make an everlasting covenant when all its contracts are limited in time and purpose? How can anarchy have a single god? There is no enforcement against deviants from the faith, because there is no common faith from which to deviate, unless one recognizes that the right to deviate is the faith. And because there are few boundaries to protect, there are few pollutions, that is, defilements to define as impermissible behavior.

Equity (Box 3) is the regime in which people are supposed to have no power over the members of their group. I call this regime an equity because of its overwhelming stress on equality. It is the sort of organization Max Weber defines as "an absolutely voluntary association."[38] Hence the equity will tolerate no hierarchy. Authority depends on the agreement of equals; any inequality is illegitimate. There must be equality of result as well as equality of opportunity.

Above equity in the diagram—still insistent on internal rewards and punishments but based on unequal power distribution—is the hierarchical regime (Box 4). It is bound up in maintaining a supportive relationship between the parts and the whole. In its full form hierarchy is like a nest of Chinese boxes with everyone ordered by rank and role. More precisely, each "box" represents a unit, with the hierarchy defining the relationship between them.

The moral basis of these regimes is part of their worldview. Voluntary organization can be sustained only by treating everyone alike. Equality in social structure is generalized to the whole way of life. This equality becomes the foundation of the equity, upon which rises the fundamental division between itself—equality as purity—and others—inequality as pollution. Whereas in a hierarchy social pollution means violation of rules specifying who can do what, in an equity pollution is pinning people down instead of allowing them to choose, just the opposite.

The moral center of hierarchies lies in their justification of inequality designed, so they say, on the divine plan (or, if preferred, on a scientific, rational basis). In return for acceptance of inequality by those below, those on top of the hierarchy must show willingness to make sacrifices for the good of the whole.

Slave regimes develop rationales for submission. Slavery differs from hierarchy in that submission is total; the rules regulating relationships cannot be used by subordinates to exert a degree of reciprocal control over superiors.

At this point, it is useful to say that though these regimes have been described as polar types, their dimensions do form a continuum. Regimes may be more or less hierarchical, in that they are somewhat more equal internally, or merge more with others externally. For instance, Moses, who finds extreme equality frustrating, moves toward hierarchy, a movement completed only much later, with the monarchical period of David and Solomon. Regimes may also combine to form hybrids. Though hierarchy and equity may be fierce opponents, they can combine to form one of a number of hybrid regimes (see the Epilogue). If I continue to emphasize the four primary regimes, that is because to do so makes sense in a book about the Bible.[39]

It is hardly necessary to say that Moses is a religious leader for whom politics is a means to a religious end. The regimes he destroys and constructs parallel the religious orders he rejects and accepts. The relation of religion to politics is central to understanding the types of regimes, with their associated difficulties, that he chooses.

Religion and Politics

"You cannot standardize the ideas without standardizing the behaviour," A.M. Hocart asserts. "Centralization of cult thus always goes with centralization in the state." He infers ideas as derivatives of institutions: "We are not dealing with metaphysics, but with practical politics.... The whole struggle of monotheism v. polytheism is meaningless as long as we look upon it as a conflict of philosophies. What does it matter whether there be one God or many? Because by abolishing minor gods you abolish minor sovereignties: monotheism means monarchy; polytheism means polyarchy."[40] Ideas and institutions, in my view, are mutually reinforcing. People want to live a certain way of life and develop ideas to suit, or they start with an idea of how to live better and develop institutions to embody that idea. Society seeks symmetry. Whether politics leads to theology or theology to politics (I suppose they are jointly chosen), religious beliefs and political regimes correspond to one another.

Since this study is about political leadership, I relate religion to politics in Model II.

Model II. Politics and Religion: Who Receives Revelation?		Source of Power	
		External Many gods	Internal One god
Division of Power	**Unequal, the Ruler(s)**	(1) Slavery Ruler as gods Revelation only to ruler NARCISSISM: Idolatry as self-love	(3) Hierarchy Rulers under god Revelation through rulers to people MONOTHEISM: One god for all people
	Equal, the People	(4) Anarchy No rulers No revelation or equal to all ATHEISM OR POLYTHEISM: Different gods for different purposes	(2) Equity Revelation to each individual within each group HENOTHEISM: A single god for a single people

Religious questions parallel cultural questions. The cultural "Who am I?" may be translated as "What is my source of inspiration?" Correspondingly, "What shall I do?" becomes "Who receives revelation?" There are different answers for different regimes—one or many gods as the source; all the people or only rulers as the receivers of revelation.

With slavery, rulers are gods; only rulers receive revelation. Their religion is narcissistic; it involves self-worship or idolatry. The internal equality of equities makes revelation available to each man individually; strongly bounded against the outside, equities nevertheless have a jealous group god; and the technical name for worship of a god to whom your group (but not necessarily others) belongs is henotheism. Hierarchies are monotheistic, tending toward belief in one universal god.[41] Revelation goes through the ruler to the people; hierarchic rulers must obey divine statutes that give prerogatives to their followers as well as themselves.

Anarchies are atheistic or polytheistic; either they have no deity or different gods for different purposes.

For a study of leadership, it is important that each regime exhibit a characteristic style of leadership. Knowing the regime, I claim, should enable an analyst to predict the style of leadership that will usually, more often than not, be associated with it. The test lies in whether readers find that the types of regimes as set forth clarify or obscure the significance of the situations in which Moses and his people find themselves.

The Scope and Duration of Leadership

Our interest is in leadership as a function (consequence, if you like) of regime. We need to know whether leaders in each regime will be obeyed over a wide or narrow spectrum of affairs (the *scope* of leadership), and whether they will exercise leadership continuously or, like the temporary dictatorships of Rome, only some of the time (the *duration* of leadership).

Under slavery, leadership is *despotic*—continuous and total; under equity, leadership is absent or *charismatic*—short-lived but unlimited in scope. Hierarchic regimes have *autocratic* leaders; within their spheres they are supreme, but their scope is limited. Anarchic regimes, to the extent that leaders exist at all, are led by *meteoric* men who flame bright and burn out quickly—the right man in the right place at the right time for the right purpose right now!

**Model III.
Styles of Leadership by
Political Regimes**

(1) Slavery	(3) Hierarchy
Unlimited	Limited
Continuous	Continuous
DESPOTIC	**AUTOCRATIC**
(4) Anarchy	(2) Equity
Limited	Unlimited
Discontinuous	Discontinuous
METEORIC	**CHARISMATIC**

Reading Model III as a series of predictions, we see that under slavery, leadership is total: it is unlimited and continuous, even though masters may change. All aspects of life, including the right to be born (Pharaoh wanted to reduce the Hebrew population), are included. As good a definition of despotism as any comes from Carlos R. Alba on modern Spain's Francisco Franco: "His position as Head of State... consisted of a power that was exceptional, arbitrary, and without limits in its exercise, except those deriving from his own will."[42]

In equities, leadership is discontinuous, but when present it is unlimited. This unusual combination occurs because charisma substitutes for authority. Endless factional struggles beset regimes with no internal hierarchy and hence no mode of settling disputes except by starting one's own equity. Ordinary leadership is anathema because it is a prima facie instance of inequality. The voluntary character of equities extends to the necessity of gaining agreement on each and every issue rather than just the most important ones. Thus there is no disposition to follow merely because an erstwhile leader says so.

Often engaged in tearing down leaders as soon as they rear their ugly heads, equities are antileadership regimes. When life sends up challenges, however, especially when foreign invasion occurs, equities get desperate. By that time, things are so bad that people attribute both virtue and heroism to their leaders, thus fitting them to exercise total power, at least until the emergency is over.

Virtue is the vice of equities. For if perfect equality makes leadership difficult, it also makes it necessary. How will children be socialized without the same strict education condemned by equities in the case of hierarchies? Having made so many enemies by attacking established authority, how will equities fight battles without generals? Thus leadership in equities, when it does appear, is charismatic—if by that is meant leadership perceived as possessing supreme virtue encompassing all aspects of life.[43] Charisma serves as a substitute for the authority equities will not recognize unless it is perceived to be perfect.

It is easy to understand why leadership is continually exercised in hierarchies; but why is it limited in scope? As the classical scholars, from Sir Henry Maine to Max Weber,[44] who studied traditional societies, maintained, obligations are reciprocal: the rules and statutes that enable the top to give orders down the line also, by virtue of their binding character, limit what leaders can do to followers: "I must obey here but you have no right to give orders there." Movies on military life which show sergeants deferential to officers but refusing encroachment on their family life—fit the picture. The military hierarchy stops at the home.

In the anarchic regime, leadership is both limited and discontinuous. It may not exist at all. When it does, leadership will be limited in duration and confined to specific purposes. Why? No one is obliged to be a leader or to acknowledge those who claim to be leaders. Before mutual obligation exists, there has to be a contract in which followers hire leaders. This contract has a narrow focus and short duration for, if leaders become permanent, they could dictate their terms, thus abrogating freedom of contract. The right to shift alliances so as to assure balance among the segments is the essence of the anarchical regime. Coalitions are reformulated until they are relatively equal in strength, leading to bargaining and stalemate. Though the family or clan may be hierarchical, it is fiercely jealous of its autonomy, coming together with others just long enough to meet immediate needs and then dissolving.[45] Anarchic regimes perform a delicate balancing act between having leaders when they are needed and getting rid of them when not.

Comparing these headless regimes (or segmentary systems, as Meyer Fortes and E.E. Evans-Pritchard named them after African experience)[46] with equities, the difference in leadership is striking. At first examination, these occasionally organized anarchies appear open to charismatic leadership. True enough, leadership is evanescent and personal. But these anarchies do not subscribe to total leadership. They give up only as much autonomy as they need for each engagement and no more. Such leaders claim no transcendent purposes. The virtue of leaders in an anarchy consists only of fighting and/or bargaining better than others. Anarchists know all too well that from the leader follows the hierarchy, among whose multitudinous ranks are found policemen and tax collectors. Not wanting the latter, they choose not to have leaders any longer than absolutely necessary.

(Anti-) Leadership

The strength of leadership exercised within political regimes flows directly from the way regimes answer basic questions about political life. Hierarchies and slave societies favor strong leadership; equities and anarchies do not. But this interpretation is too simple-minded. By addressing a common political query to these regime categories—How does the demand for leadership compare to the support for it?—we can do better. The model contains two additional dimensions—balance (the gap between demand and support) and level (the direction of the gap so as to promote or hinder leadership). The balance dimension suggests that it is not only the level of leadership desired but its relationship to the support provided that matters.

Model IV on political balance in (anti-) leadership systems (the "anti" in parentheses is a reminder that leadership may be absent as well as present) lays out the gap between demand and support for leadership.

Model IV.
Political Balance in
(Anti-) Leadership Systems

		Demand Low	Demand High	
Support	High	(1) Slavery support demand unbalanced	(3) Hierarchy support demand balanced	Leadership Systems
	Low	(4) Anarchy demand support balanced	(2) Equity demand support unbalanced	Anti-Leadership Systems

The greater the gap between demand and support, the larger the leadership problem.

In hierarchies and anarchies demand and support for leadership balance each other. The main difference between them is that hierarchies are balanced at a high, and anarchies at a low, level. So long as these regimes operate properly, leadership is not a problem. To be sure, hierarchies may be tempted to use excessive force, thereby becoming slave states, and anarchies may have so little leadership that they fall apart, becoming victims of hierarchy. Change is ubiquitous. But as long as anarchies and hierarchies last in recognizable form, too little leadership is not their problem.

Problematic leadership is a sign of unbalanced relationships—demand and support are out of whack. Slavery is unsatisfactory because it is abusive or inefficient (depending on the perspective of slave or master). Since slavery inculcates passivity, it may breed slaves who, as Moses so sadly discovered, prefer to be told what to do. A regime of equity is excessively egalitarian; too much equality leads to indecision. Because support for leadership is lacking, according to the voluntary way, the need for it becomes overwhelming in time of trouble. Anarchies do not so much reject leadership as they seek social relations that make leadership unnecessary. The little leadership they need, therefore, is roughly equivalent to what they get. Equities need much but accept little.

If leadership is a function of regime, as I claim, then it should be possible to make sense out of Moses' behavior in terms of regime requirements. But Moses is also a transformer of regimes. The challenge of grappling with Mosaic leadership is to explain both how he transformed regimes and how they, in turn, transformed his leadership.

THE UNIQUENESS OF MOSES LIES IN HIS GENERALITY

What is Moses? He is (1) *founder* of a nation; (2) *revolutionary* three times over, transforming three different regimes; (3) *lawgiver* whose laws have lasted thousands of years; (4) *administrator* of two regimes, managing the march of both an equity and a hierarchy across a desert; (5) *storyteller* whose words have become deeds; (6) *teacher* of a way of life that still lives; (7) *student* who exemplifies learning how to learn, so that his defects as well as his virtues have inspired continuous reinterpretation; and (8) *politician* balancing conflicting values within himself and among his people. Moses is a hard act to follow.

With whom may Moses be compared? No one, according to the Bible. There are founders such as Romulus of Rome and lawgivers such as Solon of Athens. There are revolutionaries galore; there are even revolutionaries who, unlike Lenin, lived on to administer regimes they created. Only a few, such as Mao Zedong (recall the Cultural Revolution) and Charles de Gaulle (the Fifth French Republic) were writers and teachers as well as transformers. The field of comparable leaders begins to seem terribly small. Winston Churchill was not a founder; George Washington, not a writer; Mahatma Gandhi, not an administrator and not a multiple transformer of regimes. In the end, no one I can think of (of course, this may be a defect of my historical imagination) dealt with anything as broad as the range of Mosaic leadership. Mao made one transformation and tried another—but not three and not all different. Even Muhammad, who comes closest, did not transform or administer as many different regimes. One can, of course, make any comparison one chooses, as I have by relating Moses to Joseph, Jacob, Aaron, and Abraham; each speaks to Moses in some, but not all, of the contexts in which we find him. Should we conclude, then, that Moses is incomparable and leave it at that? I think not.

The uniqueness of Moses, as I have been saying, lies paradoxically in his very generality, which makes him splendidly suited for political study. His experience in all major regimes encourages us to look more comprehensively at models of leadership.

Because his approach to leadership varied with regimes, we can become aware of the broad political contexts across which Moses operated and not be trapped by concern only with particular events that happened to occupy him at any moment. But if any reader thinks the purpose of studying biblical political leadership is to find out how to mold leaders in the image of Moses, I must leave him with a triple negative: Moses is against it, the Bible and tradition are opposed, and Moses' uniqueness makes it impossible. If the purpose is to learn about leadership, however—learning about learning (as the reader knows only too well by now)—the Mosaic experience has much to offer. The strengths and weaknesses of each type of regime, political personality, and style of leadership are open to appraisal. The open invitation to do-it-yourself interpretation (letting the Bible speak to current concerns) means that there is an immense array of evidence with which to contrast one's own efforts. Failures and successes are writ large, so that we may actively participate in reinterpreting their relevance to help us make our own history.

Earlier I argued both that leadership varies with type of regime and that the Torah contains teachings on leadership. Here these approaches will be combined: the leadership of Moses may be illuminated by showing how it varies with different political contexts; and the variations in Mosaic leadership may be used to probe the general problems of leadership in different regimes. By making biblical interpretation and social science mutually reinforcing, I hope to make good the promise of this book.

THE TRANSFORMATION OF REGIMES

When Moses returned to his people in Egypt, they were slaves to Pharaoh, with no say in the decisions that affected their lives. Rules were imposed upon the children of Israel by an external source, and power was distributed as unequally as could be. When Moses let his people go to enter the Promised Land, power relationships, at least among Hebrew tribes, were equal, and the source of this power lay within their own group boundaries.

Looking back, it is apparent that there was continuity as well as change, evolution as well as revolution. It is not, after all, that the Israelites liberated themselves from all restriction. Their anarchical period was short-lived. Indeed, the people ended up with many more internal rules to regulate behavior than those with which they started. So far as we know, Pharaoh was interested only in their forced labor, not in their personal practices. The hundreds of commandments to which the Hebrew people became subject when they accepted the covenant were almost unknown in Egypt, The difference presumably is that the yoke of the Torah, unlike the yoke of Pharaoh, was self-imposed.

The ruler of Egypt is a man and a god. By unifying what should be kept separate—man and certain moral knowledge (the difference between good and evil, as is said in the story of the Garden of Eden)—Pharaoh becomes a fanatic, dispensing life and death without restraint as if he were the sole owner of the universe. Pharaoh does not have to guess which way history is going; he is history, in his own eyes anyway, so that his will is the ultimate good to which all life is subject.

The radical break Moses makes is to separate what Pharaoh has joined together in one person—the human and the divine—splitting partial from complete power and understanding. For the Israelites, Pharaoh is not only replaced, but the functions he combined are divided up in Moses to guard against idolatry. Outward appearances have not changed much. The people have their deity and their ruler. The inner distance is immense, however, because there is now an impenetrable divide between man and God. No one, not even Moses, can cross that divide.

Among the extraordinary accomplishments of Moses was his transformation of three regimes—from slavery to anarchy to equity to hierarchy. How did he do it?

To escape from a slave regime, it is necessary to challenge the omnipotence of its leader. When the Egyptians are made to suffer, but the Hebrew slaves do not, the moral basis of slavery—master knows best—is gone. When the first-born of God (that is, Israel) live, but the first-born of Pharaoh (his son and all Egypt's sons) die, the slaves are freed to follow their own God, to make their own destiny.

During the brief period after leaving Egypt and before receiving the law on Mount Sinai, the Hebrews start to complain about leadership. Moses has not taken them where they were promised nor given them what they wanted. Moses, the people fear, has run out on them. So the Hebrews propose to choose another in what would then be a succession of meteoric leaders. Anarchies do produce leaders appropriate for a specific purpose. But after the immediate danger has been dealt with, the constituent elements (say, clans or tribes) feel free to make other, more suitable arrangements.

To keep the people together, therefore, Moses moves toward an equity in which he can be a charismatic leader, helping to reveal a divine law around which everyone (equals, together) can cohere. Inevitably, difficulties about interpretation of the revelation lead to quarrels over leadership. So Moses seeks to institutionalize leadership by introducing elements of hierarchy. Does the biblical narrative support this sequence of regime change?

Looking at the period immediately following the exodus from Egypt, the movement from slavery to anarchy is crystal clear. This regime depends on satisfying immediate demands; if not, its leadership will be challenged. Three days after Miriam sang of victory, there was no water, and the people murmured; God showed Moses how to provide, but the people then came to Elim and complained that there was no food. So God rained bread on them in the form of manna. Again, in Rephidim, there was no water. Water gushed out when Moses struck the rock. Enough. If this kept up, the people could keep complaining and enjoying. Why, they might make a better bargain by changing leaders every day!

Freedom turns into anarchy, and anarchy turns out to be incompatible with the goals of the revolution—the unity of God, people, and land. What Moses had done has to be undone. How? By force of arms and by force of ideas. The weak group boundaries of anarchies leave such regimes vulnerable to attack, as the episode of the Golden Calf shows all too plainly. Anarchy is overthrown because Moses can mobilize more moral and military resources than do his opponents.

Keeping his options open, Moses mediates two alternative forms of revelation corresponding to the two kinds of political leadership, and types of regimes, that are possible for a people who believe in one God. Equity corresponds with revelation direct to all the people without intermediaries; hierarchy goes with revelation first to Moses and the elders—Moses up front, the elders slightly behind—and then through them to the people at the bottom. After experience (the episodes of Korah, Abiram and Dathan, and the spies) shows Moses that equity is defective, he adds aspects of hierarchy.

Transforming equity into hierarchy is not simple. One reason is that equity, compatible with worship of a single God, does fulfill the religious mandate. Its borders are hardened and fiercely defended against external intrusion. A second reason is that equality among tribes and clans and believers produced revolutionary enthusiasm that Moses could hardly do without. A third reason, complementing Moses' personal ambivalence, is that the charismatic leadership essential to an equity (which Moses provided) is beset with contradictions. Leaders can enforce obedience only on the ground of fidelity to the divine will. When splits threaten over who has the right to interpret this will, leaders must prove that they, not their opponents, are imbued with the holy spirit. Thus, in the name of equity, rival leaders drive one another out. Carnage is the consequence.

Because external enemies are momentarily in short supply, for instance, Korah claims to see internal unholiness in Moses, who has become a usurper of power and whose advocacy of hierarchy is all the more insidious for being hidden. Moses' mediation becomes the sin—hiding God from the people, blocking out their sun, standing in their way. Where hierarchies engage in rituals affirming the divinely ordained differences among their members, equities engage in ritual destruction of leaders.

In order to retain his power in an equity, the leader can hope for (or arrange) a foreign menace to get himself off the hook—as Henry IV advised his son in Shakespeare's play. By mobilizing anger against the outside world, the equity remains united: it is the Midianites (not Moses) who are contaminated.

Internally, the leader preserves his charisma by showing that his opponents are the unholy ones. As Moses says, "the Lord will show who are his and who is holy" (Num. 16:5). There then begins a process of finding corruption among the rebels—"ye take too much upon you, ye sons of Levi… seek ye the priesthood also?" (Num. 16:7, 10). Nevertheless, the cost of unmitigated equity is too high: either the people drive out their charismatic leader or he must do in his rivals. Either the leader has to use force (as at the Golden Calf or in the episode of the spies) or the people split apart, abandoning their God with their leader.

By interpreting hierarchy as an aid to equity, though it never appears as his own overt suggestion, Moses forms a hybrid regime. Hierarchy comes first from his foreign father-in-law, its rationale being to spread the task of judging around: Moses is still to judge the hard cases, but not all of them. Hierarchy next derives from Moses' appeal to God for reduced burdens. The divine response is to institutionalize a council of elders. Somehow it is never Moses who wants hierarchy, and it is always Moses who appears to give up power to achieve it. Little by little, personal "meekness" becomes institutional strength. And Moses is not alone. The divine sanction given to kingship also came, as P. Kyle McCarter observes, "in a backhanded way," reluctantly imposed on the Lord and his prophet Samuel by an importuning people.[47]

As long as Moses is a charismatic leader in an equity (instead of the autocratic leader of a hierarchy, in which his right to issue authoritative commands is assumed), he cannot settle differences by fiat. Rather, he must call upon God to send signs—unnatural deaths, earthquake, and fire—choosing him over his opponents. The charismatic leader must show that the divine spirit is in him and that, as Moses says, he has not done the essential hard things, such as punishing his people, of his own will. By contrast, when Moses has established the hierarchical principle, he can stand up for himself.

The hierarchical Moses is less pure in principle but more humane in practice. By modifying the principle of the equality of all believers, to which, in the abstract, Moses adhered, he was able to mitigate its excesses and hence also his fierce counterreactions. A little equality was given up for a lot less fanaticism.

How did Moses manage to transform regimes without leading his people back to slavery? The answer, insofar as it may be ascertained, is that Moses was a consummate politician.

POLITICAL PERSONALITY

It is tempting to construct leaders as composites of only the admirable qualities of all those who have failed us in one way or another. If leadership does vary with regime, however, a leader for all seasons is an impossibility. For Moses to transform regimes, he had also to transform his political personality, a display of extraordinary plasticity.

Rarely, if ever, is there a firm fit between the structure of a regime, the personalities of available leaders, and the circumstances with which it must contend. The Mosaic method of leadership is not, as we know, a matter of going from one success to another but of salvaging some success from each defeat. All regimes have serious (if not fatal) flaws—the fanatical virtue of equities, the disregard of boundaries in anarchies, the heavy-handedness of hierarchies. Choice among regimes is not, therefore, choice of the unalloyedly good but consists rather in alleviating the worst consequences of the one preferred.

Moses not only designs but also tests regimes, trying but never entirely succeeding in eliminating error. As Jack Wiseman says, "The possibility of learning does not imply that through learning the future will become knowable, but only that experience will change behavior."[48] Moses' movements among regimes reveal how open he was to experience.

Leadership of the Hebrew people changes from despotic (under slavery) to meteoric (in anarchy) to charismatic (in equity) to autocratic (in hierarchy). This ability of a leader to change the regime that shapes him is not easy to understand in terms of any usual notion of social control. Surely the social context shapes the individual, including the individual leader, more than he can shape society. How can the phenomenon of Moses be understood?

The active personality wants to keep doing what he is good at.[49] It would not have taken much for Moses, having helped create a hierarchical regime, to push things to that extreme of central rule we call slavery. He must both restrain himself and be restrained by the higher principles that God offers—keeping himself out of (as the cost of getting his book, the Bible, into) the land of promise.

Many potential mismatches exist between political regimes and the personalities of leaders. Anarchies, for instance, need active, but not permanent, leaders; leaders good at the job, but not anxious to hold onto it, work there. A leader in love with his job might be too hard to throw out of office. When, after coming down from Sinai, Moses fights for the leadership, his opponents do find it difficult to displace him.

Because hierarchies are pro-leadership systems, their leaders need not be so active. Moses, the hierarchical leader, calms down considerably. Since change reverberates through the system, its pace and extent should be slow and small. Hierarchies may benefit from a reformer but are, for good reasons, endangered by the too-positive personality who will rock the boat.[50] The pace of change must be guarded carefully.

The positive personality is well suited to equity, which requires endless inputs of energy and widespread consent. Denigrating leadership in principle makes it ever more essential in practice; leaders of equities must be charismatic. It is also desirable that they should dig in their heels because the difficulties in social mobilization are so substantial and the attacks on the leadership principle so ubiquitous that only the most determined can survive. Equities cannot hold together without leaders, but neither will they tolerate them without proof, so hard to give, of perfection.

Slave societies suffer from passivity in the people. Since the master *is* the regime, he must exert continuous force. Though slave societies are the inverse of equities—the one glorifying, the other demeaning, leadership—they share one quality, the demand for leadership. That is why the one, valuing equality, so often leads to the other, glorifying obedience.

Regimes with either too much or too little authority move in the same direction—toward dependence on leadership. In transforming regimes, therefore, Moses faced a dual difficulty: exerting sufficient force to lead without leaving his followers as dependent upon him as they had been on Pharaoh, thus becoming the very evil he was sent to overcome.

Nowhere does Moses appear more revolutionary than when—fresh from meeting the Lord, his face shining with divine illumination—he punishes and purifies his people in the desert. Yet the question of whether, to what degree, and when Moses was a charismatic leader poses problems. If Moses is always charismatic, we cannot explain his behavior under regimes other than equity. His passivity under slavery, his bargaining under anarchy, and his disposition to fudge issues under hierarchy, which take up most of his life as a leader, must remain a mystery. To say that Moses was never charismatic, by contrast, would be to falsify the facts as the Bible plainly portrays them. Once we try out the hypothesis that leadership is a function of regime, however, the charisma of Moses can take its place as a sometime thing, without overwhelming his entire experience. What should be asked, since leadership is a function of regime, is what kind of leadership did Moses exercise under what regimes? Was his leadership appropriate to each regime?

In his revolutionary phase, leading a revolt against slavery, Moses was a meteoric leader in an anarchy; he led the people for a specific purpose and, so some thought, for a limited duration. The wrong leader for that regime, Moses either had to bargain for allegiance or transform anarchy into something else. After the Golden Calf, Moses transformed the regime into an equity. Throwing up a wall of virtue kept the idolaters out but allowed the idol-smashers in. God's word, delivered through Moses, was law until other interpreters argued that each man could create his own covenant. For a time, while it lasted, Moses was a charismatic leader. He had a direct line to God (the spirit was in him), he was luminous (his face shone), and he revealed exceptional personal qualities—bringing his people victories in battle, food for their stomachs, beliefs for their souls, and actions (the 613 commandments) to shape their character.

Throughout his career, Moses is not a charismatic leader. On the contrary, he begins by questioning his own competence. He continues to doubt himself. Whatever authority Moses does possess is challenged by practically everyone. Popular acclamation, to say the least, is lacking. It is posthumous rather than present, though even in the rest of the Bible he hardly looms large. Charisma, indeed! If there is such a thing as an anticharismatic force, except in a regime of equity, Moses is it. How, then, are we to understand which model—cataclysmic, or cumulative, change—demonstrates fidelity to Mosaic ideas?

EVOLUTION OR REVOLUTION?

Hierarchy was a principle to which the people had been accustomed in Egypt. A return to a modicum of hierarchy, which Moses sponsored, therefore, reduced the strain of rapid change that followed the exodus. Is it more accurate, then, to speak of Mosaic leadership as evolutionary, revolutionary, or both?

The legacy Moses imparts to future generations presents seeming contradictions—between slow and rapid, continuous and discontinuous change—as one of creative tension, the necessary dynamic of an idea's momentum in history. There is revolution from slavery to anarchy to equity and evolution toward hierarchy joined with equity. This combination of tradition and spontaneity allows us to expand the Mosaic concept of learning and relate it to the largest questions of political change.

In Cardinal Newman's view of the development of Christian doctrine, the power of an idea is measured by its capacity for expansion without disarrangement or dissolution. Metaphors of organic growth continually underscore his conservative, evolutionary scheme. The great idea, in contrast with "corrupt" or "perverse" offshoots, continues the tradition of the past rather than reversing or contradicting its course. Development is viewed primarily as a process of incorporation, a slow evolutionary expansion.[51]

In discussing historical change today, both historians and philosophers of science have called the organic model into question. Michel Foucault, for instance, underlines the ruptures among "epistemes"—the controlling historical perspectives that organize the way we view the world—rather than their continuity.[52] For Thomas Kuhn, knowledge in the sciences is won by the radical displacement of theory in revolutionary "paradigm shifts."[53] Incremental change, the slow progress of Newman's developmental scheme, gives way in Kuhn to drastic discontinuity.

If one takes these political metaphors at face value—"revolution," sudden change to entirely new forms—and "evolution," slow change to modify old forms—the ideas seem continually at odds. Each model, however, carefully provides for including its opposite. Thus, for Newman, the "assimilative power" of an idea is measured precisely by the extent to which that idea can reorganize knowledge: "Facts and opinions, which have hitherto been regarded in other relations and grouped around other centres, henceforth are attracted to a new influence and subjected to a new sovereign. They are modified, laid down anew, thrust aside, as the case may be."[54] As Richard Vernon points out in an illuminating essay, this sounds very similar to Kuhn's definition of the paradigm shift.[55] Kuhn's "revolution," moreover, is always embedded in the context of a scientific community; to become prevalent, a paradigm must be accepted by a legitimizing body. Theories may change quickly, but the people who embody principles for theorizing change much more slowly.[56] Nor does a paradigm shift simply overturn the past; Kuhn must also stress the necessity for conservation. Though new paradigms may not preserve all the explanatory power of the old, "they 'usually preserve a great deal of the most concrete parts of past achievement.'"[57] Thus, despite all the emphasis on reversal and dissolution that Kuhn's revolutionary scheme entails, the test of a new paradigm depends—as Newman might have said—on the idea's "assimilative power." There may be "astronomical change" in theoretical content, but no corresponding breach in intellectual methods occurs.[58] The shared disciplinary principles of a professional community give an "evolutionary" continuity to "revolutionary" theoretical changes.

Political metaphors, when applied to questions of historical progress, continually blur the very distinctions between change and stability they seemingly support. But suppose we take the biblical context and reinsert the metaphors, asking whether revolution in ideas and evolution in regimes are necessarily opposed? In the Mosaic tradition, as I view it, we will find them working together.

Moses' contribution was to fuse previously incompatible elements to forge a new identity for his followers. In Pharaoh's time, differences in status and power necessitated submission of the individual to the man who claimed to be a god. Pharaoh, the deity, made rules for his subjects that they could not change. Moses, on the other hand, made liberty serve authority. Instead of rules being imposed from above, they were supported from below. Subjugation to Pharaoh was replaced by self-subjugation to God. Voluntary obedience was substituted for compulsion, the family and the school for the overseers' lash. Thus Moses meets Almond's criteria for leadership: "The unusual and innovative leader is the individual who discovers or creates new options, mobilizes and combines new and old resources in creative ways."[59] The new element of separation from other peoples reinforced the notion that the rules regulating one's life come from within. And these rules were made more powerful by becoming embedded in daily life. Self-regulation came to be both more restrictive and more acceptable than domination by a foreign deity.

Moses created a hybrid regime, an amalgam of equity, to ensure criticism, and hierarchy, to maintain order. This revolution in regimes was accompanied by a transformation of political consciousness. As the transcendent replaced the human deity, human leadership lost any claim to omnipotence; infallibility belonged to God alone. Since man could make mistakes, error detection and error correction became possible. The genius of Moses lies in joining revolution with evolution. Though slavery and anarchy are prohibited, freedom and order, equity and hierarchy, are joined in a permanent tension to control each other's worst faults. By institutionalizing a method of critical consciousness—making use of experience to test practice—Moses mitigated the abuses of radical change without denying its historical importance.

The Mosaic depiction of leadership is intended to dramatize, to create a larger-than-life conception of leadership with the faults out in front. For every regime, like its leaders, brings bias into the world; each way of life concentrates on some things and ignores others, exposing itself to some dangers while guarding against others. Only the Almighty sees and lives life whole. Moses shows the way precisely by showing that there is no certain way; he combines in his own character, and spans in his own experiences, the various possibilities inherent in accepting, rejecting, exercising, and renouncing leadership. The Mosaic books teach us (as Moses himself first had to learn) to recognize, without necessarily reconciling, difficulties. If we observe Moses with all his flaws and comprehend his rule as an obstacle to as well as an opportunity for the people, if we recognize him as a source of harm as well as help, then we already have begun to learn about leadership. Emphasizing the ongoing necessity of learning from error, the Mosaic framework sets a double boundary. Even as Moses was forced to accept his human limits, the failure to reach the Promised Land, we have to accept failure in our attempts to formulate a direct, didactic theory of leadership good for all regimes under every condition. In this worldly arena of statecraft there may be specific rules but no way of enforcing them, or general principles of leadership but no specific rules for applying them. In response to his request for a clear mandate, Moses is put through some instructive rites of passage, an opportunity to test his mettle in situations. In Moses' peroration, he locates duty in this world:

> It is not in heaven, that thou shouldest say, Who shall go up for us to heaven, and bring it unto us, that we may hear it, and do it?
>
> Neither is it beyond the sea, that thou shouldest say, Who shall go over the sea for us, and bring it unto us, that we may hear it, and do it?
>
> But the word is very nigh unto thee, in thy mouth, and in thy heart, that thou mayest do it. [Deut. 30:12-14]

This tale, of course, is primarily a lesson for the people. Its theme, however, stands as a continual rejoinder to Moses' own plea for divine solutions that would absolve him from responsibility.

If leadership is supposed to vary with the regimes within which it is exercised, the very desire for a blueprint of leadership is necessarily misguided. Moses is not meant to be a paradigm of leadership. Are future leaders to be taught to try wriggling out of responsibility (as Moses does at the burning bush), or to encourage followers to take a heavy responsibility in abiding by a covenant for which they are ill-prepared? Are future leaders supposed to kill off a significant part of the people or to delay their maturity until a generation has died off? Why, if Moses is to be imitated, are we warned over and over that Moses' behavior is too special ever to be repeated? Though Moses is called to lead, his subsequent trials derive in part from the desire to escape from responsibility by getting God to give him a "How To Do It" leadership handbook. The Israelites murmur to Moses, and Moses calls for divine advice. The answer is unrelenting: "Try."

THE NURSING FATHER AMONG THE REGIMES

What have we learned about the Bible, now that I am at the end of this inquiry, that we might not have learned in any other way? What might readers see, that might otherwise have escaped their sight, by viewing the Torah as a teaching on leadership and leadership as a function of regime? The restoration of a more unified vision, a Holy Book that is more whole. Once we understand that the Bible is written from the dual premises of hierarchy and equity, both of which, in differing proportions, Moses embraced, its "binocular vision"[60] becomes explicable. These two ways of life, moreover, are deliberately left in contention so that future generations, including ours, can make their own compromises among these perennially valid but incomplete visions of the good life.

In *The Art of Biblical Narrative*, Robert Alter observes that its exposition is alternatively understandable and ambiguous. Why, he wonders, would its writer be capable of incisive commentary in one section and appear to muddle accounts in another, often in such a way as to be obvious to a schoolchild? Is this "sense of stubborn contradiction, of a profound and ineradicable untidiness in the nature of things"[61] (a pattern, Alter acutely observes, that is also present in much modern literature) a result of reediting the different sources that make up the Bible or of deliberate intent by the writers who knew better than we do how to make their points? "What, then, are we to do," Alter asks, "in reading these texts which the experts have invited us to view... as a crazy quilt of ancient traditions?" His answer is that while the Bible may not be all of a piece, "the confused textual patchwork that scholarship has often found... may prove upon further scrutiny to be purposeful pattern."[62]

Fortunately for us, as one of the two illustrations of his suggestion, Alter uses the account in Numbers 16 of Korah's rebellion, an account which has assumed central importance in this study because it evokes the basic dimensions of a regime of equity. To the documentary hypothesis of the source critics, therefore, as well as to Alter's literary sensibility, I add a cultural hypothesis: though the Bible rules out slavery and anarchy as forms of religious-cum-political organization, it purposefully includes equity and hierarchy, speaking alternately from one perspective, then another, as Moses did, so that readers can make these choices part of their own considerations. When the Bible tells the reader one thing, that is because its author is of one mind; when the Bible tells two partially complementary and partially contrasting things, that is because its author is of two minds and does not wish to foreclose choice, either then or now.

Though, in Alter's words, "The story is forceful enough to have made Korah a kind of archetype of the willful rebel against legitimate rule," it is apparent, as we saw in Chapter 4, that the episode involving Korah and the one involving Dathan and Abiram run into each other, one story being involved with the priesthood and the other with political authority. What is this uncertainty about? Alter is right to resist the charge of evident contradiction, saying, "But the writer's own editorial maneuvers indicate that he would prefer us to see the two rebellious parties... as one, or at least as somehow blurred together."[63] Alter's conclusion takes us a long way toward understanding:

> All this leads one to suspect that the Hebrew writer may have known what he was doing but that we do not. Certainly our notions about the spatial integrity of the location of a narrated action, the identity of personages, the consistency of agency and motive in the development of plot, are all flagrantly violated. Given the subject of the story,

perhaps there were compelling political reasons for fusing the two rebellions. Perhaps all these considerations of narrative coherence seemed
less important to the writer than the need to assert thematically that
the two separate events—the attempt to seize political power and the
usurpation of sacerdotal function—comprised one archetypal rebellion
against divine authority and so must be told as one tale…. In any
case… there are aspects of… biblical narrative texts that we cannot
confidently encompass in our own explanatory system.[64]

Let us see if the cultural hypothesis is a helpful addition to existing
"explanatory systems."

Why should a writer (or six writers) have trouble keeping two stories
apart? They shouldn't, unless, of course, as Alter suggests, they did not
want to do so. It is not, I suggest, the author (singular) but cultures
(plural) that are in conflict. The sects that form a regime of equity are
not only a religious and a political phenomenon but also a cultural archetype. They will attack hierarchy wherever they find it, whether secular
or religious. This much Moses came to understand from bitter personal
experience. But equity also has desirable aspects. So he sought to contain its energies by enveloping equity within a network of hierarchical
institutions. Attempting the task pulled Moses apart. No good deed, as
the aphorism says, goes unpunished.

No chance for Moses, then, no chance at all, to escape from bias.
Like other mortal men, he can live only one way of life at a time. Nor
can he entirely reconcile the conflicts built into each political regime. The
alternate denigration and glorification of leadership in equities and the
tendency toward state worship (from foreign wars to domestic injustice)
in hierarchies are inherent.

Is there, then, no way of overcoming the subjectivity inherent in living and looking one way rather than another? No, says the student of
cognitive limits on human rationality, not unless humans develop heads
on swivels. No, says the Bible, for only the Lord is all-knowing.

Yet culture shapes character. If leadership is a function of regime, the
character of the leaders who work within the regimes, even if they have
helped create their own social context, as Moses did, is also affected by
the way of life in which they and their followers are implicated. Moses
struggles for completeness. He seeks to rise above the battle, substituting
a holistic vision for the partial picture of the combatants in the social
struggle. But he does not succeed in seeing the face of God, who alone

is holy. For Moses, the land remains a promise, not a fulfillment; the rest he seeks belongs to the grave, not to life, in which contradiction is not the exception but the rule.

Precisely because regimes shape character, often for the worst, the commandments of everyday life, the mitzvot, which constitute the essence of Judaism, provide a permanent counterweight to the usual imperatives of social life. These commandments, such as the injunction to refrain from work on the Sabbath, are not justified on instrumental grounds, as if they were a means to some other end, in which case a utilitarian analysis—Is it more restful to remain at home or to drive to the seashore?—would be appropriate. Rather, the point of the commandments is precisely that they are commanded: man must recognize limits to his aspirations. There is nothing beyond them; they are ends in themselves.

Nevertheless, the commandments of Judaism are not separate from social life. On the contrary, for those who follow them, they constitute social life itself. Therefore the commandments are, like all living things, forms of bias—the social counterparts to the political regimes upon which I have focused the analysis in this book. The commandments are made up, as their very number suggests, of detailed prescriptions (for food, for clothes, for prayer, for the rhythm of daily life). Rulers as well as the ruled are subject to these laws. Hence the commandments are incompatible with the arbitrary power of slave regimes, which set themselves up above the law. Rulers are not to be gods, followers not to be slaves. These innumerable prescriptions are also incompatible with a life of anarchy in which people feel free to follow rules of their own making, rules that can be remade when new bargains become more advantageous. The virtues of anarchy lie in spontaneity, skepticism, and immediate results (the "bottom line," as we say), not in perennial commitment.

Acceptance of the commandments rules out half the spectrum of human possibilities. The answer to the question of human identity (Who am I?) is to be part of a strong group; the answer to the question of action (What should I do?) is to follow detailed prescriptions. Now this has to be hierarchical. The Ten Commandments come with graded differences in acceptable human behavior. Hierarchies are dedicated to maintaining differences among people. When Moses is referred to as the lawgiver, this means what it says: lots of laws. Only hierarchies advocate detailed prescriptions as part of the obligations imposed by the community of which they are a part. No hierarchy, no Judaism? Not quite.

There is another way: equities can combine strong group boundaries with voluntary acceptance of the commandments. The voluntariness that makes them especially fervent, however, also makes them reject authority. So they are vexatious. But they are also valuable.

Moses, the political as well as religious leader, cannot jump out of his social skin, turning in all directions simultaneously, being all things to all men, because, being human, he is limited by his social context. What he can do is combine hierarchy and equity, trying out different proportions of each, while retaining the essence of Judaism—strong groups with many prescriptions holding together their distinctive way of life.

Given the dimensions of the task—maintaining hierarchy and equity in uneasy combination—it is not surprising that Moses often fails. To the internal contradictions of equity and hierarchy must be added the incompatibilities between these regimes. Hierarchies want to maintain differences among people, equities to diminish them. Equities are suspicious of wealth; hierarchies want to enhance it for the glory of the collective. Hence hierarchies will ally themselves with other regimes (think of Solomon's foreign policy), while equities suspect that these alliances are a cover-up for introducing inequality. Despite surface similarities induced by following much the same commandments, the radical difference in principle between equity and hierarchy, between acceptance of authority for interpreting the law and rejection of that authority, leads to continuing conflict. That is why Judaism was and is a contentious community. Though Jews are an idol-smashing people, the difference is this: adherents of hierarchy smash foreign idols whereas members of equities tear down their own.

When he can no longer bear the burden of this quarrelsome people, Moses is met with the Lord's provision of a modicum of hierarchy, the council of elders, to soften the human leader's suffering. When Moses mocks himself as a "nursing father," he is only calling attention to the duty of the leader to attempt the impossible union of opposites.

When accepting existing demands, leadership consists of discovering new coalitions of interests, arranging mutually advantageous trades, and otherwise expanding the bargaining network around the political entrepreneur. Moses is politically productive; he makes much out of little. He provides largesse—food, water, spoils. He confers future benefits—promising this tribe land here and that tribe land there. The law brings cohesion as well as a portion of the patrimony set aside for the priestly order. By rejecting the existing order, Moses also transforms preferences, thus generating different demands. Once the people choose a way of life, their preferences follow from their regime. But they do not choose forever. Like Moses, they continuously evaluate their institutions. From then on, future choices become affirmations of (or departures from) the competing regimes of the people who choose.

EPILOGUE
A Speculation on the
Survival of the Jewish People

The Torah tells us a good deal more about what it is against (slavery and anarchy) than what it is for (some combination of hierarchy and equity). Pure equity is defeated with Korah in the desert, and the hierarchy that moderates it is rudimentary in form and short-lived. In order to extend the range of biblical experience with these two regimes, therefore, I will call upon the alternating anarchy and equity of the Book of Judges and the hierarchy that reached its peak under King Solomon. Here, too, we can compare the conflicts among the two covenants—Mosaic and Davidic—that compete for support in the Bible. I conclude by speculating on the part that this acceptable variety in political regimes played in Jewish survival over the centuries.

HUMAN NATURE

Let us begin with an assumption about human nature usually accepted in hierarchies: it is flawed but not so hopelessly evil that it cannot be saved by good institutions. Institutions shore up the work of the Creator. Human nature (viz., Aristotle's man as a political animal) is perfected only in institutions.

Institutions imply permanence. The placement of rewards and punishments inside hierarchic regimes enables them to undertake long-term ventures. Regime maintenance requires ability to set directions and keep to them over generations. Thus individuals must be taught to sacrifice the short term for the long run, the personal for the group interest. Momentary passions, ecstatic experiences must be eschewed in favor of sober self-sacrifice. Salvation is collective; and this applies to the people at the top as well as at the bottom.

By the same token, as good things are shared in hierarchies, so are the bad. Everyone is jointly responsible for whatever happens. Thus leaders share in the credit but are generally absolved for the blame by the diffusion of responsibility. Shoving sins on a sacrificial goat is characteristic of blame-shedding and -sharing in hierarchies; as are its standard operating procedures—secrecy, mutual protection, investigations aborted or never held. Equities, to show the difference, blame both outsiders (because they embrace inequality) and insiders (because they have secretly introduced impure practices); this explains why there may be breaches in their wall of virtue. Equities can pass blame to the outside but not share it or ignore it on the inside.

In hierarchies, human beings who love institutions are viewed as natural, and those who hate them are called unnatural. The establishment is good; if you are disloyal, you are evil.

Protection of hierarchical institutions is enhanced if individual opposition can be nullified. The rationale is that evil spreads, and the remedy—isolation—is the same as for any disease that is considered catching. The theory that moral evil (that is, antiestablishment behavior) is contagious is a standard charge in hierarchies. The weapon used is boundary maintenance. Hierarchies exert control by condemning as unworthy behavior actions in which "lowerarchs" seek to usurp the position of hierarchs, or someone somewhere plays a role for which he has not been chosen.

For the same reasons—the vulnerability of the young, their need for training in the values of the hierarchy—education assumes importance in hierarchical regimes. The young are segregated from contaminating influences and indoctrinated into prevailing practices. They must feel what is right, be able to recite the right, before they can claim to know it. Institutional allegiance is rendered automatic and the suppression of dissent, where it cannot be compromised, is justified.

Human nature is seen in equities as either perfect or perfectible. Anyone can do anything. Expertise is suspect; so is science; so is any division of labor that gives some people superiority over others. It is not people who corrupt institutions but the other way around; equities inveigh endlessly against the corrupting effect of hierarchies and anarchies. Disagreements within equities, viewed as departure from the one right way, are attributed, therefore, to the secret importation of alien practices. The characteristic accusation within the equity is hidden defilement.

Time and Memory

The stronger the hierarchy, the more effective its division of labor, and the more it is able to impose sacrifices on the present for the sake of the future. Promises of "pie in the sky" are characteristic of hierarchies. If no one thinks there will be a future or expects to be there to enjoy one (the Armageddon complex of the equity regime), all bets are off. Only the people of the future can make good the promises of the past. Thus working today to benefit tomorrow depends on trust that other people will remember their obligations. There is a name for the reproduction of patterns of reciprocal obligations, and it is "institution." This desire to project the past into the future, which is called orthodoxy, depends on the longevity of societal institutions. The memory of a people depends not only on its capacity to memorize or even to use mnemonic devices, though Moses does both, but also on its ability to preserve the institutional arrangements that make promises good.

Memory is an attribute of hierarchies whose legitimacy depends on an unbroken line of succession rationalizing the exercise of authority. Obligations are passed down and paid off. Slaves have no need of memory; they only follow orders. Nor do masters need to remember; obedience to them is automatic. Anarchies need only short-term memory, lasting only as long as their latest contract, when negotiations begin again. Equities hold a positive regret for memory as a claim of the past on the present that institutionalizes inequality. Why should some people be remembered, others forgotten? Do not the masses make history? Only distant founders, with no claim on the present generation, are recalled.

The hierarchy with its long-term goals and expected long-term gains is confident about meeting dangers that lie in the future. It has confidence that its future leaders will deal with these difficulties. Hierarchies are also reluctant to change course, partly because this implies abandonment of goals and partly because it is not easy to reprogram what has become ponderous bureaucratic machinery. Whoever threatens the long march to their distant objectives, whether it be foreign enemies or domestic deviants, will be attended to with dispatch by hierarchical regimes.

Equities reject the dead hand of the past. Traditional laws of inheritance, for example, which allow inequalities to be perpetuated into the future, are anathema. If there is to be a totally egalitarian society, no head of this or master of that, neither past nor future, must be in a position to make claims on the present. No one must be able to say he got there first. Past time is so remote there is no possible genealogy connecting it to the present. But the future is here today. The ultimate in future time is well known in secular discourse as the end of the world, or in religious language as the coming of the Messiah. By transferring the ultimate dangers of the future into the present, equities justify the severe actions they take to separate themselves from others.

HYPOCRISY IN HIERARCHY

Samuel's ambivalence about kingship—he is against it in principle but will allow it in practice—is most Mosaic. "Ye have this day rejected your God," he cries (I Sam. 10:19). Nevertheless, if the people and their king carry out the Commandments all will be well, but if not, "then shall the hand of the Lord be against you" (I Sam. 12:15). Hierarchies must be hypocritical; there is no other way. Can Moses (or any man) obey all the Commandments? Will he not say one thing and do another—unify the people and then divide them, forbid foreign wives but take one for himself, preach consent but practice coercion? Hierarchy has to cover up (because it cannot justify) the item-by-item injustice of some men deciding for others.

Why does Moses not argue the merits of his hierarchical case against the equity of Korah? For once, Moses is really tongue-tied. Is Moses against the priesthood of believers? He is not. Does he claim that he alone received the revelation? He does not. Moses' objection can be only to the consequences of purely voluntary organization, a judgment born of experience—the realization that the people will then return to Egypt or scatter—not of principle. There is a trial by fire and Korah is consumed. There is divine judgment, but not explanation, because it would justify the opposite—inequality—and that is not intended. Here spectacle is a substitute for substance.

The hierarchical Moses is secretive: no one is supposed to get more information than necessary to do his or her own jobs. Yet Moses is also a lawgiver who must teach his people a new way of life. The more they believe and understand, the less the need for coercion. Moses copes with the apparent contradiction—between the secrecy necessary for governing and the openness essential for education—by using the public setting of equity to serve the purposes of hierarchy. So long as Moses alone has direct access to the word of God, no one can successfully challenge his leadership. The problem posed by Korah is, therefore, both religious and political, in that it would deny Moses a monopoly over the word. Moses' solution is ingenious; knowledge is decentralized, but the right to interpret depends on accepting his authority; the Torah that is to be interpreted comes from Moses. In this way, sharing the power of interpretation ramifies the influence of Moses' leadership.

Hierarchies seek to prevent conflict by indoctrination and to control it by punishment. How, without a hierarchy, can equities deal with dissent?

Splits

Inside the equity life is clean; outside it is dirty. Establishing the location of rewards and punishment inside the regime, however, as our models tell us, is a dimension equities share with hierarchies. Hence the two regimes share purification rites and an obsession with cleanliness. But the kind of corruption they fear is different. Since each member of an equity claims immediate and unmediated access to higher principles, "filth" is defined as authority—imposition by others of practices equities do not accept; in short, leadership here comes close to being seen as corruption. In hierarchies, by contrast, evil is disobedience, acting against the practices imposed by hierarchical leaders.

The fraternity of equality fears fission or suppression. Yet it can neither divide its labors nor delegate its authority. Whatever hierarchies do is perceived as bad, including the plethora of rules to regulate behavior. Giving lip service to rules because they are burdensome, or stretching them to avoid difficulties, is counted as hypocrisy, the worst of vices. (The great virtue is its opposite, sincerity.) But if every man does what seems good to him, anarchy threatens and chaos may ensue. Unfortunate events tend to be blamed on the evil outside world or on disaffected members, who, it is alleged, tried to elevate themselves above their fellows.

Equities have two main modes of coping with conflict—separation and splits. The worse the outside world, the further the equitable regime removes itself from contaminating influences, the better able the regime is to justify continued adherence to its tenets. This accounts for an apparent political paradox. Regimes based on equality do not behave equitably. Though they encourage reprisal by intemperate acts, equities are unwilling to make accommodations. Indeed, the closer hierarchy comes to them, or to their position, the further they move from it. Equities appear to prefer persecution and separation to accommodation. Lacking authority, equities maintain internal cohesion through opposition to hierarchies and anarchies.

Equities are an inexhaustible source of social energy. In this sense of permanent opposition to the larger society, equities are incomplete in that they take on their chief characteristic by distinguishing themselves from hierarchies. No orthodoxy, no heterodoxy.

Equities prefer issues on which they cannot be accommodated (such as perfect ritual purity or complete physical safety) so that they can justify exclusivity. The message is not in the substance of their arguments but in the medium of disputatiousness they use to pursue it.

Yet some benefits do flow from fission. A disadvantage of hierarchy is that it requires groups of substantial size to make specialization and division of labor work. Hierarchies can be sitting ducks; they are visible and tied to one place at a time. When they are destroyed, there is nothing left. Equities are advantaged by small size and face-to-face relations; this makes inequality less likely and equality more efficient. When, as is often the case, they do not like what is happening, equities can pick up and move. They are well suited for forced marches and long exiles. The splitting style, which makes them difficult to lead, also makes them hard to suppress. For when equities are eliminated in one place, they may well spring up in others.

Both equities and hierarchies are acceptable to Judaism, but both are seriously flawed. Are there, then, some ways to combine their benefits without suffering in corresponding measure their disabilities? Possibly. As good a place to assess the prospects as any is the extraordinary continuity of the Hebrew people. If Moses had not been a leader who distrusted absolute power, whether it be the charisma of the equity or the authority of the hierarchy, he and his people would never have survived. The part Moses' political ideas played in the survival of the Hebrew people thus deserves study. We begin with the regimes of the Promised Land, the anarchy-equity of judges and the hierarchy of kings.

REGIMES WITHOUT MOSES

Life in the wilderness and in Canaan are different; there is no denying that. Nonetheless, I maintain that the similarities in regimes between the desert and the settled land are, for purposes of understanding the biblical conception of leadership, more important than the differences. To do otherwise would be to accept the proposition that Mosaic leadership, exercised in person entirely in the wilds, is irrelevant to all that comes after Moses in biblical times and in ours. On the contrary, his people's experiences immediately after his death, under judges and kings, enlarges the possibilities of learning about the central tendencies of diverse regimes, which could only be sketched in before reaching the land in which their promises (and pitfalls) would be more fully realized.

It is true that preparation for self-government is not the same as trying it. A land to conquer and defend creates a different nexus of interests than merely passing through other people's places. The maximal hierarchy permitted by settlement may be more effective and more harsh than the looser arrangements of a pastoral people. For prophets excoriating the established regime of their time, the desert period, full of discord and mayhem, may in retrospect appear rosy. As the Greeks romanticized the agora, the central place of their city-states, because its confined spaces facilitated the public life to which they were dedicated, so, too, Thomas Jefferson, who wished power distributed more evenly, saw cities as a sink of corruption. It is not surprising, given the viewpoint of most prophets, that the post-Mosaic biblical story becomes increasingly critical, almost as critical, we might say, as some of Moses' followers were of his leadership.

There is a difference between the biblical conception of leadership and that which preceded it. Before the Bible, so far as is known, there was only one right regime, and, therefore, one right kind of leadership, both good for all time. As the experiences recorded in the books of Judges and Kings recapitulate Moses' movement through anarchy, equity, and hierarchy, we will see once more that leadership varies with regime.

My theme has been that the books of Moses may usefully be regarded as instruction in leadership. This instruction was for Moses and, by recalling his struggles in their context, for us. Moses teaches us how to learn about leadership. The centuries immediately after Moses' death offer us an opportunity to observe what happened to Mosaic political ideas, allowing us to practice his method on what (in the appropriately antiseptic language of social science) could be called another "body of data." Fieldwork in the Bible is essential and available to all who come after Moses. This fieldwork requires observation of the relationship between what goes on above—man's relationship to the divine—and what is happening below in man's relationship to his own kind. The people's connection to their regime and to their God are related.

After crossing the river Jordan, the boundary between childhood and manhood, the Israelites are circumcised. That day the people also observed the Passover, eating the unleavened bread in memory of their desert period. The next day the manna they had eaten in the desert was to cease, and the people "did eat of the fruit of the land of Canaan that year" (Josh. 5:12). New life, new land, new food. The food of dependence gives way to the first fruits of maturity. "This day," the Lord told Joshua, "have I rolled away the reproach of Egypt from off you" (Josh. 5:9). Slavery gives way to choice.

Upon entering the land of promises, full of pledges and remembering their betrayal, the children of Israel lived as adults under two regimes— the alternating anarchy and equity of the judges. Each regime proved vulnerable to corruption from within and to conquest from the outside: Samuel's concern (I Sam. 4-6) that the ark containing the covenant had been captured by the Philistines signifies that vulnerability. A regime that literally cannot keep its commandments is in trouble.

It is as if, through regimes, the Hebrew people were recapitulating Moses' journey and testing anew his rejection of anarchy and his disappointment with equity. In the end, their collective experience parallels that of the people of the exodus: they fall into anarchy, choose equity, but cannot live without hierarchy.

We may take seriously the refrain of the Book of Judges: "In those days there was no king in Israel: every man did that which was right in his own eyes" (Judg. 21:25). The people of Israel governed themselves in an organized anarchy, if this is not a contradiction in terms. Between times, when judges arose to deliver Israel from evils it had brought on itself, governance became more like that of an equity. Only once—when all the other tribes fought the tribe of Benjamin because its men had gang-raped ("forced" is the biblical term) the concubine of a Levite—did the Israelites act as a unit. (He cut up her body in pieces and sent it to the tribes asking for justice.) Otherwise, the leader-judges led their own tribes and perhaps a few others. While the oft-debated question of whether the judges can be called charismatic leaders has been treated on an either-or basis, without considering alternative possibilities, attention to the regimes within which they worked should help to sort out the situation. My answer, which would explain the inconclusiveness of the debate, is that when judges ruled, they acted under a regime of equity and were charismatic leaders, but in between times there was anarchy. Since equities and anarchies share sporadic leadership, the distinguishing characteristic, according to my scheme of regimes, is whether rule is limited, as in anarchies, or unlimited, as in equities.

Everyone agrees that the judges arose in times of deep distress and by unusual—military, physical, or tactical—prowess delivered one or more Hebrew tribes from their enemies during a chronic state of war. Of most judges (both major and minor), the Bible states that the spirit of the Lord was in them; but whether the people recognized this directly or only indirectly—to the extent that these judges succeeded—cannot be ascertained. Judges are defenders of rights. Since God is the ultimate judge of Israel, it would have to be His spirit that moves men or women who protect others within the framework of Israelite religion.

Individual judges, as Abraham Malamat says in his seminal study, are representative types. They are "models of oppressors... and of deliverers."[1] Let us look at these models as clues to the character of the regimes.

The deliverer does not come immediately, but only after the people have suffered a period of abuse. Nor does he or she (Deborah) rule indefinitely. The deliverer dies; the people stray from the fold; and, in the fierce words of the Bible, they fall "into the hands of spoilers that spoiled them... so that they could not any longer stand before their enemies... and they were greatly distressed" (Judg. 2:14-15).

Coalitions are variable but limited to the tribes of Israel. Deborah, aptly called "a mother in Israel" (Judg. 5:7), had six tribes with her. But her memorable song mentions several tribes—"Gilead abode beyond Jordan: and why did Dan remain in ships?" (Judg. 5:17)—who would not serve as her sons. Gideon had three or four tribes on his side but also apparently some against him or neutral. There was always a confederacy but not always of the same size or composition, best described as shifting alliances within a religious-ethnic framework.

We are told of some (but not all) judges, as with Othniel, that "the Spirit of the Lord came upon him" (Judg. 3:10). The judges are charismatic in that the light of the Lord is in them and in them alone. Gideon alone requests and receives major public signs that it is really God who has spoken to him.

Most judges are chosen despite visible handicaps such as Jephthah's bastardy, Gideon's youth, or Deborah's sex. You do not have to be prominent to be a judge, but, like Othniel, Caleb's younger brother, you may be. No judges, except for the evil Abimelech, seize leadership; and none, with the same exception, try to pass it on. The judges, in sum, do not seek, inherit, or transfer leadership.

How are judges chosen and how do they carry out their rule? A swift summary of the careers of three judges—two good guys and a bad one—will tell us what we need to know.

How did Gideon rule? Not at all, apparently: "Then the men of Israel said unto Gideon, Rule thou over us, both thou, and thy son, and thy son's son also: for thou hast delivered us from the hand of Midian. And Gideon said unto them, I will not rule over you, neither shall my son rule over you: the Lord shall rule over you" (Judg. 8:22-23). The frequency with which younger and unlikely men prevail over their ostensible superiors in the Bible, as does Gideon, I have attributed to the desire to show that the Lord cannot be limited by precedent or expectation. From this standpoint, hierarchy, which is based on determining in advance who will rule, is a way of limiting spontaneity. McCarter writes that "from the prophetic point of view the designation of an heir to the throne (*nagid*) was a divine prerogative, and the unchecked practice of blood succession, because it seemed to interfere with Yahweh's free choice of the ruler, was one of the things that made kingship hateful."[2] The reluctance of the Bible to accept hierarchy, here as elsewhere, is grounded in its view that certainty belongs to God alone.[3]

Abimelech incites his mother's family against the house of Gideon, saying that Gideon's people are better off ruled by him than by his seventy half-brothers. He kills his brothers except for the youngest, Jotham, who hides himself. Then the men of Schechem make Abimelech king.

Hearing the news, Jotham tells the people a fable. The trees wanted to anoint a king, but one by one the better kinds refused, because they feared losing their special qualities—the oil of the olives, the sweetness of figs, or the cheer of wine—more than they desired promotion over other trees. The bramble would, however, take the job on condition that "if in truth ye anoint me king over you, then come and put your trust in my shadow; and if not, let fire come out of the bramble, and devour the cedars of Lebanon" (Judg. 9:15). Jotham's moral is that the best, who can succeed in private life, do not go into politics. But because they do not, the path is left open to the thorns and brambles of this world to wreak destruction.

Suffice it to say, in summary, that Abimelech is, as Malamat portrays him, an "anti-deliverer."[4] Abimelech seeks office not because there is a need (say, a foreign invasion) but because of a personal lust for power. His rule comes not from spontaneity but rather out of personal premeditation; not from personal prowess but because of family descent. Abimelech's military exploits are daring, but his wickedness is greater. Finally, a woman breaks his skull by dropping a piece of millstone on it.

Abimelech's wickedness is directed not only toward his own father, Gideon, but also toward God, the Father of all. Abimelech perverts proper political relationships. God, as Gideon said, should rule. Between God and His people there should be no political intermediary, not even a just ruler like Gideon, except when the survival of the people is threatened, and only then if the ruler shows signs of God's grace. Like the good trees, which serve man with olives, figs, and grapes, the righteous ruler is known by his reluctance to serve in peacetime.

The history in Judges is one of recurrent relapse into worship of ("whoring after" as biblical phraseology has it) strange gods. Anarchy leaves the people defenseless, less than whole. Having abandoned the one holy God, and with weak group boundaries, the people are open to invasion by foreign forces. To get out of these difficulties the people need stronger leadership.

Might leaders capable of such heroic feats also seek to rule permanently, turning anarchy into equity and then to hierarchy? Jephthah the bastard "was a mighty man of valor" (Judg. 11:1). His half-brothers had thrown him out of the house of Gilead because they said he was not fit to inherit. But when the Amorites attacked, the elders of Gilead asked Jephthah to return and lead them in battle. Because he had been exiled from his father's house, Jephthah bargained hard. He wanted to be the permanent tribal head. As Malamat says, "The traditional rulers were forced to accede to Jephthah and appoint him not only as 'commander,' that is, as leader for the duration of the war, but also as 'head,' that is, as supreme ruler in peace as well—all of which involved surrendering their authority and the powers vested in them."[5] The purely voluntary association could not sustain itself.

When the people demand to be ruled by kings just like everyone else, Samuel objects. With faith, the Lord will provide the right ruler. God interjects, however, saying, "they have not rejected thee, but they have rejected me, that I should not reign over them" (I Sam. 8:7). Samuel is instructed to let the people work their will but to go on exposing to them the undesirable manner of kings: "He will take your sons... take your daughters... take the tenth of your seed... take your menservants, and your maidservants... your goodliest young men, and your asses... take the tenth of your sheep" (I Sam. 8:11-17). Kings are not givers but takers. The chosen alternative, however—rule by men of righteousness—had disintegrated in confusion, the Book of Judges showing what chaos resulted when every man did what he thought best.

The people cannot bear this burden. "There was... a fatal flaw in this 'Kingdom' [of God]," Yehezkel Kaufmann asserts, "it failed to set up a stable and continuous government. It always depended on... enthusiasm... excitement... crisis, on... an inspired Savior"[6]—that is, on the charisma of judges in an equity. Hierarchy, except for tentative steps by Moses, had not yet been tried. Standing before the eternal Mount Sinai of their situation, the people cede to kings (as previously they had given

Moses) the prerogative of interpreting the voice of God. A new failure replaces the old. With few exceptions (exceptions that prove the rule but also open up messianic hopes) the kings of Israel cannot manifest in their own beings the unity of experience between God and man. Torn between abuse and abdication, between melioration and moralism, the kings of Israel bring down the people with them, like Samson proving more in death by dragging down the pillars of the state than ever in life.

In the world of behavior, of course, Israel is like other nations in its sinfulness. That is the trouble; the perversity of the people's demand to be like other nations is revealed when we recognize that that is exactly what Israel is not supposed to be.[7] The Lord's warning through Samuel, like that of the tree of knowledge in the Garden of Eden, or the Tower of Babel, is against idolatry, worship of man by man. Kingship is acceptable only reluctantly because it predisposes people to make gods out of men.

In keeping with the covenant between God and His people, kings must be anointed by a prophet or priest authorized to do so by divine will. This is how kings are said to come from God. When, at a later date, kings exert control over priests and prophets—hence the issue of false priests and prophets—hierarchy may degenerate into slavery. Each regime has its own temptations and abuses.

SOLOMON'S HIERARCHY

Saul is the man in the middle, a transitional figure, a dangling man,[8] stronger than the judges who preceded him, weaker than the kings to follow. He was, as Murray Lee Newman, Jr., calls him, "a charismatic man, not an organization man."[9] Under Saul there is monarchy but not much hierarchy. There is little division of labor. There is hardly a capital, his court, such as it is, being the pastures of his home town. Saul's rule is more akin to that of the early medieval monarchs than to the splendor and formality of the Sun King at Versailles, though even this comparison suggests more hierarchy than he had.[10]

David's rule represents the first full expression of Hebrew nationalism—one nation in one land under one God. Politically, David is a unifier. Placing the ark within the tabernacle gives his aspirations a religious cover. The ark is not moved to a permanent temple—making God's house analogous to a king's palace—because David's political aims are not yet attained. The nation is not yet entirely centralized; the succession is not yet certain; and the monarchy is not entirely secure. Of the twelve tribes, the nine that live in the north are on the verge of secession. As one uses a magnifying glass or an oversized object so as better to recognize the ordinary thing, let us learn from the rule of David's son Solomon, who enhanced the tendencies inherent in his father's hoped-for hierarchical regime.

Whatever David had done, Solomon did, and more. David had made preparations for the temple; Solomon built it—and on a lavish scale. David had concubines by the tens; Solomon by the hundreds. David had limited foreign relations; Solomon had extensive contact with other people. David began central taxation and set up a regular army; Solomon multiplied royal officials and had a much bigger army and corps of mercenaries. Forced labor or labor in lieu of taxes (the corvée), barely started by David, was extended by Solomon to include Israelites as well as tributary people. David had begun dividing the country into administrative districts; Solomon completed the task, placing relatives in outlying areas and establishing jurisdictions different from the traditional tribal areas. Hierarchy had arrived. So had civil service. As Frederic Thieberger concludes, the people were "enlisted for public services and supervised by a central administration, appointed by the king. Now it was no longer the council of city elders or the assembly of elders of the tribe who were the highest authority in matters of administration and justice, but a body of officials answerable to the king. The fact that Solomon took over David's officials shows that here, in fact, a new class had come into being. It was also very important that already under David the High Priests were appointed by the king, and in this way all priests became royal officials."[11]

The result was, at first, a more secure and more extensive kingdom; in the end, self-worship and secession. At the beginning of his reign, Solomon had a dream in which God asked what he wanted and he replied, "Give therefore thy servant an understanding heart to judge thy people, that I may discern between good and bad: for who is able to judge this thy so great a people?" (I Kings 3:9). Because Solomon had not asked for wealth, he was given "a wise and an understanding heart" (I Kings 3:12). To be able to distinguish between good and evil, however, does not necessarily mean one will act virtuously on that understanding. "King Solomon," the Bible relates, "loved many strange [foreign] women" who "turned away" his heart, so that he "did evil in the sight of the Lord" by worshiping foreign gods and allowing his wives to sacrifice to them (I Kings 11:1-8). "The Lord was angry with Solomon" and punished him, saying, "I will surely rend the kingdom from thee," leaving Solomon's son only one tribe, Judah (which had absorbed Benjamin and Simeon) for David's sake (I Kings 11:9-13).

The monarchy that issued from David failed as a result of excess, at once too strong for its citizens and too weak for its enemies. Its rulers became self-absorbed, a sign that they were confusing themselves with God. Hierarchy can lead to idolatry and begin to look like slavery. When we see not what David would have liked—an unconditional covenant with his own house—but rather the actual consequences of his hierarchical regime in Solomon's and Rehoboam's time, hierarchy appears flawed, too. But that was not the end.

Judaism is in a process of repair. Nothing noteworthy is given to Israel once and for all—not the Ten Commandments; not the covenant; not the law; not, or so Moses had to learn, his own leadership. The resilience of the Jewish people, their ability to absorb catastrophe and bounce back, deserves further consideration.

SURVIVAL

Why doesn't the Torah prescribe an ideal political regime the way it proposes an ideal religious life? When we answer this question, we are on the way to explaining the survival of the Jewish people. The behavior to be explained is not only the amazing persistence of the species, maintaining a continuous identity over thousands of years, but the coexistence over time of persecution, factionalism, and survival.

The usual explanation is certainly part of the truth: the survival of Jews is related to the practices of Judaism that make it a tightly knit community able to transmit its values over generations. Judaism has a high capacity for cultural reproduction. No doubt. But to reproduce, one first has to survive. A constant—religious values and social practices—cannot be used to explain a variable—adaptation to widely varying circumstances over thousands of years. I support Hocart's insight: "It may be in the evolution of institutions that we shall find the key to the problem of adaptation of organisms generally… seeking for it in ourselves [rather] than outside human society among animals and plants."[12] To direct this thrust, add W. Ross Ashby's "Law of Requisite Variety"—it takes variety to cope with variety.[13]

Each of the four major types of regimes has potentially fatal disabilities. Because masters do not have to pay attention to slaves, slave societies are vulnerable on grounds of ignorance. Pharaoh's lack of memory is paralleled by a trained incapacity to anticipate the future. When the master errs, everyone dependent upon him—that is, everyone—repeats the same mistake.

Unless everyone agrees to play by the same rules, anarchies are easily overwhelmed by external attack. Their weak boundaries permit information to come through but make it difficult to act together for the common defense. If there are enough groups to recombine, the game goes on. If one big group will not let the other play, it is over.

Equities suffer either from lack or excess of leadership. Either equities reject authority or they follow a leader who has to show he is perfect to maintain their allegiance. Separation from society renders equities impotent, and confrontation may kill them.

"Perseveration" is the Achilles' heel of hierarchy. Once an order is given, it keeps getting carried out. The "on" signal is stronger than the "off." Because whole phalanxes of officials have to act together, moreover, the hierarchy is often slow to adapt to changing conditions. And when it does adapt, it does so by overcommitting people to the new departure; then it becomes even harder to change back.

One can imagine structural weakness and environmental change combining to kill any type of regime. There are always things a regime cannot do or conditions to which it cannot adapt. When the infallibility of the master is challenged, or the rule of unlimited transactions is abolished, or the equity splits, or the hierarchy becomes sluggish, these regimes can crumble. Why, then, have Jewish regimes survived when other regimes have not? Or, better put, why have Jews survived though the regimes under which they lived have not?

The secret of survival lies precisely in avoiding commitment to a single type of regime. Though slavery and anarchy are prohibited by the Bible, equity and hierarchy are permitted. Since the two regimes have different disabilities and different strengths, one will survive when the other will not.

A movable hierarchy comes close to being an empirical contradiction. In order to have specialization and division of labor, there must be a structure of a certain size. Being large in size and fixed in geography, therefore, hierarchies can conceivably be wiped out with one blow. They are robust, but they can be overturned by an unfriendly environment.

Even when Jewish people have historically had a state, in biblical times or today, elements of equity have sought to separate themselves from it. The contemporary sects who love living in the Holy Land but prefer a non-Jewish state are a case in point. So long as the foreign rulers are not utterly hostile, separation from foreigners is easier than from one's own people. In moving "out of harm's way" (to use Cervantes' phrase), however, equities do have a distinct advantage: they travel light.

Small size is a distinguishing feature of equities. Lack of authority makes the division of labor difficult. Equality makes more sense (each person does possess some human qualities) in close quarters. Hence equities are characteristically small and, therefore, mobile. Since they often split, they also tend to be numerous. Beat them one place, their equivalent turns up in another. Little, quick, and dispersed, these equities are easy to attack but hard to kill off altogether.

The very diversity of its political forms saved Hebrew culture from an early demise. Along the continua between the two structural extremes are stronger and weaker versions, hierarchies modified by equity and equities affected by hierarchy. After all, both are collectives. At any one time, consequently, there are a sufficiently large number of dispersed and varied regimes adapted to different circumstances to prevent premature demise.

If an entire cultural complex is made up of constants, it can hardly adapt to change. Strands that do develop diversity, however, can vary to keep the others constant. Such is the role that political regime has played in Jewish life. No one regime but all the variants taken together have been the shock absorbers of Judaism, making up with their resilience the rigidity of religious belief and the constancy of its practice.

WHY THE TORAH DOES NOT
PRESCRIBE A SINGLE IDEAL POLITICAL FORM

Now we are in a better position to understand the view the Torah takes of government. The state, as we would call it, must not become a regime of slavery. No ruler is to be a Pharaoh. Anarchy also is proscribed, because it tends toward polytheism—different gods for different purposes. Not every voluntary transaction is allowed. For the rest, the biblical emphasis is more on limiting abuses than on widening government's ability to do good. By not specifying the ideal regime, by stating only that slavery and anarchy are impermissible, the Mosaic matrix of leaders in regimes invites us to draw our own balance between the imperfections of leaders in hierarchies and equities.

The strictures against idolatry are so powerful that there can be no overt state worship. And the covert kind is continuously undermined by prophecy, holding rulers to high ideals. The emphasis on contingency—on the unknown, on testing to discover how the leaders will behave in action—guards against reification of the state as a thing apart from, and superior to, the people. Social structure, including the structure of the state, is a product of human interaction, and it is these human beings who have goals, dominate and are dominated by others, make and break agreements. No one is to be in the grip of impersonal forces that he or she cannot control, nor subject to the inexorable forces of a history apart from human will. No regime, no state can be more perfect than the people who make it up. The state is a concession to human weakness, indispensable but not noble. It is not the best but rather the least bad that is recommended or, since none are exactly commended, at least tolerated.

What happens when the state becomes an end in itself? The people are sacrificed to it. Rulers begin by protecting the people and end, as in Solomon's time, by acting in their own interest. Government of, by, and for the governors, regimes for rulers, are inevitable unless the self-absorption of rulers, self-worship through the state, is countered by submission to the community, whose collective experience is contained in the laws of their God.

Tension is maintained between leaders and the led: rulers, by virtue of their position, are held to higher standards, and citizens are held responsible for the fate of their regimes. Rulers are to be exemplars, for they act in public. "Fortunate is the generation whose ruler brings a sin-offering for his unwitting sin," said Rabbi Johanan ben Zakkai. "If the ruler brings an offering, then need we speak of the common man?"[14] At the same time, the strain toward consistency of experience in Judaism—holiness as wholeness—suggests that ruler and ruled share a common fate. As S. Mowinckel codifies the understanding, "Just because king and people are truly one, the king embodying the supreme ego of the people, the destiny of king and people will be the same in good and evil. If the king is righteous and blessed, the whole people will be blessed, and righteous, and happy. If the king is ungodly and does what is evil in the sight of Yahweh, then the whole people will be infected with ungodliness and misfortune, and must suffer all the adversity which is the result of the king's sin."[15] The tendency to write history as if it were all political history, especially the lives of prominent men in exalted positions, may be partly responsible for this emphasis on kings. More likely, the stress on unity of experience leads Hebrew historians to view political history as the outer manifestation of the social history of their people. Biblical explanations root behavior in social relations. That is why leadership is considered a consequence of regime, not the other way around.

The Torah does not prescribe a single ideal political regime for two reasons. First, doing so would elevate politics from a means to an end. The danger that political institutions will become idols, worshiped in their own right, is thereby avoided. Concomitantly, rigidifying regimes would also be incompatible with the practice of religion in a different sense; if their politics were not pliable, there would be no Jews around to practice their religion.

ACKNOWLEDGMENTS

This book began as part of the annual Southern Regional Training Program lectures sponsored by the Program and the Bureau of Public Administration at the University of Alabama in 1974. I am grateful to Coleman Ransome, Jr., Philip Coulter, and their colleagues for the opportunity to try out these thoughts and for the enthusiastic response that encouraged me to continue.

The manuscript was written at the University of California in Berkeley and at the Van Leer Foundation in Jerusalem. No one could have had better working conditions or more genuine interest from the leaders of the organizations concerned—Yehuda Elkana in Jerusalem, Sandy Muir in the Political Science Department, and Percy Tannenbaum at the Survey Research Center in Berkeley.

My research assistants were especially gifted. Caroline Newman, a doctoral student in comparative literature at the University of California, helped concentrate my thought by raising one objection after another to every hypothesis I tried. Our conversations were a high point in my education. She is responsible for whatever grammatical sophistication this book possesses. Rabbi Avi Weinstein, who teaches Talmud at Yeshivat Hamivtar in Jerusalem, helped me trace sources among the traditional interpreters. Our lively discussions about the principles of rabbinic commentary have informed my perspective. A student in the Near Eastern

Studies Department at Berkeley, Susan Rattray, and Yael Gir, a student at the Hebrew University, searched for and discussed a variety of interpretations, adding substantially to the range of views considered.

Distinguished biblical scholars on the Berkeley campus—David Daube and Jacob Milgrom—and in Israel—Abraham Malamat, Moshe Weidenfeld, and Avraham Wolfensohn, set me straight on many matters. Yehoshua Leibowitz's characteristically incisive criticism made me face up to the importance of daily practice as over against merely reading the Bible. They read early drafts of the first five chapters. Rabbi George Vida, who married me off, gave me a good feel for the relationship between my interpretation and traditional values. Murray Baumgarten of the University of California at Santa Cruz wrote a detailed literary critique that sharpened my perception. Alouph Hareven at Van Leer allowed me to read his own creative interpretations and spent hours discussing my own with me. As a newcomer to the field, it was indispensable that I learn from those who know more about the Bible than I can ever hope to understand.

Colleagues in the political science profession were acute in their critical comments on leadership. I benefited greatly by comments from Gabriel Almond, James Barber, Eugene Bardach, Reinhard Bendix, Walter Berns, Steve Brams, Gerald Caiden, Rufus Davis, Lewis Dexter, Yaron Ezrahi, Fred Greenstein, Herbert Kaufman, Martin Levin, Arnold Meltsner, Robert Parker, Nelson Polsby, Allen Schick, Lester Seligman, Elaine Spitz, and Michael Walzer. Anthropologists Mary Douglas and Michael Thompson were especially helpful in commenting on my models of regimes. David Cohen, a leader as well as a student of leadership, and Mitch Allen, an editor of social research, brought their special perspectives to bear.

Thinking privately is one thing and trying ideas out in public is another. I am, therefore, most appreciative of the opportunity to give lectures on the leadership of Moses at the Van Leer Foundation, the Political Science Department of the Hebrew University, the Bible meeting at the home of Prime Minister Begin, and Daniel Elazar's continuing meeting on covenantal relationships at the Center for Jewish Community Studies in Jerusalem. I leave it to the reader to imagine what it is like carrying Moses to Jerusalem. I gave seminars on the same subject at the Miller Center at the University of Virginia, the University of Iowa, and the Columbia University Seminar on Political and Social Thought.

In one respect, if no other, this book reflects a Mosaic theme; it has been revised more times than I care to think. Doris Patton, my secretary, has borne this travail with calm and has never let me lose track of what I once thought I was doing. Along the way, "Moses" has been edited and re-edited with distinction by Peter Dreyer, Marie-Anne Seabury, and Trudie Calvert, though those familiar with my style will have no doubt about the original and final author.

Family and friends have been more interested in "Moses" than in any other book I have written. My wife, Mary, read material on Moses in French. Her questions on what it all meant were more fundamental (and thus more useful) than she may have realized. My son Ben improved the public lectures by pointing out failures to explain sufficiently. Gershon and Elisa Rivlin, cousins in Israel, who set up the Ben Gurion archives at Sede Boker after retirement age, took us to Kadesh Barnea, which is reputed to have been the place where much of the desert wanderings took place. Our cousins from Kibbutz Gesher, Ben Ami and Channa Rivlin, showed us other historic places not only with loving care but with appreciation of their significance in the life of the people. Ronald Winton, an active layman in the Church of England and a mentor from Australian days, gave me an invaluable sense of how a practicing Christian might look at the text. Raphaella Bilsky, Fred Simons, and Janet and Mikey Aviad made Israel bloom for us.

If it were possible, I would give my greatest thanks (the kind that can never be adequately acknowledged) to the subject of this study. Whether he would thank me is another matter. There is need to accept responsibility for the many inadequacies of my own account, for Moses did not absolve himself of his own errors. One thing is incontrovertible: without Moses, this book could not have been written.

NOTES

FOREWORD

1. See George H. Sabine and Thomas L. Thorson, *A History of Political Theory* (Hinsdale, Ill.: Dryden, 1973); Leo Strauss and Joseph Cropsey, *History of Political Philosophy* (Chicago: Chicago, 1987); Sheldon Wolin, *Politics and Vision: Continuity and Innovation in Western Political Thought* (Boston: Little, Brown, 1960).

2. For an overview of this period, see Fania Oz-Salzberger, "The Jewish Roots of the Modern Republic," *Azure* 13 (Summer 2002), pp. 88-132.

3. Leon Kass argues that Rousseau's *Discourse on the Origin of Inequality* is in fact written as a commentary on the early chapters of Genesis. See Kass, *The Beginning of Wisdom: Reading Genesis* (New York: Free Press, 2003), p. 10n, and various references throughout.

4. Sigmund Freud, *Moses and Monotheism* (New York: Random House, 1967), p. 30.

5. For example, Brevard Childs, *Introduction to the Old Testament as Scripture* (Philadelphia: Fortress, 1979).

6. For example, Robert Alter, *The Art of Biblical Narrative* (New York: Basic Books, 1981).

7. Donald Harman Akenson, *Surpassing Wonder: The Invention of the Bible and the Talmuds* (New York: Harcourt Brace, 1998).

8. Aaron Wildavsky, *Assimilation Versus Separation: Joseph the Administrator and the Politics of Religion in Biblical Israel* (New Brunswick: Transaction, 1993).

9. Michael Walzer, *Exodus and Revolution* (New York: Basic Books, 1985), p. xii.

10. Walzer, *Exodus and Revolution*, pp. 7-8.

11. Adrian Hastings, *The Construction of Nationhood: Ethnicity, Religion, and Nationalism* (Cambridge: Cambridge, 1997).

INTRODUCTION

1. "What the social scientific approach contributes," as Norman K. Gottwald says, "is the recognition that all ideas, even the highest and most encompassing, have social matrices and are... shaped in the dynamics of cultural and social development." In this study, I attempt to connect the social science and biblical interpretations, so that each serves the other. See Norman K. Gottwald, *The Tribes of Yahweh: A Sociology of the Religion of Liberated Israel, 1250-1050 B.C.E.* (Maryknoll, N.Y.: Orbis, 1979), p. 912.

2. A sketch of my father's life may be found in Aaron Wildavsky, "The Richest Boy in Poltava," *Society* 13 (November-December 1975), pp. 48-56.

3. By "Mosaic," I mean "pertaining to Moses," as in "Mosaic community" (referring to Jews) or "Mosaic law" (signifying the body of rules laid down through him in the Bible). I also intend the other dictionary definition—the process of making pictures or designs by inlaying small bits of colored stone, glass, or other materials in mortar, by which apparently disparate parts form a coherent whole. "Mosaic" belongs to Moses in this second sense also, because Moses learns and changes by reacting to experiences under different regimes, yet remains recognizable.

4. See "Leadership Varies with Regimes," below, in this Introduction.

5. Martin Buber, *Israel and the World* (New York: Schocken, 1948), pp. 127, 133.

6. Alfred D. Low, *Jews in the Eyes of the Germans* (Philadelphia: Institute for the Study of Human Issues, 1979), p. 77.

7. Buber, *Israel and the World*, p. 119.

8. If the Lord's covenant with Israel is regarded as perpetual, lasting as long as history, Moses still might be considered in a class by himself. For all time, he remains the only founder, the only leader of the exodus, the only authoritative lawgiver. Can one, then, derive a rule from an exception? One might argue that Moses' seminal act of leadership was the founding of a people tied to a written teaching (that is, the people of the book). But Moses himself is not more or less unique for being ensconced in a book. On the contrary, the open and public character of the Bible makes Moses' leadership more general, not more particular. To learn from the experiences of the people of the book cannot mean conferring antiquarian status on an ancient text but rather making it part of our lives. It is our ability to find a framework for analysis connecting Moses' experiences with ours that is decisive.

9. Based on a suggestion by Herbert Kaufman.

10. Unless an author writes only for specialists, which I do not, he probably cannot count on an audience that knows more than the basic outlines of Bible stories. Certainly, one cannot expect potential readers to fill in any of the many details necessarily left unstated. Thus I risk telling the specialist too much and the general reader not enough. Nor am I the one to judge whether this balancing act has been carried out successfully. What is there to work with? First, last, and always, there is the Bible itself. Then there is an immense body of commentary. Most major works have been translated into English. Interpretations of the Bible by classic rabbinic commentators are arrayed with insight and learning in the multi-volume contemporary classic by Nehama Leibowitz, *Studies in Genesis* (1972); *Studies in Exodus*, Part 1 and Part 2 (1976); *Studies in Leviticus* (1980); *Studies in Numbers* (1980); and *Studies in Deuteronomy* (1980), published in Jerusalem by the World Zionist Organization. Traditional and scholarly approaches to topics and people are found in the excellent *Encyclopaedia Judaica* (Jerusalem: Keter, 1972). My favorite studies of the Pentateuch are Nahum Sarna, *Understanding Exodus* (New York: McGraw-Hill, 1966); Brevard S. Childs, *The Book of Exodus* (Philadelphia: Westminster, 1974); Jacob Milgrom, *Commentary on the Book of Numbers* (Philadelphia: Jewish Publication Society, forthcoming); Leibowitz, *Studies in Leviticus*; and Moshe Weinfeld, *Deuteronomy and the Deuteronomic School* (Oxford: Clarendon, 1972).

Inevitably, interpreters do not always agree. How does one choose among them? The standards are the same as for any intellectual inquiry—cohesiveness, persuasiveness, inclusiveness in subsuming sufficient episodes under a given theory, and power in leading to more interesting future investigations.

11. Gerhard von Rad, *Old Testament Theology*, vol. 1, *The Theology of Israel's Historical Traditions*, trans. D. M. G. Stalker (New York: Harper & Row, 1962), p. 3.

12. In its extreme form, this skepticism corrodes all meaning to the extent that, evidence aside, anything goes. Freud, for example, feels justified in disregarding contrary findings because he claims everyone else does! In a footnote, Freud says something the like of which cannot be found anywhere else in his writing: "When I use Biblical tradition here in such an autocratic and arbitrary way, draw on it for confirmation whenever it is convenient, and dismiss its evidence without scruple when it contradicts my conclusions, I know full well that I am exposing myself to severe criticism concerning my method and that I weaken the force of my proofs. But this is the only way in which to treat material whose trustworthiness—as we know for certain—was seriously damaged by the influence of distorting tendencies. Some justification will be forthcoming later, it is hoped, when we have unearthed those secret motives. Certainty is not to be gained in any case, and, moreover, we may say that all other authors have acted likewise." Sigmund Freud, *Moses and Monotheism* (New York: Random House, 1967), p. 30. Uncertainty is one thing and nihilism another.

13. John Henry Cardinal Newman, *An Essay on the Development of Christian Doctrine* (New York: Longmans, Green, 1949), pp. 65-66.

14. *The Babylonian Talmud*, ed. Rabbi Dr. I. Epstein (London: Soncino, 1936), Tractate Baba Metzia, p. 596.

15. Leibowitz, *Studies in Exodus*, Part 1, p. 69.

16. From an anonymous reviewer.

17. Hermann L. Strack, *Introduction to the Talmud and Midrash* (New York: Atheneum, 1969).

18. Edmund Leach, "The Legitimacy of Solomon: Some Structural Aspects of Old Testament History," in Edmund Leach, *Genesis as Myth* (London: Jonathan Cape Ltd., 1969), p. 29.

19. Leach, "Legitimacy of Solomon," p. 45.

20. Strack, *Introduction to the Talmud*, p. 95.

21. Strack, *Introduction to the Talmud*, pp. 94, 98. "There is no early and late in the Torah"—Mishnah, Pesahim, ch. 6.

22. Leach, "Legitimacy of Solomon," pp. 42-43.

23. Strack, *Introduction to the Talmud*, pp. 96-97.

24. Strack, *Introduction to the Talmud*, p. 97.

25. Leach, "Legitimacy of Solomon," p. 80.

26. Leach, "Legitimacy of Solomon," p. 37.

27. Strack, *Introduction to the Talmud*, p. 94.

28. Leach, "Legitimacy of Solomon," pp. 45, 53.

29. Hyam Maccoby, "No Further Word," review *The Exile of the Word: From the Silence of the Bible to the Silence of Auschwitz*, by Andre Neher, in *The Times Literary Supplement*, December 25, 1981, p. 1506.

30. Samson Raphael Hirsch, trans. and commentary, *The Pentateuch*, 2nd ed., trans. into English by Isaac Levy (Gateshead, England: Judaica, 1973), p. 299.

31. Throughout this book, I use the King James version of the Bible because it is incomparably the most beautiful. It is also the version that sounds most biblical to a modern ear, no small thing in a book that proposes so many departures from past approaches. Throughout this book I have quoted from *The Holy Bible* (New York: American Bible Society, n.d.). Since the King James translation is also centuries old and, therefore, inaccurate in some respects, I have checked every passage against several other standard texts. Critical portions have also been compared to translations made by scholars especially interested in them. My favorite recent translation, because of its accuracy, clarity, and colloquial character, is the Jewish Publication Society's *New Translation*, done by Harry M. Orlinsky, assisted by a committee of seven. In keeping with the spirit of the enterprise, differences of opinion among committee members were settled in the traditional manner of rabbinic academies—by majority vote. A couple of comparisons between the best of the modern translations and the King James version will give the grounds for my preference. At the burning bush, for example, Moses, in a desperate effort to reject the Lord's mission, says he cannot go because he is "a man of impeded speech" (Exod. 6:12, *New Translation*). The King James version has the same phrase refer to Moses as a man "who am of uncircumcised lips." Again, in regard to Moses' difficulties with his people in the desert, the *New Translation* has him ask the Lord wearily whether he must bear their burden "as a nurse carries an infant?" (Num. 11:12), whereas the King James has Moses speak of himself acting "as a nursing father beareth the sucking child." Finally, without further comment, let us look at the translations of Numbers 23:19 side by side:

> King James version: "God is not a man, that he should lie; neither the son of man, that he should repent."
>
> *New Translation*: "God is not man to be capricious, or mortal to change His mind."

The elegance, indeed, the majesty of the King James Bible is evident. Even more important is its evocative character, the associations it suggests. A speech impediment is one thing, a thing that does not go beyond itself. To refer to oneself as a man of "uncircumcised lips," however, knowing that circumcision is the chief sign through which a male became a member of his people and joined with them in a covenant with their God, is also to say that there and then Moses is not ready to carry out the mission the Lord assigns him. Similarly, any man may carry an infant, but comparing oneself to a nursing father who supports a sucking child conveys images of the people's dependence on Moses and his being burdened by them, images strengthened by the overlap in which Moses is both father and mother, playing a feminine as well as a masculine role, suggesting both the completeness to which the leader aspires and the impossibility of being all things to all people. For an illuminating discussion of recent translations, see Dewey M. Beegle, "What Does the Bible Say?" *Biblical Archaeology Review* (November-December 1982), pp. 56-61.

32. "We all know about the paucity of archaeological evidence concerning the Exodus," Yehuda T. Radday writes. "As a result, this sparse evidence has little explanatory value." "A Bible Scholar Looks at BAR's Coverage of the Exodus," *Biblical Archaeology Review* (November-December 1982), pp. 68-71. As John D. Currid of the Oriental Institute of the University of Chicago concluded, "On the basis of the extant evidence, however, I do not see the historian on firm ground in regard to the 'exodus' question. (There exist no pertinent archaeological data.) I wonder if scholarship would be better off to conclude that the evidence, at this time, does not warrant an answer." Review of *The Bible and Recent Archaeology* by Kathleen M. Kenyon, in *Journal of Biblical Literature* 99 (December 1980), pp. 585-586.

33. Martin Buber and Franz Rosenzweig, *Die Schrift und Ihre Verdeutschung* (Berlin: Im Schocken Verlag, 1936). Adopting a sly suggestion by Franz Rosenzweig, the "R" that stands for Redactor in the notation of source critics may stand instead for "Rabbenu" as in "Moshe Rabbenu"—"our teacher Moses" (p. 322).

34. For a view of the immense size and scope of this literature, including a bibliography of more than ninety pages, the reader should consult *Stogdill's Handbook of Leadership*, revised and expanded edition by Bernard M. Bass (New York: Free Press, 1981).

35. We can appreciate these regimes if we consider their principal characteristics, as described below.

A Model of Slavery

Source of Power
External

Division of Power — Unequal

Regime: Slavery
Religion: Narcissism; ruler as god, self-love as idolatry
Revelation: Only to rulers
Rule of leadership: Despotic
Scope of power: Unlimited
Duration of power: Continuous

A Model of Anarchy

Source of Power
External

Division of Power — Unequal

Regime: Anarchy
Religion: Atheism or polytheism; different gods for
different purposes
Revelation: To no one or different for everyone
Rule of leadership: Meteoric
Scope of power: Limited
Duration of power: Discontinuous

A Model of Equity

Source of Power
Internal

Division of Power — Equal

Regime: Equity
Religion: Henotheism (a single god for a separate
people)
Revelation: To each individual
Rule of leadership: Unanimity or charisma
Scope of power: Nonexistent or unlimited
Duration of power: Discontinuous

A Model of Hierarchy		Source of Power
		Internal

Division of Power	Unequal	Regime: Hierarchy
		Religion: Monotheism, one God for all people
		Revelation: Through ruler(s) to people
		Rule of leadership: Autocratic
		Scope of power: Limited
		Duration of power: Continuous

36. Evidently, there are differences between the hierarchy Pharaoh headed and the one David ruled, between Nazi and Leninist hierarchies, between caste and class hierarchies, and so on. To introduce these would be to bring in more variety than is necessary for the study of Mosaic leadership. The main difference concerns the presence or absence of independent centers of power acting as restraints on those who rule. Pharaoh accepted none. Moses acknowledged the law. This difference is bound up with the admixture of political cultures that coexist at a given time and place. Hierarchies constrained by equities must be more responsive to criticism. Hierarchies in coalition with anarchies must recognize some element of competition, including the right to switch support. Rival hierarchies competing for office are quite different from a single one that systematically excludes opposition. David acknowledged the internal constraint of the Torah, but in Solomon's time this proved insufficient. Only the ability of the northern tribes to secede prevented further abuse at the hands of Solomon's successors. But all this belongs to another book, not this one.

For a discussion of eight regimes, four primary and four hybrid (social democracy, American individualism, state capitalism, and totalitarianism), see my "Conditions for Pluralist Democracy, or Cultural Pluralism Means More Than One Political Culture in a Country" (paper presented at a conference, "The Meaning of American Pluralism," Center for the Study of Federalism, Temple University, May 16-19, 1982). Michael Thompson and I are writing a book, to be titled *A Theory of Political Regimes*, which will carry the study of regimes much further.

37. See the valuable article by Melvin Seeman, "Role Conflict and Ambivalence in Leadership," *American Science Review* 18 (August 1953), pp. 373-380.

CHAPTER 1

1. Nahum M. Sarna, *Understanding Genesis* (New York: Schocken, 1970), p. 24.

2. Alouph Hareven, "A Secular Midrash," *Forum on the Jewish People, Zionism, and Israel* 32 (Fall 1978), p. 69.

3. Umberto Cassuto, *A Commentary on the Book of Genesis, Part I from Adam to Noah* (Jerusalem: Magnes, 1961), p. 112.

4. Cassuto, *Commentary on the Book of Genesis*, p. 112.

5. On identity, see Erik H. Erikson, *Childhood and Society*, 2nd ed. (New York: Norton, 1963); and *Young Man Luther* (New York: Norton, 1962).

6. In order to remove the onus from Moses, various commentators have suggested that he was not acting guilty but looking around to see if anyone else would help. Nice try. But the point is that he took the law into his own hands. See Rabbi Yehuda and Maharzu, quoted in Leibowitz, *Studies in Exodus*, Part 1, pp. 43-45.

7. After the Hebrew people entered the Promised Land, at the end of the time of Judges, when "the word of the Lord was precious" because "there was no open vision," the Lord called Samuel and he also answered, "Here am I" (I Sam. 3:1, 4).

8. See Chapter 5 on why Moses does not go to the Promised Land. Appropriating the name of God for oneself would be idolatry.

9. Childs, *Exodus*, p. 45.

10. Martin Buber, *Moses: The Revelation and the Covenant* (New York: Harper & Brothers, 1958), p. 51.

11. Gerhard von Rad develops these parallels in *Moses* (London: Lutterworth, 1960), pp. 19-26.

12. Von Rad, *Moses*, p. 21.

13. There is a rabbinic story that Moses asked God to promise to do everything Moses wished; God did promise, with two exceptions: to let him into Canaan and to postpone his death. Gerald Friedlander, trans., *Pirke de Rabbi Eliezer* (New York: Block, 1916), p. 352. My interpretation is different, as the reader will see. Moses' limits are an integral part of his leadership.

14. Martin K. Hopkins has a neat summary of interpretations: (1) "He Who is"—i.e., Existence itself; Self-existent Being (this interpretation is popular with philosophers). (2) "He causes to happen"—perhaps, "Watch and see what I shall do!" "Let My actions be the answer to your question." (3) "I am Who

I am"—i.e., "It's none of your business Who I am." *God's Kingdom in the Old Testament* (Chicago: Henry Regnery, 1964), p. 104.

15. The now widely accepted argument that the divine name was based on a causative form of the verb "to be" was first developed by W. F. Albright in *From the Stone Age to Christianity*, 2nd ed. (Baltimore: Johns Hopkins, 1957). Analyses of possible translations and the history of the scholarship may be found in Bernhard W. Anderson, *Understanding the Old Testament*, 3rd ed. (Englewood Cliffs, N.J.: Prentice-Hall, 1975), pp. 53-56; Childs, *Exodus*, pp. 61-64; J. Philip Hyatt, *Commentary on Exodus* (London: Oliphants, 1971), pp. 75-76.

16. Scholars have frequently noted the connection between "Yahweh," the particular form by which Israel is to address God, and the Hebrew word for "I am." The name of the God of Israel is the third person singular form of the same verb *ehyeh*, which marks the beginning and end of God's tautology (*Ehyeh asher ehyeh*). This view is held by Anderson, *Understanding the Old Testament*. See also Dewey M. Beegle, *Moses, the Servant of Yahweh* (Grand Rapids, Mich.: Eerdmans, 1972), p. 71. Thus the "name" granted Israel is no proper substantive, but once again a copulative without the completed equation, "He is...." This ingenious syntax forecloses any limitation because Hebrew tenses can be established by context alone.

17. I have left out the obvious connection between the use of God's name and the Fifth Commandment prohibition: "Thou shalt not take the name of the Lord thy God in vain." Exodus 20:7.

18. This is not, I think, a modern meaning, denigrating magic. My point is not that magic is only for fools (we have so many contemporary equivalents), but that tricks are no substitute for faith.

19. For this and other legends about Moses' rod, see "Rod of Moses" by Shlomo Hasson and the editorial staff, *Encyclopaedia Judaica*, 14:219.

20. Exodus Rabbah 3:12.

21. Reluctance is typical on the part of those named to leadership: compare Gideon's and Jeremiah's calls. But Moses is the only one who makes his acceptance conditional. For further literature on the structure of call narratives, see Harry Orlinsky, *Essays in Bible Culture and Bible Translation* (New York: Ktav, 1973), p. 11; James Plastaras, *The God of Exodus* (Milwaukee: Bruce, 1966), p. 80; "Moses" entry in *The Jewish Encyclopedia* (1904; reprinted, New York: Ktav, 1964), p. 374.

22. Upon being entrusted by his master with the most important task in finding a wife for Isaac from among his kinfolk, Abraham's steward, Eliezer, after completing the task, refuses to delay his return (Gen. 24:56). How much more important for the servant of God to do his work earlier rather than later.

23. "This paragraph," Umberto Cassuto writes, "does, in truth, contain much that is strange and obscure." *A Commentary on the Book of Exodus* (Jerusalem: Magnes, 1967), p. 58. "Few texts contain more problems for the interpreter," Childs tells us, "than these few verses which have continued to baffle throughout the centuries." *Exodus*, p. 95. "This is the most obscure passage in the Book of Exodus," Hyatt concludes. *Commentary on Exodus*, p. 86.

24. "The early state of Israelite religion knows no Satan; if a power attacks a man and threatens him, it is proper to recognize God in it or behind it... and it is proper to withstand Him." Buber, *Moses*, p. 58.

25. For a stronger statement, see Elias Auerbach, *Moses* (Detroit: Wayne State University, 1975), p. 48.

26. *Babylonian Talmud*, ed. Epstein, Tractate Nedarim, p. 93.

27. This suggestion comes from Henri Cazelles, *A la recherche de Moise* (Paris: Editions du Cerf, 1974), p. 43.

28. Cf. Isaiah 6:2, where the angels in Isaiah's vision use two of their six wings to hide their "feet."

29. Killing is a form of consecration. This God says in no uncertain terms: "Because all the first-born are mine, for on the day that I smote all the first-born in the land of Egypt I hallowed unto Me all the first-born in Israel, both man and beast: Mine they shall be: I am the Lord" (Num. 3:13).

30. Menahem Kasher, ed., *Torah Shlemah* (Jerusalem: Torah Shlemah Institute, n.d.), 8:199.

31. Rashi says the term means "closed-mouthed." Hence I think the word "uncircumcised" everywhere means "shut" (Exod. 6); "uncircumcised ears" is thus "shut from hearing" (Exod. 9). By contrast, "circumcised" signifies self-awareness, that is, openness to experience.

32. Edmond Fleg, *The Life of Moses* (Paris: Albin Michel, 1956), p. 40.

33. See David Daube, *Ancient Hebrew Fables*, Inaugural Lecture of the Oxford Centre for Postgraduate Hebrew Studies, delivered at Corpus Christi College, May 17, 1973 (Oxford: Oxford, 1973), pp. 14-15.

34. See the illuminating discussion of the views of Arama, Rashi, Nahmanides, and others, in Leibowitz, *Studies in Numbers*, pp. 309-313.

35. Daube, *Ancient Hebrew Fables*, pp. 14-15.

36. From Leibowitz, *Studies in Numbers*, p. 311.

37. Bamidbar Rabbah 20:12, from Leibowitz, *Studies in Numbers*, p. 313.

38. Buber, *Moses*, p. 109.

39. Sarna, *Genesis*, p. 195.

40. According to commentators, Jacob's faults included vulgarity—"Give me my wife," he demands of Laban in regard to Rachel, "that I may go in unto her" (Gen. 29:21), marrying sisters, which was later prohibited, and much more. (A larger list may be had from Moses Aberbach, "Jacob," *Encyclopaedia Judaica*, 9:1200-1201.) Here I would observe that the faults mentioned all stem from deceit, only this time it is Jacob who is on the receiving end.

41. Franz Rosenzweig, *The Star of Redemption* (New York: Holt, Rinehart & Winston, 1971), p. 266.

42. A good example is Lot's fear of leaving Sodom and his running in and out of refuge in Zoar to a cave where ostensibly no one can hurt him. Here, as Lot's daughters dupe him into drunken intercourse with them, he loses control of his own body. The children of this incestuous encounter were Moab and Ammon; the first-born founded a people who (like their ancestor, Balaam) enticed the Hebrews into a mass sexual frenzy at Baal Peor; the second, the Molech who practiced passing through fire (Lev. 18:21). Loss of faith is made equivalent to lack of self-control. For further discussion, see Derek Kidner, *Genesis* (London: Tyndale, 1967), p. 136.

43. A midrash captures the underlying feeling superbly well: "All that night she (Leah) acted the part of Rachel. As soon as he arose in the morning, 'and behold it was Leah.' Said Jacob to her: Daughter of the deceiver! Wherefore has thou deceived me? Said she to him: And thou—wherefore didst thou deceive thy father?! When he said to thee: 'Art thou my very son Esau?' thou didst say to him: 'I am Esau thy firstborn.' Yet thou sayest: 'Wherefore then hast thou deceived me!?' Thy father did he not say of thee: 'Thy brother came with deceit'?" Leibowitz, *Studies in Genesis*, p. 266.

44. Sarna, *Genesis*, p. 184.

45. Leibowitz, *Studies in Genesis*, p. 369.

46. Hirsch, *Pentateuch*, vol. 1, p. 459.

47. Leibowitz, *Studies in Genesis*, p. 300.

48. Leibowitz, *Studies in Genesis*, p. 300.

49. Solomon Zeitlin, "Religious Faith and Practice," in *The Rise and Fall of the Judaean State* (Philadelphia: Jewish Publication Society, 1962), 1:271-272.

50. Leibowitz, *Studies in Genesis*, pp. 368-369.

51. Leibowitz, *Studies in Genesis*, p. 367. Yes, but Jonah actually refuses; Moses, Balaam, and Jacob, on the other hand, say they will go and pretend to be wholehearted. Jonah's doubts are out in the open.

52. Leibowitz, *Studies in Genesis*, p. 369.

53. Sarna, *Genesis*, pp. 170-171; see also E.A. Speiser, introduction, trans., and notes, *The Anchor Bible, Genesis* (Garden City, N.Y.: Doubleday, 1964), p. 183.

54. After Jacob meets Esau in peace, an apparently unrelated incident interrupts the narrative. Jacob's daughter Dinah was noticed by a local prince who "saw her... took her, and lay with her, and defiled her" (Gen. 34:2). The man loved Dinah and wanted her as his wife. Because of the defilement, Jacob's sons replied "deceitfully" (Gen. 34:13) that they could not allow marriage to one who was uncircumcised. If all the men of Schechem were circumcised, Jacob's clan would give them the clan's daughters. "And it came to pass on the third day, when they were sore, that two of the sons of Jacob, Simeon and Levi, Dinah's brethren, took each man his sword, and came upon the city boldly, and slew all the males" (Gen. 34:25). Jacob's mild complaint that the action had made him offensive and exposed him to attack was met with "Should he [the prince] deal with our sister as with a harlot?" (Gen. 34:31). Fornicating with foreigners (equivalent to whoring after their gods) leads to disaster. The sign of the circumcision, even the holiest objects, we are told, may be used for immoral purposes. Once more Jacob is driven from the Promised Land by deception.

55. Hirsch, *Pentateuch*, p. 219.

56. Hirsch, *Pentateuch*, vol. 2, p. 504.

57. Michael Fishbane, "Composition and Structure in the Jacob Cycle (Gen. 25:19-35:22)," *Journal of Jewish Studies* 26 (Spring-Autumn 1975), p. 28.

58. Andre Neher, *Moses and the Jewish Vocation*, trans. Mary Wildavsky (Paris: Editions du Seuil, 1956), pp. 84-85. [French]

59. Moshe Greenberg, *Understanding Exodus* (New York: Behrman, 1969), p. 59.

60. Greenberg, *Understanding Exodus*, p. 59.

61. Auerbach, *Moses*, pp. 21-24.

62. The sages have not failed to notice that though the people say they believe (after Moses and Aaron do their magic show), the elders do not accompany them to see Pharaoh. Shemot Rabbah and Rashi simply say the fearful elders slipped away by ones and twos until there were none. Leibowitz, *Studies in Exodus*, Part 1, pp. 87-88.

CHAPTER 2

1. For extensive illustration, see E.W. Heaton, *Solomon's New Men* (London: Thames & Hudson, 1974). See also J.L. Crenshaw, "Method in Determining Wisdom Influence upon Historical Literature," *Journal of Biblical Literature* 88 (June 1969), pp. 129-142.

2. See Roland De Vaux, *The Early History of Israel* (Philadelphia: Westminster, 1978), pp. 295-296, for a detailed discussion.

3. Steven J. Brams, *Biblical Games: A Strategic Analysis of Stories in the Old Testament* (Cambridge, Mass.: MIT, 1980), p. 83.

4. Cassuto, *Exodus*, p. 56.

5. David Daiches, *Moses: The Man and His Vision* (New York: Praeger, 1975), p. 69.

6. See the discussion in Plastaras, *God of Exodus*, p. 137.

7. Childs, *Exodus*, p. 85.

8. Childs, *Exodus*, p. 152.

9. A midrash says that Pharaoh was spared so he could continue to be chastened. Again, the point is better applied to Israel.

10. The English word "plague" covers a variety of meanings. Sometimes the Hebrew word is used to signify a "wonder," something extraordinary that could be done only by God. At other times, God's presence is attested to by the words "sign" or "act of judgment." When the death of the first-born is spoken about, the words used are "blow" and "strike." In Deuteronomy the plagues become "tests," "trials," and "provings." Only after the exodus did it become clear that a plague on the Egyptians might also be a test for the Israelites.

11. Why, the great commentators ask, was Moses brought up by Pharaoh's daughter? Abraham ibn Ezra (Tudela, Spain, 1089-1164, known for his grammatical analysis of the Bible) argues that the purpose is to teach Moses the leadership lacking in a slave people. Isaac Arama (1420-1494, Spain, author of *Akedat Yitzhak*, a philosophical commentary on the Bible) has an equally valuable explanation: God's purpose is to have Pharaoh defeated by a member of his own household (Louis Jacobs, "Moses," *Encyclopaedia Judaica*, 12:400). The implication for Israel is that each people is its own worst enemy.

12. The phylacteries (*tefilin*), placed on the hands and between the eyes during prayer, are another token. "And it shall be for a sign unto thee upon thine hand, and for a memorial between thine eyes, that the Lord's law may be in thy mouth: for with a strong hand hath the Lord brought thee out of Egypt" (Exod. 13:9). As the distinguished late Chief Rabbi Avraham Kook of

Israel interpreted the *tefilin*, their purpose is "to subdue the profane and grosser elements of existence which constituted the struggle in Egypt." Quoted in Leibowitz, *Studies in Exodus*, Part 1, p. 229, from Rabbi Kook's commentary on the Siddur, *Olat Re'iya*.

13. David Daube, *The Exodus Pattern in the Bible* (London: Faber & Faber, 1963), p. 44.

14. Dewey M. Beegle offers an alternative translation that is more striking: "And you do wrong to your own people." Beegle, *Moses*, pp. 88-89.

15. For discussion see Greenberg, *Understanding Exodus*, pp. 85ff.

16. It may be all right, but it may also be unfair. Thus another king was forgiven in advance by the Lord, who intervened to prevent him from sinning with Sarah because he had been denied relevant information—she was Abraham's wife, not, as Melchizedek thought, his sister. See Genesis 20 and, for a similar incident involving a different Pharaoh, Genesis 12:11-20.

17. See Thomas C. Schelling, *A Strategy of Conflict* (Cambridge: Harvard, 1960), pp. 37-38.

18. On power see Robert A. Dahl, *Modern Political Analysis* (Englewood Cliffs, N.J.: Prentice-Hall, 1965), pp. 39-54.

19. Exodus 8:8; for the timing of the plagues see Exodus 8:8-10, 8:23, 8:29, 9:5, 9:29, 11:4.

20. I am indebted to Cassuto, *Exodus*, p. 145, for the emphasis on the terror of night.

21. See Mary Douglas, *Purity and Danger: An Analysis of Concepts of Pollution and Taboo* (New York: Praeger, 1966). David Daube has suggested to me that the dietary provisions are, nevertheless, invoked by a medical formula (as in regard to leprosy): symptom, diagnosis, prescription. In those days, priests may well have passed for doctors. That they were primarily doctors of the social structure that must be fed by pure categories is Douglas' point, which, to me, is persuasive.

22. Leibowitz, *Studies in Leviticus*, p. 203.

23. Nehama Leibowitz's discussion of the distinction between clean and unclean foods in Judaism reveals both the promise and the difficulty of a social interpretation. Leibowitz begins by showing that medical and health reasons cannot account for the prohibitions. "The most acceptable motivation of these prohibitions appears to be the very fact that they are forbidden." *Studies in Leviticus*, p. 84. Rationalization leads one only further "from the true reason—the fulfillment of the will of God." In support, Leibowitz cites Rabbi Eleazar ben Azariah: "Whence that a man should not say... it is impossible for me to commit incest, but rather, I can, but what shall I do when my Father in

Heaven has declared such things out of bounds for me?—from the text 'I have separated you from the peoples to be Mine.' He thus separates himself from transgression and accepts upon himself the yoke of Heaven." The purpose of separation is to remove oneself from contact with evil. Social separation, eating different foods, serves a moral purpose. Leibowitz will go this far but no further, for she disagrees with those "who maintain that the dietary laws were designed as a barrier to separate us from the nations (just as our Sages forbade the partaking of bread baked by a heathen because of their wine and their wine because of their daughters to prevent social intercourse and intermarriage)" (p. 83). Why not argue that a social practice is established to fulfill a social purpose? Leibowitz uses an excerpt from Hoffman's commentary on Leviticus to prove her point that the wording of the text presents a contrary view. Hoffman writes that the Bible does not say "that certain foods were prohibited Israel in order to separate them from the nations. On the contrary, it is stated that since God has separated the Jewish people from other peoples, Israel is obliged to observe the Divine precepts, that teach us to make a difference between clean and unclean beasts, just the same as Israel is obliged to keep other precepts." Whether keeping clean serves to separate the Jewish people, or they keep kosher because they are separated, the explanation contains a significant social element.

24. Leo Strauss, "Interpretation of Genesis" (lecture in the Works of the Mind series at the University of Chicago, January 25, 1957).

25. *Pentateuch with Targum Onkelos, Haphtaroth and Prayers for Sabbath and Rashi's Commentary*, translated into English and annotated by Rev. M. Rosenbaum and Dr. A. M. Silbermann, in collaboration with A. Blashki and L. Joseph (London: Shapiro, Vallentine, 1946), p. 2.

26. For a variety of interpretations, see Childs, *Exodus*, p. 176.

27. Daube, *Exodus Pattern*, pp. 50-51, 69.

28. An earlier episode, Abraham's attempt to pass off Sarah as his sister (she was his half-sister) rather than his wife, indicates that gift-giving was then regarded as absolving the victim of culpability. Thus the King James version tells of Abimelech giving Sarah a thousand pieces of silver so as to constitute a "covering of the eyes" (Gen. 20:16), which the *New Translation* recites as "this will serve you as a vindication... and you are cleared before everyone." The gifts enable the Israelites to pass through the Egyptians, who, affording them a new status, no longer regard them as slaves.

29. See Cassuto, *Exodus*, p. 165.

30. *Babylonian Talmud*, ed. Epstein, Tractate Sota, p. 183.

31. Childs, *Exodus*, p. 292.

32. Speiser, *Anchor Bible, Genesis*, p. 86, n. 1 and references.

33. It took several readings to convince me that childhood memories of Abram as a boy smashing the idols in his father's house were legends not included in the Bible.

34. Hirsch, *Pentateuch*, vol. 1, p. 276.

35. Gerhard von Rad, *Genesis: A Commentary* (London: SCM, 1963), p. 196.

36. The biblical phrase "within the city" led S. R. Hirsch to add that Abraham's righteous man is to be found "'in the midst of the city' and in lively connection with everything and everybody. He never leaves off admonishing, teaching.... He never despairs, is never tired of trying, however distant the hope of success may be" (Hirsch, *Pentateuch*, vol. 1, p. 326). In a phrase, the righteous man is engaged with civic life.

37. See Leibowitz, *Studies in Genesis*, pp. 183-186.

38. See W. Gunther Plaut, *The Torah: A Modern Commentary: Genesis* (New York: Union of American Hebrew Congregations, 1974), 1:185.

39. Though circumcision was common among other peoples, its early administration (eight days after birth) means that it is not an entry into manhood but a "commitment to God's people." Kidner, *Genesis*, p. 130.

40. The lamb's blood on the doorpost during Passover, which saved the inhabitants from the plague and the slaughter of the first-born, may be regarded as protection provided by the blood of the covenant.

41. This clue of comparability may help us try to interpret the most obscure of stories about Abraham that put him and his wife in an unfavorable light. Learning he might be killed for the beautiful Sarai, Abram passes her off in Egypt as his sister—a technicality, since she is a half-sister. A Pharaoh of that time, favoring Abram by reason of his sister's beauty, takes Sarai into his palace as his wife. (Translations differ as to whether Sarai merely went to Pharaoh's palace or became his wife. The context of the story and the *New Translation* [Genesis 12:19] suggest the latter.) The Lord then plagues Pharaoh and his people until Pharaoh, who somehow discovers Abram's deception, sends him away richer than he came, with his wife and all his possessions (Gen. 12:10-17). Though deceit can be countenanced in a good cause, where power relationships are asymmetrical (cf. the excuses of the midwives about failing to kill Hebrew boys), there is no evidence here of bad intent on the part of Pharaoh. And innocent bystanders—Abimelech, king of the Philistines, with Abraham (Gen. 20) and Abimelech with Isaac and Rebekah (Gen. 26:6)—do get hurt. The stories, including their repetition, make more sense when they are viewed as prefiguring the exodus. Israel as a people is the beautiful woman who is taken by Pharaoh until he discovers that she belongs to another, her God, after which she is sent away better off than she came.

CHAPTER 3

1. See Sarna, *Genesis*, p. 55.

2. God's remembrance, Derek Kidner writes, "combines the ideas of faithful love... and timely intervention." Kidner, *Genesis*, p. 92. See also Brevard S. Childs, *Memory and Tradition in Israel, Studies in Biblical Theology*, No. 37 (Naperville, Ill.: Alec R. Allenson, Inc., 1962), p. 34.

3. The relation between types of covenant and regime can be depicted as follows:

Regimes Related to Covenants		Perpetual	
		No	Yes
Unconditional No		(1) Slavery No covenant: ruler is god who remakes rules at will	(3) Hierarchy Covenant through leaders to people: perpetual within group but subject to performance
Unconditional Yes		(4) Anarchy No covenant or many; no conditions but not same covenant for all time	(2) Equity Covenant with each individual within group; unbreakable; direct access to God

4. George E. Mendenhall, *The Tenth Generation: The Origins of the Biblical Tradition* (Baltimore: Johns Hopkins, 1973), p. 20.

5. See Buber, *Moses*, p. 102, for comment.

6. See Childs, *Exodus*; Peter C. Craigie, *The Book of Deuteronomy* (Grand Rapids, Mich.: Eerdmans, 1976); Anderson, *Understanding the Old Testament*; Walter Eichrodt, *Theology of the Old Testament* (Philadelphia: Westminster, 1967), vol. 2; and Mendenhall, *Tenth Generation.*

7. This is well put in *Pirke de Rabbi Eliezer*, p. 355: "Whilst Israel had not yet sinned before Thee, Thou didst call them 'My people,' as it is said, 'And I will bring forth *my* hosts, *my* people' (Exod. 7:4). Now that they have sinned before Thee, Thou sayest unto me, 'Go, get thee down, for *thy* people have corrupted themselves.' As it is said, 'Yet they are thy people and thine inheritance' (Deut. 9:29)."

8. Saul D. Alinsky, *Rules for Radicals: A Practical Primer for Realistic Radicals* (New York: Random House, 1971), pp. 88-91.

9. Gerhard von Rad, *Deuteronomy: A Commentary* (Philadelphia: Westminster, 1966), p. 78.

10. Moshe Weinfeld, "Covenant," *Encyclopaedia Judaica*, 5:1020.

11. *Jewish Encyclopedia*, p. 376.

12. See Leivy Smolar and Moshe Aberbach, "The Golden Calf Episode in Post-Biblical Literature," *Hebrew Union College Annual* 34 (Cincinnati, 1968), pp. 91-116.

13. Smolar and Aberbach, "Golden Calf Episode," p. 114 and references.

14. Fleg, *Life of Moses*, pp. 104-105.

15. "Breaking the law" is not a play on words in Hebrew as in English, but the image is the same.

16. See Hyatt, *Commentary on Exodus*, p. 307. God repents a number of times in the Bible, not only of doing harm, but of helping. Hyatt states that "the bases of Yahweh's repenting are three: (i) intercession, as here and in Amos 7:1-6; (ii) repentance of the people (Jeremiah 18:3ff.; Jonah 3:9f.); and (iii) Yahweh's compassionate nature (Judges 2:18; Deuteronomy 32:36; II Samuel 24:16)."

17. By Second Temple times, the test had fallen into disuse. According to Rabbi Johanan ben Zakkai, the test was designed to determine whether a woman was an adulterer. "Since adulterers became common," the Rabbi said, "the ordeal of the waters has been dropped, for it was needed only in cases of doubt." Gedaliah Alon, *The Jews in Their Land in the Talmudic Age* (Jerusalem: Magnes, 1980), 1:90.

18. Childs, *Exodus*, p. 564.

19. Cassuto, *Exodus*, p. 420.

20. Smolar and Aberbach, "Golden Calf Episode," pp. 91-92.

21. For full citation of the rabbinic literature, see Smolar and Aberbach, "Golden Calf Episode," pp. 91-92, from which this account is taken.

22. Cf. Rosenbaum and Silbermann, *Pentateuch*, where it is deduced from the words "these be your gods, O Israel" that it must have been foreigners who made the Calf and led Israel astray; otherwise they would have said "these are our gods" (p. 180b).

23. Cf. Rosenbaum and Silbermann, *Pentateuch*, p. 180. According to this interpretation, everything Aaron does is a delaying tactic: by asking for the gold earrings he hopes the women and children will hesitate to give up their ornaments; he builds the altar himself and dawdles, so that the people will not build one quickly, and calls out, "tomorrow is a festival to the Lord," so that nothing will happen that day.

24. Rosenbaum and Silbermann, *Pentateuch*, p. 184, goes so far as to read into Exodus 32:24 the words "I cast it into the fire and I *did not know* that

this (i.e., this living) calf would come out but it did come out"; emphasis added.

25. Cassuto, *Exodus*, pp. 411, 413, 408.

26. Ramban explains that Aaron did not intend to make a substitute for God but merely a substitute for Moses, since they were complaining that they did not know what had become of Moses. Were this so (assuming one could imagine being led by an idol), Moses would have had to be something of a god. Ramban (Nahmanides), *Commentary on the Torah: Exodus*, trans. and annotated by Rabbi Dr. Charles B. Chavel (New York: Shilo, 1973), pp. 549-550.

27. Auerbach, *Moses*, p. 126.

28. Eli Davis, "Golden Calf," *Encyclopaedia Judaica*, 7:711.

29. See Martin Noth, *Exodus, A Commentary* (Philadelphia: Westminster, 1974), p. 246.

30. Smolar and Aberbach, "Golden Calf Episode," p. 100.

31. Smolar and Aberbach, "Golden Calf Episode," and references, pp. 100-101.

32. Origen, "Against Celsus," in Smolar and Aberbach, "Golden Calf Episode," p. 99.

33. Moses Aberbach, "Golden Calf," *Encyclopaedia Judaica*, 7:712.

34. Quoted in Aberbach, "Golden Calf," *Encyclopaedia Judaica*, 7:712. Also compare Rosenbaum and Silbermann, *Pentateuch*, "Genesis," p. 186, where the phrase "nevertheless in the day when I visit, I will visit their sin upon them" (Exod. 32:34) is interpreted to mean that whenever God punishes them for any sin, He will also be partly punishing them for this sin.

35. Smolar and Aberbach, "Golden Calf Episode," p. 104.

36. *The Interpreter's Bible* (New York: Abingdon-Cokesbury, 1952), 1:1063-1064.

37. Leibowitz, *Studies in Exodus*, Part 2, p. 676.

38. Instead of the first-born, who should have done so, having already been sanctified (Exod. 13). The substitution of the Levites for the first-born is also apparent in the choice of the Levites to be the guardians of the sanctuary. See Hirsch, *Pentateuch*, vol. 4, p. 28.

39. Ramban, however, has it that God's command, not written in the Torah, was "Since you do not want Me to destroy them, you should slay its worshippers by the sword." *Commentary on the Torah*, pp. 568-569.

40. Yehezkel Kaufmann, *The Religion of Israel: From Its Beginnings to the Babylonian Exile* (Chicago: University of Chicago, 1960), p. 230.

41. See Nahum M. Waldman, "The Breaking of the Tablets," *Judaism* 27 (Fall 1978), p. 446.

42. See von Rad, *Old Testament Theology*, p. 318, where David is said to have "flung himself through the thick curtain to the divine anger directly on God's heart."

43. Nahmanides writes that Moses approved the idea "since the Torah does not intend man to depend on miracles, but demands that those who fight, help themselves, keeping guard and laying ambush." Quoted in Leibowitz, *Studies in Numbers*, p. 144.

44. If "brought up" means "spread," it could suggest "they invented a lie" according to *The Soncino Chumash*, ed. A. Cohen (London: Soncino, 1966), p. 863. My interpretation differs. Fearful of entering the land, the spies see their fears in exaggerated form. What they say is true to their own unfortified understanding.

45. For a different interpretation, stressing "the numerous incongruities in detail," see George B. Gray, *A Critical and Exegetical Commentary on Numbers* (1903; reprinted, Edinburgh: T. & T. Clark, 1965), p. 129. For attribution of these difficulties to different sources, see Martin Noth, *Numbers: A Commentary* (Philadelphia: Westminster, 1968), pp. 101ff.

46. In his great work *Nuer Religion* (Oxford: Oxford, 1956), E.E. Evans-Pritchard reports that the Nuer people speak of themselves as being "like little ants in the sight of God" (p. 12); but, note, not ants in the sight of other men.

47. N. H. Snaith, ed., *The Century Bible: Leviticus and Numbers* (London: Nelson, 1967), p. 256.

48. Note the similarity to another episode of ingratitude, in which Jacob tells Laban that "thou has changed my wages ten times," that is, frequently (Gen. 31:41).

49. John Sturdy, *Numbers* (Cambridge: Cambridge, 1976), p. 103.

50. See the discussion in Snaith, ed., *Century Bible*, p. 248.

51. Von Rad, *Moses*, p. 70.

52. Quoted in Leibowitz, *Studies in Numbers*, pp. 188-189.

53. Speiser, *Anchor Bible, Genesis*, p. 166.

54. For references to child sacrifice as an abomination of the Canaanites and King Moab's sacrifice of his first-born in a vain effort to bring victory, see Sarna, *Genesis*, pp. 157ff.

55. *No'am Elimelech* on Genesis 22:7; see Louis Jacobs, "Akedah," *Encyclopaedia Judaica*, 2:483.

56. Sören Kierkegaard, *Fear and Trembling and the Sickness Unto Death* (Princeton: Princeton, 1954), p. 37.

57. Kierkegaard, *Fear and Trembling*, p. 41.

58. Kierkegaard, *Fear and Trembling*, p. 90.

59. Speiser, *Anchor Bible, Genesis*, pp. 165-166.

60. Von Rad, *Genesis: A Commentary*, p. 244.

61. The main clue about Isaac is that there are so few. Isaac stands for submission. He serves to reveal God's will. His birth shows that God can work His will contrary to nature by letting an old woman conceive. Isaac accepts the possibility of sacrifice, so far as can be read, without protest. He is married inside, not outside the clan. Isaac's wife, Rebekah, is brought to him by Abraham's faithful servant, Eliezer, who gives thanks for divine aid. Isaac stays in Canaan at God's urging, receiving in return a reiteration of the covenant with Abraham. Even in death, Isaac serves to give his blessing to the wrong one of his two sons, guided, in blindness, by forces greater than himself.

Alone among the patriarchs, Isaac's name is not changed, having been ordained by God before his birth (Sarna, *Genesis*, p. 131). Speiser concludes, "Isaac, who can scarcely be described as a memorable personality in his own right, is important chiefly as a link in the patriarchal chain" (Speiser, *Anchor Bible, Genesis*, p. 182). But there is more. Caught between the imposing figures of the father who went to sacrifice him and the son who deceived him, Isaac shares the plight of many another man (cf. Denis Diderot's *Rameau's Nephew* [New York: Bobbs-Merrill, 1964], who lacked even his own name, his identity squeezed out by events larger than himself). Isaac's name may signify laughter, but he does not have too much to laugh about.

62. Geza Vermes, "Redemption and Genesis XII," in *Scripture and Tradition in Judaism* (Leiden: E.J. Brill, 1961), p. 208.

63. On the Akedah and the Passover, see Shalom Spiegel, *The Last Trial: On the Legends and Lore of the Command to Abraham to Offer Isaac as a Sacrifice—The Akedah* (New York: Pantheon, 1967).

CHAPTER 4

1. Jacob Licht, *Testing in the Hebrew Scriptures and in Post-Biblical Judaism* (Jerusalem: Magnes, 1973). [Hebrew] I generally follow Licht's interpretation. But I have also sharpened and shaped it to fit in with the general theme being advanced—namely, that the stubborn complaint of the people is an essential part of how they come to terms with their God and their God with them. They cannot be confirmed in their way of life without trying out alternatives.

2. Licht, *Testing in the Hebrew Scriptures*, passim.

3. Licht, *Testing in the Hebrew Scriptures*.

4. Fleg, *Life of Moses*, pp. 148-149.

5. Buber, *Israel and the World*, pp. 117-118.

6. Wilfried Diam, "Moses in the Wilderness," *Jewish Spectator* 38 (January 1973), p. 11.

7. Lincoln Steffens, *Moses in Red: The Revolt of Israel as a Typical Revolution* (Philadelphia: Dorrance, 1926), p. 72.

8. Steffens, *Moses in Red*, p. 124.

9. Snaith, *Century Bible*, p. 226.

10. What we do have, without any intervening consideration, is the Lord's statement to Moses: "The man shall be surely put to death: all the congregation shall stone him with stones without the camp" (Num. 15:35).

11. Buber, *Moses*, p. 87.

12. See the discussion in Snaith, *Century Bible*, p. 258. Saying that he had neither defrauded nor oppressed the people, Samuel cried out, "Behold, here I am: witness against me before the Lord, and before his anointed; whose ox have I taken? or whose ass have I taken? or whom have I defrauded? whom have I oppressed? or of whose hand have I received any bribe to blind mine eyes therewith? and I will restore it you" (I Sam. 12:3).

13. Louis Ginzberg, *The Legends of the Jews*, 7 vols. (Philadelphia: Jewish Publication Society, 1909-1938), 3:290-291.

14. Rabbinical commentators, by and large, have sided with Moses. Instead of taking "holy people" as "demand notes" to "honour by deeds of holiness," Nehama Leibowitz writes, "they took them to be titles of distinction conferring privileges on them." *Studies in Numbers*, p. 183.

15. Dewey M. Beegle approves of the version in the New England Bible— "Do you think you can hoodwink men like us?" Beegle, *Moses*, p. 293.

16. Jacob Liver, "Korah, Dathan and Abiram," in *Studies in the Bible*, vol. 8, ed. Chaim Rabin (Jerusalem: Magnes, 1961), pp. 203-207. "Coming up" is roughly equivalent to submitting a case for decision in court. *Soncino Chumash*, p. 880.

17. Hirsch, *Pentateuch*, vol. 4, p. 278.

18. The phrase "of mine own mind" is, literally, "from my heart," which Snaith describes as "that centre from which all thought and all action proceed." Snaith, *Century Bible*, p. 259.

19. Noth, *Numbers*, p. 128.

20. Snaith, *Century Bible*, p. 260.

21. Another interpretation is that Korah died in the fire that consumed the princes.

22. Frederick V. Winnett, *The Mosaic Tradition* (Toronto: University of Toronto, 1949), p. 143.

23. Jacob Milgrom, "The Rebellion of Korah (Num. 16): A Study in Redaction," in *De la Torah au Messie*, eds. J. Doré et al., Melanges Cazelles (Paris: Discleé, 1981), pp. 135-146.

24. Perhaps the sons of Aaron were hoisted by this (their very own) petard when they were killed for offering strange and unauthorized fire before the Lord (Lev. 10:1-2). Possibly their death proved that the principles of the law did indeed apply to all, however high, thus exemplifying the injunction that judges not be respecters of persons.

25. Leibowitz, *Studies in Numbers*, p. 231. She quotes Moses Mendelssohn: "According to the laws of my faith miraculous acts are no touchstone of truth, and a miracle cannot be accepted with moral certainty as evidence that a prophet has been sent by God." Leibowitz, *Studies in Exodus*, Part 1, p. 167.

26. A.S. Yahuda, *The Accuracy of the Bible* (New York: E.P. Dutton & Co., 1935), p. 112.

27. The root of "cease from me" is used to describe the subsiding of Noah's ark. It means either "once and for all" (Snaith, *Century Bible*, p. 263) or "gradually"; the former appears most likely linguistically, the latter more realistic.

28. Yahuda, *Accuracy of the Bible*, p. 112.

29. Noth, *Numbers*, p. 129.

30. Snaith translated the relevant portion as "But they did so no more." *Century Bible*, p. 232.

31. "The subcharacters, the most numerous agents of an allegory, may be generated by the main protagonists, and the finest hero will then be the one who

most naturally seems to generate subcharacters—aspects of himself—who become the means by which he is revealed, facet by facet.... They are like those people in real life who 'project,' ascribing fictitious personalities to those whom they meet and live with. By analyzing the projections, we determine what is going on in the mind of the highly imaginative projector." Angus Fletcher, *Allegory: The Theory of a Symbolic Mode* (Ithaca, N.Y.: Cornell, 1964), pp. 35-36.

32. Childs, *Exodus*, p. 327. I do not disagree with Childs; it is only that the reminders of kinship mean more if they are telling us something about leadership.

33. Letter from Professor David Jay Beier, Middle Georgia College.

34. Buber, *Moses*, p. 99.

35. Max Weber, *Ancient Judaism*, eds. and trans. Hans H. Gerth and Don Martindale (New York: Free Press, 1952), p. 225.

36. For the argument, understandable but unbelievable, that "eye for eye" refers only to monetary compensation, see Leibowitz, *Studies in Leviticus*, pp. 245-248.

37. Henry George, *Moses: The Crime of Poverty* (New York: International Joseph Fels Commission, 1918).

38. Hirsch, *Pentateuch*, vol. 4, p. 185.

CHAPTER 5

1. See J. Lindblom, *Prophecy in Ancient Israel* (Philadelphia: Fortress, 1962).

2. The emphasis on memory in the Pentateuch has been noted by many commentators. Peter C. Craigie, for instance, writes, "The renewal of the covenant in Moab has two focal points: (1) the remembrance of the past, specifically the forming of the covenant at Horeb (Sinai); (2) the anticipation of the future, when again the covenant would be renewed. This perspective is a part of the Hebrew understanding of history.... The general principle is given, namely that in the future there would have to be a further renewal of obedience and commitment to God's law, which had just been declared and expounded." Craigie, *Deuteronomy*, p. 327.

3. Von Rad, *Deuteronomy*, p. 189.

4. Brevard S. Childs, *Introduction to the Old Testament as Scripture* (Philadelphia: Fortress, 1979), p. 134.

5. Two accounts are given of water-drawing at Meribah. In the first (Exod. 17:5), Moses smites the rocks, water flows, and no punishment follows. In the first episode, Moses obeys God's command; in the second, he takes matters into his own hands.

6. Quoted in Leibowitz, *Studies in Numbers*, p. 241.

7. M. Margaliot, "The Sin of Moses and Aaron at Me Meribah," *Bet Mikra* 58 (1974), pp. 374-400.

8. Eugene Arden, "How Moses Failed God," *Journal of Biblical Literature* 76 (March 1957), pp. 50-52.

9. Jacob Milgrom, "Magic, Monotheism and the Sin of Moses," in *Quest for the Kingdom of God*, eds. M.B. Huffman et al. (Chico, Calif.: Scholars, 1983).

10. Milgrom, "Magic."

11. Cassuto, *Exodus*, p. 203; Hyatt, *Commentary on Exodus*, pp. 180-182.

12. On this incident in general, see Karen Randolph Joines, "The Bronze Serpent in the Israelite Cult," *Journal of Biblical Literature* 87 (September 1968), p. 245.

13. Snaith, *Century Bible*, p. 279.

14. Hugo Gressmann, *Mose und seine Zeit: Ein Kommentar zu den Mose-Sagan* (Göttingen: Vandehoeck und Ruprecht, 1913), pp. 174-175.

15. *Babylonian Talmud*, Tractate Rosh Hashana, p. 134.

16. Fleg, *Life of Moses*, pp. 205-206.

17. Mendenhall, *Tenth Generation*, p. 116.

18. Martin Noth, *A History of Pentateuchal Traditions* (Englewood Cliffs, N.J.: Prentice-Hall, 1972), p. 157.

19. For evidence of deliberate intent on the rabbis' part, see David Daube, "The Significance of the Afikoman," *Pointer* 3 (Spring 1968), pp. 4-5.

20. Murray Baumgarten, "That Stutterer Moses," *Western Political Quarterly* 32 (June 1979), p. 153.

21. There was an evocative Mayan custom in which a man was chosen to be treated as a god for a time, only to be subject to ritual slaughter afterward. His heart was cut out, and his skin was stripped from his body. Those who wished to be living gods then would take that sanctified skin and place it over their own so as to claim the outer appearance of divinity. Barrie M. Biven, "A Violent Solution: The Role of Skin in a Severe Adolescent Regression," in Ruth Eissler et al., *The Psychoanalytic Study of the Child* 32 (New Haven: Yale, 1977), p. 346. How different is Aaron's transfer of his office?

22. Genesis Rabbah 19:10.

23. Craigie, *Deuteronomy*, p. 127.

24. Winnett, *Mosaic Tradition*, p. 140.

25. Von Rad, *Deuteronomy*, p. 124; see also Anthony Phillips, *Deuteronomy* (Cambridge: Cambridge, 1973), p. 19.

26. "No one ever challenged the view held by Rabbi Akiba that man was not allowed to inflict bodily harm upon his own person, not even when sanctifying the name of God during martyrdom." E.E. Urbach, "The Talmudic Sage—Character and Authority," *Journal of World History* 11 (1968), p. 140.

27. See David Daube, "Limitations on Self-Sacrifice in Jewish Law and Tradition," *Theology* 72 (July 1969), pp. 291-304.

28. Craigie, *Deuteronomy*, p. 126.

29. Von Rad, *Deuteronomy*, p. 85.

30. "Torah" itself means primarily not "law" but "instruction."

31. Throughout the Bible the first-born are rarely adequate to the task. Among others, Esau, Ishmael, and Reuben come to mind. This observation is part of a larger theme in which those who have the presumed right do not measure up. The lesson for leadership is twofold: leading is much more than formal authority, and followers must be able to generate new leaders because they are so often inadequate. Of course, if appearance and reality were too often together, man would be in less need of God.

32. Kenneth Boulding, "Pathologies of the Public Grants Economy" (paper presented to the International Economic Association Conference, Cambridge, England, September 1-5, 1979).

33. Alexander Hamilton, John Jay, and James Madison, *The Federalist* (New York: Modern Library, n.d.), p. 337.

34. Hamilton, Jay, and Madison, *The Federalist*, pp. 470-471.

35. Benedict de Spinoza, *The Political Works*, ed. and trans. A.G. Wernham (Oxford: Clarendon, 1958), pp. 171-173.

36. Ahad Ha-am, "Al Parashat Derakhim," quoted in Louis Jacobs, "Moses," *Encyclopaedia Judaica*, 12:401.

37. Throughout Deuteronomy, as Daube shows in his seminal study "The Culture of Deuteronomy," there is a strong "shame-cultural" element. *Orita* (a religious journal published at the University of Ibadan), 3 (June 1969), pp. 27-52.

38. On this theme see Jacob Z. Lauterbach, "The Belief in the Power of the Word," *Hebrew Union College Annual* 14 (Cincinnati, 1939), pp. 287-302.

39. See the discussion in Buber, *Israel and the World*, pp. 122-123.

40. Louis Jacobs, "Moses," *Encyclopaedia Judaica*, p. 400.

41. Ever anxious to claim credit for his people, "Philo maintains that Heraclitus snatched his theory of opposites from Moses 'like a thief'" (*Jewish Encyclopedia*, p. 389).

42. A suggestion from David Daube.

43. David C. Rapoport, "Moses, Charisma, and Covenant," *Western Political Quarterly* 32 (June 1979), p. 137.

CONCLUSION

1. Cecil A. Gibb, "Leadership: Psychological Aspects," in *International Encyclopedia of the Social Sciences*, ed. David L. Sills, 17 vols. (New York: Macmillan, 1968), 9:91-101.

2. Leaders were thought to be generally heavier and taller, though in two of nine studies some turned out to be shorter. In 1915 E.B. Gowin found that university presidents were taller than college presidents; railroad presidents, than station agents; and insurance executives, than policyholders. Cecil Gibb, "Leadership," in *Handbook of Social Psychology*, 2nd ed., eds. Gardner Lindzey and Elliot Aronson, vol. 4, *Group Psychology and Phenomena of Interaction* (Reading, Mass.: Addison-Wesley, 1969), pp. 216-217.

3. Alvin W. Gouldner, introduction to *Studies in Leadership*, ed. Alvin W. Gouldner (New York: Russell & Russell, 1965), p. 25.

4. Gibb, "Leadership: Psychological Aspects," pp. 98-99.

5. Quoted in Gouldner, Introduction to *Studies in Leadership*, p. 23.

6. Daniel Bell, quoted in *International Encyclopedia of the Social Sciences*, 9:102.

7. Robert Tannenbaum, Irving R. Weschler, and Fred Massarik, *Leadership and Organization: A Behavioral Science Approach* (New York: McGraw-Hill, 1961), p. 23.

8. Quoted in Tannenbaum, Weschler, and Massarik, *Leadership and Organization.*

9. Quoted in Gibb, "Leadership," p. 228.

10. Quoted in Gibb, "Leadership: Psychological Aspects," p. 93.

11. A. Paul Hare, "Situational Differences in Leader Behavior," *Journal of Abnormal and Social Psychology* 55 (July 1957), p. 134.

12. Gibb, "Leadership," p. 207.

13. See Harold Proshansky and Bernard Seidenberg, *Basic Studies in Social Psychology* (New York: Holt, Rinehart, and Winston, 1965), p. 377.

14. Kenneth F. Janda, "Towards the Explication of the Concept of Leadership in Terms of the Concept of Power," *Human Relations* 13 (November 1960), pp. 345-363.

15. Quoted in Gibb, "Leadership: Psychological Aspects," pp. 93, 94.

16. Gibb, "Leadership: Psychological Aspects," p. 94.

17. Quoted in Gibb, "Leadership," pp. 224, 239.

18. Gibb, "Leadership," p. 268. Gibb adds, "No doubt Sanford (1952) was right when he predicted that studies focusing on any one of these aspects alone will continue to yield 'positive but unexciting correlations.' What is needed is a conception in which the complex interactions of these factors can be incorporated." This I have tried to supply with "regimes."

19. Edward Shils, "Charisma, Order, and Status," *American Sociological Review* 30 (April 1965), pp. 199-213.

20. See the lengthy list in Janda, "Explication of the Concept of Leadership."

21. Robert T. Morris and Melvin Seeman, "The Problem of Leadership: An Inter-Disciplinary Approach," *American Journal of Sociology* 56 (September 1950), pp. 152-153.

22. "Although students of the subject are often troubled by the obvious differences in the phenomena selected for study by these various criteria," Janda reports wryly, "they reluctantly do what Festinger did and include studies under a heading of leadership 'only because those reporting such studies call it leadership.'" Janda, "Explication of the Concept of Leadership," p. 350.

23. Janda, "Explication of the Concept of Leadership," p. 353.

24. See Robert A. Dahl, *Who Governs?* (New Haven: Yale, 1961).

25. John C. Harsanyi, "Measurement of Social Power, Opportunity Costs, and the Theory of Two-Person Bargaining Games," *Behavioral Science* 7 (January 1962), pp. 67-80.

26. Herbert Simon, *Models of Man* (New York: Wiley, 1957).

27. Andrew S. McFarland, *Power and Leadership in Pluralist Systems* (Stanford: Stanford, 1969), pp. 157-158, 161.

28. Fred I. Greenstein, "The Impact of Personality on Politics: An Attempt to Clear Away Underbrush," *American Political Science Review* 61 (1967), pp. 629-641.

29. One can readily agree with Gibb that "individual personality cannot be left out of the leadership picture" ("Leadership," p. 218), even without knowing precisely how to put it back in.

30. Carl J. Friedrich, "Political Leadership and the Problem of the Charismatic Power," *Journal of Politics* 23 (February 1961), pp. 3-24.

31. James M. Burns, *Leadership* (New York: Harper & Row, 1978), p. 417.

32. Quoted in Burns, *Leadership*, p. 455.

33. Lewis J. Edinger, "Political Science and Political Biography: Reflections on the Study of Leadership (I)," *Journal of Politics* 26 (May 1964), pp. 431-432.

34. John A. Miller (Management Research Center, University of Rochester), "Structuring, Destructuring Leadership in Open Systems," Technical Report No. 64, Office of Naval Research (March 1973), p. 3.

35. Elihu Katz and his colleagues approach, but do not quite reach, this understanding. Inquiring into the conditions under which leaders survive from this to that situation, they conclude that "leaders change not with every change of activity, but only with changes to markedly different *kinds* of activity—that is, to activities which may no longer be compatible with the leader's talents." Elihu Katz et al., "Leadership Stability and Social Change: An Experiment with Small Groups," *Sociometry* 20 (March 1957), p. 37. Such qualitative changes in kind would be changes in regime.

36. Gabriel Almond, "Approaches to Developmental Causation," in *Crisis, Choice, and Change: Historical Studies of Political Development*, eds. Gabriel A. Almond, Scott C. Flanagan, and Robert J. Mundt (Boston: Little, Brown, 1973), pp. 1-42, quote on p. 18.

37. See Lewis A. Dexter's splendid introduction to Arthur F. Bentley's *Process of Government* (New York: Transaction, 1982).

38. Max Weber, *Economy and Society: An Outline of Interpretive Sociology*, eds. Guenther Roth and Claus Wittich (Berkeley and Los Angeles: University of California, 1978), 2:1204. Weber describes religious sects as I do their political counterparts: "The sect does not want to be an institution dispensing grace, like a church, which includes the righteous and the unrighteous and is especially concerned with subjecting the sinner to Divine law. The sect adheres to the ideal of the *ecclesia pura* (hence the name 'Puritans'), the *visible* community of saints, from whose midst the black sheep are removed so that they will not offend God's eyes. The typical sect rejects institutionalized salvation."

39. See note 34 to Introduction for further reading.

40. A.M. Hocart, *Kings and Councillors: An Essay in the Comparative Anatomy of Human Society*, ed. Rodney Needham (Chicago: University of Chicago, 1970), pp. 249, 85.

41. Hierarchies may be of two forms, according to whether they operate in such a way as always to align power and status or to keep them separate. The hierarchies with which we in the West are most familiar always align power and status, and they are monotheistic. But the hierarchies of caste systems keep power and status divorced and do so by resisting monotheism. Thus they separate themselves from others by imposing prohibitions that they alone must obey, not, as in class-based regimes, by imposing their rules on lower classes. The Hindu equivalents of nonconformity—the Sikhs, for instance—reject the caste hierarchies and allow power and status to come together. As they do this, they become monotheistic. In a Hindu system, the ruler is at the head of the power hierarchy, but the Brahmin is at the head of the status hierarchy. Hence the problems with revelation.

42. Carlos R. Alba, "The Organization of Authoritarian Leadership: Franco's Spain," in *Presidents and Ministers*, eds. Richard Rose and Ezra Suleiman (Washington, D.C.: American Enterprise Institute for Public Policy Research, 1980), p. 258.

43. Max Weber's idea of the routinization of charisma is tempting but troublesome. If leadership is regularized, it is not charismatic. Leaders may want to disperse their charisma, as Moses did, but when the carriers of the creed become an institution, regular and predictable, they are, in my opinion, better called a hierarchy. If charisma is, as I think, a substitute for the authority of hierarchy, confusion results from speaking of the "institutionalization of charisma."

44. What is here called a hierarchic regime is a combination of Max Weber's traditional and rational legal authority. Since the rational-legal mode had hardly emerged in Mosaic times, barely beginning under David and Solomon, the distinction between it and the traditional regime does not seem worth making. On more general grounds, I think the concept of hierarchy serves well enough in discussions of leadership without loading it with distinctions that have proved elusive in practice. See Reinhard Bendix, "Reflections on Charismatic Leadership," in *State and Society*, ed. Reinhard Bendix (Boston: Little, Brown, 1968), pp. 616-629; and Shils, "Charisma, Order, and Status."

45. The classic description of anarchies, from which I have taken the designation, is from E.E. Evans-Pritchard, *The Nuer: A Description of the Modes of Livelihood and Political Institutions of Nilotic People* (Oxford: Oxford, 1977). The political puzzle Evans-Pritchard seeks to explain is that "the lack of governmental organs among the Nuer, the absence of legal institutions, of developed leadership,

and, generally, of organized political life is remarkable.... The ordered anarchy in which they live accords well with their character, for it is impossible to live among Nuer and conceive of rulers ruling over them.

"The Nuer is a product of hard and egalitarian upbringing, is deeply democratic, and is easily roused to violence. His turbulent spirit finds any restraint irksome and no man recognizes a superior. Wealth makes no difference. A man with many cattle is envied but not treated differently from a man with few cattle. Birth makes no difference. A man may not be a member of the dominant clan of his tribe, he may even be of Dinka descent, but were another to allude to the fact he would run a grave risk of being clubbed" (p. 181).

46. Meyer Fortes and E.E. Evans-Pritchard, eds., *African Political Systems* (London and New York: International African Institute and Oxford University, 1940, reprinted 1955).

47. P. Kyle McCarter, Jr., *I Samuel: A New Translation with Introduction, Notes, and Commentary* (Garden City, N.Y.: Doubleday, 1980), p. 162.

48. Jack Wiseman, "Costs and Decisions," in *Contemporary Economic Analysis*, eds. David A. Currie and Will Peters (London: Croom Helm, 1980), 2:475.

49. On the active-passive dimension of leadership see the seminal study by James David Barber, *Presidential Character: Predicting Performance in the White House*, 2nd ed. (Englewood Cliffs, N.J.: Prentice-Hall, 1977).

50. Michael Oakeshott's philosophy of politics, especially the images of the captain of the ship of state keeping it on an even keel, fits this model hierarchy well. *Hobbes on Civil Association* (Berkeley and Los Angeles: University of California, 1975); *On Human Conduct* (Oxford: Clarendon, 1975); *Rationalism in Politics and Other Essays* (New York: Basic Books, 1962).

51. Newman, *Christian Doctrine*, pp. 157-191.

52. See Georg G. Iggers, *New Directions in European Historiography* (Middleton, Conn.: Wesleyan, 1975), p. 6.

53. Richard Vernon, "Politics as Metaphor: Cardinal Newman and Professor Kuhn," *Review of Politics* 41 (October 1979), pp. 513-535.

54. Quoted in Vernon, "Politics as Metaphor," p. 522.

55. Vernon, "Politics as Metaphor," p. 523.

56. Stephen Toulmin, *Human Understanding* (Princeton: Princeton, 1972), vol. 1.

57. Quoted in Vernon, "Politics as Metaphor," p. 524.

58. Toulmin, *Human Understanding*, pp. 117-118.

59. Almond, "Approaches to Developmental Causation," pp. 19-20.

60. Robert Alter, *The Art of Biblical Narrative* (New York: Basic Books, 1981), p. 148.

61. Alter, *Art of Biblical Narrative*, p. 154.

62. Alter, *Art of Biblical Narrative*, pp. 132-133.

63. Alter, *Art of Biblical Narrative*, pp. 135-136.

64. Alter, *Art of Biblical Narrative*, pp. 136-137.

EPILOGUE

1. Abraham Malamat, "Charismatic Leadership in the Book of Judges," in *Magnalia Dei: The Mighty Acts of God*, eds. Frank Moore Cross, Werner E. Lemke, and Patrick D. Miller, Jr. (New York: Doubleday, 1980), pp. 152-168.

2. McCarter, *I Samuel*, p. 187.

3. Moses is younger than Aaron, Joseph younger than all but one of his brothers; Jacob gives the blessing to the youngest of Joseph's children; Solomon and David are younger brothers, and so on.

4. Malamat, "Charismatic Leadership," p. 163.

5. Malamat, "Charismatic Leadership," p. 160.

6. Yehezkel Kaufmann, "The Biblical Age," in *Great Ages and Ideas of the Jewish People*, ed. Leo W. Schwarz (New York: Random House, 1956), p. 45.

7. For a parallel interpretation, see McCarter, *I Samuel*, pp. 160-161.

8. See Saul Bellow's novel, *Dangling Man* (New York: Vanguard, 1944).

9. Murray Lee Newman, Jr., *The People of the Covenant: A Study of Israel from Moses to the Monarchy* (Nashville: Abingdon, 1962), p. 130.

10. See Albrecht Alt, *Essays in Old Testament History and Religion*, trans. R.A. Wilson (Garden City, N.Y.: Doubleday, 1968), especially "The Formation of the Israelite State in Palestine," pp. 185ff.

11. Frederic Thieberger, *King Solomon* (Oxford and London: East and West Library, 1947), p. 165.

12. Hocart, *Kings and Councillors*, p. 299.

13. W. Ross Ashby, "Variety, Constraint, and the Law of Requisite Variety," in *Modern Systems Research for the Behavioral Scientist: A Sourcebook*, ed. Walter Buckley (Chicago: Aldine, 1968), ch. 15.

14. Quoted in Leibowitz, *Studies in Leviticus*, p. 30.

15. S. Mowinckel, *He That Cometh* (Oxford: Basic Blackwell, 1959), p. 74.

INDEX

Aaron, 67, 151-152, 154-155, 175-177, 199, 227; challenge to Moses' authority, 151, 162, 199; comparison to Jacob, 121; comparison to Moses, 124-125, 176, 178; denied Promised Land, 124, 183; at Mount Sinai, 112, 120-126; passivity of, 121, 123-125, 126, 162; priesthood of, 122, 158, 162; as representative leader, 121, 209-210; rod of, 159; role in Golden Calf episode, 112-113, 120-126; as voice for Moses, 46, 162, 204

Abraham (Abram), 98-100, 139, 227; comparison to Moses, 98-100, 202; God's covenant with, 100

Akedah (binding of Isaac), 48, 133-136, 202; as parallel to Golden Calf episode, 129, 136, 202; as parallel to spies episode, 129; as parallel to Zipporah's intercession for Moses, 48; social significance of, 136

Anarchy, regime of, 24-25, 79, 87, 101-102, 105, 197, 210, 218-219, 224-226, 229, 232, 235, 236-237, 241, 246-247, 249-255, 259-261; gods in, 151, 221-222; meteoric leadership in, 143, 147, 222, 229, 234; shame in, 184

Angel of God: Abraham in the binding of Isaac, 133; Balaam on his way to Balak, 50-51; Jacob on his way to Haran, 40, 57-60; Moses on his way to Midian, 48

Authority: central, 166; challenge to (see

Korah, rebellion of); charismatic, 210-211; delegating, 188, 249; division of, 162-163, 165-166, 193; general principles of, 152; non-centralized, 165-166; organization of, 147-148; in political regimes, 218-220, 233, 246, 248-250, 260; rational-legal, 210; sharing, 161-162, 193, 195, 197; struggle over, 157-158; traditional, 210

Balaam's ass episode, 50-55, 65; ambivalence of Balaam, 52; meekness in compared to Moses, 199; as parallel to Jacob wrestling with the stranger, 55; as parallel to Moses on his way to Midian, 52-54; as parallel to Zipporah episode, 50

Beth-el, 56, 59-60, 63

Bible: conflict in, 139; fieldwork in, 251; origins (authorship), 12-15; as teaching on political leadership, 3, 10, 20, 54

Blood: as a sign, 43, 48, 68, 89, 110, 136

Bloody husband (bloody bridegroom): Moses as, 48; God as, 190

Boundaries: between man and God, 35, 39-41, 90, 108-110, 156, 186-187, 228; in social legislation, 168, 217

Brazen serpent (Nehushtan): Christian versus Jewish interpretation, 180; as divine irony, 180, 204; as idol, 179-180, 204; as spiritual reminder, 179

Burning bush, 35-42, 45-46, 49, 74, 99, 186, 194, 208, 238

Canaan. *See* Promised Land
Charisma in leaders, 102, 106, 143, 150-152, 160, 197, 210-211, 222, 223, 225-226, 229-234, 250, 252-253, 255-256; contradictions of, 230; as substitute for authority, 211, 223. *See also* Equity, regime of
Child sacrifice, 134, 136
Circumcision, 47-49, 61, 64, 89, 100, 251; as sign of covenant, 49, 202
Commandments (Ten Commandments; the laws), 205-206, 112, 149, 173, 192, 201, 228, 242, 247, 252, 258; shattering of, 112, 116-119; significance of shattering, 117; as social legislation, 106-110, 217, 241-242
Covenant, 167-168, 181, 183; with Abraham, 39, 100; community, 181; conditional, 108, 119; as conditions of rule, 106; Davidic, 244-258; as elements of culture, 106; history of, 172-174; with Jacob, 39, 57-62; Mosaic, 244; with Moses, 39, 48; at Mount Sinai, 101, 106-112, 165; with Noah, 104; perpetual, 190, 202; in regimes, 106; renewal of, 105, 136, 173, 190, 196; renewal at Mount Sinai, 118-119, 126-127, 129
Craftsmanship, 125; specialization in, 164

Division of labor (dividing power), 155, 161, 163-165, 193, 208-209, 246, 247-250, 260

Elders, seventy, 161-162, 166, 231, 242; hierarchy established, 162-166
Equity, regime of, 25-26, 87, 102, 105-106, 139, 143-144, 147, 151, 155, 160-161, 204, 210, 218-219, 221, 223, 225-226, 230, 234, 236-243, 246, 248, 260; blame in, 246; charismatic leaders in, 147, 197, 222-223, 229, 231-232, 252; combined with hierarchy, 220, 236-244; memory in, 246; shame in, 184; splits in, 249-250, 259
Esau, 55-56, 60

Fanaticism, 6-7, 34, 126, 183, 232
Fire: signaling God's presence, 148
Followers: choosing regimes, 215-216; dilemma of leadership for, 193, 216; learning about behavior, 184; learning about leadership, 186; of Moses, 80; need for leaders, 189; new identity for, 236; of Pharaoh, 80; rebellion of, 144-145; sharing power, 140; in "situation" theory, 207-208
Free will, 111, 115, 141

Garden of Eden, 31, 256; as first exodus, 32; as parallel to Jacob's inner struggle, 63; as parallel to slavery in Egypt, 32, 169
Golden Calf, 56, 92, 100, 111, 124-126, 139-140, 148, 162, 167, 176, 178, 186, 190, 202, 209-210, 229, 231, 234; issues in, 129; as parallel to the Akedah, 129, 202; as parallel to the spies episode, 129-133, 148, 167; in Christian commentary, 123. *See also* Mount Sinai

Hierarchy, regime of, 26-27, 79, 106, 139, 144, 147-148, 151, 155-161, 165, 167, 193, 219-226, 229-234, 246-247, 248-249, 255-258; combined with equity, 220, 236-244; division of labor in, 144, 249, 260; hypocrisy in, 247-248; institutions in, 245-246; salvation in, 245; shame in, 184

Intercession: Aaron for Miriam, 152; Abraham at Sodom and Gomorrah, 100; Balaam's ass, 50-51; Moses for Aaron, 124; Moses for the Hebrews, 113-115, 132,

164-165, 182, 201; Samuel for the Hebrews, 182; as teaching, 189-190; Zipporah for Moses, 35, 47-48

Isaac: binding of (see Akedah); birth of, 100; as "child of the promise," 135

Jacob, 139, 227; ambivalence in, 35, 55, 57-58; comparison to Moses, 35, 40, 46, 55-64, 202; flight to Laban, 56; inner struggle as parallel to the exodus and Garden of Eden, 63; Jacob's ladder (wrestling with a stranger), 57-60; lack of faith compared to Hebrews at Mount Sinai, 56; name changed to Israel, 58; passivity, 57-58; split personality, 55, 61; thigh wound as parallel to Zipporah episode, 61

Jethro, 163-166; as origin of administrative division of labor, 162-164

Joseph, 227; call for continuity, 66; contrast to Moses, 66, 71-73; serving Pharaoh, 71-73

Joshua: Moses teaching, 161-162, 169; as successor to Moses, 161, 190, 195

Judaism: boundaries of, 242; commandments in, 241-242, 258; communal religion, 100; equity and hierarchy in, 27, 238-243; faith in, 49; obedience in, 11; practices of, 258-259; regimes of, 259-262; resilience in, 258; survival of, 244-262

Judges: Abimelech, 254; anarchy and equity under, 244, 250-252; Deborah, 253; as deliverers, 253; Gideon, 253-254; Jephthah, 253-255; learning under, 250; Oth-niel, 253

Kadesh, 175, 185, 189-190; lack of faith at, 160

Kibroth Hattaavah, 149

Kings: David, 59, 198, 220, 256-258; hierarchy in, 244, 250; Samuel,

247, 251-252, 255; Saul, 256; Solomon, 244, 257-258

Korah, 138, 165, 166, 169; as exemplifying regime of equity, 154, 167-168, 204, 239, 244, 248; rebellion of, 145-146, 149, 154-159, 167, 175-176, 204, 209, 230, 239, 247-248

Leaders: as administrators, 226-227; as cause or effect, 111; fate of, 52; as founders, 193, 226-227; humanness of, 185; indispensability of, 188, 197-198; as lawgivers, 226-227, 248; learning by, 190, 201; as politicians, 226-227; as revolutionaries, 226-227; as storytellers, 226-227; as students, 226-227; as teachers, 184, 226-227; traits of, 21, 206-207, 210-211; as transformers of regimes, 22-27, 232, 255

Leadership: abuse of, 192-194; ambivalence in, 10, 35, 44, 50, 52, 54, 196, 247; (anti-), 223-226; bargaining and compromise in, 84, 196-198; biblical conception of, 250-251; as cause, 211-214; centralized, 167; coercion in, 213-214, 216, 247; continuity of, 188; as corruption, 248; dilemmas of, 3, 10-11, 28, 33-34, 127, 150, 168, 193; group-centered, 210; identification with followers, 133, 176, 178, 202; initiative in, 125-126; institutionalization of, 183, 188, 229; limitations on, 186, 188, 193; Lord's search for, 137; mediation in, 101, 118, 154, 165, 186, 215, 230; models of, 8, 222, 227; Moses chooses, 105; persuasion in, 197, 216; principle of, 193, 237; pro-, 233-234; representative, 124-126, 252; scope and duration of, 222-224; situations in, 207-211, 215-216; task-centered, 210; teaching, 202-203; testing in, 129-130, 139-141, 261; transferring, 195; using force

in, 136, 160, 176, 207; using time
in, 85-86; variations in, 212

Leadership, call to: Abraham, 98-99,
133; Moses, 36-42, 201, 238

Leadership, as a function of regime: 3,
8, 9, 21, 105, 139, 143, 193, 196-
197, 205-243, 250-258, 261-262

Leadership, learning about, 54, 82-83, 126,
186, 205-206, 227, 237, 251

Leadership in the social sciences, 3-4,
7-9, 21, 205-216; interaction
theory, 210; situationists, 207-
211, 217

Learning, 174, 184, 188-190, 201-202;
from failure (error) 8-9, 11, 227,
237; from success, 9, 227

Macropolitics of regimes, 4, 215-216

Manna, 96-98, 229, 251

Marxist ideology, 145-147

Massah, 97, 177-178

Memory, 114-115, 168; in hardening
of Pharaoh's heart, 76-78; in
Judaism, 78-79; Pharaoh's lack of,
98, 259; in regimes, 246; role in
learning, 76-78, 161, 189

Meribah, 8, 175-176, 178-179, 189-190

Micropolitics of regimes, 4, 215-216

Minyan, 100, 135

Miriam, 43, 151-152, 154-155, 199,
229; criticism of Moses, 151

Mixing: of cultural categories, 87, 91,
114; Judaic abhorrence of, 86-87;
of people, 91, 151

Moab, 171-172; kiss of death at, 189

Moses: character of, 36-38, 198-201;
compared to Aaron, 122-125,
176, 178; compared to Abraham,
98-100, 202; compared to Jacob,
35, 40, 46, 55-64, 202; compared
to Joseph, 66, 71-73; compared to
other leaders, 226-227; God and,
101-102, 202-204; Hebrews retreat
from, 94-98; murmuring against
(see Murmuring); rebellion at
Meribah, 175-178; as transformer

of regimes, 22-27, 228-243. See
also Charisma in leaders, Covenant,
Intercession, Leadership, Leadership (call to), Leadership (learning
about), Mount Sinai, "Nursing
father," Passivity in leadership,
Promised Land, Rod, Teaching

Mount Sinai, 52, 101, 104, 107, 140-
141, 165, 208, 229, 255; lack of
faith at, 120, 160; theophany at,
110. See also Golden Calf

Murmuring, 24, 68, 95-98, 131, 148-149,
161, 165-166, 175-176, 229, 238

Noah, 103-104; rainbow as sign of
covenant, 63-64, 104

"Nursing father," Moses as, 51, 64-66,
188, 203, 238, 242

Passivity in Hebrews, 34-35, 203

Passivity in leadership: Aaron, 121, 123-
125, 162; Jacob, 62; Moses, 3, 35,
62, 66-69, 97-98, 167, 220, 233

Passover, 251; departure from Egypt,
68, 89; as forging of a people, 79;
Hagada, 182; remembering in, 78;
separating pure from impure, 89

Peniel, 56, 62

Pharaoh: during plagues, 67-69; hardened heart of, 74-76; lack of
memory in, 76-77; in Moses, 67;
served by Joseph, 72-73; as teaching on negative leadership, 201

Phinehas: initiative of, 126, 180-181;
priesthood of, 159; as reprimand
to Aaron, 126; teaching of, 181

Plagues, 43, 68, 74-76, 84-85, 98, 158;
as threat to Hebrews, 43

Promised Land (Canaan), 63, 64, 84,
129-131, 141, 143-144, 148, 159-
160, 162, 167, 169, 171, 209-210,
228, 250-251; denial to Aaron,
183; denial to Moses, 9, 171-172,
175-178, 182-189, 193-196, 237

Prophesying: Eldad and Medad, 83,
161, 169; elders, 161

Rebellions, 161; Dathan and Abiram,

155-160, 230, 239; Korah, 145-146, 149, 154-159 (*see also* Korah, rebellion of); as lack of faith, 97-98; Moses at Meribah, 8, 176

Regimes: evolution in, 234-236; gods in, 220-222; hybrid, 231, 236; as political cultures, 8; revolution in, 229, 235; in shaping character, 240; transformation of, 215, 228-243. *See also* Anarchy, regime of; Equity, regime of; Hierarchy, regime of; Slavery, regimes of

Remembering, 142, 178, 188, 210, 246, 251; the covenant, 172; in learning, 78, 161, 189; Pharaoh's lack of, 77; as signs to Hebrews, 78; Torah as aid to, 189

Rephidim, 97, 163, 179

Rod, Aaron's, 159; Balaam's, 51; of leadership, 183, 185, 204; at Meribah, 175-176, 179; Moses', 9, 43-45, 49; Moses at Rephidim, 97, 163; as serpent, 43-44, 178 (*see also* Brazen serpent); as shepherd's staff, 44, 178; as symbol of power, 43, 175-176

Sabbath: as sign, 63; work prohibited, 96, 149, 181

Sarah (Sarai), 99

Sea of Reeds, 24, 44, 68, 76, 95, 97, 140, 148, 158, 168, 172, 179, 182, 208

Separation: between God and man, 31-32, 90, 108-110, 136; functions of, 155; in plagues, 88; of pure from impure, 89-90, 117, 155, 167; sign of, 88; significance of, 89; sinners from the people, 149-152, 156-158. *See also* Mount Sinai, Promised Land, Sea of Reeds, Spies episode

Slavery, 200, 204; Joseph serving Pharaoh, 72-73; Moses replacing Pharaoh, 177; passivity in, 226, 233

Slavery, regimes of, 23-24, 87, 93, 151, 207-208, 217-222, 228-229, 232, 235, 241, 246, 258-259, 261; despotic leaders in, 147; shame in, 184

Spies episode, 129-131, 148, 175, 185, 188, 230; as parallel to the Akedah, 129; as parallel to the Golden Calf, 129-131, 148, 167

Spoiling: of Egyptians, 92-94; as social legislation, 93

Survival of Jewish people, 244-250, 254, 258-262

Taberah, 148

Teaching: as circular process, 189; on failure, 200; about leaders, 189; leaders as teachers, 184; on leadership, 193; by Moses, 170, 188-189, 196, 200; as storytelling, 182; Torah as, 20, 186, 189, 202, 251, 262; in wanderings, 132

Testing: of faith in the spies, Akedah, and Golden Calf episodes, 129; God testing man, 140-142; of ideas, 139, 145; man testing God, 140-142; at Meribah, 177-178; at Mount Sinai, 141; in rebellions, 160; in wanderings, 141

Torah, 145, 228, 258, 261-262; as book of the law, 190-191; contradictions in, cultural hypothesis, 238-241; contradictions in, documentary hypothesis (source critics), 239; interpretation of, 192, 248; oral tradition of, 192-193; as teaching, 20, 186, 189, 202; as teaching on leadership, 23, 205, 227, 251

Tower of Babel, 90-91, 211, 256

Zipporah, 38, 178, 202; as intercessor for Moses, 35, 47-48